Towards New Developmentalism

The global financial and economic crisis starting in 2007 has provoked the exploration of alternatives to neo-liberalism. Although neo-liberalism has been critiqued from various perspectives, these critiques have not coalesced into a concrete alternative in development economics literature. The main objective of this book is to name and formulate this alternative, identify what is new about this viewpoint, and project it on to the academic landscape.

This book includes contributions from many prominent development economists who are unified by a form of "developmental pragmatism." Their concern is with the problems of development that preoccupied the pioneers of economic development in the mid-twentieth century, known as the developmentalists. Like the developmentalists, the contributors to *Towards New Developmentalism* are policy-oriented and supportive of institutional development. This collection has an over-arching concern with promoting social justice, and holds the general view of the market as the means to affect an alternative program of development rather than as a master whose dictates are to be obeyed without question.

This important collection sets the agenda for new developmentalism, drawing on issues such as industrial policy, technology, competition, growth and poverty. In broad terms, the economic development debate is cast in terms of whether the market is the master, an ideological neo-liberal perspective, or the means to affect change as suggested by the pragmatic perspective that is being termed neo-developmentalism. This book will be valuable reading to postgraduates and researchers specializing in the area of development studies including within economics, international relations, political science and sociology.

Shahrukh Rafi Khan is currently a Copeland Fellow at Amherst College, USA.
Jens Christiansen is a Professor of Economics at Mount Holyoke College, USA.

Routledge Studies in Development Economics

Towards New Developmentalism

Market as means rather than master

Edited by Shahrukh Rafi Khan and Jens Christiansen

LONDON AND NEW YORK

First published 2011
by Routledge
2 Park Square, Milton Park, Abingdon, Oxon OX14 4RN

Simultaneously published in the USA and Canada
by Routledge
711 Third Avenue, New York, NY 10017

Routledge is an imprint of the Taylor & Francis Group, an informa business

© 2011 Selection and editorial matter; Shahrukh Rafi Khan and Jens
Christiansen, individual chapters; the contributors

Typeset in Times by Wearset Ltd, Boldon, Tyne and Wear
First issued in paperback in 2013

British Library Cataloguing in Publication Data
A catalogue record for this book is available from the British Library

Library of Congress Cataloging in Publication Data
Towards new developmentalism: market as means rather than master/
edited by Shahrukh Rafi Khan and Jens Christiansen.
p. cm.
Includes bibliographical references and index.
1. Economic development. 2. Economic policy. 3. International relations.
I. Khan, Shahrukh Rafi. II. Christiansen, Jens.
HD82.T646 2010
338'9–dc22
                                                            2010008374
ISBN13: 978-0-415-74677-9 (pbk)
ISBN13: 978-0-415-77984-5 (hbk)
ISBN13: 978-0-203-84431-1 (ebk)

Contents

Figures

xiv *Figures*

Tables

Contributors

Luis Abugattas is with the UNDP

Yves Ekoué Amaïzo is with the Knowledge for Interdependency Consulting and the think tank "Afrology"

Ha-Joon Chang is with the Faculty of Economics, Cambridge University

Jens Christiansen is with the Department of Economics, Mount Holyoke College

Kevin P. Gallagher has a joint position at the Department of International Relations, Boston University and the Global Development and Environment Institute, Tufts University

Ilene Grabel is with the Josef Korbel School of International Studies, University of Denver

Rainer Kattel is with the Department of Public Administration, Tallinn University of Technology, Estonia

Shahrukh Rafi Khan is with the Department of Economics, Amherst College

Leonce Ndikumana is with the Development Research Department, African Development Bank

Eva Paus is with the Department of Economics and the McCulloch Center for Global Initiatives, Mount Holyoke College

Erik S. Reinert is with The Other Canon Foundation, Norway

Mehdi Shafaeddin is with the Institute of Economic Research, University of Neuchatel, Switzerland

Helen Shapiro is with Sociology Department, University of California Santa Cruz

Gus Van Harten is with the Osgoode Hall Law School, York University

Robert Wade is with the Development Studies Institute (DESTIN), The London School of Economics and Political Science

Lyuba Zarsky is with the Graduate School of International Policy and Management, Monterey

Acknowledgments

This book is an outcome of a conference held at Mount Holyoke College on November 14–16, 2008. First and foremost, we would like to thank Dawn Larder, Senior Administrative Assistant to the Economics Department, and Unika Shrestha, our student assistant, for their part in making this conference so successful. Dawn Larder continued to be very helpful in the manuscript preparation stage. We also acknowledge financial support for the conference from the Economics Department's Morrison Fund, the Purington Fund, and the McCulloch Center for Global Initiatives (all at Mount Holyoke), Five College Inc., the Political Economy Research Institute at the University of Massachusetts, the economics departments at Smith and Amherst College, and the School of Social Science at Hampshire College. We thank Elizabeth Dewar and Maisha Islam for providing exceptional research assistance. Elizabeth Dewar's text editing, formatting, as well as her substantive comments, have all been outstanding. Maisha Islam was prompt and conscientious in formatting the tables and figures. Thanks also go to four anonymous referees for their insightful and valuable comments. Last but not least, we are very grateful for the conscientious engagement, timely responsiveness, and continued interest of Thomas Sutton, our editor, and for Louisa Earls' timely helpfulness and cooperation in the manuscript preparation and submission stages.

Part I
Introduction

1 Exploring and naming *an* economic development alternative[1]

Shahrukh Rafi Khan

Introduction

In the last three decades, a substantial body of scholarship has emerged that collectively represents an alternative development program to neo-liberalism. However, this research, exemplified by the contributions of Amsden (1989), Chang (2002), Johnson (1982), and Wade (2004) on East Asia, has not coalesced into a distinct alternative in the development economics literature.[2] The global financial and economic crisis of 2007–09[3] has created a climate to explore alternatives and a validation of the alternative proposed by the above scholars. For example, the nationalization of a substantive part of the automobile industry in the US, a bastion of free market capitalism, is one prominent example of such validation as will be explained below. The main objective of this volume is to explicate and name an alternative, identifying what is new in this program, and projecting it onto the academic landscape.

This volume has emerged from a conference at Mount Holyoke College, November 14–16, 2008, that brought together development economists supportive of an alternative program. Our focus is on an economic development strategy that evidence has proven superior to neo-liberalism, which is at best ineffective and at worst destructive. The discussion at the Conference on naming of an alternative produced a consensus around the term "new developmentalism" to characterize the program proposed in this volume. The call for "new developmentalism" was made by Alice Amsden at the UNCTAD "High Level Round Table on Trade and Development: Directions for the Twenty First Century," February, 2000, Bangkok.[4]

What unifies these new developmentalist economists is a form of "developmental pragmatism": they are concerned with the problems of development that preoccupied the developmentalist pioneers of the mid-twentieth century, chief among them Rosenstein-Rodan (1943), Nurkse (1953), Lewis (1954), and Hirschman (1959); they are policy-oriented and largely endorse the policy solutions recommended by the early developmentalists; they support institutional development and engagement with economic globalization; they are concerned with promoting social justice; and they view the market as a means to be harnessed for this alternative program of development rather than as a master whose dictates are to be obeyed.

4 *S. R. Khan*

Developmentalism generally refers to an activist state engaged in selective industrial policy. Industrial policy is defined as strategically creating comparative advantage in industries that embody dynamic efficiencies in low- and middle-income countries. Dynamic efficiencies include increasing returns and potential for technological development, learning by doing, training, raising labor productivity and energy efficiency, and externalities (including diffusing managerial and marketing skills). Thus central to this program is a pro-active state and such states have been referred to as developmental.[5]

While some have criticized development state theorists as "ahistorical" and "technocratic" (Berger 2004: 209), contributors to this volume view their scholarship as building on historical studies, welcoming of institutional and political economy approaches, and often drawing upon inter- and multi-disciplinary methodologies. Even so, the theory of the state and state autonomy are central challenges for an alternative program if one is to argue that the East Asian experience can be more generally replicated. Chang (2006: 47–52) very effectively refutes the standard arguments concerning non-replicability including the lack of a competent economic bureaucracy in most low-income countries and the changed global economic scenario relative to when the East Asian economies took off.

Evans' (1995) comparative institutional analysis classifies states as either developmental or predatory, though most fit into an intermediary category. In Evans' conceptualization, developmental states are embedded in the political and economic milieu with open channels of communication between the political administration, business, and the economic bureaucracy, but such that the latter has sufficient autonomy to act in the public interest. Thus, the presumption is that the economic bureaucracy is reasonably efficient and honest. Such economic bureaucracies are able to perform various functions as circumstance requires, including custodian, demiurge (production), midwifery, and husbandry. Evans also views the state's role in the development process as complex, dynamic and unique to the country in question and with outcomes that are uncertain. For example, the outcomes of a national project, with ostensible buy-ins from other stake holders, may still be unexpected and may result in constituencies that challenge state action. Hence, there is a constant need for the state to transform itself to remain relevant for the broader industrialization project.

This view of the state is implicit in most of the chapters in this volume although Khan in Chapter 12 of this volume proposed that a new development program could be pursued with much less stringent requirements on state capacity. Chang (2006: 48) points out that the capacity of the economic bureaucracy concomitantly develops and should not be viewed as a pre-requisite. He points out that Korea sent its economic bureaucrats for training to the Phillipines and Pakistan in the late 1960s. However, Shapiro, in Chapter 5 of this volume, criticizes Evans' concept of "embeddedness" as somehow emerging from above rather than evolving organically from the "social and political dynamics of state-society relations."[6]

Fine (2005: 17–18), makes an important distinction between scholars writing about the developmentalist state from a political or an economic perspective; the latter is the focus of this volume.[7] Based on the Asian financial crisis of 1997, Fine viewed developmentalism as declining and thus saw the time as opportune to present radical political economy as an alternative. He views such decline as inevitable following the contradictions that emerge between the state and empowered capital, once "catch up" has occurred. The focus of this volume is on catch-up development, rather than on processes and tensions that arise after the fact.

Exploitation, class struggle, and social transformation are central to a radical political economy approach. A more reformist agenda that includes land reform, just wages (at least tied to productivity), and industrial labor empowerment via economic democracy complements industrialization by promoting productivity growth and boosting domestic demand. New developmentalist scholars have pointed out that both Korea and Taiwan benefited from land reform in their industrialization efforts, and Amsden (1989) shows how the military regime promoting industrialization in Korea did not rely on wage repression. However, both these governments were authoritarian and are noted for repressing labor and so attaining development without labor repression is a key challenge to this approach as an alternative to neo-liberalism.

Neo-liberalism or the "Washington Consensus" has been characterized as an unlikely amalgam of neo-classical economics, which provides the intellectual rigor, and the Austrian school, which provides the political and moral philosophy (Chang 2002: 540). Calclough (1991: 17–22) distinguishes it from neo-classical economics and argues that neo-liberals are more likely to engage in policy advocacy. Williamson (2008), credited with coining the term Washington Consensus, points out that this term has acquired meanings not intended by him when he first identified what he viewed the consensus to be in 1989. Williamson had initially distanced the Washington Consensus from the neo-liberalism of the Mount Pelerin Society or the Reagan–Bush focus on supply side economics, monetarism, and minimal government. The original ten-point consensus he outlined included fiscal discipline, re-ordering public sector priorities (to be pro-growth and pro-poor), tax reform (raising the base and reducing rates), interest rate liberalization, competitive exchange rate regimes, trade liberalization, foreign direct investment liberalization, privatization, deregulation, and expanding property rights. It does seem, however, that the strong emphasis on privatization, liberalization, and deregulation of this program is suggestive of minimal government.

The developmentalist critique of neo-liberalism is not the only critical narrative, and new developmentalism is not the only proposed alternative. There is a large literature that critiques neo-liberalism and presents progressive alternatives.[8] While it presents alternative policies, much of this literature does not take the step to develop a coherent alternative to neo-liberalism. Baker *et al.* (1998: 3), for example, note that they did not intend to present "a unified theoretical alternative to neo-classical economics." This volume, by contrast, not only shows how neo-liberalism perpetuates itself, shrinks policy space, and constricts turning to an alternative, but also strives for a unified, operational, alternative economic development policy to neo-liberalism. Further, the alternative we develop in this volume is pertinent to contemporary industrialization efforts in low- and middle-income countries. Similar to Cimoli *et al.* (2009), this volume focuses on various aspects of industrial policy, but our project seeks to identify a broader alternative development program.

In making a case for working towards "new developmentalism" as a coherent alternative, this book draws on the thinking of early developmentalists. As mentioned in the opening paragraph, a distinctive aspect of new developmentalism is the conceptual breakthroughs that emerged from the insightful observations of scholars like Robert Wade and Ha-Joon Chang, among others, about how development, defined as transforming production structures and achieving an endogenous technological capacity, actually happened in East Asian economies.

This concept differs from development as defined by Sen (2000) or the UNDP's *Human Development Reports*. While Sen (1999) praises Korea and Taiwan for their achievements in human development and their approach for achieving these outcomes, the human development approach tends to focus on defining the possible outcomes of successful development and not necessarily development itself – "the missing prince of Denmark" as Ha-Joon Chang puts it in his chapter of this volume. The exploration of *process* using various empirical tools, including the case study (inductive) method, is what put an alternative explanation onto the academic landscape. The process of development has entailed "governing the market," as Wade (2004) put it, and thus examination of the tools of pro-active government will be an important overarching theme of this volume.

The developmentalists indicated much of what was needed for industrialization in the post Second World War context in which they wrote, but fell short of exploring how it could be achieved in terms of specific design principles. This gap has been addressed in the emerging literature of new developmentalism. Robert Wade, in setting the agenda for new developmentalism in the opening chapter, emphasizes governance capacities of the state. These could be viewed as akin to agricultural extension services, but targeted at industry; an apex body with real power and a Weberian merit-based bureaucracy for implementation that subordinates short-term to long-term interests. The pro-active state needs to use performance criteria and, at times, sanctions to achieve developmental objectives. Ha-Joon Chang stresses the state's political ability to mediate losses and socialize risk, as was done by the US in 2009 when it took over a large part of the automobile industry. Another important insight of new developmentalism is that export promotion (EP) and import substitution industrialization (ISI) are complementary and synergistic rather than alternative policies. Finally, while developmentalists tend to be inward-oriented, Robert Wade and others mention that globalization needs to be engaged with. Thus, Kevin Gallagher and M. Shafaeddin show in Chapter 9, while comparing Chinese and Mexican economic development, that policy must be pro-active to derive benefits from economic globalization.

Ha-Joon Chang in Chapter 3 of this volume sees the move to new developmentalism as a synthesis of the "productionist" focus of the developmentalists with key subsequent insights in the development economics literature that did not or could not (in the case of climate change) get a sufficient emphasis in early developmentalist writings. Nonetheless he indicates that the core aspect of development is transforming productive structures (moving to higher productivity activities) based on superior technology and knowledge and organizational capability embodied in institutions. He points out that development is essentially a collective endeavor, in contrast to, for example, micro-credit that targets the individual.

Erik S. Reinert, Yves Époque Amaïzo, and Rainer Kattel in Chapter 4 argue from the same vantage point in their prescription for a country to avoid a failed, failing or fragile status and argue that the economic history of currently high income countries provides substantial support for the core of a new developmentalist position. They also define development as the move to high productivity activities in the process of achieving an indigenous technological capacity. In their view, much else that is desired, such as human development, transparency in governance, a clean environment, and solid institutions may be concomitantly achieved so that they question the general view of causality that proposes objectives as prerequisites.

As earlier mentioned, much of the new developmentalist literature focuses on industry, as did the developmentalists, because of the potential dynamic efficiencies. Within industry, manufacturing is most likely to provide these dynamic efficiencies. The concern of new developmentalists with manufacturing remains well placed, as an extensive analysis of the data in the concluding chapter suggests a decline or no change in manufacturing for two thirds of the low- and middle-income countries in the post-WTO period (1995–2007) compared to the 1980–94 period. However, in principle, there is no need for an exclusive focus on industry, with the important qualification made above that, in order to be fundamentally wealth creating, activities need to generate increasing returns and embody learning and technical change.

The world has changed much from the time developmentalists wrote and new developmentalists need to address the important changes. For example, it has reached tipping points with regards to climate change and other ecological challenges and thus technology and production structures need to be ecology-sensitive. There is also a greater realization that increasing returns activities (industry) and sustainability can be at odds and Lyuba Zarsky addresses the issues of ecological and social justice in her chapter in the concluding section.

Based on the brief review above of the thinking of the authors in Part II of this volume, it may be that the most important contribution they make would be to change the focus of attention to what development is really about, i.e., that it is a *process* rather than a set of objectives. I turn below to a fuller account of the contributions of all authors to this volume.

Overview

Part II of the book focuses on the broad theme of new developmentalism, and the chapters by Robert Wade, Ha-Joon Chang, and Erik S. Reinert *et al.* address this. Essentially they propose and define a new developmentalist agenda. Robert Wade presents extensive evidence that the widespread adoption of the neo-liberal program by the governments of low- and middle-income countries – with its focus on raising "market efficiency" – has failed to generate catch-up growth, reduce national income inequality, or even to reduce the number of people living in "ordinary" (as distinct from "extreme") poverty. Nor are the outcomes much improved by adding on the standard "good governance" program, with its focus on defining property rights, strengthening the rule of law, and curbing corruption (extended Washington Consensus). He outlines a new developmentalist or growth enhancing agenda that is more likely to succeed in this regard (in contrast to the "market enhancing" agenda). This requires acquiring governance capacities that make the state effective in ways that matter most for growth.

Effective policies require the state's ability to move resources from unproductive to more productive sectors and to play a sustained role in acquiring technology and ensuring their local mastery. Specific mechanisms to implement a growth enhancing program include a high level apex coordination point, selective use of incentives, and disciplining beneficiaries by making incentives conditional of performance. Wade argues for pragmatism and flexibility so that, depending on context, the state can simply "follow the market" (assist ventures that private entrepreneurs would want to undertake anyway, without state assistance), or "lead the market" by undertaking new investments in new areas with more or less involvement of private entrepreneurs. The balance within any one sector, and within an economy, would change over time. Given limited resources, the state would have to focus on key sectors or industries.

Thus an important difference in new developmentalist thinking from the early developmentalists is the focus on governance capacities to make the state effective. In addition, unlike the closed economy approach advocated by many developmentalists, the new developmentalist approach, as practiced by successful East Asian economies (including China), includes a strategic openness.

Wade illustrates, with reference to East Asian examples, the approach in action. Finally, he explains why neo-liberalism prevailed over the last three decades despite the ambiguity of supportive evidence, and why the new developmentalist alternative has not yet received broad acceptance, despite evidence from several success stories.

Ha-Joon Chang shows that many current development discourses, such as those revolving around the UN's Millennium Development Goals or the NGO-led microcredit focus on poverty alleviation, are individual level human investments rather than fundamental structural transformations involving enterprises as "collective" ventures; true developmentalism. Viewing investments in education and health, the provision of credit, and the creation of property rights as adequate is "ersatz development." The WTO's Doha Development Round development discourse is actually anti-development because it sharply restricts the ability of low-income countries to change their production structures. Chang shows that none of these discourses meet the criteria of development as indicated above and suggests that they amount to *Hamlet* without the Prince of Denmark! Most of what is viewed as development in these discourses is little more than "the provision of basic needs and poverty reduction."

Chang concludes that a return to the original definition of development is needed to ensure the correct policies are adopted, while being more sensitive to concerns such as human development, gender equality, politics, environment, technological development and institutions than was true for the original developmentalists. Doing so represents progress as characterized by new developmentalism.

Reinert *et al.*'s chapter complements Ha-Joon Chang's by drawing on economic history, both recent and past. They point out that getting on a growth trajectory requires economic structures that produce virtuous circles, just as the absence of such structures creates vicious circles in low-income countries. These structures include sufficiently diffused, high value added, increasing return activities. The subsequent virtuous circles then generate the self-sustaining economic growth. Drawing on recent history, these authors argue that former US Secretary of State, George C. Marshall, essentially understood this point when he advocated for his reconstruction plan of Europe, but that this lesson has been lost on those who view his plan as a hand out. Though Marshall specifically argued against a palliative, his plan is frequently cited as an inspiration by aid advocates of initiatives such as the MDG (Millennium Development Goals), which engages in palliative economics.

Drawing on economic history, these authors show that industrialization and production systems that revolve around increasing returns activities and the synergies they create are essential for the convergence of low-income countries to higher levels of income. Industrialization and knowledge creation demand strong industrial policy and governmental administrative capacity. Trade theory that does not include the synergies of knowledge production makes it probable that nations will specialize according to a comparative advantage in being poor and ignorant. The economies of failed, failing and fragile states must be restructured away from their present dependence on raw materials (diminishing returns) activities. They point out that "the absence of an increasing returns sector creates zero-sum-game societies of static rent-seeking," one reason for states becoming failing, failed and fragile (FFF).

The identification of constraints to productive networking, innovation and the building of competencies and administrative capacity are absent from current donor initiatives such as the African Growth Opportunity Act (AGOA), the Economic Partnership Agreement (EPA), Everything But Arms (EBA), the Aid for Trade package of the World Trade Organization, and other bilateral and multilateral initiatives. The authors advocate a new developmentalist agenda as an alternative.

Part III of the book is both critical and prescriptive. The chapters explore how the low- and middle-income country policy agenda and institutions are constricted by neo-liberalism and hence make a case for new developmental alternatives to address these constraints. Helen Shapiro shows that in recent years, development theory and practice have moved in opposite directions. The theoretical literature has revived market failure arguments from the early 1960s, turning full circle from the market-based approach back to state intervention to attain industrialization. In contrast to that earlier period, however, this theoretical turn has not led to a change in policy direction, even though the empirical results on the economic and social achievements of liberal reforms have not been impressive.

Her chapter argues that the rent-seeking critique of state intervention, first elaborated in the 1970s and 1980s, continues to shape mainstream policy recommendations in two ways. First, it has successfully shifted the focus from markets to states, so that the untested counterfactual that state failure is worse than market failure still holds sway. Second, it has influenced the recent emphasis on state reform.

The initial rent-seeking paradigm provided the theoretical basis for a minimalist state. Based on countries' experiences with economic liberalization, mainstream policy makers now argue that a reformed and strengthened state is required to implement these policies – hence, the "second-wave" of reforms, following the initial wave of liberalizations. However, these reforms are motivated by an instrumental view of politics and institutions, in which the "right" institutions are those that deliver the "right" policies.

Yet, the nature of those policies remains unquestioned and they are promoted not for the underlying economic logic but because of their potential to contain rent-seeking. Moreover, the empirical underpinnings of the contention that rent-seeking constrains economic development have been challenged.

An appropriately reformed state is essentially considered to be one whose policy-making apparatus is staffed by "enlightened" technocrats and limited to non-targeted programs in order to remain insulated from rent-seeking pressures. Once again, the motivation of technocrats remains unquestioned even though the rent-seeking critique was targeted at the self-interest of optimizing government functionaries when industrial or regulatory policies were the issue. Also, empirical evidence rejects the contention that the technocrats are disinterested.

Shapiro argues that legacies of the rent-seeking approach, including the simplistic dichotomization of "winners" and "losers," exercise a powerful hold on development economists and policy makers. Thus, despite important theoretical developments indicating the non-optimality of market-driven outcomes, the economic importance of using rents and temporary protection as policy tools and the need for policy co-ordination, mainstream scholars are reluctant to press to the logical conclusion and endorse a role for the state in industrialization.

This reluctance is all the more surprising since these scholars have demonstrated that it was often macro imbalances rather than import substitution industrialization (ISI) related micro inefficiencies that resulted in economic setbacks;

that, in both East Asia and Latin America, many exports were based on the productive capacity and expertise developed during import substitution; that the
evidence shows greater productivity gains associated with selective protection;
and that industrialists working closely with government bureaucrats produced
better outcomes than the neo-liberal arms length prescriptions and rules regarding the role of the state. Thus, neo-liberal state theory remains unchallenged
despite having been theoretically and empirically undermined.

Ilene Grabel shows how ideologically driven concepts and the interlocking
policies and institutions they shape lead to the ever expanding sway of neo-
liberalism, which includes paring back the role of the state. At the policy level,
concepts such as "policy credibility" and "policy coherence" constrain policy
autonomy. For example, policy credibility justifies the creation of independent
"non-partisan" technocrat run central banks or currency boards following rule
based policies and hence not answerable to elected representatives. The more
recent and aggressive concept of policy coherence binds low- and middle-
income countries to a common neo-liberal policy agenda, particularly with
regards to the trade liberalization mandate of the WTO.

Coherence is imposed with the leverage and policy conditionality of multilateral organizations such as the IMF and WB, yet other UN agencies, the OECD,
and bilateral donors are also on board. Other tools used to implement the neo-
liberal agenda, particularly by the USA, are bilateral or small group investment
or trade agreements such as NAFTA, which are even more stringent in constraining policy space. Like the WTO, these agreements have a binding and disciplining dispute settlement mechanism. The investment and trade agreements provide
foreign investors the right to constrain or re-interpret much economic policy that
they claim is harmful to them.

In short, ideologically driven concepts and the policies and institutions that
emanate from them restrict the ability of governments in the developing world to
pursue financial, exchange rate, trade and industrialization policies that support
new developmentalist strategies. Grabel shows that evidence in support of neo-
liberal policies and institutions is mixed at best (such as for an independent
central bank and inflation targeting) in some cases and there is considerable
evidence suggesting that the policies and institutions are damaging in other cases
(such as the obsession with inflation, monetary and fiscal stringency, and trade
liberalization).

In conclusion, Grabel discusses and re-defines coherence so that it represents
an expansion rather than a constriction of policy space for adopting alternatives
such as new developmentalism. On a positive note, she observes signs of change
accompanying the 2007–09 financial and economic crises that have undermined
the legitimacy of neo-liberal prescriptions. In these changed circumstances, low-
and middle-income countries are becoming more assertive and stand a good
chance of succeeding in asserting their right to choose their own development
path.

Luis Abugattas Majluf and Eva Paus argue that a new developmentalist
capability-based strategy has to "bring the state back in" to achieve structural

change and improve the living standards of the poor in developing countries. At the core of a capability-based strategy is the expansion of knowledge-based assets, i.e., the capabilities to move production up the value chain and generate productivity growth that can sustain an increased standard of living. In addition to providing investment in basic infrastructure and education, governments – in some areas in collaboration with the private sector – need to implement pro-poor policies, provide support for productive sectors with high spill-over potential, and build institutional capacity (among others).

Whatever the country-specific combination of new developmentalist policies, a substantial increase in fiscal revenue is often central to governments' ability to implement the new strategy. But in the current global-national context, the increased need for public revenue conflicts with the declining ability of governments to raise it. Governments face a fiscal space dilemma as actual fiscal space is much smaller than the potential fiscal space.

While developing country governments have *always* faced constraints on fiscal space, Abugattas and Paus argue that the current globalization process combined with the legacies of the Washington Consensus have significantly changed the nature and intensity of these constraints. The authors propose an analytical framework for understanding the fiscal space dilemma which incorporates the sources of constraints and the channels through which they affect the fiscal space. They use it to analyze the fiscal space dilemma in Latin America.

The main constraints from globalization are international financial institution conditionality, international trade agreements, global market constraints, and competition for foreign direct investment including tax incentives, tax stabilization agreements, and investment agreements. The principal internal constraints are the size of the informal sector, institutional capacity for tax collection, tax evasion, and political economy considerations.

The authors explore possible national and international policies to broaden the fiscal policy space for development. Based on the internal and external constraints identified above, the authors suggest appropriate multi-lateral, regional and domestic policy actions. In particular, the theme of social justice, introduced in Part I of the book, recurs here because to break the Gordian knot, legitimacy has to be established to generate resources. The state is in a catch-22 because it needs legitimacy to collect revenue and deliver services. In many countries, state credibility has been shrinking as public service delivery is often poor and exclusionary. A way out necessitates the forging of a new social contract around effective budget reform that will have to include more taxes on the rich through property taxes and more effective, broader provision of public services. Concomitantly, supra-national action will be needed to relax some of the constraints stemming from economic globalization; for example, collective action is needed to overcome the perilous budgetary effects of inter-country competition for foreign direct investment. Such collective action will help governments adopt domestic policies that level the playing field between foreign and domestic producers, which is currently biased unequivocally in favor of foreign producers (through tax exemptions, investment treaties, etc.).

Gus Van Harten's chapter complements the preceding ones in Part III and shows how, because of a lack of legal capacity, interfacing with economic globalization can be problematic as low-income countries get overwhelmed by the litigation investment treaties expose them to. This can result in a serious loss of policy space and a regulatory chill.

The theme of "strong states, free markets" informs the neo-liberal project for the restructuring of government and its regulatory relationship to capital. Van Harten points out that, at the international level, this is represented by steps taken by major capital-exporting states (i.e., states whose nationals own more foreign direct investment [FDI] abroad than are owned within the state by foreign nationals) to establish investment treaty arbitration as a lever to constrain the democratic choice and policy space of capital-importing countries.

The lever is more powerful than comparable legal mechanisms for five reasons. First, it requires capital-importing states to consent to mandatory arbitration of disputes with any foreign investor (multinational firm) whose assets are subject to regulation by the state. Second, it assigns to foreign investors the triggering authority for the arbitration mechanism. Third, it creates a structural bias in favor of foreign investors by delegating to private arbitrators, rather than judges, the authority to determine the legality of regulatory acts of the state and the state's obligation to pay public funds to foreign investors. Fourth, to discipline states, it relies on broadly framed standards giving arbitrators wide discretion in their interpretation. Fifth, it utilizes the remedy of state liability and permits enforcement of damages awards against the unsuccessful state's assets abroad.

Recipient states bind themselves to ambiguously framed treaties with asymmetric terms vastly in the favor of investors, without knowing what they are binding themselves to. Moreover, the arbitrator's interests are aligned with the investors, to generate more business for the arbitration industry. Thus, it is not surprising that arbitrators often adopt an expansive reading of standards like "national treatment," "like treatment," "most favored nation" or "fair and equitable treatment." Standards of investor protection are applied at the expense of the recipient state in ways that would not be applied to high income states.

Other aspects of the Bilateral Investment Agreements (BIT) also disadvantage the host country. Many investment treaties contain an "umbrella clause" that obligates the state parties to observe or respect their "obligations" to foreign investors, beyond the obligations contained in the treaty itself. Performance requirements on FDI, used very successfully by East Asian economies, are ruled out. Finally, a liberal approach to forum-shopping, furthered in the treaties themselves, enables investors to design their corporate structure so as to maximize opportunities to bring treaty claims on the most favorable terms against a state in which they own assets.

In case of disputes, the treaties relegate authority to organizations whose power resides with capital exporting states or the investors. Many awards to date under investment treaties have disciplined states for general regulatory measures that affect foreign investors only indirectly and in unintended ways. In principle, when a state refuses to pay, the investor can pursue assets of the state in the territory of other states pursuant to the relevant arbitration treaties that provide for extra-territorial enforcement of awards.

Part IV of the volume is devoted to case studies of pro-active government using new developmentalist prescriptions. Kevin Gallagher and M. Shafaeddin show that China's industrial development is occurring at an unprecedented rate, as evidenced by the increasing level of value added in its products and its export competitiveness. The policies and performance of China stand in stark contrast to those of Mexico, where China's development is seen as "threatening" Mexican manufactured exports and development. Both countries sought to attract foreign direct investment into manufacturing and high technology sectors to gain access to technology and export success. Yet, while Mexico and China share similar export structures, the share of world exports for many Mexican export sectors is contracting while China's share in the same sectors is expanding at an unprecedented rate.

Gallagher and Shafaeddin conduct a comparative analysis of government policy to examine the extent to which China and Mexico's industrial policies affect industrial learning and upgrading in the manufacturing sector. They examine how policies regarding foreign direct investment, science and technology, R&D, and training as elements of industrial policy determine the relative decline in value added and world export markets that Mexico is experiencing vis-à-vis China, despite its privileged market access to the USA and Canada via NAFTA since 1995. In each case, they find that Mexico followed a neo-liberal "hands off" approach while China's openness to globalization was conditioned by a pro-active state. In particular, the Chinese state is pro-active in ensuring industrial learning, technological acquisition, diffusion and capability, and moving up the value chain in commodity production.

This analysis is used to provide general lessons on the merits of neo-liberal development policy versus what we term as a new developmentalist industrial strategy currently being practiced in China. Indeed, such policies were utilized by countries like Japan and Korea, who recently acquired high income status, as well as by those who achieved this status much earlier.

Since the turn of the century, and until the 2007–09 financial and economic crises, African countries experienced substantial improvement in economic performance marked by higher GDP growth rates, increased exports and better macroeconomic balances. This growth recovery represented a major turnaround from the history of economic stagnation and decline suffered over the ("lost") decades of the 1980s and 1990s. However, despite this encouraging growth recovery, African countries still face serious challenges of growth volatility, deep poverty, mass unemployment, exposure to external shocks, marginalization despite engagement with globalization, and low share in foreign capital and trade. Thus much is needed to both accelerate growth and increase its developmental impact. Leonce Ndikumana examines the sources of the recent growth recovery, analyzes its weaknesses, and discusses strategies for increasing growth rates, broadening the growth base and accelerating progress towards reaching national development goals.

He concludes that without a structural transformation that diversifies economies (and ends resource dependence), a productivity take-off in both agriculture and manufacturing, addressing structural constraints such as a shortage of physical and social infrastructure, and a growth-oriented macroeconomic framework, African countries are unlikely to generate adequately high or sustainable growth rates. Emphasizing pragmatism, flexibility, and good leadership, he also proposes forward looking strategies for achieving sustained growth which substantially resemble those proposed in Part II of the book.

These would not, however, be enough to address mass poverty and inequality; the latter would require pro-active employment and anti-poverty policies. Ndikumana refers to this as "mainstreaming poverty reduction in national development policies" with a major focus on agriculture and consciously redressing exclusion based on political power dynamics. It would also require scaling up aid, honoring commitments, and timely and predictable disbursements and new strategically managed regional and global partnerships (such as the emerging one with China). Finally, Ndikumana calls for a greater African voice in global policy debates which might be achieved via equitable representation in global development policy shaping institutions.

Lyuba Zarsky's chapter is the first in the concluding section of the book and brings to attention that industrial policy needs to be climate and social justice sensitive. She starts by reviewing the recent evidence put forth by climate science and demonstrates that global climate instability is unfolding faster than the most pessimistic scenarios projected in 2007 by the UN-IPCC (United Nations Intergovernmental Panel on Climate Change) in its Fourth Assessment Report. These scientific reports and vulnerability studies make clear that mitigation of climate change is urgent – and that adaptation is unavoidable. They also show that the greatest impacts of a warming and unstable global climate will be experienced by the least developed countries. While the climate is warming mostly due to the historical green house gas emissions of the OECD countries, many of the poorest (2.4 billion), who are the most vulnerable to climate change, lack affordable, efficient and reliable energy.

Zarsky argues that the "climate change imperative" – the need to both mitigate and adapt to climate change – points to the need for a fundamental shift in underlying development models and strategies. Despite evidence of poor performance, the dominant, neo-liberal development model remains fixated on promoting growth, primarily through globalization. She argues that the central goal of "climate resilient development paths" should instead be to provide sustainable livelihoods.

The provision of sustainable livelihoods, Zarsky suggests, requires the development of endogenous productive capacities that are ecologically sound – including low or no carbon energy sources – and that promote equity and social solidarity. To achieve this goal will require both a greater and more effective role for public policy, and more effective and innovative partnerships between private and public sectors. She then sets out five design principles for climate-resilient development paths: (1) proactive industrial policies; (2) industrial diversification; (3) the promotion of investment in public goods (including innovative engagement with foreign direct investment); (4) knowledge-intensive local adaptive management, and (5) partnerships between business, government and civil society.

Zarsky then evaluates climate resilience in three development models, namely, the neo-liberal globalization model, the sustainable globalization model and a new developmentalist model. She goes on to show that the neo-liberal model, with its emphasis on growth and hostility to pro-active industry policy, is most unsuited to climate resilient development. The strength of this model, however, is recognition of the potential benefits of trade and investment, including foreign direct investment. Zarsky argues that there is ample evidence that the marriage of pro-active and effective public policy with FDI has generated both growth and sustainability.

The sustainable globalization model, based on the notion of corporate social responsibility, has substantial overlaps with the neo-liberal model, including the emphasis on growth. It also has strengths including the call for standards, public private partnerships (PPPs), and the endorsement of "social businesses" to attain sustainable development objectives. However, despite these strengths, it is limiting, particularly with regards to the call for a "neutral" industrial policy, as in the neo-liberal case, and very limited in achievements.

She goes on to show that a new developmentalist model, which is context specific and institution based, has advantages and the ability to introduce climate resilient industrial policies, since it is based on pro-active government, for building endogenous technological and productive capacity. These traits are essential for climate resilient industrial development and make the new developmental model the best starting point for climate resilient development paths.

Nonetheless, much more work is needed to incorporate the insights of sustainability research in general and climate science in particular into new developmentalist theory and practice. Moreover, much of the new developmentalist literature has been poverty and gender blind. Finally, much of the focus of its industrial policies has been on the collaboration of the state and private sector, whereas it needs to be open to broader collaboration including municipal governments, labor, community groups and other civil society organizations, and international development organizations for attaining its objectives.

The title of Robert Wade's chapter in the first section is "The Market as Means rather than Master" and it sets the tone for this book. Wade argues that the global financial and economic crisis that began in 2007 is likely to lead to a search for alternatives that centers on an appropriate role for governments and markets. He presents an alternative that the other chapters of the volume build on. The concluding chapter of the book bears the title "Towards New Developmentalism" and takes up several of the issues highlighted in this introduction and also provides a synthesis of the major findings and conclusions in the volume.

This ambitious project is merely a point of departure. Issues such as the possibilities of adoption of an alternative program under weak governance conditions (corrupt bureaucracies in quasi democracies) and those having to do with embodying social, gender and ecological justice in the program need much more work and we hope that researchers will be stimulated to take on such work. I also hope that the introduction and overview in this chapter have whetted the reader's appetite to continue reading.

Notes

1 Thanks are due to Guseli Berik for providing extensive and invaluable comments on the introduction.
2 Other notable contributions include Alam (1989), Luedde-Neurath (1986) and ed. White (1988).
3 As of end-February 2010, it is far from clear that the global economic crisis is over. In the US for example, there is some speculation of a double dip recession emanating from a continuing weakness in residential construction, household and state level debt, and the expected termination of fiscal and monetary stimulus. Nonetheless, by early 2010, economic growth rates in most high and middle economies had turned positive and hence the reference throughout this volume to the 2007–09 financial and economic crisis.
4 New developmentalism has also been used by Al Bresser-Pereira (2006). The contending term was "neo developmentalism" proposed by Khan (2007). Both terms appeared earlier in the "grey literature" that showed up in *Google* searches, but often in the context of disciplines other than economics.
5 Khan (2005) presents a thoughtful account of what a developmental state represents and the structural transformation it brings about, but not necessarily how to get there. One could argue that whether or not a state is developmental is more a question of degree than an absolute.
6 Evans does not explore the historical origins of the state in depth. Kohli's (2004) comparative historical analysis addresses the question of why different state types emerge. His typology includes *neo-patrimonial, fragmented multi-class* and *cohesive capitalist* states. His approach is both historical and political. It is historical in that it explores the specific state's experience with colonialism, which in his view leaves the largest imprint on the type of state to emerge in the post-colonial period. It is political in that it gauges the state's ability to muster and effectively use power most critical to state success.
7 Also refer to Noguchi (2005: 2–4) on the origins of developmentalism.
8 See, in particular, Calclough and Manor (1991), DeMartino (2000), Lapavitsas and Noguchi (2005), and Ruccio (2008), and Cimoli *et al.* (2009).

References

Alam, M. S. 1989. Governments and markets in economic development strategies: Lessons from Korea, Taiwan and Japan. New York: Praeger.

Amsdem, A. H. 1989. *Asia's Next Giant.* New York: Oxford University Press.

Berger, M. T. 2004. The Battle for Asia: From decolonization to globalization. New York: RoutledgeCurzon.

Baker, D., Epstein, G., and Pollin, R., eds. 1998. *Globalization and Progressive Economic Policy.* Cambridge: Cambridge University Press.

Bresser-Pereira, L. C. 2006. "The New Developmentalism and Conventional Orthodoxy." *Economie Appliquee*, 59(3), 95–126.

Calclough, C. 1991. "Structuralism vs. Neo-Liberalism." In: Calclough C., and Manor, J., eds. *States or Markets? Neo-Liberalism and the Development Policy Debates.*" Oxford: Clarendon Press.

Calclough, C. and Manor, J., eds. 1991. *States or Markets? Neo-Liberalism and the Development Policy Debates.*" Oxford: Clarendon Press.

Chang, H.-J. 2006. The East Asian Development Experience: The Miracle, the Crisis and the Future. London/Penang: Zed Books/Third World Network.

Chang, H.-J. 2002. "Breaking the Mould: An Institutionalist Political Economy Alternative to the Neo-Liberal Theory of the Market and the State." *Cambridge Journal of Economics*, 26(5), 539–559.

Cimoli, M., Dosi, G., and Stiglitz, J. E., eds. 2009. *Industrial Policy and Development: The Political Economy of Capabilities Accumulation*. Oxford: Oxford University Press.

DeMartino, G. F. 2000. *Global Economy, Global Justice: Theoretical Objections and Policy Alternatives to Neo-liberalism*. London: Routledge.

Evans, P. 1995. *Embedded Autonomy: States and Industrial Transformation*. Princeton, New Jersey: Princeton University Press.

Fine, B. 2005. "The Development State and Political Economy of Development." In: Fine, B., and Jomo, K. S., eds., *The New Development Economics: Post Washington Consensus Neo-Liberal Thinking*. London: Zed Books.

Hirschman, A. O. 1959. *The Strategy of Economic Development*. New Haven: Yale University Press.

Johnson, C. 1982. *MITI and the Japanese Miracle*. Stanford: Stanford University Press.

Khan, S. R. 2007. "WTO, IMF and the closing of development policy space for low-income countries: a case for neo-developmentalism," *Third World Quarterly*, Vol. 28, No. 6, 1073–90.

Khan, M. H. 2005. "The Capitalist Transformation." In: Jomo, K. S. and Reinert, E. S., eds., *The Origins of Development Economics*. New Delhi and London: Tulika and Zed Books.

Kohli, A. 2004. *State-Directed Development: Political Power and Industrialization in the Global Periphery*. Cambridge: Cambridge University Press.

Lapavitsas, C. and Noguchi, J., eds. 2005. *Beyond Market Driven Development: Drawing on the Experience of Asia and Latin America*. New York: Routledge.

Lewis, W. A. 1954. "Economic Development with Unlimited Supplies of Labor." The Manchester School, 22(2), 139–91.

Luedde-Neurath, R. 1986. *Import Controls and Export Oriented Development: A Reassessment of the South Korean Case*. Boulder Colorado and London: Westview Press.

Nurkse, R. 1953. *Problems of Capital Formation in Underdeveloped Countries*. Oxford: Basil Blackwell.

Noguchi, J. 2005. "Introduction." In: Lapavitsas, C. and Noguchi, J., eds., *Beyond Market Driven Development: Drawing on the Experience of Asia and Latin America*. New York: Routledge.

Rosenstein-Rodan, P. N. 1943. "Problems of Industrialization of Eastern and South-Eastern Europe." Economic Journal, 53(June–September), 202–211.

Ruccio, D. F. 2008. *Economic Representations: Academic and Everyday*. New York: Routledge.

Sen, A. K. 2000. "What is Development About?" In: Meier, G. M. and Stiglitz, J. E., eds., *Frontiers of Development Economics: The Future in Perspective*. New York: Oxford University Press, 506–513.

Wade, R. 2004. *Governing the Market: Economic Theory and the Role of Government in East Asian Industrialization*. 2nd edn. Princeton: Princeton University Press.

Williamson, J. 2008. "A Short History of the Washington Consensus." In: N. Serra and Stiglitz, J. E., eds., *The Washington Consensus Reconsidered: Towards a New Global Governance* (New York: Oxford University Press).

White, G., ed. 1988. *Development States in East Asia*. London: Macmillan.

Part II

Conceptual issues and a new developmentalist agenda

2 The market as means rather than master

The crisis of development and the future role of the state

Robert Wade

"Convictions are more dangerous enemies of truth than lies."
(Nietzsche 1996 [1878]: 483)

"One day I asked a friend: 'What is life all about? Why are we working so hard?' My friend could not answer."

A book about the invisible foot soldiers who man China's production lines.
(Chang 2008: 174)

Introduction

The First World debt crisis, which started in 2007, may serve to waken minds from "the deep slumber of a decided opinion" (Mill, 2008) and direct attention to ways of "governing the market," including in developing countries as the crisis sweeps through them too. In this chapter, I first establish why the prevailing approach to development strategy (variously called neo-liberalism, the Washington Consensus, or the globalization consensus) needs to rethink its assumptions about the role of the market and the state. One important reason is evidence of (a) the failure of catch-up growth since the global shift towards neo-liberalism in the 1980s, and (b) the plight of Southeast Asian economies, which appear to be leading contenders to enter the ranks of the "rich" countries, but which are in fact caught in a "middle income" trap. This evidence challenges the argument that market liberalization should still be the microeconomic core of development strategy.

I then show that the prevailing neo-liberal position on the appropriate role of the state in a developing market economy – to enhance the efficiency of markets and reduce transaction costs by strengthening the rule of law, increasing transparency of public bodies, curbing corruption, reducing the regulatory burden, maintaining political stability, and so on – rests on weak empirical foundations. Next, I elaborate an alternative new developmentalist or "growth-enhancing" role, which embraces both policies and governance arrangements, and suggest that this role is important for rapid growth and diversification. Northeast Asian governments provide many examples of growth-enhancing governance mechanisms in action.

Finally, I turn to the question of why the neo-liberal approach has been so widely accepted in western development circles and subsequently integrated into these circles within the developing world. The answer leads back to the fall in the share of labor and the rise in the share of capital in western GDP, as well as to the New Wall Street System (NWSS) which evolved in response to these changes in income shares and further intensified them. Neo-liberal ideology about the market and the government has provided a powerful narrative to legitimize these changes. Western development agencies translated this ideology into policy agendas and projected them onto the developing world, helping to produce the instabilities and failure of catch up described earlier.

As of 2007–09 we are in the midst of a crisis *of* the global economy, not a crisis *in* the global economy – the first since the Great Depression. In a crisis of the system, the circuit breakers and built in stabilizers do not work, and the system does not readily reset. It has changed from a liquidity crisis (credit crunch) into a solvency crisis; from one in which most banks, firms and households are solvent but short of credit, to one in which a large proportion of banks, firms, and households are insolvent, their assets worth less than their debts. We do not have or cannot deploy the policy instruments which might steer us out of a solvency crisis in short order. It will continue to morph unpredictably around the world for several years, during which time world economic growth will be very low. Even developing countries not directly entangled in the inverted pyramid of credit-debt relations at the heart of the First World debt crisis will be badly hit.

To see how the dynamics of a "crisis of the system" are playing out, consider Britain as an uncontrolled experiment. At first sight, everyday life continues as normal. In London, West End theaters and opera houses remain fully booked. Yet the country underwent the fastest fall in house prices ever recorded in its history (down by 15 percent on average in the year to October 2008, as compared with the previous highest annual fall of 8 percent in 1992); the stock market fell some 47 percent between the peak in June 2007 and end-October 2008; consumption fell; the number of people made redundant or put on short-time work rose across almost all sectors other than fast food. The British state, hitherto famous for its advocacy of free markets and light regulation, crossed multiple red lines in a panicky "interventionist" direction. The Bank of England set the central bank interest rate to the lowest in its 300-year history. The state assumed a large ownership share in the banking system. The state also raised spending by borrowing, in lieu of raising direct taxes, to the point where fears mounted of a UK sovereign default, which jeopardizes the continued financing of government debt. Yet despite this "shock and awe" response, banks still hoarded cash, rather than lent, because of a pervasive lack of confidence in counter parties. The slump ground on...

As we begin to rebuild the global financial system, societies will no longer tolerate the practice of privatized gains and socialized losses, which has been the *modus operandi* of the financial sector for the past 20 years (Icelanders call it "the devil's socialism"). We will end up with a more stable, but less "innovative," system in which the state has a bigger role. More of the financial sector will be operated like a public utility (rather than like a casino) and subject to a similar kind of regulation as for pharmaceuticals, alcohol, gambling, explosives and other products with large "externalities," or even kept in public ownership to protect the public good of stable financial intermediation. Regulation will have to be much more multilateral than it has been, on the principle that the domain of regulation must coincide with the domain of the market. The G7/8 has already been superseded by the G20 which includes China, India, Brazil, Mexico, Turkey and South Africa.

The economics profession for the most part slept into the crisis. It bears a good part of the blame for brainwashing millions of people around the world that (a) governments hamper economic growth, (b) private markets create the wealth, and therefore, in terms of my title, (c) markets should be "master" rather than "means."

The argument – expressed in the admittedly extreme terms of a *Wall Street Journal* editorial entitled "Keynes really is dead" – is that:

> [G]overnment spending is less efficient, and thus less productive, than private spending. The government tends to spend on items (welfare, subsidies) that produce less economic growth than private investment does. The profound point about government spending is that the money has to come from somewhere, which means the private sector. The government must take it either through taxation or borrowing. "But either way," says University of Chicago Professor of Finance John Cochrane, *"no new wealth is created."*
>
> ("Keynes Really Is Dead," 2001: A14; emphasis added)

Surveys of American economists' opinions carried out in 1980, 1990 and 2000 confirm that propositions of this kind – based on the assumption that government "intervention" in markets typically has higher costs than "market failure" – command wide agreement (Frey *et al.* 1984: 986–94; Fuller and Geide-Stevenson 2003: 369–87).

Moreover, these beliefs are combined with an epistemology which claims that economics – or mainstream American economics – is based on "laws" of universal validity. Harvard economics professor and former Treasury Secretary Larry Summers expressed it well when he said, "The laws of economics, it's often forgotten, are like the laws of engineering. There's only one set of laws and they work everywhere" (Green 1995: 27).

However, these mathematically tractable "laws" apply to "markets," and part of the reason economists presume that "markets work best" is simply that they can analyze markets through the beautiful mind of mathematics. Unpicking the racking and mauling, which is the government process, is for them a Piranesian nightmare.

In some formulations the trajectory of income inequality between countries takes the shape of a Kuznets inverted-U: initially it widens as the lead countries race ahead while the others remain stuck in "tradition" or "pre-modernity," but eventually it falls as the laggards begin to catch up – their catch up propelled by the establishment of liberal market institutions and by earnings from land- or labor-abundant exports to rich countries. The growth of the richer countries therefore helps the poorer countries become less poor. Mutual benefit in the open world economy dominates conflicting interests.

The agendas of western-dominated multilateral organizations like the World Bank and the World Trade Organization rest on this argument of mutual benefit. They equally rest on the epistemological assumption that the unit of observation and prescription is the country (as in the marathon race metaphor). Though both the Bank and the Fund do some analysis of the international economy, it is not integrated into the core of their work, which is analysis and advice for countries treated separately. So while one part of the Bank urges country X to increase exports of cocoa another part is urging countries Y and Z to also increase exports of cocoa. Most strikingly, the 30 year run of the World Bank's flagship publication, the annual *World Development Report*, shows almost no effort to integrate the analysis of country-level trends and policies into the analysis of the international system in which country policies have to operate (Yusuf 2009). In an important sense, the Bank and the Fund are not global organizations.

The 2007–09 global crisis is a wake-up call, and these new circumstances provide more room for rethinking the appropriate role of states and markets in developing, as well as developed, countries. That is what happened after the last great crisis of capitalism, in the 1930s and on through the Second World War. It encouraged an opening of minds to arguments that we know today as Keynesianism and paved the way for acceptance of a more active role of the state in newly independent developing countries after the Second World War.

The general failure of catch-up growth

The editor of the British journal *Prospect*, David Goodhart, declared that "We have had 15 fantastic years, when almost everyone in the world enjoyed vast improvements in living standards. Unless this crisis turns out to be very bad, it will have been worth it."[1]

Martin Wolf, columnist for the *Financial Times* and one of the most influential economics commentators in the world, conveyed the same sense of vast improvements in material well-being over the past quarter-century in his book, *Why Globalization Works* (Wolf 2004). Wolf showed how the process of globalization – meaning the ascendance of neo-liberal policies, the resulting increase in economic integration across national borders, and subsequent increase in competition affecting all producers – has caused large falls in poverty and in income inequality between countries and between individuals on a world scale.[2] These findings pack a powerful punch: they show that to make development work we need to shift the world in the direction of neo-liberal capitalism, which is the only system able to produce a sustained rise in living standards for just about everyone.

David Goodhart and Martin Wolf articulate "facts" which form the conventional wisdom of our time. I shall suggest that the "facts" are substantially wrong. I have space for only a bald summary of an argument made at length elsewhere (Wade 2008).

Poverty

The World Bank's figures on the incidence of extreme poverty indicate that the world saw a substantial fall in the *proportion* of the developing world's population living in households with an average income of less than about PPP (purchasing power parity) $1-a-day or $365-a-year between 1981 and 2004, as well as a fall in the *absolute number* of people in extreme poverty.[3] On the face of it, this is good news – but the story cannot end there. The absolute number of people in extreme poverty *increased* globally between 1981 and 2004, when one country, China is excluded. The number of people in "ordinary" poverty (living on less than about PPP $2-a-day) *increased* substantially between 1981 and 2004, whether China is in or out, including in every developing region except East Asia (Ferreira and Ravallion, 2008). The surge in food prices in 2007 and the global economic crisis, which began in the summer of 2008, have almost certainly caused the poverty head count to rise substantially since 2004.

Moreover, it is not clear that the World Bank's numbers can be taken at face value, because it is not clear that the "extreme" or "ordinary" poverty line reflects the basic needs that would have to be met before it could plausibly be said that a person was not extremely poor. Calculations by the Economic Commission for Latin America (2001: 51) based on a poverty line defined by demographic and calorific criteria (unlike the World Bank line) suggest extreme poverty rates in Latin America often twice as a high as the World Bank rates for the same country at the same time.

Income inequality

Determining trends in income (or consumption) inequality is problematic because there are multiple measures of income inequality, none of which is "best," and different measures give not only different rates of change but different directions of change. Here, I argue that by plausible measures of income "catch up," development has failed; the large majority of poor countries are not catching up with the rich countries. Indeed, the average income of the large majority of states has been diverging or "falling behind," not converging or "catching up" with the rich countries.

Figure 2.1 shows the average income of several regions relative to that of the North, expressed in PPP dollars, from 1950 to 2001.[4] If the big increase in globalization starting in the early 1980s had produced catch-up growth, we should see these ratios *rise* during the 1980s and continue until the end of the series. For the most part we do not. Latin America and Africa display a relative decline *before and after* 1980, and Eastern Europe tracks Latin America. China, at the bottom of the graph for most of the period, starts to rise in the 1980s and continues to rise, reaching the average of the South by 2001. The Asia line (excluding China) rises a bit as well, also from a relatively low-income level. The conclusion is that developing regions outside Asia have not been catching up with the North, and that Asian catch up is occurring from a very low-income level, and has been sufficient to bring average income to no more than the average of the South by the turn of the millennium.

Figure 2.2 shows the average income of the developing world as a share of the North's, expressed in *market exchange rates*, from 1960 to 2007 – almost half a century.[5] The top line represents the whole of the global South, the bottom line the global South minus China. The ratio was higher before 1980 (during the era of "bad" state intervention), fell steeply during the 1980s (the decade of the worldwide shift towards neo-liberalism), flattened out at a much lower level during the 1990s, and had a small uptick after 2004 largely because of the commodity boom induced by fast growth in China. The trend is not consistent with catch-up growth, and with reference specifically to China and India, they show hardly any catch up on US average GDP between 1980 and 2006, and remain well under 10 percent. By this measure it is difficult to herald them as development success stories.

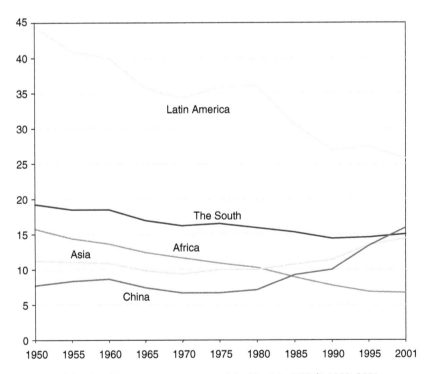

Figure 2.1 Regional income as percentage of the North's (PPP $) 1950–2001.

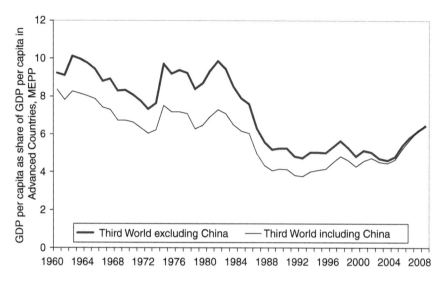

Figure 2.2 Third World income relative to the North's, including and excluding China (market exchange rates), 1960–2007 (source: International Monetary Fund (World Economic Outlook), World Bank).

Figure 2.3 shows the same information as the previous figure, but with incomes expressed in PPP $s. Here, the trend line of the average income of the global South relative to the North's *is* consistent with the globalization story: it turns up in the early 1980s and keeps rising. Exclude China, however, and the trend is much the same as in Figure 2 (which uses market exchange rates).[6]

So the claim that we know how to do development, because the evidence shows that the global switch towards neo-liberal or market liberalizing policies has generated catch-up growth, depends, empirically, on (a) one country, China, and (b) incomes measured in PPP $. Change either of these and the global South has been *falling behind* the North, rather than catching up. China, of course, has pursued a policy regime a long way from that endorsed by the neo-liberal approach, even while it has engaged intensively in international trade and investment. Furthermore, if we do not weigh countries by population, inter-country income inequality (measured by the Gini coefficient) increases substantially between 1970 and 2000 (from about 0.47 to 0.55).

A related, and striking, piece of evidence is shown in Table 2.1, as a "state mobility" matrix for the period 1978–2000.[7] It classifies countries into four average income bands (in PPP $). "Rich" countries are those in Western Europe, North America, and Oceania. "Contender" countries are those with average income two-thirds or more that of the poorest Rich country (Portugal in 1978, Greece in 2000). "Third World" countries are those with average income between two-thirds and one-third that of the poorest Rich country. "Fourth World" countries have average income less than one-third that of the poorest Rich country.

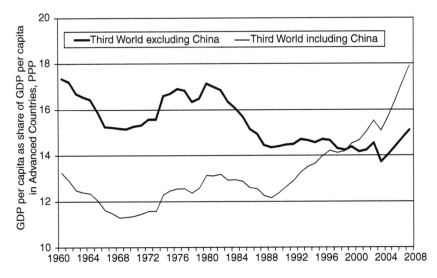

Figure 2.3 Third World income relative to the North's, including and excluding China. (PPP exchange rates), 1960–2007 (source: International Comparison Project (ICP)).

Table 2.1 classifies countries according to these categories in 1978, with Portugal's average income as the denominator, and again in 2000, with Greece's average income as the denominator. So a country like Venezuela, whose average income in 1978 was above Portugal's (hence "Rich"), but whose average income in 2000 had fallen to between one-third and two-thirds that of Greece (hence "Third World"), would go into the "Rich-decrease" cell (which contains 20 percent of the countries that started out "Rich" in 1978). A country like South Korea, whose average income in 1978 was between one-third and two-thirds that of Portugal and whose average income in 2000 was above that of Greece, would go in the "Third World-increase" cell (which contains 10 percent of countries that started out Third World in 1978).

Table 2.1 State mobility matrix, 1978–2000 (rounded %)

	Increase	*No change*	*Decrease*
Rich	–	**80**	20
Contender	15	5	**80**
Third World	10	30	**65**
Fourth World	5	**95**	–

Source: Derived from Milanovic (2005: Chapter 7).

Note
The table shows that 80% of countries which were rich in 1978 stayed rich in 2000; 20% went down. 15% of countries which were contenders in 1978 went up (to rich category), 5% remained contenders, 80% went down. 95% of Fourth World countries in 1978 remained Fourth World in 2000.

The table shows three important facts.

- The Rich countries have a low probability of going down, as though held aloft by magnetic levitation.
- The Fourth World countries have a very low probability of moving up – the Fourth World is like a slump from which escape is unlikely, as though subject to powerful gravity. China and India were in the Fourth World in 1978 and remained in the Fourth World in 2000.
- The Contender countries have a high probability of going down – most countries which were Contenders for Rich country incomes in 1978 fell into a lower category by 2000, as the Contender category hollowed out. It is as though the Contender countries too are subject to strong gravitational pulls. Similarly for Third World countries. In other words, the large majority of countries which could have gone up or down or stayed constant went *down* (into a lower income category relative to the Rich countries). Korea and Taiwan are quite exceptional in rising from Third World to Rich World in this period.

In short, several measures suggest that inter-country income distribution between 1978 and 2000 became more bipolar or twin peaked. Recall, however, that there is one measure which does show convergence, with developing countries in aggregate closing the gap with rich countries from the early 1980s onwards. It uses PPP incomes, and the catch-up trend depends entirely on China. If China is removed, even this measure shows developing country divergence from the North since the start of the 1980s for all but the past few years, not catch up.

All these measures use average national income. If we divide national populations into deciles and calculate the average income of each decile, then locate each country's deciles in the deciles of world income distribution, we get more bad news about catch up as shown in Table 2.2. All the developed countries have their deciles compressed within the top two world deciles. Korea's extend over

Table 2.2 Location of country deciles in relation to world deciles, 2006

	Top (10th) decile	*Bottom (1st) decile*
US	10th	9th
Sweden	10th	9th
Spain	10th	9th
Korea	10th	8th
Mexico	10th	4th
Brazil	9th	3rd
China	8th	2nd
India	7th	1st

Source: Derived from Korzeniewicz and Moran (forthcoming: Figure 5.2).

Note
The table reads: the US's top decile is in the top decile of world income distribution, its bottom decile is in the 9th decile of world income distribution; China's top decile is in the 8th decile of world income distribution, its bottom decile in the second decile of world income distribution.

the top three world deciles. The deciles of "middle income" developing countries, like Mexico, Brazil, and Argentina, extend over six or seven world deciles, as do the "success stories" of China and India. Such evidence as is available about movement across time suggests that the bottom half of developing countries' distributions have gained little or nothing as a fraction of the income of the North over the past 20–30 years.

Yet another piece of bad news for the neo-liberal or "gains from globalization" argument comes from the recent World Bank revision to the PPP income figures, based on a comprehensive price survey of 2005 (Chen and Ravillion 2008). Almost 60 percent of the world's population lives in countries whose Gross National Income (GNI) expressed in PPP $ was revised by more than 25 percent. In the large majority of cases, GNI was revised downwards, including China (−38 percent) and India (−36 percent). Thirty-seven countries had revisions of more than 40 percent. The new figures raise the Gini coefficient of inter-country PPP income inequality to close to the inter-country exchange rate Gini and raise the extreme poverty head count significantly (by two times or more in the case of China and India). It is not clear how the new numbers affect the *trends* in intra-country, inter-country, and global interpersonal income inequality, or in extreme and ordinary poverty. The statements about PPP incomes made above were based on the World Bank's earlier numbers (Beja 2007).[8]

Southeast Asia

More evidence about the failure of development – in terms of catch up with the North – comes from Southeast Asia (Malaysia, Thailand, Indonesia, Philippines, combined population 400 million). Of all developing regions, apart from China, Southeast Asia looks to be the most promising for upward mobility in the terms of Table 2.1. I shall argue, however, that Southeast Asia is stuck in a "middle income" trap and subject to strong downward gravitational pulls.

Since 1970, the structure of these economies has been transformed from natural resource-based activities to manufacturing, such that they now have substantial manufacturing capacities in electronics, electrical engineering, textiles, and automobiles. In 1970, Malaysia, the leading developer of the four, had 95 percent of its exports based on natural resources; by 2006, less than 30 percent. Few other developing countries have experienced so much structural change in 35 years (Yusuf and Nabeshima 2009; Doner 2009). Indeed, in Table 2.1, Malaysia and Chile were the only countries that jumped from the Third World income band in 1978 to the Contender band in 2000. At the firm level, Southeast Asian firms have been able to assimilate technologies from the West and match Western labor productivity in standardized manufacturing.

Yet all is not well and Southeast Asia seems to be stuck in a middle income trap. In terms of Table 2.1, Southeast Asia, apart from Malaysia, remained either constant between 1978 and 2000 or fell (Thailand stayed in Third World, Indonesia stayed in Fourth World, Philippines descended from Third World to Fourth World).

Since the Asian crisis of 1997–98, growth rates in Southeast Asia have fallen to around 4–6 percent, in contrast to 7–9 percent earlier in the 1990s. The recovery trajectory has been L shaped, with none of the Southeast Asian crisis-affected countries coming close to regaining the pre-crisis trend level of per capita output (Beja 2007: 57–72). Rates of investment have fallen. Unlike in Northeast Asia, the countries of Southeast Asia do not show indigenous design and innovation capacity sufficient to sustain diversification into new and more profitable sectors. Very few indigenous firms have created regional, let alone global, brands. Not a single firm in the whole region has embarked on a strategy for improving competitiveness based on innovation.

There has been little development of backwards linkages from multinational corporations (MNCs) to indigenous firms, signifying industrial deepening, as happened in Northeast Asia and is happening in China. Hence the domestic value-added in manufacturing remains low. Neither Malaysia nor the other three have established high quality universities or research institutes, to make a national innovation system worthy of the name.

If this is the story for Southeast Asia, the story for poorer countries is worse. As UNCTAD's *Least Developed Countries Report 2007* shows, the flow of knowledge from rich to poor countries, which can lead to new processes and products, is extremely limited, and the spillovers from foreign companies to domestic companies are slight. The Trade-related Intellectual Property (TRIPs) agreement of the WTO is one of many obstacles to bigger flows of knowledge.

In short, evidence about regional income relative to the North's, and about the diversification and innovation capacity of promising middle-income developing countries, calls into question the optimism of the "globalization works" argument, as seen in the remarks of *Prospect* editor David Goodhart, Martin Wolf of the *Financial Times*, and most of the policy advice of the World Bank and the IMF.

The debate about the appropriate role of government

The "globalization works" argument contains a policy prescription for "more market and less state." How well does the evidence support this? Ever since the neo-liberal revolution in development economics in the early 1980s it has been widely accepted – at least in western organizations which claim to think for the world, such as the World Bank, the IMF, and US Treasury. This argument states that developing countries should follow free market principles and that the direction of "reform" should always be towards the liberalizing of markets (though it was recognized that the liberalization of a few markets – finance in particular – would have to be accompanied by stronger regulation). This policy reform agenda has often been referred to as the Washington Consensus.

At first, all the attention was on *policies*. Specifically, on changing policies to shift the economy towards free markets and get the state out. But then, influenced by evidence that free market policies often do not work and by the research of New Institutional Economists like Douglass North about the role of economic *institutions*, the development community began to give more attention to institutions and governance as the next best thing. The argument gained currency that it was not enough to move towards free market policies because the institutions required for free markets to work well were typically weak in developing countries.

Free market policies therefore had to be complemented by governance reforms which would increase the *confidence* of market actors to invest, or "throw resources into the future." So the reform agenda of western development organizations came to give high priority to governance reforms, where the content of these reforms came from the market institutions prevailing in *already developed countries*, mainly the Anglo-American variety. To develop faster, developing countries had to bring their institutional matrix more closely in line with that already established in developed countries (as earlier modernization writers had argued).

Through the 1990s, the World Bank hired experts in governance who could advise governments on how to bring the market institutions of developing countries closer to those of developed countries, on the assumption that this would accelerate their development by exploiting the complementarities of free market policies and the institutions of efficient markets. At the same time, the World Bank was getting rid of its experts on industrial policy and industrial technology.

Market-enhancing governance

Evidence is now available which allows us to test the standard prescription that developing countries should give high priority to improving market institutions and governance across the board. We can score countries on several indicators of institutions and governance, and then on their growth rate in the subsequent period. The expanded neo-liberal argument predicts that countries which score higher on market institutions and governance will have higher subsequent growth. If this is confirmed, it supports the case for efforts to improve what we could call – following Mushtaq Khan – "market-enhancing governance."

There is now a sizable literature on the relationship between governance and economic growth. The indicators of governance include:

1   The rule of law (the quality of contract enforcement, the quality of the police and the courts, and the likelihood of crime and violence).
2   The regulatory burden (the incidence of market-unfriendly policies).
3   Control of corruption (both petty and grand corruption, and private entities' capture of the state).
4   Government effectiveness (competence of the bureaucracy, and quality of public service delivery).
5   Political instability and violence.
6   Voice and accountability (political and civil rights).

We could summarize these indicators by calling them indicators of the formalization of economic, social, and political regulation, or indicators of impersonal, as distinct from personal, mechanisms to sustain trust. The core argument is that societies which have a higher degree of formalization provide economic actors with more confidence to invest, and hence will show higher growth than those with lower formalization.

Figure 2.4 shows a large number of countries plotted in a scatter diagram, with governance scores on one dimension and subsequent decadal growth rates on the other. The linear regression line shows a slightly positive relationship between governance indicators and economic growth: higher governance scores go with higher economic growth. This seems to confirm the neo-liberal institutional argument, and to confirm that the World Bank, and other development organizations are right to emphasize "good governance" programs, because movement along the horizontal axis towards the higher governance scores of the developed countries will then enable them to move up the vertical axis towards higher growth rates.

Closer inspection shows that the positive slope of the linear regression line is due largely to the high governance scores of the developed countries, whereas our interest is in knowing whether, *among developing countries*, those with higher governance scores have higher subsequent growth. This is the test which Mushtaq Khan applies (Khan 2005: 69–80). He distinguishes three categories of countries: high income countries (the old OECD); converging developing countries, whose growth rate was above that of the median of the high income countries in the relevant period; and diverging developing countries, whose growth rate was below that of the median of the high income countries. It turns out that there are many more diverging countries than converging countries, as we would

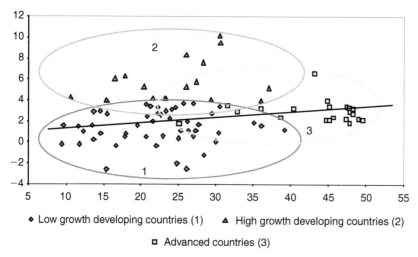

Figure 2.4 Stability of property rights and economic growth (source: Khan (2005: 69–80)).

expect from Table 2.1. Figure 2.4 shows the results for one governance indicator, pertaining to the strength of property rights in different countries, and Khan presents similar figures for the other indicators.

The results are clear: there is no difference between converging and diverging developing countries in terms of the median of all six of the above governance indicators, and no difference in the range of variation. In other words, *converging countries do not have better market-enhancing governance scores than diverging countries.* On the one hand, one cannot then say – as just about all the literature does say – that improvements in market-enhancing governance will increase the rate of growth. On the other hand, the difference in growth rates between developing countries does suggest the possibility that *other kinds* of governance capacities may be important in explaining the differences, and that programs to improve these other kinds of governance capacities may lead to improvements in economic growth.

New developmental or growth-enhancing governance

On the margins of the development community, a rival approach to economic governance has been elaborated, which could be called the "new developmental" or "growth-enhancing" approach. It rests on the assumption, first, that market efficiency in developing countries is typically low; and second, that it will typically remain low until quite late in the development process because causation runs more from development to market efficiency rather than from market efficiency to development (Wade 2004; Wade 2009a).

The new developmental approach rests, second, on the assumption that giving high priority to policies that raise market efficiency – like anti-corruption agencies or judicial reform – will give relatively little "bang for the buck." Indeed, the World Bank's publication, *Economic Growth in the 1990s: Learning from a Decade of Reforms*, published in 2005, buried the following observation deep within its headline platitude that "good progress has been made but challenges remain": "most of these interventions [to promote judicial reform] produced little change, as did the attempted reforms of other public sector institutions during the 1990s" (World Bank 2005: 280).

Third, even if the measures did make markets more efficient, efficient markets would not solve the problems of a developing country needing to shift resources out of unproductive sectors and into productive sectors, and to acquire and master more advanced technologies. For this, a more active role of the state is needed.

The underlying rationale is that the move out of sunset activities and technologies into new ones is commonly subject to large-scale market failure when these moves are not profitable for uncoordinated agents in the short run.

The state can potentially help to overcome this market failure and accelerate the move of resources into more productive sectors or activities. This approach can sanction a range of trade and investment interventions, such as selective protection, credit subsidies, capital controls, and hard bargaining with incoming foreign investment, which the neo-liberal model cannot. It can also sanction more coercive methods of transferring resources from unproductive uses to more productive uses, such as appropriative land reform.

However, these policies have to be carried out in a way which builds the confidence of economic agents that investments made today will yield returns to the agents who made the investments, provided the rules of the game are followed. Until the country has reached upper middle average income it may be difficult to provide the required level of confidence across the *whole* of the economy, but it is possible in selected sectors with more targeted interventions. The principle of the government giving more support to some sectors or to some functions than to others should be fundamental, given acute shortage of relevant resources in developing countries. Once the principle is accepted, it can be applied pragmatically, on a smaller or bigger scale depending on the resources available and on the capacity of the state; the suit can be cut according to the cloth available. Also, the government can "bet on success" (bet on some private sector ventures which look as though they could be successful with a bit more support), a role which could be called "government followership of the market"; or it can "lead the way" (commit public investment to a venture which private entrepreneurs would not otherwise want to undertake), which we could call "government leadership of the market." Hence, one can generate a two by two matrix with "big/small" on one axis and "followership/leadership" on the other. Korea's Posco steel plant would be in the "big-leadership" cell; but plenty of East Asian industrial policy would be in the "small-followership" cell (Wade 1990: 231–66; 2005: 196–213; 2008a; 2009; Kohli 2004).[9]

Interventions of this selective kind have to be complemented by a set of governance capacities which are different from those needed to expand the efficiency of markets across the board. The growth-enhancing governance capacity has to provide an extra-market source of discipline over the behavior of market actors to ensure that resources are transferred to growth sectors and that those who receive them use them to good effect.

The first key component of the governance capacity needed for growth-enhancing policies is what could be called an apex coordination point in the state, comprising a small number of individuals and organizations. In South Korea, during the catch-up phase, the apex coordination point included President Park, the Blue House, the top echelons of the military, and the Economic Planning Board. In Singapore, it included Prime Minister Lee Kuan Yew, the Cabinet, the Economic Development Board and the National Wage Council, and the American Chamber of Commerce.

The function of this apex coordination point is to draw in key elites and constrain their short-term profit seeking by a wider and longer term interest, curbing negative sum games between them. From their interaction comes the strategic vision of development, which the apex body causes to be widely shared outside the circle of insiders.

The second key component of growth-enhancing governance capacity is incentive schemes, including fiscal incentives, credit incentives, and others, targeted at priority production chains – such as the Heavy and Chemical Industry production chains in Korea and Taiwan during the 1950s to the 1980s. The aim is to stabilize confidence and to help obtain western technology in these priority sectors, not across the board.

The third important growth-enhancing governance capacity is discipline over the beneficiaries, and in particular, the ability to withdraw assistance either when the performance of assisted producers remains poor, so that industrial policy does not become a matter of "betting on losers," or when the assisted producers no longer need assistance to be competitive against foreign producers. This capacity requires assistance to be conditional on the attainment of stipulated performance conditions, such as bringing price and quality close to international standards (Amsden 1989; Wade 2004; Weiss 2003).

Of course, improving growth-enhancing governance does not exclude attention to the market-enhancing measures of the neo-liberal model. There is a trade-off, however: more attention and resources to market-enhancing measures (reining in corruption) causes less attention and resources to growth-enhancing measures.

At the level of global organizations this "new developmental" or "growth-enhancing" model of the role of government has had little support over the past 30 years. As mentioned, over the 1990s the World Bank cut its employment of experts in industrial policy and industrial technology, and replaced them with experts in the social sectors and in (market-enhancing) governance.

The development approach proposed here has a long history, going back at least to Alexander Hamilton in the late eighteenth century, concerned with how the US could catch up with Britain, and to Friedrich List in the mid nineteenth century, concerned with how Germany could catch up with Britain. In addition, the post Second World War "pioneers" of development economics, like Rosenstein-Rodan, Myrdal, Nurkse and Hirschman, as well as the UN's Economic Commission for Latin America headed by Raul Prebish, supported this approach to the role of the state.

However, from today's standpoint we can see that all these pioneer development economists remained too focused on interventionist *policies* and not enough on improving the governance capacities needed to make those policies effective. They also tended to favor relative closure of economies rather than strategic openness. In retrospect they were mistaken.

Ignorance of governance capacities and opportunities to expand exports helps explain the observation of many neo-liberal champions – like Gottfried Harberler, Peter Bauer, Jagdish Bhagwati, and many others – that many governments of developing countries which attempted to "intervene" in the market to raise investment and technology proactively by using protection and other kinds of industrial policy, had little success. On the one hand, consider India for most of the period from Independence to around 1990, for example, and Argentina for decades after the Second World War. In these and many other cases, growth-enhancing policies failed to raise investment and productivity, but succeeded in raising corruption and in raising the wealth and power of established elites. On the other hand, many scholars of East and Southeast Asian development in the postwar period claim that "growth-enhancing" prescriptions better reflect what the governments of these successful developing countries actually did than do market-enhancing prescriptions.[10]

The Japanese government in the early 1990s paid the World Bank over $1 million to finance a research project on East Asian development, in the hopes it would endorse something like the growth-enhancing model, which it said was the Japanese model. The World Bank published the study with the title, *The East Asian Miracle* in 1993. The Bank's researchers, caught between the wishes of Japanese financiers and pressures to confirm the World Bank's ideology, split the difference much closer to the Bank's ideology (though the study contained enough nods to the Japanese position to allow the Japanese government to claim a measure of victory). The preface says, for example, "[The study] concludes that in some economies, mainly those in Northeast Asia, some selective interventions contributed to growth," without even the protective cover of "may have contributed to growth" (Wade 1996). This is what the Japanese government paid $1.2 million to hear the Bank say.

Examples of growth-enhancing governance in East Asia

Here are some examples of new developmentalist or growth-enhancing governance mechanisms in operation in East Asia. The point to emphasize is that the capacities required to carry out these growth-enhancing tasks are rather different from the capacities needed to carry out market-enhancing tasks. For the several decades in which Korea and Taiwan were growing fast, they would have scored quite low by market-enhancing governance criteria; their formalization of rules was low, trust depended on personal rather than impersonal mechanisms, and corruption was rife, both petty and grand. However, within the generally lowly scoring institutional environment, strategic sectors brought within the circle of the apex coordination point had a high level of transactional security, even if achieved by mechanisms beyond the standard western approach.

First, the governments of Japan, Taiwan, and Korea contained departments which closely monitored the quality, price, and purchasers of imports down to the six digit level. When I did my research in Taiwan in 1983, the Board of Foreign Trade had daily information about what had been imported into Taiwan in the previous 24 hours and by whom. The information enabled industrial policy officials to compare the quality and price of imports against domestic substitutes, as a way of judging the performance of domestic producers in receipt of industrial policy assistance. It also enabled them to identify which import-buying firms to target for special encouragement to switch to domestic sources of supply (when the import figures were not clear inspectors could be sent to the docks to identify the destination of strategic imports). The assistance – whether in the form of protection, credit subsidies, fiscal incentives, or other – was explicitly or implicitly given against the condition of coming close to the quality and price of imports within a stipulated period of time. In this way, international competitive pressure was applied to domestic producers in receipt of industrial policy assistance, but in a mediated way.

Second, new producers in strategic and capital-intensive sectors (such as petrochemicals) would be assured that provided prices moved down towards international levels they would receive quantitative protection against imports for between two and five years, after which the protection would be removed. My research in Taiwan revealed many cases in which the Industrial Development Bureau gave assistance against conditions, the conditions were not met, and the government withdrew the assistance.

This being the most difficult of the growth-enhancing governance capacities, let me give an example from Taiwan (Wade 2004: 132). In 1982 the government wished to encourage investment in the new product of videocassette recorders (VCRs). It granted an import ban to help two of the main domestic electronics companies build their own production capacity. A year later, their prices were still significantly above Japanese imports. Warnings began to appear in the business press that, "If domestic manufacturers do not achieve international standards for technology and price within the period of guidance [note that word] ... then the government might consider bringing in foreign companies for joint investment ventures." Sure enough, 18 months after the start of the import ban the government announced it was allowing Sony to form a joint venture with a local firm (not one of the initial two), on the condition that 50 percent of production be exported after three years; the import ban was lifted.

Third, all these governments took an active and sustained role in obtaining important foreign technologies and ensuring their local mastery. Alice Amsden described many examples of growth-enhancing governance of this kind in Korea (Amsden 1989). Enos (1984) showed how the Korean government maximized the acquisition and mastery of foreign technology, much more actively than other governments, in the petrochemical industry from the early 1960s onwards. He compared the adoption of the same petrochemical technology (for ethylene) from the same US supplier (Dow) in Korea, Hong Kong and Chile and he compared the construction of three successive ethylene crackers in Korea from the same supplier.

With regard to output performance, he found that Korean facilities were brought to full capacity much faster than in Hong Kong and Chile, and subsequently exceeded design capacity by more than in the other countries. In terms of "indigenization" of skills, he found that the government bargained hard with Dow to increase the proportion of Korean engineers in each stage of development, especially in the more highly skilled jobs of design and procurement. He also found a significant increase of Koreans in these jobs over the three successive ethylene plants (even in the first ethylene plant the large majority of the engineers in the less skill-intensive construction, startup and operation stages were Korean).

More broadly, Enos showed that from the initial conception of a national petrochemical complex in the early 1960s to the semi-coerced transfer of ownership of the three ethylene plants from Dow to the government in 1982, the government was continually "on the stage," guiding the process as other actors came and went. Enos was in no doubt that the government's role was towards the "more influential" end of the spectrum from "unimportant" to "controlling," and further along to that end than the governments of Chile and Hong Kong. The story illustrates the Korean adage, "We never learn anything twice."

In a comparison between China and India, China scores no better than India when it comes to market-enhancing governance capacities referred to earlier (such as the rule of law, corruption, business regulation), but its economic performance has been much better. China's superior economic performance reflects the combination of more growth-enhancing policies and better governance mechanisms – such as the ability of local and central government to make land and infrastructure available to investors in critical sectors (often after existing owners or occupiers have been coercively dispossessed), and to offer fiscal and other incentives to foreign investors in these sectors. The Chinese government is also devoting significant resources to helping Chinese firms engineer their way around western patents.[11] The Indian government has done much less to improve growth-enhancing governance.

Why has neo-liberalism won out?

The neo-liberal narrative has been persuasive to the point of hegemony over the past 20–30 years. It has shaped the agenda of the World Bank and IMF, and that of successive governments in the US and UK. In the name of the "rational expectations theory" and the "efficient markets hypothesis," which say that financial markets tend to reach efficient equilibrium "by themselves," the US and UK governments have encouraged the growth of a lightly regulated financial sector, while remaining unconcerned about the decline of most manufacturing sectors. Yet the empirical foundations of the neo-liberal narrative are weak, as I have shown, at least when examined on a global scale. So why has it been so widely accepted? Much of the counter-evidence I have drawn on has been "out there" for a long time, but eclipsed by the "confirmation bias" established by the neo-liberal consensus. Some points are particularly noteworthy.

First, an intuitively appealing intellectual argument is at hand to make neo-liberalism the default position, irrespective of evidence. In its sophisticated form it says, to quote William Easterly, former World Bank economist and author of *The Elusive Quest for Growth*,

> Systems that respect individual rights do the best in the long run on economic development. Such individual rights include property rights, rights to dissent from prevailing conventional wisdom, rights to trade whatever with whomever you want, rights to enter new industries and start up new firms, rights to advocate new political directions, and so on [notice no mention of rights to work, employees' rights to participate in the governance of their firms and to form associations that limit the freedom of employers]. The theoretical appeal of this hypothesis is that individual rights can handle

systemic uncertainty by exploiting individuals' superior *localized* knowledge and powerful incentives to solve their own *local* problems, which will
lead to superior performance even if no policy maker at the top knows how
to raise growth rates.

(Easterly 2009: 136)

The flaw is clear from the italicized words. Individuals may have superior localized knowledge for solving local problems; but many kinds of market failure
endemic in developing countries require knowledge and coordination at a non-
local scale, which agencies of the state may be better equipped to provide.

Second, evidence which might upset the neo-liberal presumptions tends to be
simply ignored, or else treated as inexplicable. Here is William Easterly again,
who acknowledged in an interview in 2002,

> Things had gone very well in the 1960s and 1970s in developing countries.
> They had grown about as fast as the rich countries, and some of them con-
> siderably faster.... [T]here was a huge reversal of fortune just at the time
> when much of the advice that is standard today was becoming fashion-
> able.... And just as all of these efforts [of reform] should have been bearing
> fruit, they failed.

So the interviewer asked Easterly why the typical developing country did well in
the 1960s and 1970s when there was so much government intervention, often in
the form of import substituting trade regimes. He replied, "It is a bit of a mystery
why they did well ... the growth had a lot of mystery for me.... It is mysterious
to those [like me] who advocate hands-off markets" (Easterly 2002: 88–103).

By saying that the relative success of developing countries under regimes of
import substitution or other forms of "government intervention" was a "mystery"
and leaving it at that, Easterly protects the Washington Consensus from re-
examination and helps opinion-makers continue to advocate neo-liberal economic policies for all, while keeping talk of industrial and technology policy off
the agenda.

A third reason the neo-liberal paradigm has remained dominant is that the
number of "success stories" is far too small to support confident general conclusions about how to achieve superior long-run performance; in particular because
of the difficulty in separating robust, persistent causes from transitory and non-
replicable causes. Much of the evidence adduced for the success of a directive
role of the state in East Asia and in some other developing countries (including
Brazil in certain periods) is case study evidence, which carries little weight with
those who accept only econometric data as "real" evidence. Thus it is open to
jeers of Easterly's kind: "[T]he track record of dictators picking winners is very
poor, so why are we so sure that this factor contributed to the success of the
Gang of Four [East Asian tigers]?" (Easterly 2009: 129). Note the rhetorical
trick, commonly employed in the neo-liberal literature, of reducing industrial
policy to "picking winners," the easier to dismiss it with the phrase, "govern-

ments can't pick winners." However, these reasons for neo-liberal dominance all operate at the level of ideas and knowledge, as though in an academic debating chamber.

The fourth reason is more compelling because it is based on hard, material interests. In the 1980s, governments around the world (first in the West and then in the Rest) abolished exchange controls and other capital controls, allowing capital to flow freely wherever it could find the highest profit. This weakened labor in relation to capital, resulting in a fall in the share of wages in GDP and a rise in the share of profits. Then, after the collapse of the Soviet Union around 1990 and enhanced trade with China, India, as well as other large developing countries at around the same time, the global labor force roughly doubled almost overnight (Freeman 2007) with three main effects. One was to raise growth rates, a second was to depress the costs of everyday manufactured goods and hence depress inflation (the combination producing fairly high inflation-free growth), and a third was to raise further the share of profits in world GDP.

Top-level income inequality soared in most OECD countries, especially in the US and UK, to levels last seen in the 1920s. At the same time, intergenerational social mobility in the US and UK has remained low, relative to continental European countries. Remarkably, neither rising top-level inequality nor low social mobility has become a political issue (except Wall Street and City bonuses as the banks were bailed out by taxpayers in 2008). In Britain, for example, people tend to be clueless about income distribution and social mobility. When asked if they agreed that, "In this country the best people get to the top whatever start they've had in life," 49 percent of respondents agreed and only 43 percent disagreed in a poll in 2008. In fact, a middle-class child is 15 times more likely to stay middle-class than a working-class child is likely to move upwards.[12]

The advent of fast, inflation-free growth was interpreted by those who benefited most, as the result of the adoption of neo-liberal policies, especially the principles of limited financial regulation and getting other nations to open up to free trade and capital movements. They argued that the performance of the West and the wider world economy showed that (neo-liberal) globalization worked. At the individual and household level, those at the top interpreted their swelling prosperity as the result of their own clever judgment – which rightly should be rewarded by the market – rather than as the result of a general run-up of asset values and their disproportionate holdings of such assets.

No one benefited more from neo-liberal principles than the people and firms of the emerging New Wall Street System (NWSS). The system comprised commercial and investment banks, which increasingly traded on their own account as well as on behalf of clients, and which operated the "originate to distribute" business model (whereby they took fees for packaging debts into securities and selling the securities around the world, shifting some of the risks from their own balance sheets). It was also composed of a growing, unregulated, "shadow" banking system of hedge funds, private equity funds, Special Investment Vehicles and the like. The NWSS was phenomenally successful in generating much higher rates of return on capital than anywhere else in the economy, and much higher remuneration to the people engaged in it. It became a powerful lobbyist for the neo-liberal view about the appropriate role of government.

Of course, the regime under which the NWSS operated was, in reality, a long way from neo-liberalism in the sense that the financial industry was highly oligopolistic, with only a small number of big players who frequently colluded. But neo-liberalism provided the justification for regulators to adopt a narrow view of their function and for the US and UK governments to push the rest of the world to open up to their financial service industry.

Perhaps the most important reason why the neo-liberal narrative has been so widely accepted, then, is that it provides a coherent rationale for governments to act in ways which bring hugely disproportionate material benefits to the elites of a few sectors of the Anglo-American economy and its overseas offshoots. These elites devote resources and effort to promulgate this (Toynbee 2008 and Irwin 2008). In other words, the explanation lies mainly in the answer to the oldest social science question of all: "*cui bono?*" coupled with an ideology claiming that mutual benefit dominates conflicting interests. Or, as British Prime Minister Tony Blair put it, "If you end up going after those people who are the most wealthy in society, what you actually end up doing is in fact not even helping those at the bottom end" (Lansley 2006: 24).

However, the neo-liberal perspective obscured emerging problems in the world economy, which have come home to roost in the current global economic crisis. As investment rose as a share of GDP worldwide and output grew faster than wages, an "over production" or "under consumption" problem was created, or what Keynesians would call a lack of effective demand. Investment was increasingly driven into asset markets; first in Japan, where asset prices soared in the second half of the 1980s only to crash in 1990 and usher in deflation and a decade long recession; then in East Asia, where asset markets boomed through the 1990s until the crash of 1997–98; and finally in the US, where the stock market boomed in the 1990s with the rise of information technology, followed by the tech-stock crash at the turn of the millennium. All of these were debt-fueled bubbles in asset prices and investment, which then turned into what we could call "trubbles," or bubbles going down.

Around the turn of the millennium, with Asia contracting domestic demand and increasing exports, the US would have contracted after the tech-stock crash. But salvation came in the threefold combination of the New Wall Street System, which had emerged since the 1980s, plus the Fed's sharp cut in interest rates to ease the recession of 2000–01, plus the financing of US external deficits from East Asian surpluses. The combination enabled a big increase in property lending (since stocks were down), which fueled a property boom in many countries. With house prices rising, households could run up debt without making their household balance sheet appear unsound since the run up of debt was matched by rising asset values.

Eventually this bubble, too, became a "trubble," and the over-indebted had to sell or be foreclosed. Property prices tumbled. The New Wall Street System had sold securities containing property debt all around the world, and with these securities falling in price, banks and other financial organizations that had borrowed and lent on the basis of inflated asset valuations crumbled into bankruptcy or worse.

One of the upsides to the crisis is that there is now much less confidence in the existing Anglo-American model of banking, making substantial changes more feasible. However, most of the discussion about policy response assumes the roots of the crisis are in the financial sphere, and that some combination of tighter prudential regulation and making parts of the banking system operate more like utilities is the way forward, without touching the rest of the economy. It is certainly true that redesigning the financial system so that it is less prone to take excessive risks must be part of the solution.

Yet proposals for change in the financial system fail to address one of the main engines of instability which is the rising share of profits and the falling share of wages that create overproduction or lack of effective demand. For this deeper problem, higher taxation of profits is one solution. Development of domestic demand in developing countries (to lessen reliance on export demand) is another, for which higher minimum wages and enforcement of labor standards are helpful (Weller 2009: 67–86). Internationally, the governments of developing countries need to protect their economies from NWSS efforts to blow up bubbles around the world by treating exchange controls as a normal part of economic management. The evidence is all too strong that international capital markets do sometimes behave like drunken air traffic controllers. It is a fair bet that the combination of the financial market failure represented by the 2007–09 global crisis and the growing assertiveness of some developing countries in global economic governance will cause a shift in global policy norms towards thinking of the market more as means than master, much as happened in the 1930s. A program of action for this has been proposed in this chapter.

Notes

1 David Goodhart, personal communication, November 10, 2008.
2 Wolf (2006) explained why some countries are prosperous and others are not as follows: The "prosperous countries" achieved prosperity because they instituted "remorseless, pervasive, fair and open competition," while the poor countries did not.... "Policymakers need to understand that the aim of policy must not be to nurture specific producers, but to promote the interests of consumers and, so, competition." Of course, he takes as given that the competition takes place in the context of well defined and well defended property rights, so that competition does not take the form of piracy or other forms of illegal dispossession; and that the government has an important role to play in protecting property rights and fostering competition (which is why this view is called *neoliberal* rather than just liberal, which in the European sense denotes something closer to laissez faire).
3 On the purchasing power parity (PPP) methodology see Wade (2008, box 12.1).
4 Countries weighted by population, excluding "transitional economies."
5 Incomes expressed in market exchange rates smoothed over three years.
6 (Freeman 2009). Wolf (2004) does not present evidence of this kind. The nearest he comes is a table (8.1) giving regional growth rates for seven regions and several time periods from 1820 onwards. The table shows that, between 1950–73 and 1973–98

(the latest), six out of the seven regions had *lower* growth rates in the era of globalization and outward orientation than in the previous era of state intervention and "bad" import substituting industrialization. Wolf does not comment on the fall in growth rates.

7   Derived from Milanovic (2005 Table 7.3.).

8   It is not clear whether the new numbers are more reliable than the old. A source close to the International Comparison Project (ICP), which sponsored the data collection in 2005 and undertook the analysis (and is housed in the World Bank), said that the China price data comes from 11 cities (rural areas were hardly sampled) and that the surveyors interpreted the instruction in the ICP handbook to sample "internationally comparable" goods and services to mean they should sample prices in department stores. On the one hand the results showed, unsurprisingly, that "prices in China" were much higher than had been thought, and hence the purchasing power of the Chinese currency much lower, and hence China's GDP was much lower. On the other hand, the previous estimates for China were not based on any systematic price surveys, the Chinese government having refused to undertake one for the ICP going right back to the first round of ICP surveys in 1980.

9   On how to conceptualize "state capacity" see Kohli (2004).

10   Indeed, the Korean economist Kuen Lee, the Australian economist John Matthews, and I published a short piece on FT.com in 2007 outlining an argument along these lines and declaring a Beijing-Seoul-Tokyo Consensus as an alternative to the Washington Consensus – Beijing-Seoul-Tokyo in that order because the acronym is BEST (Lee, Matthews, and Wade 2007). Also refer to Wade 2009a.

11   Also refer to Gallagher and Shafaeddin, Chapter 11 in this volume.

12   Refer to Toynebee (2008) and Irvin (2008). The UK Labour Party government's Chancellor Alistair Darling declared "I'm not offended if someone earns large sums of money. Is it fair or not? It is just a fact of life." When he was then asked to define his politics, he replied, "Pragmatic. I believe passionately in living [in] a fair country and treating people properly, with proper respect and fairness" (Aitkenhead 2008).

References

Aitkenhead, D. 2008. "Storm Warning," *Guardian Magazine*, August 30th.

Amsden, A. 1989. *Asia's Next Giant*. Oxford: Oxford University Press.

Beja, E. 2007. "A retrospective on East Asian economic performance," *Challenge*, 50(5), 57–72.

Chang, L. 2008. *Factory Girls: From Village to City in a Changing China.* New York: Spiegel and Grau.

Chen, S. and Ravallion, M. 2008. "The developing world is poorer than we thought, but no less successful in the fight against poverty." Policy Research Paper 4703, World Bank, Washington D.C. (http://econ.worldbank.org/docsearch).

Doner, R. 2009. *The Politics of Uneven Development: Thailand's Economic Growth in Comparative Perspective.* Cambridge: Cambridge University Press.

ECLA (Economic Commission for Latin America). 2001. Panorama Social de America Latina 2000–2001, Santigao.

Easterly, W. 2009. "The indomitable in pursuit of the inexplicable: The World Development Reports' Failure to Comprehend Economic Growth Despite Determined Attempts, 1978–2008." In: Yusuf, S. ed., *Development Economics through the Decades: A Critical Look at Thirty Years of the World Development Report.* Washington D.C: World Bank Publications.

Easterly, W. 2002. "The failure of development economics," *Challenge*, 45(1), 88–103.

Enos, J. 1984. "Government intervention in the transfer of technology: the case of South Korea," *IDS Bulletin*, 15(2), 26–31.

Ferreira, F. H. G. and Ravallion, M. 2008. "Global poverty and inequality: a review of the evidence," Policy Research Working Paper 4623, Washington, D.C.: World Bank, http://www-wds.worldbank.org/external/default/WDSContentServer/IW3P/IB/2008/05/19/000158349_20080519142850/Rendered/PDF/wps4623.pdf.

Freeman, R. B. 2007. "The Challenge of the Growing Globalization of Labor Markets to Economic and Social Policy." In: Paus, E. ed., Global Capitalism Unbound: Winners and Losers from Offshore Outsourcing. New York: Palgrave Macmillan.

Freeman, A. 2009. "The poverty of statistics." *Third World Quarterly*, 30(8), 1427–48.

Frey, B., Pommerehne, W. Schneider, F., and Gilbert, G. 1984. Consensus and Dissensus among Economists: An Empirical Inquiry. *American Economic Review*, 74(5), 986–94.

Fuller, D. and Geide-Stevenson, D. 2003. Consensus among economists: revisited. *Journal of Economic Education*, 34(4), 369–87.

Green, D. 1995. *The Silent Revolution: The Rise of Market Economics in Latin America.* London: Cassell.

Irvin, G. 2008. *Super Rich: The Rise of Inequality in Britain and the United States.* Cambridge: Polity Press.

Khan, M. 2005. "The Capitalist Transformation." In: Jomo, K. S. and Reinert, E. S., eds., *The Origins of Development Economics: How Schools of Economic Thought Have Addressed Development.* New Delhi and London: Tulika Books and Zed Press, 69–80.

Kohli, A. 2004. *State-directed Development*, Cambridge: Cambridge University Press.

Korzeniewicz, R. P. and Moran, T. 2009. *Unveiling Inequality: A World-Historical Perspective* New York: Russell Sage Foundation.

Lansley, S. 2006. *Rich Britain: The Rise and Rise of the New Super-wealthy.* London: Politico's Publishing.

Lee, K., Matthews, J., and Wade, R. 2007. "Rethinking development policy: from Washington Consensus to Beijing–Seoul–Tokyo Consensus," *Financial Times.com*, October 19th.

Mill, J. S. 2008. *On Liberty.* Sioux Falls, SD: Nuvision Publications.

Milanovic, B. 2005. *Worlds Apart: Measuring International and Global Inequality.* Princeton: Princeton University Press.

Nietzsche, F. 1996. *Human, All Too Human.* Translated by R. J. Hollingdale. Cambridge: Cambridge University Press.

Rodrik, D. 2007. *One Economics, Many Recipes: Globalization, Institutions, and Economic Growth.* Princeton: Princeton University Press.

Toynbee, P. 2008. "Without the facts on pay, how can we judge what is fair?" *The Guardian*, December 9th.

Wade, R. 2009. "Rethinking Industrial policy in low-income countries," *African Development Review*, 21(2), pp. 352–66.

Wade, R. 2009a. "The Washington Consensus," in *International Encyclopedia of the Social Sciences*. Oxford: Elsevier Science, forthcoming.

Wade, R. 2008. "Globalization, growth, poverty, inequality, resentment and imperialism." In: Ravenhill, J., ed., *Global Political Economy*. Oxford: Oxford University Press, Chapter 12.

Wade, R. 2008a. "How can Middle-Income Countries Escape 'Gravity' and Catch up with High Income Countries? The Case for Open Economy Industrial Policy," CEEOL (Central and Eastern European Online Library), Frankfurt, www.ceeol.com.

Wade, R. 2005. "Escaping the squeeze: lessons from East Asia on how middle-income countries can grow faster," In: B. Laperche and D. Uzunidis, eds., *John Kenneth Galbraith and the Future of Economics*. New York: Palgrave Macmillan.

Wade, R. 2004. *Governing the Market*. Princeton: Princeton University Press.

Wade, R. 1996. "Japan, the World Bank, and the art of paradigm maintenance: The East Asian Miracle in Political Perspective," *New Left Review*, 217 (May/June), 3–36.

Wade, R. 1990. "Industrial policy in East Asia: does it lead or follow the market?": In Gereffi, G., and Wyman, D., eds., *Manufacturing Miracles: Paths of Industrialization in Latin America and East Asia*. Princeton: Princeton University Press.

The Wall Street Journal, 2001, "Keynes Really is Dead," October 19th, p.A14.

Weiss, L. 2003. *States in the Global Economy: Bringing Domestic Institutions Back in*, Cambridge: Cambridge University Press.

Weller, C. 2009. In trade, you can eat your cake and have it, too. *Challenge*, 52(1), 67–86.

Wolf, M. 2006, "Competition would overthrow the tyranny of vested interests," *Financial Times*, January 18th.

Wolf, M. 2004. *Why Globalization Works*. New Haven: Yale University Press.

World Bank. 2005. "Improving public sector governance." In: *Economic Growth in the 1990s*, Washington D.C.: World Bank, Chapter 9.

Yusuf, S. 2009. *Development Economics through the Decades: A Critical Look at 30 Years of the World Development Report*. Washington D.C.: World Bank Publications.

Yusuf, S. and Nabeshima, K. 2009. "Tigers Under Threat: The Search for a New Growth Strategy by Malaysia and Its Southeast Asian Neighbors," World Bank, forthcoming.

3 *Hamlet* without the Prince of Denmark

How development has disappeared from today's "development" discourse[1]

Ha-Joon Chang

Introduction

The definition of "development" has always been a contentious one. Income level is of course one of the most widely accepted measures of development, but most people would agree that development is more than providing higher material standards of living. The most well known in this respect is the UNDP's human development index (HDI) and its variations, which try to incorporate non-income dimensions of human welfare, such as education, health, and gender equality. HDI and similar measures of development (e.g., the physical quality of life index – a 1970s predecessor of HDI) are useful in pointing out that the possession of material goods alone cannot fulfill our lives – we need self-realization and dignity. The "humanistic" dimension of development emphasized by these indicators is essential in reminding us that material progress is only the ends and not the means of development. There is another dimension to development that used to be central in its definition in the early days of development economics but has become increasingly forgotten: the "production" side of development.

Before the rise of neo-liberalism in the late 1970s, there was a general consensus that development is largely about the transformation of the productive structure (and the capabilities that support it) and the resulting transformation of social structure – urbanization, dissolution of the traditional family, changes in gender relationships, rise of labor movement, the advent of the welfare state, and so on. This was mainly, though not exclusively, to be achieved through industrialization. Even though they radically disagreed on how exactly this was to be done, most commentators – ranging from Walt Rostow on the right and the Dependency Theorists on the left – shared the view that development centers around a process of transformation in the productive sphere.

Most of us still hold such a view of development at the instinctive level. For example, most people would not classify some oil-rich countries with incomes higher than those of some "developed" countries as "developed." In refusing to classify these countries as "developed," we are implicitly saying that achieving a high income through a resource bonanza is not "development" – the high income should be somehow "earned." At the other extreme, following the

Second World War, Germany's income level fell to that of Peru or Mexico, but few people would argue that Germany should have been reclassified as a "developing" country, because we know that Germany still had the necessary technologies and organizational capabilities to regain its prewar level of living standards quickly.[2] These examples show we implicitly believe that to qualify as "developed," an economy's high income should be based on superior knowledge, embodied in technologies and institutions, rather than simple command over resources.

However, during the last quarter of a century, at the more formal level, "development" has come to mean something quite different from what it used to mean. As I shall show below, "development" has come to mean poverty reduction, provision of basic needs, individual betterment, and sustenance of existing productive structure – that is, anything but "development" in the traditional sense. In other words, development discourse has turned into *Hamlet* without the Prince of Denmark!

In this chapter, I analyze the use of the term, "development," in some of today's key "development" discourses – the Millennium Development Goals of the United Nations, the Doha Development Agenda (DDA) of the WTO (World Trade Organization), and the discourse on micro-finance. I will argue that these discourses have a view of "development" that lacks a vision of transformation in productive structures (and the development of social and technological capabilities that are both the causes and the consequences of such transformation). Consequently, they are unable to promote development and can even be anti-developmental. At most, today's mainstream view of development is that of *ersatz* development, which relies upon uncoordinated individual initiatives. I conclude by arguing that a discourse on "new developmentalism" should be constructed by reviving the "productionist" concern of the old development economics while paying greater attention to the issues of human development, politics, technological development, institutions, and the environment than was the case in the old days.

Development without development: the MDGs

Since the rise of neo-liberalism in the late 1970s and early 1980s, many people in rich countries, both inside and outside of academia, have adopted the view that developing countries are what they are only because of their own inabilities and corruption and rich countries have no moral obligation to help them. Indeed, there is a growing view that helping developing countries is actually bad for them because it will only encourage a dependency mentality.

Fortunately, the aforementioned is not a mainstream view in all rich countries. Most people still believe that, with strong help from rich countries, developing countries can pull themselves out of poverty. The most "progressive" and comprehensive of the mainstream discourses on development along this line is arguably embodied in the United Nation's Millennium Development Goals (MDGs). According to the UN, the eight broad goals are as follows:

Goal 1: Eradicate extreme poverty and hunger.

Goal 2: Achieve universal primary education.

Goal 3: Promote gender equality and empower women.

Goal 4: Reduce child mortality.

Goal 5: Improve maternal health.

Goal 6: Combat HIV/AIDS, malaria, and other diseases.

Goal 7: Ensure environmental sustainability.

Goal 8: Develop a global partnership for development.

There are many different elements to the MDGs, especially as each goal has a number of "targets" that span different sub-issues, but most of them relate to reducing poverty and improving education and health in poor countries. This is obvious in the case of Goals 1–6, but even Goal 7 (environmental sustainability) is partly about health (improving access to safe drinking water and increasing access to improved sanitation).[3]

Laudable as these goals and targets may be, their sum does not amount to development in a meaningful sense, as they pay no serious attention to the transformation of productive structure and capabilities. The only explicit "development" dimension to the MDGs is embodied in Goal 8. The targets under this heading include: development of an "open, rule-based, predictable, nondiscriminatory trading system"; reduction or even writing-off of developing country foreign debt; increase in foreign aid from rich countries, including trade related technical assistance; provision of access to affordable essential drugs for developing countries; and the spread of new technologies, mainly information and communications technologies.

The emphasis in this vision is very much on the trinity of increased aid, debt reduction, and increased trade. Debt reduction and increased aid (unless they are on a very large scale, which is unlikely) are simply enabling conditions, rather than those that determine the contents of development. The view of the relationship between trade and development is central to understanding the vision of development underlying the MDGs. So what are the contents of an "open, rule-based, predictable, nondiscriminatory trading system" that the MDG agenda refers to?

From the concrete indicators that measure the "developmental" contribution of the world trading system in the MDG discourse, we see that the "pro-developmental" trading system boils down to one in which rich countries reduce their tariffs and subsidies on agriculture, textile, and clothing exports from developing countries, especially the least developed countries (LDCs).

However, the understanding of the relationship between trade and development implicit in this vision is non-developmental. In this vision, the best way to make trade spur development is by liberalizing rich country markets so that developing countries can sell more of what they are already selling – or "trade their way out of poverty," as a popular slogan puts it. There is no notion that developing countries need to get out of what they are doing now (their current specialization is after all what keeps them poor) and move into higher-productivity activities, if they are to achieve development.[4]

Thus seen, the MDG envisages "development without development." Most of what it takes as "development" is really the provision of basic needs and poverty reduction. What little attention is paid to the question of production is a result of the view that development can be achieved by specializing more in the products in which a country has comparative advantage (supported by the rich countries reducing debts and giving more aid).

However, doing more of the same thing in terms of productive activities is not how today's developed countries developed. Starting from eighteenth-century Britain through nineteenth-century USA, Germany, and Sweden, down to twentieth-century Japan, Korea, and Taiwan, history has repeatedly shown that development is achieved by upgrading productive capabilities and moving into more "difficult" industries *before* they acquire comparative advantages in those new activities, by using protection, subsidies, and other means of market-defying government intervention (Chang 2002, 2007).[5] Let me give some prominent examples.

In 1960, when Nokia entered the electronics industry, the per capita income of Finland was only 41 percent that of the US, the frontier country in electronics and overall ($1,172 vs. $2,881). It was thus not a big surprise that the electronics subsidiary of Nokia ran losses for 17 years and remained in business mainly because of cross-subsidization from mature firms in the same business group (helped by government procurement programs).

In 1961, the per capita income of Japan was a mere 19 percent that of the US ($563 vs. $2,934), but Japan was then protecting and promoting all sorts of "wrong" industries through high tariffs, government subsidies, and a ban on foreign direct investment – automobile, steel, shipbuilding, and so on.

To take an even more dramatic example, take the case of South Korea. Its (then) state-owned steel mill, POSCO, which had been set up in 1968, started production in 1972, when its per capita income was a mere 5.5 percent of US income ($322 vs. $5,838).[6] To make matters worse, in the same year, South Korea decided to deviate even further from its comparative advantage by launching its ambitious Heavy and Chemical Industrialization program, which promoted shipbuilding, (home-designed) automobile, machinery, and many other "wrong" industries. Even as late as 1983, when Samsung decided to design its own semi-conductors, Korea's income was only 14 percent that of the US ($2,118 vs. $15,008).

By discussing these examples of countries that defied the market and entered activities where they did not have a comparative advantage, I do not mean that all forms of "traditional" activities, such as agriculture or textile/clothing, are incompatible with development. After all, the Netherlands is still the world's third largest exporter of agriculture despite not having much land (it has the fifth highest population density in the world, excluding city states or island states with territories less than, and including, that of Hong Kong).[7] Germany used to be the world's fifth largest exporter of textiles and clothing until as late as the early 1990s. However, this was possible only because these countries applied advanced technologies to these "traditional" activities and upgraded them – hydroponic culture in the case of Dutch agriculture and specialty textiles and high-class design in the case of German textile/clothing. At the other extreme, countries like the Philippines export a lot of high-tech products, like electronics, but no one calls it developed because the production uses someone else's technologies, is organized by someone else, and has few roots in the domestic economy. Should all the multinational companies decide to leave the Philippines tomorrow, it will be reduced to exporting primary commodities.

Again, these examples confirm my earlier point that it is *not what one has but how one has got it* that determines whether a country is developed or not. Without any vision of transformation in productive structure and the upgrading of the productive capabilities that make it possible, the vision of development behind the MDGs can only be described as "development without development."

Anti-developmental development agenda: the DDA

The "non-developmental" nature of the MDGs is bad enough. However, the "development" discourse becomes positively anti-developmental when it comes to the Doha "Development" Agenda (DDA) of the WTO talks.

Launched in November 2001 in the Doha ministerial talks of the WTO, the DDA claims to provide special attention to the needs of developing countries, compared to previous rounds of trade talks. There are many different elements to its agenda, which comprises 21 areas such as agricultural subsidies and e-commerce. However, the core of the DDA is what we can describe as the "agriculture-industry swap" between developed countries and developing countries – basically the former countries lower their agricultural tariffs and subsidies, in return for the latter lowering their industrial protection under the so-called non-agricultural market access (NAMA) negotiations.

The negotiations are stalled at the moment (and could collapse, given the current global economic crisis), mainly because of the magnitude of the cuts on both sides. Even as they disagree on who should cut their tariffs and subsidies in which areas by how much, most people seem to accept the principle behind the agenda itself – that the developed countries should specialize in industry and developing countries should specialize in agriculture and therefore whatever makes that specialization difficult should be criticized.

The first problem with this vision is that an agriculture-industry swap is not going to help "development" very much even in the anodyne MDG sense. In reality, many developing countries are net agricultural importers and thus unlikely to benefit from agricultural liberalization in developed countries. They may even get hurt as a result of agricultural liberalization in developed countries, if they happen to be importers of those agricultural products that are heavily subsidized by developed countries. This could directly hinder MDG goals regarding hunger and health.

Overall, the main beneficiaries of the opening of agricultural markets in the developed world will be other developed countries with strong agriculture –

the USA, Canada, Australia, and New Zealand.[8] Most developing countries export agricultural products that are not protected very much by developed countries for the simple reason that they do not have any domestic producers (e.g., coffee, cocoa). Only two developing countries, Brazil and Argentina, are likely to benefit from this in a major way because they are major exporters of the "temperate" products where developed country tariffs and subsidies are concentrated (e.g., beef, wheat). Moreover, some (although obviously not all) of the prospective losers from agricultural trade liberalization within the developed countries will be the least well-off people by their national standards (e.g., hard-pressed farmers in Norway, Japan, or Switzerland), while some of the prospective beneficiaries in developing countries are rich even by international standards (e.g., agricultural capitalists in Brazil or Argentina). In this sense, the popular idea that agricultural liberalization in the developed countries mainly helps poor peasant farmers in developing countries is totally misleading.[9]

More importantly, in the long run, the DDA is likely to hinder, rather than help, development, by making it structurally difficult for developing countries to transform their productive capabilities. This is because, in return for the liberalization of agriculture and textile/clothing by developed countries, developing countries are required to reduce their industrial tariffs (which ironically demonstrates that developed countries do not really believe in free trade theory, which asserts that trade liberalization does not require any compensation – unilateral trade liberalization is always beneficial, whatever one's trading partner does).

Of course, the reduction of industrial tariffs may bring some benefit to consumers within developing countries, but these gains are unlikely to be more than (a one-off gain of) 1.5 percent of developing country income even according to the optimistic scenarios envisaged by the World Bank (Chang 2005, p. 28). Moreover, these short-term gains are likely to be quickly overwhelmed by the long-term losses that come from the inability (due to tariff cuts) to promote "infant" industries. In addition to the historical evidence discussed in the previous section, there are many respectable economic theories that show a transformation in the productive structure of a developing country is highly unlikely without some sort of "infant" industry protection (and other supportive policies) (Chang 2005).

The potential long-run damages to development from the NAMA negotiations are great, as the cuts in industrial tariffs of developing countries proposed by the developed countries in the NAMA negotiations are on historically unprecedented scales. Even though the US proposal to abolish all industrial tariffs by 2015 is considered a deliberately radical opening gambit, the core US proposal is to bring average industrial tariffs in developing countries down to 5–7 percent by 2010, the lowest level since the days of colonialism and unequal treaties when weaker countries were deprived of policy autonomy, especially the right to set tariffs (on colonialism and unequal treaties, see Chang 2002, pp. 51–4).[10] With very few exceptions, they will be also lower than the rates that had prevailed in current developed countries until the early 1970s (see Chang 2005, for further details).[11]

Moreover, the context in which industrial tariff cuts are to be made magnifies their potential negative impacts. The range of policy tools available to developing countries has shrunk sharply in the last two decades. During this period, through the WTO and various bilateral and regional FTAs (free-trade agreements), subsidies, quantitative restrictions, foreign investment regulations (such as local content requirements), directed credit programs, foreign exchange rationing, and many other tools of industrial promotion have become either impossible to use or very circumscribed. Given this shrinkage in policy space, the relative importance of tariffs as a policy tool has, unintentionally, increased significantly in the recent period (on the question of policy space, see Chang 2005, and Gallagher (ed.) 2005). If the ability to use tariffs is curtailed significantly, there will be few other policy tools that developing countries can use to engineer the transformation of their productive structure and capabilities.

To make matters worse, the tariff cuts are to be made in a much more stringent manner than before. For example, in the Uruguay Round, tariff cuts involved only cuts in (trade-weighted) average tariffs. This time, a "Swiss" formula, which requires higher tariffs be cut most steeply and that tariffs are cut *line-by-line*, is to be employed. This means that developing countries are not even going to have the freedom to protect some key sectors while cutting tariffs in others. In contrast, in agriculture, where they are largely on the defensive, developed countries advocate a much less draconian tariff reduction formula and are refusing to put caps on agricultural tariffs.

Thus seen, the DDA deal is not simply non-developmental (like the MDGs) but is deeply anti-developmental in the sense that it not only encourages developing countries to stick to their current production structure but also makes it impossible for them to move away from it in the future.[12]

Ersatz developmentalism: the MDGs and micro-finance

Having shown how the dominant vision of development fails to see development as the process of transforming a country's productive structure and capabilities, it would be unfair to suggest that there is no attempt whatsoever to increase productive capabilities in that vision. After all, improvements in health and education emphasized by the MDGs should increase the productive capabilities of individuals, especially the poor.

However, today's mainstream development discourse sees these increases in productive capabilities as happening mainly through individual betterment. For example, six of the eight MDGs are about improving the income, health, and education of individuals (with the partial exception of Goal 3 – gender equality and female empowerment – which by definition is a "relational" goal). There is relatively little discussion of the need to improve social institutions, except in the vague assertion that developing countries should be encouraged, or even required, to adopt "global standard" institutions (for a critique of the global standards discourse, see Chang 2007a and 2007b). Micro-finance, which, according to today's orthodoxy, is supposed to promote development by helping people lift themselves out of poverty through their own entrepreneurial efforts (for a "productionist" critique of microfinance, see Bateman and Chang 2009). Even the mainstream discourse on institutions emphasizes the protection of private property rights, partly because it is seen as crucial in inducing rational self-seeking individuals into entrepreneurial activities (Chang 2007a).

At one level, there is nothing wrong with all this. Entrepreneurship is an important force behind the increase in a country's productive capability. When the capabilities of individuals in a country – whether in terms of education, health, or ability to acquire credit (as in microfinance) – are enhanced, the country's productive capabilities are likely to increase. However, there are only so many productive capabilities that can be developed through improvements at the individual level. This is because development in productive capabilities mainly occurs in (public, private, and cooperative) productive enterprises. However well-educated and healthy individuals may be, they cannot produce the rapid, lasting, and sustainable productivity growth that makes development possible, unless they are employed by firms engaged in production activities with large scopes of productivity increase.

Even if the capabilities of the individuals involved are the same, more and better ideas will be produced by individuals working together in a productive enterprise through the cross-fertilization of ideas than isolated individuals running their own one-man operations. Moreover, because much of the knowledge in productive enterprises is acquired in a "collective" manner, in the context of a complex division of labor and deposited in the form of organizational routines and institutional memories, when the individuals are organized into productive enterprises, productivity growth stops being dependent on individuals and acquires a self-sustaining dynamic that individual entrepreneurship cannot produce.

To put it more graphically, 1,000 extra street food stalls or 1,000 one-man TV repair shops are not going to enhance national productive capabilities in the same way that one modern supermarket or one electronics manufacturer employing 600 workers and supplied by 20 small enterprises that employ 20 people each on average. Even if those 1,000 owners of the food stalls or TV repair shops all have Ph.Ds in food technology or electronics and even if most of the 1,000 employees working in (large and small) modern enterprises have only primary education, the former are still unlikely to enhance the country's productive capabilities as much as the latter can.

Thus seen, the emphasis on individual capabilities and entrepreneurial energy dominating today's mainstream development discourse is largely misplaced. To put it another way, what really distinguishes the US or Germany, on the one hand, and the Philippines or Nigeria, on the other hand, are their Boeings and Volkswagens, not their economists or medical doctors (which the latter countries have in large quantities). Similarly, what really distinguishes Ecuador or Vietnam from the US or Japan is not the raw entrepreneurial energy of the people that neo-liberals so often talk about but the ability of a society to set up and manage productive enterprises that can channel that individual energy into raising productivity.

What little developmentalism there is in the dominant vision of development is *ersatz* developmentalism – the belief that, if you educate them, make them healthier, and give them security of property rights and credit, rational self-seeking individuals will exercise their natural tendency to "truck and barter" and somehow create a prosperous economy. However, this vision is fundamentally at odds with the reality of development. In reality, development requires collective and systematic efforts to acquire and accumulate better productive knowledge through the construction of better organizations, the cross-fertilization of ideas within it, and the channeling of individual entrepreneurial energy into collective entrepreneurship.

Towards a new developmentalism

I have argued that the currently dominant discourse on "development" lacks any real notion of development in the sense of the transformation of productive capabilities and structure (and the accompanying social changes). In line with the comparative advantage argument, it emphasizes the need for developing countries to stick to their existing specializations in agriculture and textile/clothing. It is believed that this should be encouraged by the lowering of trade barriers in rich countries vis-à-vis products in which poor countries have comparative advantage, such as agricultural products and textile/clothing. Sometimes, as in the DDA, the discourse can even be anti-developmental, when it demands that developing countries give up their industrial tariffs in return for rich countries lowering their trade barriers in agriculture. This amounts to no more than an *ersatz* developmentalism, where uncoordinated efforts by individuals with better health, more education, and greater access to micro-credit will somehow produce development (but again based on existing specialization). This is why I call the mainstream discourse on development *Hamlet* without the Prince of Denmark.

Predictably, the dominant agenda has failed to deliver any lasting development. To move forward, therefore, we need to go back to the "productionist" tradition of old development economics and put the transformation in productive capabilities that go beyond individuals back at the heart of our development thinking.

Of course, by saying this I am not suggesting that we go back to development economics of the 1950s and the 1960s. For there are issues that it largely (if not entirely) neglected but that are crucial to properly understand development. The list can be made longer, but here are the five issues I think are the most crucial.

First, going back to the productionist tradition should not mean that we focus only on the material aspects of development. Early development economists were aware of these additional dimensions (hence the fierce debate on the "meaning of development" amongst them), but it is true that this dimension was not fully brought into their analyses. The "humanistic" dimension of development, which has been highlighted by the human development approach of the UNDP and Amartya Sen's capability approach, should be more explicitly incorporated into the "new developmentalist" approach, without losing emphasis on the "productionist" view. Development in the humanistic sense is not sustainable without a robust transformation in the underlying productive structure and capabilities.

Second, not enough attention was paid to politics by the development economists of the past, although it is unfair to say that all of them were like that – Albert Hirschman and Gunnar Myrdal are obvious exceptions. Of course, the political economy discourse that has emerged since (allegedly) to address this shortcoming has been dominated by the so-called Neoclassical Political Economy, which has serious problems. Therefore, anyone interested in developing a "new developmentalist" approach needs to develop a more sophisticated approach that can capture the complexities of the modern political process (for an attempt along this line, see Chang 2002a).

Third, the old school development economics did not pay enough attention to the issue of institutions. Once again, we should not under-estimate the sophistication of old development economists in this regard. For example, Simon Kuznets, when discussing his famous "inverted-U" relationship between the level of income and the degree of inequality, emphasized that improvement in income distribution is not automatic but depends on the development of institutions like trade unions and the welfare state. However, it is true that institutions were not discussed in a theoretical way very much in the old development literature. Therefore, we need to develop theories of institutions and institutional change, especially as the currently mainstream discourse on institutions has serious limitations (Chang 2007a, for a critical review of the mainstream literature; Chang 2002a, is an attempt to develop an "institutionalist political economy" alternative to it).

Fourth, development economists of the old vintage did not pay much attention to technological development in the process of productive transformation. Productive transformation was seen mainly in terms of capital accumulation and the transfer of investible surplus and labor force from the traditional sector. The "technological capabilities" literature, which has emerged from the 1980s, has highlighted issues like the complex nature of technological learning, the role of productive enterprises as the main vehicles of such learning, and the role of trade, industrial, and technology policies in promoting it (Lall 1992, is a classic on this). Any "new developmentalist" approach needs to put these issues at the heart of its transformative strategy.

Last but not least, environmental sustainability was more or less ignored in the old-style development economists. Especially, the issue of global warming was simply not on anyone's mind at the time. However, it is increasingly recognized that an environmental catastrophe could strike the world, especially the developing countries (many of which are poorly located and, more importantly, have very low capacity to cope with the consequences), unless a major transition is quickly made away from carbon-based technologies that have so far driven the developmental process. Therefore, the "new developmentalist" agenda has to think of ways to make the transition to a post-carbon economy before disaster strikes while allowing continued industrialization of the developing countries. The technological, institutional, and distributive issues that will arise in the process will tax our understanding to the limit.

Developing and enriching the traditional "productionist" perspective of development with the addition of these new elements will not be easy. However, unless we develop a "new developmentalist" discourse by doing that and overcome the poverty of vision in the currently dominant development discourse, the future of the developing world would be bleak.

Notes

1 I would like to thank Shahrukh Rafi Khan for his help in conceptualizing the paper. I would like to thank Solava Ibrahim and Luba Fakhrutdinova for their able research assistance. Milford Bateman and Philipp Lepenies made helpful comments on the first draft of the paper. I also benefited from the participants at the Mount Holyoke conference, Cambridge History of Economic Thought seminar at Clare Hall, and the Monday discussion group of my research students.
2 In 1946, Germany's per capita income in PPP terms was $2,217 – a huge fall from the wartime peak of $6,084 in 1944. In the same year, per capita income in Peru was $2,046 and that in Mexico was $2,211. Ten years later, in 1956, German per capita income surpassed the wartime peak of $6,177, but the Peruvian and the Mexican per capita income remained at $2,731 and $2,843. The data for Germany are from Table 1c and that for the Latin American countries are from Table 4c of Maddison (2003).
3 Detailed targets under each goal of the MDGs can be found at the United Nations website and Reddy and Heuty (2006), Appendix 1.
4 Moreover, it is not as if the reduction in tariffs/subsidies for agriculture and textile/clothing is going to help the developing countries very much. As I will show in the next section when I discuss the DDA, the benefits of these reductions are going to be quite modest and concentrated among the rich farmers in some of the richer developing countries, such as Brazil and Argentina.
5 Also refer to Renert *et al.*, Chapter 3 in this volume.
6 Even in PPP terms, its income was only 16 percent that of the US ($2,561 vs. $15,944).
7 Only Bangladesh (1,045 persons per km²), Taiwan (636 persons per km²), Mauritius (610 persons per km²) and South Korea (498 persons per km²) have higher population densities.
8 See Stiglitz and Charlton (2005), pp. 121–2 and Appendix 1. For various numerical estimates of the gains from agricultural liberalization in the rich countries, see Ackerman (2005). Two World Bank estimates cited by Ackerman (2005) put the share of the developed countries in the total world gain from trade liberalization in agriculture by high-income countries at 75 percent ($41.6 billon out of $55.7 billion) and 70 percent ($126 billion out of $182 billion).
9 The other main beneficiaries of agricultural liberalization in rich countries, that is, their consumers, do not gain very much. As a proportion of income, their spending on agricultural products is already pretty low (around 13 percent for food and 4 percent for alcohol and tobacco, of which only a fraction is the cost of the agricultural produce itself). Moreover, the trade in many agricultural products they buy is already liberalized (e.g., coffee, tea, cocoa).
10 The EC proposal will bring average industrial tariffs down to 5–15 percent.
11 The exceptions are Britain and the Netherlands between the late nineteenth and the early twentieth centuries, Germany briefly in the late nineteenth century, and Denmark after the Second World War.

12 Supplementary to the MDGs and the DDA is the "aid for trade" deal, supported, among others, by the WTO. In this deal, developing countries are asked to liberalize their trade in return for the additional foreign aid that will enable them to make extra investment in skills and infrastructure. However, trade liberalization will destroy, and make it very difficult to newly set up in the future, the very locales of accumulation of productive capabilities, namely, productive enterprises in high-productivity industries.

References

Ackerman, F. 2005. The Shrinking Gains from Trade: A Critical Assessment of Doha Round Projections, Global Development and Environment Institute Working Paper, No. 05–01, October, 2005, Tufts University, Boston, Massachusetts.

Bateman, M. and Chang, H.-J. 2009. Microfinance Illusion, mimeo, University of Juraj Dobrila Pula, Croatia, and University of Cambridge, Cambridge.

Chang, H.-J. 2007. *Bad Samaritans – Rich Nations, Poor Policies, and the Threat to the Developing World.* London: Random House.

Chang, H.-J. 2007a. "Understanding the Relationship between Institutions and Economic Development – Some Key Theoretical Issues." In: H.-J. Chang, ed., *Institutional Change and Economic Development.* United Nations University Press, Tokyo and London: Anthem Press.

Chang, H.-J. 2007b. "Globalisation, Global Standards, and the Future of East Asia." In: J.-S. Shin, ed., *Global Challenges and Local Responses: The East Asian Experience.* London and New York: Routledge.

Chang, H.-J. 2005. *Why Developing Countries Need Tariffs – How WTO NAMA Negotiations Could Deny Developing Countries' Right to a Future,* South Centre, Geneva, and Oxford: Oxfam International.

Chang, H.-J. 2002. *Kicking Away the Ladder – Development Strategy in Historical Perspective.* London: Anthem Press.

Chang, H.-J. 2002a. "Breaking the Mould – An Institutionalist Political Economy Alternative to the Neo-Liberal Theory of the Market and the State," *Cambridge Journal of Economics,* 26(5), 539–59.

Gallagher, K., ed. 2005. *Putting Development First – The Importance of Policy Space in the WTO and IFIs,* London: Zed Press.

Lall, S. 1992. "Technological Capabilities and Industrialization," *World Development,* 20(2), 165–86.

Maddison, A. 2003. *The World Economy: Historical Statistics.* Paris: OECD.

Reddy, S. and Heuty, A. 2006. "Achieving the Millennium Development Goals: What's wrong with existing analytical models?," DESA Working Paper, No. 30, Department of Economic and Social Affairs, United Nations, New York.

Stiglitz, J. and Charlton, A. 2005. *Fair Trade for All – How Trade Can Promote Development.* Oxford: Oxford University Press.

4 The economics of failed, failing, and fragile states

Productive structure as the missing link

Erik S. Reinert, Yves Ekoué Amaïzo, and Rainer Kattel[1]

Introduction: lost theoretical insights from US Secretary of State George Marshall

More than 60 years ago on June 5, 1947, US Secretary of State George Marshall gave a speech at Harvard University announcing what was to be called the Marshall Plan.[2] The Marshall Plan was probably the most successful development plan in human history, re-industrializing and industrializing countries from Norway and Sweden in the North to Greece and Turkey in the South-east. At about the same time, a similar process based on the same principles, re-industrialized and industrialized East Asia, spreading from Japan in the North-east towards the South-west. In this way, a *cordon sanitaire* of wealthy countries was created around the communist world to stem the communist tide that was rising at the time of Marshall's speech. One country to benefit from the Marshall-type ideology was South Korea, a country that in 1950 was poorer (GDP per capita estimated at $770) than Somalia (GDP per capita estimated at $1057; Maddison 2003), today's example of a failed state (see Figure 4.1).

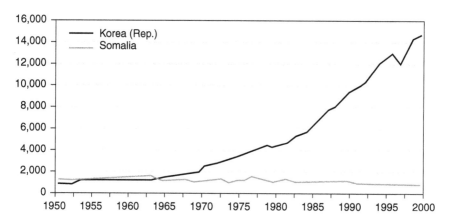

Figure 4.1 Korea–Somalia, GDP per capita, 1950–2001, in 1990 $s (source: Original data extracted from Maddison (2003)).

Although it is sometimes misunderstood as a scheme for giving away huge sums of money rather than a re-industrialization scheme, the Marshall Plan is well known. What is less known is that the relatively short speech contained three key theoretical insights with strong relevance to today's situation.

The first insight is the link between a certain type of productive structure and what George Marshall calls "modern civilization," what in a more politically correct language today could be called "development and democracy":

> There is a phase of this matter which is both interesting and serious. The farmer has always produced the foodstuffs to exchange with the city dweller for the other necessities of life. *This division of labor is the basis of modern civilization.* At the present time it is threatened with breakdown. The town and city industries are not producing adequate goods to exchange with the food-producing farmer [italics added].
>
> (Source: Endnote 2)

During the time of European nation-state growth, it was common knowledge that democracies and "civilization" were both products of certain economic structures associated with "city activities" (Reinert 2009). It was not lost on Enlightenment Europe that the first democracies – Venice and the Dutch Republic – were also the states where artisans and manufacturing were the dominant professions. Agricultural states meant feudalism and lack of political freedom. As early as 1613, an Italian economist, Antonio Serra, identified the "glue" that creates the common weal of cities and nations as a large division of labor in activities all subject to increasing returns (falling costs as volume of production goes up, which excludes agriculture) (Serra 1613; Reinert and Reinert 2003). As city-states grew first into dynamic agglomeration, then as nation-states, the phenomenon described by Marshall could be observed.

Marshall's second insight pertains to the vicious circles created in societies without manufacturing activities:

> The remedy lies in *breaking the vicious circle* and restoring the confidence of the European people in the economic future of their own countries and of Europe as a whole. The manufacturer and the farmer throughout wide areas must be able and willing to exchange their product for currencies, the continuing value of which is not open to question. [italics added]
>
> (Source: Endnote 2)

It is notable that Marshall used the term vicious circle, which became fashionable only later – in the 1950s and 1960s – with development economists like Gunnar Myrdal.

Marshall's third insight is that development assistance must provide a cure rather than a mere palliative:

> Such assistance, I am convinced, must not be on a piecemeal basis as various crises develop. Any assistance that this Government may render in

the future should provide a cure rather than a mere palliative. Any government that is willing to assist in the task of recovery will find full cooperation.

(Source: Endnote 2)

In this chapter we argue that the root causes of poverty lie in a certain type of economic structure which fails to produce the virtuous circles of economic growth. The latter require increasing returns and sufficient diffusion of value added solutions in order to become self-sustaining. Increasing returns produce barriers to entry into an economic activity, which again allow a degree of imperfect competition that produces capital accumulation. We argue that economic development requires dynamic imperfect competition under increasing returns, rather than the standard assumptions of perfect competition and diminishing returns.

During the decades following the Second World War, world development followed the strategic outline of the 1947 Marshall Plan, the principles of which also were at the core of the 1948 Havana Charter, signed by all the members of the United Nations at the time. These principles were abandoned in the 1980s however, and at the end of a sequence of unsuccessful "Development Decades" the Millennium Development Goals were launched. The latter are – in the view of the authors – heavily biased towards palliative economics, treating the symptoms of poverty rather than addressing its root causes.

Ibn-Khaldun: pre-industrial rent-seeking as a zero-sum-game

Muslim historian and philosopher Ibn-Khaldun (1332–1406) described society's development from the nomadic tribes of the desert, organized in clans originating in blood relationships, to agriculturalists and ultimately into town dwellers. The town dwellers become luxurious, and as their wants increase, the city must resort to increasing taxation. Resenting the claims of their clansmen to equality, they rely on foreign supporters for aid, who become necessary because of the decline of clansmen as warriors. Thus the state grows decrepit and over time becomes prey to a fresh group of nomads, who then undergo the same experience. In Ibn-Khaldun's pre-industrial setting, history logically becomes a cyclical sequence of tribal wars – with foreign supporters – fighting over the static and non-productive rents that accrue to the capital.

Pre-increasing returns and pre-common-weal productive systems that specialize in raw materials create a type of feudal political structure. Yet even where no real feudalism is involved, as in some African agriculture, the state seems to continue the extraction of economic surplus characteristic of colonialism, and gives very little back. The sharing of economic growth becomes a fundamental issue in the identification of responses to poverty alleviation. Under such conditions, pre-capitalist production and political structures are very durable, and for good reason. The Swede Göran Hydén, an advisor to Tanzanian president

Julius Nyerere, talks about Africa's "un-captured peasantry." Similarly, NATO and the West today face an "un-captured peasantry" in Afghanistan. Our suggestion is that Nyerere's African socialism may have failed for the very same reason NATO and the West are failing in Afghanistan and in the Middle East in general. The absence of an increasing returns sector creates zero-sum-game societies of static rent-seeking.[3] These nations are prime candidates for developing into failing, failed and fragile (FFF) states.

Indeed, as Clark (2007) argues, the world before the industrial revolution and that of today's failed states is characterized by what he calls a Malthusian trap: higher standards of living bring increasing population growth that, without significant productivity increases, lowers the standards of living back to subsistence level. In many ways today's poorest countries are worse off than ever before in history. As Clark argues,

> the subsistence wage, at which population growth would cease, is many times lower in the modern world than in the preindustrial period.... Given the continued heavy dependence of many sub-Saharan African countries on farming, and a fixed supply of agricultural land, health care improvements are not an unmitigated blessing, but exact a cost in terms of lower material incomes.
>
> (2007: 45)

There are essentially two options to escape the Malthusian trap: decreasing population or significant and continuous productivity increases (through diversification into increasing returns activities). We have argued that the genocide in Rwanda cannot be understood except in this perspective (Reinert 2007).

It is increasingly clear that there is a strong connection between economic growth and states failing or not failing. As Collier (2007: 19) argues, "civil war is much more likely to break out in low-income countries: halve the starting income of the country and you double the risk of civil war." However, in the same book Collier goes on to argue that "globally, we now know what produces productivity growth in manufacturing: it is competition" (160). This is a startlingly simplistic view from someone who repeatedly admires East Asian economies that have escaped the bottom billion of poorest people on earth in the last century. Clearly, productivity increases alone do not solve the problem of poverty, the fruits of productivity increases may easily disappear as lowered prices to foreign customers (Singer 1950; Reinert 2007). In order to remain in the producing country, productivity increases must take place inside the synergies of a finely woven web of diversified economic activities, all subject to increasing returns (a "National Innovation System"). The lack of competition and growth does not explain state failure. It is rather the lack of the specific composition of the economic structure that characterizes all rich and middle-class nations. Failed, failing and fragile states exhibit decidedly different economic structures compared to developed countries.[4] The FFF states have common economic factors that distinguish them from, e.g., Canada, Finland, Norway, Germany, or Singapore (see Appendix 4.1 for detailed data and figures).

We have argued that economic retrogression – a development process in reverse – is a common phenomenon that requires much more attention that it actually gets (Reinert 2007). The former Soviet Republics in Central Asia, Moldova, and Mongolia offer examples of how ill-guided liberalization (premature exposure to global free trade) can reverse the long-term building of productive forces in just a few years. With the breakdown of the Soviet Union and the following rapid liberalization of trade and economy in general, most Central Asian countries transformed within a few years from relatively developed countries to fragile and poor states that by now exhibit often feudal patterns of political and socio-economic behaviour (see Figures 4.2 and 4.3).

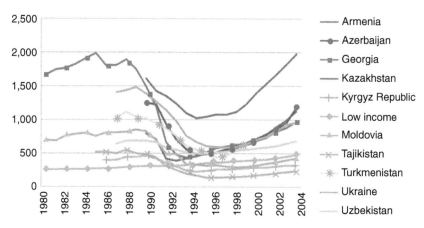

Figure 4.2 GDP per capita in constant 2000 US$ in Central Asia and selected former Soviet economies, 1980–2005 (source: World Bank WDI online database; calculations by the authors).

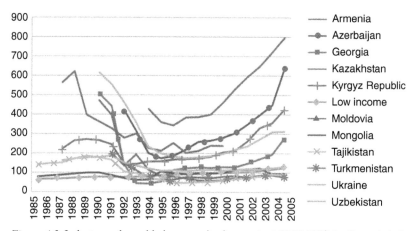

Figure 4.3 Industry value added per capita in constant 2000 US$ in Central Asia and other selected former Soviet economies, 1985–2005 (source: World Bank WDI online database; calculations by the authors).

It is also exceedingly important to understand the qualitative difference between developed states and FFF-states when it comes to absorbing "wealth shocks" from oil, mining, and other natural resources into the economy. Developed countries normally manage to integrate these activities into their innovation systems, while the same type of activities in FFF states tend to create economic enclaves that are isolated from the rest of the economy.

In the case of former Soviet republics depicted in figures above, we see state collapse accompanied by a heavy fall in GDP per capita and industry value added per capita. While before 1990 most of these countries had income levels well above what the World Bank calls "low income,"[5] countries like Tajikistan, the Kyrgyz Republic and Moldova have fallen well below most low-income countries and stayed there throughout the 1990s and early 2000s. It is thus not a coincidence that we find Georgia, the Kyrgyz Republic, Moldova, Tajikistan, Turkmenistan, and Uzbekistan among states listed in *Foreign Policy*'s failed state index.[6]

The development that broke the Ibn-Khaldunian circle of rent-seeking tribal violence was the simultaneous development of a large division of labor and growth of increasing returns industries. With these activities, the national capital became an asset to the countryside and vice-versa; the nation-state was no longer a zero-sum game. Nations displaying these types of characteristics became the first democracies (Italian and Dutch city states).

Three main periods could be identified for increasing divergence between FFF States and industrialized countries:

First, the divergence among regions was marginal during the first period, i.e., from 1000 to 1870, ending with the geographical segmentation of the colonial world among former colonial powers (see also Clark 2007, 303–70).

Second, during the second period, between 1870 and 1950, developing regions such as Africa, Latin America, and Asia (excluding Japan) were unable to boost their GDP per capita on a sustainable basis above the world average. An important explanation for this is colonialism, which at its very core has been a technology policy prohibiting manufacturing in the colonies (Reinert 2007). Asymmetry among these regions is mainly due to the fact that regions which managed to become economically independent or directly integrated in the productive structure of the regional economic locomotive (such as Japan for Asia) could gradually re-appropriate their economic wealth with special reference to Friedrich List's theory of "productive power" (List 1856: 394). Whenever visionary leaders were dedicated to the promotion of public goods for their respective population, the country or the region experienced a convergence with industrialized countries in terms of GDP per capita, share of manufacturing value added (MVA) in GDP, and growth of MVA per capita (see Appendixes 4.8, 4.9, and 4.10). Bad governance usually leads to a convergence among FFF states, which is another form of the race to the bottom. (See also Collier 2007: 53–63.)

Third, between 1950 and 2001, economies with productive structures in place benefited from the gradual acceleration of the globalization process. The globalization shock that started in the 1980s accelerated the divergence between poor FFF economies and rich industrialized countries: nations that had achieved a dynamic increasing returns economy above a certain threshold prospered (*forging ahead*), while those below that threshold were made poorer by globalization (*falling behind*). In parallel, middle-income economies, even though sometimes considered fragile, are gradually experiencing a convergence with the world average (see Appendixes 4.5 and 4.6).[7]

In sum, the gap between the poorest and richest countries in the world has grown from a 4:1 ratio in 1800 to more than 50:1 (Clark 2007: 319–20).

The need for a holistic view of economic and political structures

Six main differences distinguish today's approach to economic development – as represented by the Washington Institutions – from previous theories of the development process (Renaissance to Marshall Plan). Today's theories fail:

- to approach economic development from a multidisciplinary standpoint, as was done in the German tradition of *Staatswissenschaft*;
- to study and tailor-make policy-recommendations to the specific *context* in which a nation finds itself (insisting that "one size fits all");
- to observe and classify qualitative differences between economic activities (e.g., increasing or diminishing returns, perfect or imperfect competition, etc.);
- to investigate differences between the productive structures of nations;
- to conceive of development as a dynamic synergetic phenomenon propelled by self-reinforcing mechanisms (e.g., Collier's static development "traps" compared to the dynamic virtuous and vicious circles of classical development economics);
- to understand the role of the state in economic growth from any standpoint other than "market failure."

These weaknesses all reflect the standard methodology of economics today (see also Clark 2007: 145–7). In particular, the latter failure leads to a highly simplistic juxtaposition of free market vs. government intervention. Such a dichotomy fails to capture how real markets work: markets are often bundles of rules, institutions, regulations, enforcements (or lack thereof) and thus highly intricate webs of transaction costs and externalities that create context-specific motivators for particular economic behavior. This failure, in turn, leads to an overly primitive understanding of the role of the state and in particular of public administration in development (see below) and thus to policy solutions and advice (e.g., get market institutions right) that are often completely alien to the country they are meant to help (Fukuyama 2004; Doornbos 2002; Rodrick 2008).

The important trend of divergence between FFF states and industrialized countries appears a major source of concern, which cannot be reduced to security related issues. In 1950, Singapore was poorer (GDP per capita estimated at $2,219) than Peru (GDP per capita estimated at $2,263, see Figure 4.4). A clear indication of a non-failed state is its ability to perform productive activities by awarding growing value-added achieved through industrial diversification under increasing returns. Our contention is that any policy aimed at preventing nation-states from failing, should – in order to avoid treating mere symptoms rather than causes – include an analysis of how to make the productive structure of such states resemble the structure of developed ones. The overall approach of the Millennium Development Goals should be revised to include productive structure as the core variable (Reinert 2007: 239–70). Poor countries ought to emulate the productive structure of rich countries, not their economic policies.

Common economic characteristics of failing states are, among others, very few if any urban increasing returns industries, very little division of labor (i.e., monoculture), no urban middle class bringing political stability, no important artisan class that is economically independent, engaged in commodity competition (perfect competition) in their export activities, a comparative advantage in supplying cheap labor to the world markets, and a low demand for educated labor combined with a very low level of education. This complex of symptoms cannot be cured by attacking isolated symptoms: a focus on education will tend to increase the brain drain rather than improving the economic structure, as the local demand for jobs requiring education is so low. All symptoms must be attacked simultaneously through the only solution that has proved historically viable: that of changing the underlying economic structure.

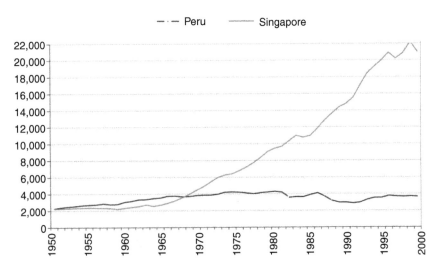

Figure 4.4 Peru–Singapore, GDP per capita, 1950–2001, in 1990 international Geary–Khamis dollars (source: Original data extracted from (Maddison 2003)).

The following governance characteristics define FFF states:

- The central government does not control the whole territory and has lost authority over selected zones (including cross-border areas).
- Internal conflicts move to violent confrontations and get out of control. New leaders emerge with the objective of siphoning off wealth from natural resource extraction in a process much resembling the cycles described by Ibn-Khaldun. This circulation of elites is based on static rent-seeking rather than, as in Schumpeter's version of elite circulation, on a succession of families that create national industrial wealth in one generation and live on financial income in subsequent generations (e.g., the Ford family). Abuse of power and deficit of democracy on the one hand and a pre-industrial economic sector on the other are factors that mutually reinforce each other, locking nations into very strong vicious circles.
- Human rights, the control of media, lack of free speech, and the democratic deficit reach a critical point where the lack of productive powers leads to hunger, poverty, and inequality. This raises the concern of the international community, which, however, only moves in to attack the symptoms of the crisis, not its root causes (by sending food, troops, etc.);
- The international community focuses almost exclusively on how governments are elected, rather than on what kind of economic policies they promote. This locks the FFF-states into economic structures in which the natural way to create personal wealth is either by siphoning off rents from raw material extraction or from the international aid-industry, rather than by engaging in the kind of productive activities that are necessary to create real national wealth. Rent-seeking in the international aid sector seems to crowd out productive rent-seeking in industrial activities. Corruption becomes an inevitable and integral part of such a system, whereupon the international community turns around and blames poverty on corruption – which they themselves have created – rather than on the sub-optimal productive structures that are the heritage of colonialism. Moyo (2009) provides a good analysis of the evils of aid dependence, but unfortunately her recommendations largely represent the same policies that created the problem in the first place;
- Inability to actively participate in regional integration processes through Africa's "spaghetti bowl" of trade agreements that makes focused trade policies virtually impossible.

In nations with this type of economic and governance structures a particular type of regionalism tends to evolve, which in Latin America is referred to as *caudillismo* and in Somalia and Afghanistan is referred to as the rule of war lords. The economic structure that provides the "bonding agent" for a functioning nation-state is not there. Schmoller (1897/1967) provides a description of how European nation-states were consolidated, i.e., the very process that FFF states lack.

In some cases, a productive system specialized in raw materials creates a type of feudal political structure. But even where no real feudalism is involved, like in some African agriculture, the state seems to wish to continue the extraction of economic surplus characteristic of the colonial and post-colonial paradigm. These patrimonial states afflicted by rent-seekers' syndrome can give very little back. Under such conditions pre-capitalist production structures are very durable, and probably for good reason (see also Collier 2007: 34). Nevertheless, neo-feudal governance cannot become a reference for FFF states because of their present delay in upgrading their productive structure; the industrial policy tools of the Marshall Plan and the Havana Charter have in effect become outlawed and the artisan/industrial class is too weak to induce a change in this direction. Enlightenment economics of the 1700s clearly distinguished between "parasitic" administrative capital cities, surrounded by inefficient agriculture, and "synergy-creating" industrial capitals surrounded by efficient agriculture. Spain's Madrid was the classical example of the first kind of capital, and Lombardy's Milan of the second. As George Marshall stated "the synergy between city and country-side forms the core of economic development." And we must not forget that in order for this system to work, the countryside's city customers must be part of the same labor market as the farmers themselves. Farmers' customers in faraway countries cannot trigger these mechanisms.

The positive-sum-game between city and countryside referred to by George Marshall can only be created through a large division of labor and increasing returns. Only then the "common weal" that was the goal of Italian Renaissance city states can be observed. Only then the state ceases to be a parasite that takes away in taxes less than it brings back. This synergy-based understanding of successful states is found already in Florentine state theory, with Brunetto Latini, in the thirteenth century (see Reinert 2005). In order to escape pre-capitalist zero-sum games – negative-sum game from the point of view of the subsistence sector – the nation-state must operate under synergic increasing returns. The argument of increasing returns was, according to Schumpeter, also a key argument in eighteenth-century national economic policy promoting industrialization.

We also suggest going back to the literature at the time when early viable states with some kind of democracy were created. In Giovanni Botero (1588) and the *Staatsraison* ("reason of state") tradition there are clear links between economic structure and the viability of states. Botero's *Ragion di Stato* (reason of state) and *Sulle grandezze delle Città* (on the wealth of cities), are, after all, parts of the same work (1588). This tradition was continued by eighteenth-century social scientists, including Montesquieu. As one German author said at the time: "it is not so that a primitive people become civilized, and then found industries, it is the other way around!" (Meyen 1770) Friedrich List continues this core eighteenth-century argument of linking manufacturing and "civiliza-tion" directly. In early German social science, Veit Ludwig von Seckendorff (1626–92) found that Germany did not have the economic basis to create a society like the one observed and so admired in the Dutch Republic. Seckendorff's approach to making the state function better was intimately tied to changing the economic basis of the state itself, its mix of professions and industries and their geographical relocation within the realm. In the tradition started by Seckendorff, the *Fürsten* (Princes) became modernizers by arguing that their *Recht* (right) to govern was accompanied by a *Pflicht* (duty) to modernize and in the long term created the conditions where the *Fürsten* became obsolete and the conditions needed for a functioning democracy were created. A successful Principality carried with it the seeds of its own destruction and the birth of democracy (Reinert 2005).

The first wealthy states with some kind of republican rule were often islands, like Venice and the Dutch Republic. The absence of arable land led to both an absence of a feudal structure and the creation of a diversified economic structure including activities subject to increasing returns. This therefore makes the case of Florence, where landowners also had power, particularly interesting. There the *corporazioni* (guilds) and burgers fought for power among themselves, but very early (twelfth to the thirteenth century) they had banned land-owning families from participating in politics (these families continued to trouble Florence for centuries through alliances with other cities).

There is, then, a long history of trying to move the vested interests of the ruling class from land into manufacturing. The rulers who had a manufacturing strategy, starting with Henry VII in England in 1485, also tended to have a policy against the landed nobility. The goal of converting the "useless" landed nobility to something else was an important reason for Johann Heinrich Gottlob von Justi's appointment in Vienna in 1752, and for the establishment of the *Theresianum* there. Sometimes, however, the urban non-feudal modernizers lost, as in the *War of the Comuneros* in Spain in 1520–21. This kind of strife between landed upper classes – with their economic interests vested in diminishing return activities – and the generally urban classes promoting artisans and manufacturing – has been very common over the last 500 years. The politics of economic development evolve around these crises. The US Civil War was one such conflict of interests when the manufacturing North defeated the raw-material producing South. In many ways the history of Latin America is the history of nations where the "South" has won the civil wars, and where the military, at times, has sided with a weak industrial bourgeoisie and contributed to creating development.

Palliative industrialization: from "primitivization" to "de-industrialization"

De-industrialization as an accident, or alternatively as a planned process of colonialism, should always be considered an integral part of our understanding of FFF states. The international community's focus on palliative economics – on "development aid" – rather than on wealth creation may push economically fragile states towards the failed states group. Particularly in Africa, top-down policies aimed at "fixing" developing countries' problems have produced poor results and many failures. (See, for example, Easterly 2001, Collier 2007, Moyo

2009). At the core of the problem of these Washington Institution policies is the failure to perceive the activity-specific nature of economic development: it does not take off in the absence of increasing returns and the synergies created around them. There is an urgent need to reverse the counterproductive policies that the Washington Consensus established in many weakly industrialized countries.

Based on a continuous policy of industrialization starting in the late 1940s, China and India have stubbornly improved their industrial structure and productive capacities and capabilities (see Appendix 2 and 3), based on an economic policy diverging from the one advised by the so-called Washington Consensus. The present relative success of these nations cannot be understood without taking into account a more than 50-year history of industrial policy in both India and China. Without a re-definition that puts industrial policy at its core, the Millennium Development Goals will fail as being overly palliative rather than constructive. When the G8 group of countries calls for "an improvement of global investment climate as well as taking the social dimension of globalization into account," they must go one step further and re-introduce the building of productive structure in FFF states as a means both to create profitable investment opportunities *and* to improve the social conditions in these states. Only a changed economic structure will start a process leading them to become middle-income countries. After all, it is the fragile countries that suffer the most from the globalization process (see also Collier 2007: 79–96). Approaching the problem exclusively from the collateral effects which could be defined as an additional lack of predictability in terms of security threats for the international community, one may fail to address the root of the problem. Attacking the symptoms of poverty and conflict rather than its causes prevents security- and peace-building processes and increases the cost of building trust in FFF states. This "palliative economics" in effect produces a new type of colonialism that we have dubbed "welfare colonialism" (Reinert 2006). While the World Bank models normally assume full employment, the latter is what Africa needs most of all. In order to create employment the vicious circle of "no purchasing power" and "no productive power" must be broken. Studying 500 years of the history of economic thought we argue that the only way to escape this type of vicious circle has been through heavy doses of industrial policy (Reinert 2009).

Just like in eighteenth-century Latin America, Africa achieved decolonization but not real independence. Keeping Africa de-industrialized also carries a huge price tag both in terms of human suffering and in monetary terms. According to the International Crisis Group,

> civil war in a low-income country costs that country and its neighbours on average 42 billion euro in direct and indirect costs. That is for a single conflict. To put that in perspective, the worldwide aid budget in 2004 was 60 billion euro.

Between the 1870s and 1950s (see Appendix 4.4), most poor regions faced difficulty addressing people's real life conditions. Emerging economies are following an interesting path which focuses on getting out of the vicious circle through the mastering of their productive structure. Declining aid in real terms and window-dressing debt relief embedded in donor-driven solutions have been unable to radically change the situation on the ground for the better.

Today Africa is being split up into different trading areas (the so-called "spaghetti bowl") much as it was split up and divided by the colonial powers in the 1880s. The lack of collective governance in Africa, and regular external interventions to promote external interests, generates social pressure. This pressure is often kept under control by powerful political regimes supported by military powers, which use the democratic deficit as a new management tool of governance. Failing to discuss and negotiate new terms to improve the sustainable development process, the international community has often adopted palliative measures. Some of them were agreed upon and structured around the United Nations Millennium Development Goals with no clear reference to wealth creation. Long-term vision and strategies using bottom-up approaches should reverse the dominant donor-driven approaches which often facilitate poor country leadership with little concern for the well-being of the local population. Positive impacts on poverty reduction cannot be de-linked from wealth creation and synergic growth.

Recently the globalization process has been reduced to issues of direct interest to rich and powerful countries. After the cold war, countries such as China, Korea, India, Japan, Brazil, and Russia (see Appendix 4.3) have become major players using alternative approaches to neo-liberalism. However, for poor countries, globalization in reality means they should not enter into any industrialization process but continue to take advantage of temporary measures such as the Economic Partnership Agreement (EPA),[8] Everything-but-Arms (EBA) of the European Union, or the Africa Growth Opportunity (AGOA)[9] of the United States of America, to name a few. Preferential trade access to rich countries' markets through the promotion of labor-intensive manufactures, void of any learning potential, bereft of any scale effects and with obsolete technology, creates a race to the bottom. This is becoming an obsolete and unsustainable option that essentially leaves the poorest countries trapped in a Malthusian world.

From divergence to convergence: building and upgrading productive agglomeration

Divergence and convergence exist even at the regional level. Benchmarking selected regions based on GDP per capita reveals that regions with a large number of poor and FFF countries are also regions which face difficulty generating wealth and sustained development (see Appendix 4.4, Benchmarking selected world regions).

Collapsed, weak or healthy, a nation-state is continually engaged in a building process towards wealth creation. From that perspective, FFF states should be considered incomplete, unfinished, and unsuccessful states in securing wealth for their population. The question then becomes: how do we give a new impetus to long-term over short-term perspectives while searching for development and progress? This main issue should not be overshadowed by military and security related actions. The latter should of course not be underestimated as a key issue in breaking the vicious circle of security in failed states.

The missing link in the economics of FFF states is the lack of increasing returns based on "coo-petitive" (a mix of competition and cooperation) diffusion of means (technology, know-how, innovative culture, entrepreneurship, and information sharing) in a predictable and conducive environment.

Cumulative approaches to economics or productive "governance" often enforce the development of sustainable productive structures usually based on a participatory system. However, what is more important than the difference in statistical figures is to identify appropriate indicators capturing trends towards convergence or divergence in productive capacity building. In order to acknowledge a country's performance in relation to productive agglomeration, it is suggested that performance in value addition in productive sectors be analyzed using at least the following five main indicators:

Trend of GDP (or gross national income – GNI) per capita over a long period;

Share of manufacturing value-added (MVA) and the knowledge-intensive service sector (or other measure of knowledge-intensity) in GDP over a period and in comparison with (a) the world and region average, (b) the best performer at the level of sub-regions and (c) countries with a similar convergence starting point. The share of MVA in GDP should be equal to or above world average on a sustainable basis to ensure the effective development of productive structures in a country (or a region). It is important to explain the divergence or convergence of performance in productive agglomeration over an agreed period;

Growth rate of MVA per capita which indicates the real commitment of a government to promote industrialization; this indicator avoids being misguided by countries failing to promote productive structures because of unforeseen rent activities based on a few commodities or minerals;[10]

Benchmarking business environment indicators which should be better than the region (or sub-region) average. Most data is available from the World Bank (business environment databank);[11]

Selected competitiveness index[12] with special focus on the existence of a pool of human capital expertise structured around value chains (indicator of capability and capacity of absorption), productivity, innovation, and technology content especially at the local level. Special references should be made to proxy-indicators related to the industrial complexity and the level of regional/global integration of processed goods and the impact on services of know-how and technology at the local level (indicator of capability);

Real wage and social inequality dynamics.

Based on the six groups of indicators mentioned above, an integrated index which could be called "Poverty reduction index" or preferably "Wealth creation index" or "Knowledge creation index" will be required to generate an "early alert" on states failing economically. Such a mechanism, which will not have a "security bias," should identify correlations between effective states' commitment to promote productive structures and the real chances to escape the vicious circles of the failing states process.

The wealth creation index (WCI) should benchmark the performance of FFF states and prevent countries from falling from the status of Fragile States to Failing and Failed States. WCI should then be used to benchmark the fragility of a country. Fragility is a dynamic concept which enables states to be classified as committed, partially committed or irresponsible in implementing effective governance. The WCI classification should avoid spreading the usual "good or bad" donor approach, as donors' agencies often do.[13]

The convergence (or lack thereof) of economies could be attributed to a type of governance where the building of an "entrepreneurial organization at the level of the country" becomes part of an effective vision, strategy, and objective of a country or a region. An entrepreneurial organization at the country level could be defined here as the awareness of countries' leaders to structure a country or a region as a collection of resources (including capital, people, and productive assets) and to regularly identify new combinations of those resources based on a network of relations and information with the objective of sharing economic growth at all levels. The key concept here, however, is that of administrative capacity: to what degree a country's administration (in terms of structures, coordination, competencies and real achievement) can handle the problems it faces. It is important to note that administrative capacity is highly contextual.

The Washington Consensus and its underlying neo-liberal ideology have had great impact on the way the development community understands administrative capacity. Perhaps the main idea behind the Washington Consensus understanding of administrative capacity is that government intervention more often than not has a negative impact on private sector transaction costs and market externalities and thus hampers market forces and free trade which could otherwise bring development. Thus, according to the Washington institutions, government intervention is justified only in cases of market failure. Coase (1988) is often credited as the intellectual founding father of this approach and, despite his explicit warnings that he has been misunderstood, the impact has been huge both in developing and developed countries. First, we see a growing trend to privatize government functions and encouragement to use more market-like mechanisms in public sector management (e.g., performance pay) even though there is almost no empirical evidence to suggest that such reforms have ever made the public sector or the government perform better (see Pollitt and Bouckaert 2004, and Katula and Perry 2003 on performance pay). Second, there is a growing emphasis on "governing by networks," which generally means using more partnerships with private and the third sectors to govern specific fields, from policy design to implementation (e.g., setting up a development agency as a NGO, where government, private companies, and other NGOs have more or less equal footing).[14] While such an approach to governing can indeed bring substantial gains (e.g., tapping into new human and/or financial resources, utilizing local initiative, etc.), there is strong evidence to suggest that unless there is a very high administrative capacity present the impact of using networks is increasingly negative.

This is because there tends to be a high degree of difference between private and public sector goals.[15] In addition, networks as organizations often operate outside the public law domain and thus are under different standards of accountability and legality. This often entails outright corruption and high-jacking of the agenda by private interests.

At the same time, there is strong evidence to suggest that developing countries profit strongly from classical Weberian bureaucratic structures, particularly in terms of administrative capacity. Weberian administration relies on strict legal principles (government actions are regulated by public law), there is a strong emphasis on merit, competence, and achievement in public service and there are clear hierarchies that enhance accountability.[16] Weberian bureaucracy tends to focus on long-term strategic goals and thus provides developing countries with direly needed stability in policy planning and design. Indeed, previous lack of strategic capacities in policy making is perhaps the strongest reason why many developing countries should be careful in experimenting with more recent administrative reform fashions like "governing by networks." However, we also see a growing trend towards what has been termed a neo-Weberian state in developed European countries, where notions of legality and accountability, competence and merit are re-entering both academic discourse and actual changes in public sector reforms (Pollitt and Bouckaert 2004; Drechsler 2005).

Conclusion

The policies of the Washington Consensus precipitated a process of de-industrialization in many poor countries, from Mongolia via Africa to Latin America (Reinert 2007). This process, strengthened by the many "conditionalities" imposed on these countries, weakened their productive agglomerations, making them more fragile. Contemporaneously with an effort to build peace and security in FFF states, the process of deindustrialization produced exactly the opposite effect as the one desired: the creation of a system of vicious circles of reducing wealth, employment, and the middle class. The centuries-old understanding of the relationship between the "urban sector" and "democracy," so well explained by George Marshall announced the Marshall Plan was lost: the division of labor between the farmer and the city dweller (agriculture and manufacturing) "is the basis of modern civilization."

In post Second World War Europe, the Marshall Plan followed the Morgenthau Plan, a plan to de-industrialize Germany. Reinert (2004) argues that the free trade shocks promoted by the Washington Institutions in practice created a Morgenthau Plan, a de-industrialization plan, for the world periphery, starting in the late 1970s. Now is the time to start a real Marshall Plan for the de-industrialized Third World, but recognizing that probably the most important element of the Marshall Plan – without which the transfer of funds would have been much less efficient – was that the Plan was accompanied by tariff autonomy. Heavy industrial policy interventions, including prohibitive tariffs and import prohibitions, were key elements in the reconstruction of Europe after the Second World War. Africa, starting from a much weaker base than Europe did, will probably need an even stronger tonic of policies. Pan-African economic integration must be an integrated element in any such long-term policy.

The virtual absence of a manufacturing sector seems to explain the lack of convergence between the FFF least industrialized countries and industrialized countries. Improving industrialization and knowledge creation needs an enabling governance system with a strong administrative capacity. Trade in diminishing return activities without knowledge production is not sustainable, and the economics of failed, failing and fragile states must be re-engineered with performing productive structure.

The identification of constraints to productive networking, innovation, and the building of competencies and administrative capacity should be given more importance when looking for the creation of decent jobs in the global economy. Therefore, most of the present concepts linking trade to development aid, including trade preference mechanisms (the African Growth Opportunity Act (AGOA), the Economic Partnership Agreement (EPA), the Everything But Arms (EBA), the Aid for Trade package from the World Trade Organization, or any bilateral and multilateral aid lacking non-wealth generating considerations) should be redesigned and adjusted to enable effective wealth and knowledge creation in developing countries through the upgrading and integration of productive economic structures to regional and global markets. Importantly, the MDGs should be revisited to ensure that wealth creation becomes more explicit and supported by the promotion of effective productive structures in the least industrialized countries.

At the core of fragile, failing, and failed states is a productive system where the glue that creates national unity in a positive-sum game is missing: a large increasing returns sector with a large division of labor (i.e., many different professions and manufacturing activities). The relation between economic structure and political stability and peace – or instability and armed strife – was well understood during the Enlightenment (Reinert 2007 and 2009). As long as this key relationship is not recognized, long-term peace building and poverty alleviation will fail. Five hundred years of historical record is crystal clear.

Appendix

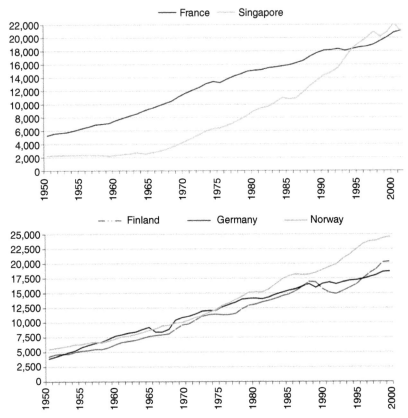

Figure A4. 1 Selected countries, GDP per capita, 1950–2001 (source: Original data extracted from Maddison (2003)).

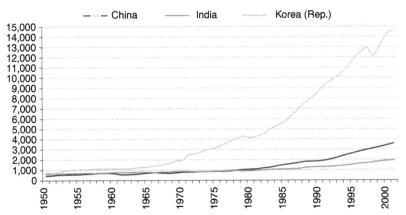

Figure A4.2 South Korea, China, and India, GDP per capita, 1950–2001 (source: Original data extracted from Maddison (2003)).

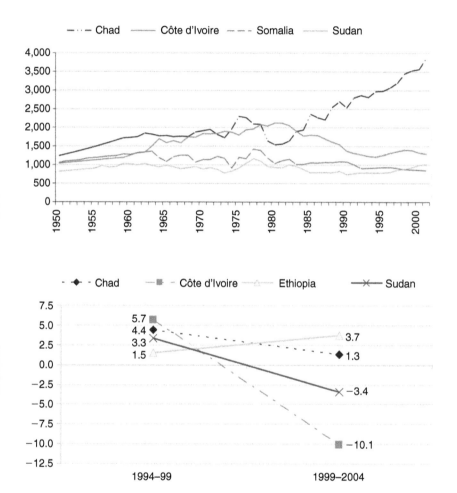

Figure A4.3 GDP and manufacturing value added per capita for Chad, the Ivory Coast, Somalia, and Sudan (source: UNIDO (2009)).

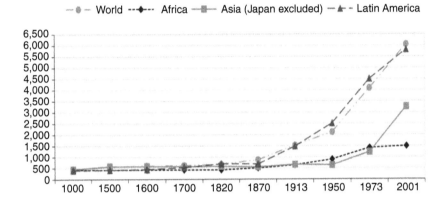

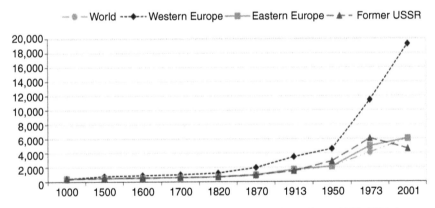

Figure A4.4 GDP per capita (average) for selected world regions: 1000–2001 (source: Original data extracted from Maddison (2003)).

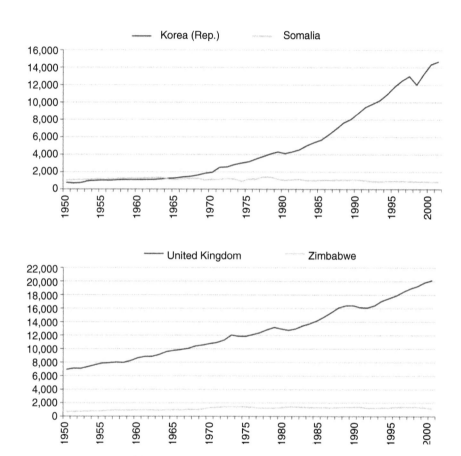

Figure A4.5 Benchmarking per capita GDP: selected failed, failing, and fragile (FFF) states versus industrialized and emerging countries, 1950–2001 (source: Original data extracted from Maddison (2003)).

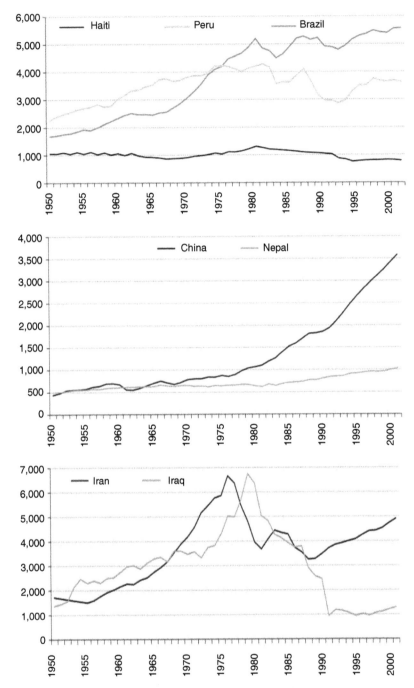

Figure A4.6 Benchmarking per capita GDP: failed, failing, and fragile (FFF) states versus neighbouring countries, 1950–2001 (source: Original data extracted from Maddison (2003)).

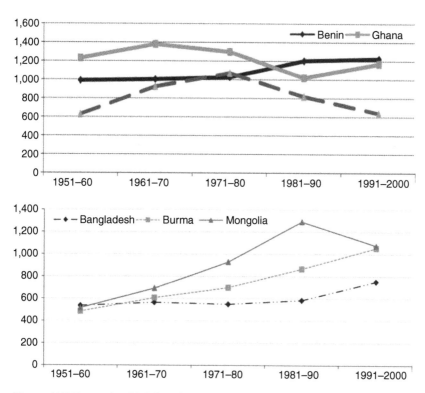

Figure A4.7 Per capita GDP in selected countries: convergence and divergence in the same region, 1951–2000, average evolution per decade (source: Original data extracted from Maddison (2003)).

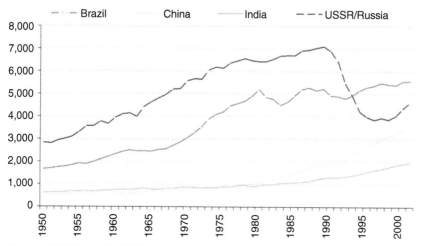

Figure A4.8 Per capita GDP in selected countries, 1950–2001: Average evolution per decade, convergence and divergence in the same region (source: UNIDO (2006)).

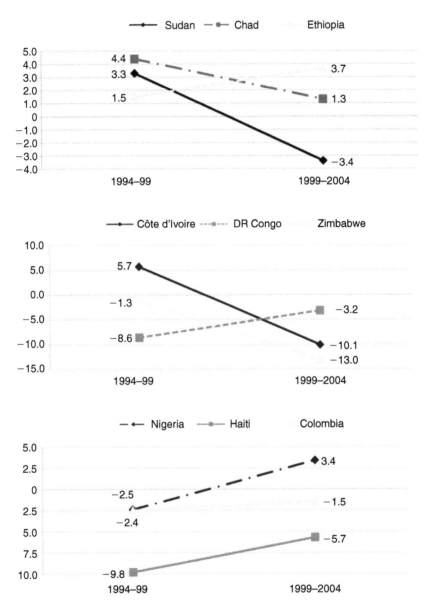

Figure *A4.9* Share of manufacturing value added in GDP for selected countries and regions 1995–2004 (percentages) (source: UNIDO (2006)).

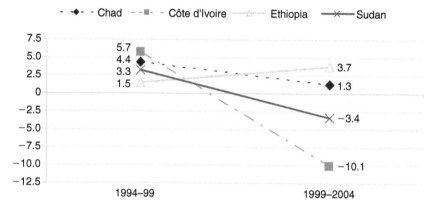

Growth rate manufacturing value added per capita for Chad, Côte d'Ivoire, Ethiopia, and Sudan, 1994–1999 and 1999–2004 (percentages).

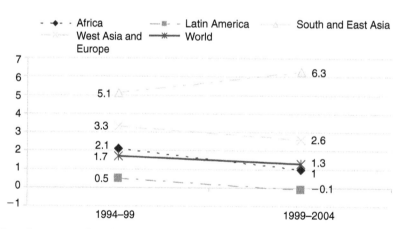

Growth rate manufacturing value added per capita for Africa, Latin America, South and East Asia, West Asia and Europe, and the World, 1994–99 and 1999–2004.

Figure A4.10 Average annual growth rate of MVA per capita for selected countries and regions (source: UNIDO (2006)).

Notes

1 Contact authors: esr@nifo.no, yeamaizo@yahoo.com, and kattel@staff.ttu.ee. The research for this chapter was partially funded by the Estonian Science Foundation, grant no 6703.
2 The text of the speech is available on OECD website, see www.oecd.org/document/1 0/0,3343,en_2649_201185_1876938_1_1_1_1,00.html.
3 It is, however, important to note that increasing returns can today easily characterize knowledge-intensive services as well. In the manufacturing industry outsourced low-end activities are often subject to constant or negative returns to scale and have very limited scope for learning. What used to be a simple system, where manufacturing activities are always "good," has developed into something more complex, but the key characteristics of "good" activities remain the same: increasing returns, imperfect competition, and a large scope for learning and technical change (Reinert 2007).
4 Another important aspect in state failure and fragility is the fast pace of urbanization in many poor regions of the world. (Davis 2006; UNHSP 2003) These are urban agglomerations where increasing returns are few and limited in scale and scope. The rise of such slums in poor countries indicates an interesting phenomenon: state failure and fragility are often preceded, or at least accompanied, by failure and fragility of cities. In fact, such failed cities are often surviving on resource-based activities from the country-side (large-scale agriculture, natural resources such as minerals, mining, etc.) and petty commerce (often selling imported goods). State and city failures reverse the development logic (city does not support surrounding areas but vice versa) and thus create huge dependencies and vicious circles. In such human settlements many survive in illegal activities and lodgings that enforce the vicious circles.
5 According to World Bank WDI online database, low-income economies are those in which 2005 GNI per capita is $875 or less.
6 See www.foreignpolicy.com/articles/2009/06/22/the_2009_failed_states_index.
7 Robert Wade in Chapter 2 in this volume refers to the "middle income trap" and is less optimistic about such convergence.
8 EPA: Economic Partnership Agreement (EPA) is essentially a free trade area agreement, which is consistent with WTO rules on free trade areas, see www.epawatch.net/general/abc.php?menuID=62#175.
9 AGOA: The African Growth and Opportunity Act (AGOA) was signed into law on May 18, 2000 as Title 1 of The Trade and Development Act of 2000. The Act offers tangible incentives for African countries to continue their efforts to open their economies and build free markets, see www.agoa.gov/.
10 See example of Chad with an improved economic growth rate and a MVA per capita of 1.1 percent between 1999–2004. (UNIDO 2006 38).
11 See www.doingbusiness.org.
12 See further Porter *et al.* 2007.
13 For example, the UK Department for International Development (DFID) classifies fragile states into four categories: Good performers with capacity and political will to sustain a development partnership with the international community; Weak but willing states with limited capacity; Strong but unresponsive states that may be repressive and Weak-weak states, where both political will and institutional capacity pose serious challenges to development. (DFID 2005).
14 A well-balanced overview of the topic is Goldsmith and Eggers 2006.
15 See further Goldsmith and Eggers 2006; Collier 2007, 118–19 offers instructive discussion of using networks/agencies in FFF states.
16 See in particular Evans and Rauch 1999, Rauch and Evans 2000, also Wade 2004.

References

Botero, G. 1588. *Sulle Grandezze delle Città*. Rome: Vicenzo Pellagallo.

Clark, G. 2007. A *Farewell to Alms. A Brief Economic History of the World*. Princeton: Princeton University Press.

Coase, R. 1988. *The Firm, the Market and the Law*. Chicago: University of Chicago Press.

Collier, P. 2007. *The Bottom Billion. Why the Poorest Countries Are Failing and What Can Be Done About It*. Oxford: Oxford University Press.

Davis, M. 2006. *Planet of Slums*. New York: Verso.

DFID. 2005. "Why We Need to Work More Effectively in Fragile States," UK Department for International Development, January 2005, London.

Drechsler, W. 2005. "The Rise and Demise of the New Public Management." *Post-Autistic Economics Review*, 33(14), 17–28. www.paecon.net/PAEReview/issue33/Drechsler33.htm.

Doornbos, M. 2002. "State collapse and fresh starts." *Development and Change*, 33(5), 797–815.

Easterly, W. 2001. *The Elusive Quest for Growth: Economists' Adventures and Misadventures in the Tropics*. Cambridge: MIT Press.

Evans, P. and Rauch, J. E. 1999. "Bureaucracy and Growth: A Cross-National Analysis of the Effects of 'Weberian' State Structures on Economic Growth." *American Sociological Review*, 64(5), 748–65.

Fukuyama, F. 2004. *State-Building. Governance and World Order in the Twenty-First Century*. London: Profile Books.

Goldsmith, S. and Eggers, W. 2004. *Governing By Network: The New Shape of the Public Sector*. Washington, DC: Brooking Institution Press.

Katula, M. and Perry, J. 2003. "Comparative Performance Pay." In: Peters, B. G. and Pierre, J. eds, *Handbook of Public Administration*. London: Sage, 53–61.

List, F. 1856. *The National System of Political Economy*. Philadelphia: J.B. Lippincott and Co.

Maddison, A. 2003. *The World Economy: Historical Statistics*. Paris: OECD Publishing.

Meyen, J. 1770. "Wie kommt es, dass die Oekonomie bisher so wenig Vortheile von der Physik und Mathematik gewonnen hat; und wie kann man diese Wissenschaften zum gemeinen Nutzen in die Oekonomie einführen, und von dieser Verbindung auf Grundsätze kommen, die in die Ausübung brauchbar sind?" A winning prize essay to the Royal Prussian Academy, Berlin.

Moyo, D. 2009. *Dead Aid. Why Aid is not Working and How There Is Another Way for Africa*. London: Allen Lane.

Pollitt, C. and Bouckaert, G. 2004. *Public Management Reform: A Comparative Analysis*. 2nd ed., Oxford: Oxford University Press.

Porter, M., Schwab K., and Sala-i-Martin X. 2007. *The Global Competitiveness Report 2007–2008*. London: Palgrave Macmillan.

Rauch, E. and Evans, P. 2000. "Bureaucratic Structure and Bureaucratic Performance in Less Developed Countries." *Journal of Public Economics*, 75(1), 49–71.

Reinert, E. S. 2009. "Emulating Success: Contemporary Views of the Dutch Economy before 1800." In: O. Gelderblom ed., *The Political Economy of the Dutch Republic*. Aldershot: Ashgate, pp. 19–40.

Reinert, S. 2007. How *Rich Countries Got Rich ... and Why Poor Countries Stay Poor*. London: Constable.

Reinert, E. S. 2006. "Development and Social Goals: Balancing Aid and Development to Prevent 'Welfare Colonialism'," United Nations, DESA Working Paper No. 14, ST/ESA/2006/DWP/14, January 2006.

Reinert, E. S. 2005. "A Brief Introduction to Veit Ludwig von Seckendorff (1626–1692)." *European Journal of Law and Economics*, 19(3), 221–30.

Reinert, E. S. 2004. "Globalisation in the Periphery as a Morgenthau Plan: The Underdevelopment of Mongolia in the 1990's." In: E. Reinert (ed.), *Globalization, Economic >Development and Inequality: An Alternative Perspective*. Cheltenham: Edward Elgar, pp. 157–214.

Reinert, E. S. and Reinert, S. 2003. "An Early National Innovation System: the case of Antonio Serra's 1613 'Breve Trattato'." *Institutions and Economic Development/Istituzioni e Sviluppo Economico*, 1(3), 87–119.

Reinert, S. 2005. "Italian tradition of political economy: Theories and Policies of Development in the Semi-Periphery of Enlightenment." In: Jomo, K. D. and E. S. Reinert eds., *The Origins of Development Economic: How Schools of Economic Thought Have Addressed Development*. New Dehli: Tulika, pp. 24–47.

Rodrik, D. 2008. "Second-Best Institutions." *American Economic Review*, 98(2), 100–4.

Schmoller, G. 1897/1967. *The Mercantile System and its Historical Significance*. New York: Macmillan/Kelley.

Serra, A. 1613. Breve trattato delle cause che possono far abbondare li regni d'oro e argento dove non sono miniere con applicatione al Regno di Napoli. Naples: Lazzaro Scoriggio.

Singer, H. 1950. "The Distribution of Gains between Investing and Borrowing Countries." *American Economic Review*, 40(2), Papers and Proceedings of the Sixty-second Annual Meeting of the American Economic Association (May), pp. 473–85.

UNHSP (United Nations Human Settlements Programme). 2003. "The Challenge of Slums. Global Report on Human Settlements 2003," London.

UNIDO. 2009. *International Yearbook of Industrial Statistics*. Vienna.

UNIDO. 2006. *International Yearbook of Industrial Statistics*. Vienna.

Wade, R. 2004. *Governing the Market: Economic Theory and the Role of government in East Asian Industrialization*. 2nd ed., Princeton, NJ: Princeton University Press.

World Bank. 2007. World Development Indicators 2007. Washington D.C: The World Bank.

Part III

Neo-liberal constraints on the policy agenda

5 The pernicious legacy of the rent-seeking paradigm

Helen Shapiro

Introduction

In recent years, development theory and practice have moved in opposite direc-tions. The theoretical literature has revived market failure arguments from the early 1960s, coming full circle from a market-based approach back to state inter-vention for attaining industrialization. In contrast to that earlier period, however, this theoretical turn has not led to a change in policy direction, despite the unim-pressive results on the economic and social achievements of liberal reforms.[1]

I will argue in this chapter that the rent-seeking critique of state intervention, first elaborated in the 1970s and 1980s, continues to shape mainstream policy recommendations in two ways. First, it has successfully shifted the focus from markets to states, so that the untested counterfactual that state failure is worse than market failure still holds sway. Second, it has influenced the recent empha-sis on state reform. The initial rent-seeking paradigm provided the theoretical basis for a minimalist state.[2] However, based on countries' experiences with eco-nomic liberalization, mainstream policy makers now argue that a reformed and strengthened state is required to implement these policies, hence the "second-wave" of reforms following the first wave of liberalization reforms.

The second wave of reforms, however, is motivated by an instrumental view of politics and institutions, in which the "right" institutions are those that deliver the "right" policies. Yet, the nature of those policies remains unquestioned. Moreover, an appropriately reformed state is essentially considered to be one whose policy-making apparatus is staffed by enlightened technocrats and limited to non-targeted programs in order to remain insulated from rent-seeking pres-sures. I will argue that these legacies of the rent-seeking approach have ham-pered the promotion of industrial policies.

The rise of the rent-seeking paradigm

In the post-war period, the crux of the debate in development economics con-cerned the extent of market failure and whether state intervention was necessary. The efficacy of that intervention was not an issue. Even for those who viewed the state as an antidote to widespread market failure, its ability to be just that remained an unexamined article of faith.

In the 1970s and 1980s, this implicit assumption about state capacity was critiqued. Different models depicting the interaction between state and private actors predicted that "bureaucratic failure" could be worse than "market failure," thereby shifting the terms of debate. Demonstrating market failure would no longer be sufficient to legitimate interventionist policies; it would now be required to show ex ante that state intervention wouldn't be worse.[3]

Therefore, even when it became generally accepted that selective industrial policies, rather than relatively free trade and non-interventionist policies, led to East Asia's success, the political conditions that allowed for their efficacy were deemed unreplicable. Most states' capacity to enforce reciprocity commitments was questioned, thereby requiring market mechanisms to discipline firms.[4]

Subsequently, the balance of payments crises of the 1980s, which affected many countries that had followed more inward-oriented industrialization strategies, were attributed to inadequate political institutions. Overspending and the ongoing protection of inefficient industries were seen as resulting from the capture of state bureaucrats by the industries they regulated and the unwillingness of politicians to make budget cuts unpopular with vested interests. The recommended solution was to alter the political landscape by eliminating the potential for rent-seeking activity. A "good" state was defined essentially in a negative sense by what it did not do. As many pointed out, the neoclassical political paradigm posited a peculiar counterfactual combining a non-politically organized society with an ideal liberal state.[5]

It was quickly recognized, however, that moving from theory to practice with respect to state reform contained an inherent contradiction. A strong state, defined as one that could insulate the policy making apparatus from vested interests, was required to implement liberal economic reforms (Evans 1995). So instead of the minimalist state of traditional neoclassical theory, a state with sufficient autonomy and capacity was now required. As editors Bates and Krueger (1993: 463, 467) concluded in a volume of case studies on the political economy of reform, "Economic policy reforms are not 'anti-state.' Rather, they appear to strengthen the powers of the core of the state, the executive branch, and to enhance its control over key economic policy variables which affect the outcome of economic activity." Their policy recommendation was to create "political and economic institutions that enable politicians to withstand the temptation to employ distributive political strategies and that give power over economic policy making to technocrats."

These recommendations were echoed in many subsequent studies along similar lines. For example, Haggard and Kaufman (1995) found that successful reform efforts were due to institutional arrangements that insulated reformers from distributional pressures. Based on Olson's view of collective action, whereby minorities are more likely to organize in their own self-interest, they argued that these pressures were likely to be particularly intense given that the losses from economic liberalization were readily apparent while the benefits were more diffuse and uncertain.[6]

The technocratic fix

In virtually all these assessments, the appropriate economic policies were assumed to be self-evident. The only question remaining was instrumental: how to create conditions whereby the technocrats, particularly those in the finance ministries, would have the autonomy to implement these policies? In fact, these technocrats were heralded as the "heroes" of the story by Wall Street, the international financial institutions, and many academics (Harberger 1993). A few from Latin America, such as Pedro Aspe of Mexico and Domingo Cavallo of Argentina, became financial media celebrities.

The reliance on enlightened technocrats is reminiscent of the tilt towards authoritarianism that some of the original neoclassical authors revealed. Lal (1985: 33), for example, suggested "A courageous, ruthless, and perhaps undemocratic government is required to ride roughshod over these newly created special interest groups." Much subsequent work was done on the relationship between authoritarianism and economic development, showing in fact an indeterminate relationship between economic outcomes and political regimes.[7] However, there has been little analysis of the technocrats' motivations or why they would act towards the common good. While the assumption is that those with ties to a particular industry will represent that sector's interests, the self interest of technocrats – particularly those in charge of macro and monetary policy – is never an issue.

Ironically, it was precisely this kind of implicit faith in government functionaries that neoclassical political economy identified as a weakness of early development theorists. Indeed, much of that critique was based on an analysis of the optimizing behavior of all actors, including those within the state apparatus. In contrast to venal politicians and corrupt bureaucrats, however, the technocrat's own self-interest is left unquestioned.

Interestingly, Bhagwati (1998: 11–12), a staunch supporter of free trade and economic liberalization, challenged this notion of disinterested technocrats responsible for financial policy. In 1998, he compared the Wall-Street-Treasury Complex to the military-industrial complex, and argued that it hijacked the ideas of free trade to support free capital mobility:

> Wall Street has exceptional clout with Washington for the simple reason that there is, in the sense of a power elite *à la* C. Wright Mills, a definite networking of like-minded luminaries among the powerful institutions – Wall Street, The Treasury Department, the State Department, the IMF, and the World Bank.... They equate the interests of Wall Street with the good of the world.[8]

Yet, these are precisely the "heroes" often given credit for the macro-stabilization of the 1990s. While many came from academia or international agencies, some came directly from the financial sector. Moreover, in many less-developed countries, virtually all of the top financial appointees ultimately landed in finance upon leaving the government.[9]

This doesn't mean that these technocrats necessarily acted in their own self-interest or that they intentionally implemented policies at odds with the imagined national interest. Nor does it mean that some of the policy mistakes can be attributed only to their self-interested behavior. Clearly, ideology as well as domestic and international pressures played a role. Nevertheless, the possibility that they promoted policies that served the interests of the financial sector from which they came, or that enhanced their own careers, cannot be ruled out. It is also inconsistent to make different assumptions about the supposed impartiality of technocrats in the financial ministries as compared to that of other state functionaries, particularly those with ties to other sectors or involved with industrial and regulatory policies.

There is also an empirical problem with this depiction of liberalization as a process carried out by disinterested technocrats, holding rent-seekers at bay – it is not historically accurate. In some instances, rather than eliminating opportunities for rent-seeking, liberalization simply generated new ones and bestowed benefits on different groups. As described by Schamis (1999: 238), in several Latin American countries, the politics of economic adjustment was not about "neutralizing the losers" but "empowering the winners." "Policy-making elites did, in fact, insulate themselves ... but often by forming alliances with groups of beneficiaries."[10]

Others have pointed out that the policy-making apparatus did not always need to insulate itself from the supposed "losers," because they did not always oppose liberalization. Kingstone (2001: 1000) describes how some industrialists who had benefited from trade protection and subsidies recognized that they could no longer count on the state for such support. Their preferences were not determined by static market positions. Moreover, firms were not dichotomously divided between winners and losers, or those that sold for the domestic market and those that exported; big conglomerates did both. Therefore, "the bulk of important economic actors at the start of the reform process remained important economic actors seven years later."

The obsession with institutions

When it became clear that the policies leading to macro-stabilization did not always generate growth, attention turned to broader institutional reform. In establishment policy-making circles, it was recognized that institutions matter and that markets only exist and function within an appropriate institutional context. While this was by no means an original idea,[11] taking institutions seriously marked a new direction in policy-making spheres.

Unfortunately, the way in which institutions have been considered is extremely problematic. Economic development has often been reduced to an institutional problem, in that autonomous state institutions are portrayed as the key determinants of economic performance. The correct policies are given; the problem lies in their implementation. This follows the historic pattern of searching for *the* determining factor in economic development. As stated in World

Bank (1996: 49), "Although the recipe for good policies is well known, too many countries still fail to take it to heart, and poor performance persists. This often signals the presence of political and institutional incentives for maintaining 'bad' policies." Easterly and Levine (2003) found that the quality of institutions was the only indicator that could reliably account for economic development. A similar approach is seen in the World Bank (2001) and its discussion of the so-called second generation of the Washington Consensus reforms.[12]

The rationale for institutions and the policies they promote is rooted in the assumptions of neoclassical political economy and the notion that bureaucratic failure is worse than market failure. The general message of this literature is that institutions need to channel information, define and enforce property rights, and increase market competition. Policies are promoted not only for their economic logic, but for their potential impact on rent-seeking and corruption. For example, World Bank (1996) states:

> In general, any reform that increases the competitiveness of the economy will reduce incentives for corrupt behavior. Thus policies that lower controls on foreign trade, remove entry barriers to private industry, and privatize state firms in a way that ensures competition will all support the fight. If the state has no authority to restrict exports or to license businesses, there will be no opportunities to pay bribes in those areas. If a subsidy program is eliminated, any bribes that accompanied it will disappear as well.[13]
>
> (World Bank 1996)

This echoes the arguments put forth to support export-promotion strategies in the 1970s and to explain the success of South Korea once it had to be acknowledged that the state was interventionist. The pressures of international competition supposedly mitigated the worse types of rent-seeking.[14]

Implications for industrial policy

While the policy-making literature has been focused on the failure of the state and institutions, the theoretical development literature has been moving in the opposite direction. Many of the theoretical assumptions about market failure which motivated industrial policies of the 1960s have made a comeback in development economic theory. Moreover, novel approaches to innovation have challenged previous assumptions about firm behavior. This has generated a new literature, which describes how market forces will not produce optimal results and provides a theoretical justification for the need for state intervention to promote industrialization. Some argue for the need to coordinate investment, others argue that countries can be stuck in a low-level equilibrium trap, and still others acknowledge that all sectors are not equal in a world of differential returns. Rodrik (2004) makes the case that firms will only invest in nontraditional activities if they are assured that their rents won't be competed away through foreign or domestic competition. Indeed, the notion that rents are at the heart of technological change and not simply politically derived is ubiquitous in the literature on the micro-foundations of development (see Shapiro 2007, 2008).

In contrast to the 1960s, however, a kind of schizophrenia has emerged between theory and practice. The reticence to immediately recommend state intervention is clearly due to past failures, as well as to different political-economic realities. However, it can also be argued that the unwillingness to even consider such strategies is due to the legacy of the rent-seeking paradigm.

For example, proposals for institutional reform go in precisely the opposite direction. They argue that institutions should foster domestic and international competition not only because of the economic benefits, but because of the impact on rent-seeking. Therefore, theoretical arguments demonstrating market failure and empirical challenges to the gains from free trade are not sufficient. Preventing rent-seeking has become an end in and of itself.

In this climate, theorists are often quick to disavow the policy implications of their findings. Traca (2002: 15) argues that temporary protection, which would allow firms to keep market share, is warranted for firms that are far from the technological frontier. Otherwise, they would not be able to maintain the returns necessary to sustain the costs associated with research and development. Yet he concludes by saying,

> this paper has not taken into account the difficulties of policy implementation by imperfect governments, e.g. rent-seeking, lobbying or lack of credibility, which are frequently used as an argument against the protection of infant industries. Addressing these, in the context of our analysis, remains a challenge for future research.

Likewise, Murphy *et al.* (1989: 1006) write, "We stress, however, that because all our models are highly stylized and capture what we can only hope to be one aspect of reality, policies suggested by these models should be interpreted with caution."

Another legacy of the rent-seeking mindset has been the confluence of micro and macro phenomenon. The crises that followed import substitution in many countries resulted from macro imbalances rather than micro inefficiencies.[15] However, the political analysis of rent-seeking behavior is fundamentally a sectoral approach.

It is important to underscore, therefore, that the outcomes of sectoral policies were not all disastrous. In Latin America, many of the successful sectors post liberalization are precisely those that originated under import-substitution. Natural resource processing industries received state support in the form of financial and technical assistance to nontraditional agriculture and forestry or as subsidies in the 1970s and 1980s to help firms invest in capital intensive processing plants. In manufacturing, in both East Asia and Latin America, many exports were based on the productive capacity and expertise developed during import substitution. Furthermore, to the extent that nontraditional exports were distinct from products initially made for the domestic market, they were often produced by the same firms that matured under the ISI regime. To the extent that managerial and technological capabilities at the firm level are essential to development, recognizing this continuity is critical. Amsden (2001: 266) also points out that to the extent that free trade did not lead to massive restructuring in most late-industrialization countries, "the resource allocation of the developmental state appears to have been efficient enough to withstand the market test."

Rodrik's study of export subsidy programs also found results that contradicted those predicted by rent-seeking assumptions (Rodrik 1995). The programs with the clearest rules and least chance of private manipulation were not the most successful; those that were (in South Korea and Brazil, for example) had government bureaucrats working closely with exporters. Finally, in Latin America, although the productivity gap with the US narrowed more quickly in the 1970s and 1980s than in the 1990s, exceptions were found in those sectors that grew quickly and which continued to benefit from protectionist policies, such as the auto industry. Import-competing sectors facing external competition fared the worst (Katz 2001; Ocampo 2004).

Finally, despite these shortcomings, no alternative theory of the state has successfully challenged either that of neoclassical political economy or the recent literature on institutions. As a result, they still define the discourse, and proponents for more activist industrial policies start in a defensive posture. Invariably, they offer caveats about the need to minimize rent-seeking. For example, even Rodrik, who argues that rents are central to the development process and that *all* policies, not just trade and industrial policies, generate them, introduced a paper on industrial policy with, "The objective of this paper is to develop a framework for conducting industrial policy that maximizes its potential to contribute to economic growth while minimizing the risk that it will generate waste and rent-seeking" (Rodrik 2004: 2).

In fact, a peculiar and contradictory theory of the state is implicit. On the one hand, the state is still presented as a passive, pluralist one acted upon by rent-seeking groups. On the other hand, the state institutions called for are portrayed as autonomous from society and as the key variables that explain economic outcomes. There is no theorizing about the nature of the state in less-developed countries to support either of these approaches. For all the talk about rent distribution, there is no mention of the political and distributional struggle in society and how that power struggle is reflected in the state, or alternatively, how the state may derive autonomy from it.

The underlying social dynamic is not even considered when discussing budget deficits. Instead, a technocratic fix – either strong, insulated state agencies or a hard, external budget constraint – is suggested to "resist demands from interested constituencies for the expansion of spending" (World Bank 2001). The notion that macro policy in general reflects underlying social dynamics is unexplored.

Even those with a more nuanced approach fail to address this dilemma. Many who have written about the need for government support to solve information externalities and to engage in coordination with the private sector refer to Evan's (1995) notion of "embedded autonomy" – an arrangement whereby coordination can occur without the lack of information caused by full autonomy and the corruption and rent-seeking of full partnership. Rodrik credits this type of embeddedness as the reason for the success of South Korea's and Brazil's export programs. Others also cite South Korea's ability to impose performance requirements on the private sector as an example. Rodrik (2004: 17) argues that once this institutional balance is found, "we need to worry considerably less about appropriate policy choice." But in contrast to Evans and an earlier literature on state autonomy, there is virtually no mention of the determinants of "embedded autonomy." It is presented as something to construct from above as opposed to reflecting the social and political dynamics of state-society relations.

Conclusion

Until recently, the mainstream literature ranked institutional frameworks according to how well they could deliver the correct economic policies, which were taken as a given. This approach has been shown to be problematic – not only is the correlation between "quality" institutions and development unproven, but the determinants of institutions are all but ignored. Even the assumption that there is a single recipe for growth has been questioned. As The Commission on Growth and Development (2008) acknowledged, there is "no general formula" for growth.

The recognition that neither the appropriate policies nor institutional framework is predetermined is a welcome shift. It will hopefully lead to more country – and context-specific approaches which reflect underlying social and economic dynamics. It may also provide an opportunity to question the way in which developmental goals are determined and to challenge the one-size-fits-all approach towards institutional reform.[16] Finally, it will hopefully lead to a more complex understanding of rents, which would take into account the conditions under which so-called rent-seeking may or may not be detrimental to development.

Notes

1 Refer to the evidence provided by Wade in Chapter 2 of this volume.
2 Refer to Krueger (1974).
3 See Lal (1985).
4 For a discussion of reciprocity, see Amsden (1989), and Wade in Chapter 2 in this volume.
5 For a review, see Shapiro and Taylor (1990).
6 See also Alesina and Drazen (1991).
7 See Haggard (1985).
8 Bhagwati (2008) reiterated this critique in the context of the 2007 financial crisis.
9 For example, Arminio Fraga had been fund manager for George Soros and a bond trade for Solomon Brothers before heading the Brazilian Central Bank from 1999–2002. As Gowland (1999) wrote, "His appointment is a further step in putting

control of the Brazilian central bank into the hands of the international banks and speculators." Upon leaving the government, Fraga went to investment banking, as did many of his team. The same was true of Pedro Aspe and many others involved in the Salinas administration and NAFTA negotiations. There are countless other examples throughout the developing world of the revolving door for technocrats between international financial institutions and financial and economic ministries in the home country.

10 Bates and Krueger (1993: 465) also acknowledge that new economic institutions may represent new interests, i.e., exporters over older interests.

> The role of economic institutions ... is to institutionalize these reform programs – i.e., to so empower the technocrats that their reforms are left beyond political challenge. The empowerment of the economic bureaucracy represents, then, an attempt to stabilize the fortunes and protect the political triumph of particular interests.

11 See North (1990) and Williamson (1985).
12 Other studies have found no close association between growth and institutional reform. See Rodrik (2001, 2003) and Wade, this volume.
13 This sentiment was repeated in the World Bank (2001: 107) which states that there is growing evidence that "countries that are more open to international trade have lower corruption."
14 Kang (2002) challenges the wide-spread assumption that growth is incompatible with corruption. In the case of South Korea, he argues that rent-seeking was rampant, but took place within a particular institutional context which promoted development. He focuses on the underlying class dynamics and the balance of power between the government and economic elites.
15 Ocampo (2004); Rodrik (1996).
16 See Evans (2005).

References

Amsdem, A. H. 2001. *The Rise of "The Rest": Challenges to the West from Late-Industrializing Economies.* Oxford: Oxford University Press.
Alesina, A. and Drazen, A. 1991. "Why are Stabilizations Delayed?" *The American Economic Review*, 81(5), 1170–88.
Bates, R. H. and Krueger, A. O. eds. 1993. *Political and Economic Interactions in Economic Policy Reform: Evidence from Eight Countries.* Malden: Blackwell Pub.
Bhagwati, J. 2008, October 17. "We Need to Guard Against Destructive Creation." *Financial Times*, 11.
Bhagwati, J. 1998. "The Capital Myth: The Difference between Trade in Widgets and Dollars." *Foreign Affairs*, 77(3), 7–12.
Easterly, W. and Levine, R. 2003. "Tropics, Germs, and Crops: How Endowments Influence Economic Development." *Journal of Monetary Economics*, (50)1, 3–39.
Evans, P. B. 2005. "The Challenges of the 'Institutional Turn': New Interdisciplinary Opportunities in Development Theory." In: Nee, V. and Swedberg, R. ed., *The Economic Sociology of Capitalist Institutions.* Princeton: Princeton University Press.
Evans, P. B. 2004. "Development as Institutional Change: The Pitfalls of Monocropping and the Potentials of Deliberation." *Studies in Comparative International Development*, 38(4), 30–52.
Evans, P. B. 1995. *Embedded Autonomy.* Princeton: Princeton University Press.
Gowland, R. 1999. February 10. "Brazil: Privatising a Nation's Reserves," *Guardian* (London), 940. Retrieved from www.cpa.org.au/z-archive/g1999/940braz.htm.

Haggard, S. 1985. "The Politics of Adjustment." *International Organization*, 39(3), 505–34.

Haggard, S. and Kaufman, R. R. 1995. *The Political Economy of Democratic Transitions*. Princeton: Princeton University Press.

Harberger, A. 1993. "Secrets of Success: A Handful of Heroes." *American Economic Review*, 83(2), 343–50.

Kang, D. C. 2002. *Crony Capitalism: Corruption and Development in South Korea and the Philippines (Cambridge Studies in Comparative Politics)*. New York: Cambridge University Press.

Katz, J. M. 2001. *Structural Reforms, Productivity and Technological Change in Latin America (Libros de la CEPAL)*. New York: United Nations Publications.

Kingstone, P. R. 2001. "Why Free Trade 'Losers' Support Free Trade: Industrialists and the Surprising Politics of Trade Reform in Brazil." *Comparative Political Studies*, 34(9), 986–1010.

Krueger, A. O. 1974. "The Political Economy of the *Rent-Seeking* Society." *American Economic Review* 64(3), 291–303.

Lal, D. 1983. *Poverty of Development Economics*. Cambridge, MA: Harvard University Press.

Murphy, K., Shleifer, A., and Vishny, R. 1989. "Industrialization and the Big Push." *The Journal of Political Economy*, 97(5), 1003–26.

North, D. 1990. *Institutions, Institutional Change and Economic Performance*. Cambridge, UK: Cambridge University Press.

Ocampo, J. A. 2004. "Beyond the Washington Consensus: What Do We Mean?" *Journal of Post Keynesian Economics*, 27(2), 293–314.

Rodrik, D. 2004. "Industrial Policy for the Twenty-First Century," CEPR Discussion Papers 4767, Center for Economic Policy Research, London, http://papers.ssrn.com/sol3/papers.cfm?abstract_id=666808.

Rodrik, D. 2003. *Growth Strategies*. Cambridge: Harvard University.

Rodrik, D. 2001. "Development Strategies for the 21st Century." In: Pleskovic, B. and Stern, N. eds., *Annual World Bank Conference on Development Economics 2000*. Washington, D.C.: World Bank.

Rodrik, D. 1996. "Understanding Economic Policy Reform." *Journal of Economic Literature*, 34(1), 9–41.

Rodrik, D. 1995. "Taking Trade Policy Seriously: Export Subsidization as a Case Study in Policy Effectiveness," in Deardorff, A., Levinson, J., and Stern, R., (eds.), *New Directions in Trade Theory*, Ann Arbor, University of Michigan Press, 1995.

Schamis, H. E. 1999. "Distributional Coalitions and the Politics of Economic Reform in Latin America." *World Politics*, 51(2), 236–68.

Shapiro, H. 2008. "Industry and Industrial Policy." In: Dutt, A. K. and Ros, J. eds. *International Handbook of Development Economics, Volume One*. Cheltenham, UK: Edward Elgar.

Shapiro, H. 2007. "Industrial Policy and Growth." In: Ocampo, J. A., Jomo, K. S., and Vos, R. eds. *Growth Divergences: Explaining Differences in Economic Performance*. London: Zed Books.

Shapiro, H. and Taylor, L. 1990. "The State and Industrial Strategy." *World Development*, 18(6), 861–78.

Traca, D. 2002. "Imports as Competitive Discipline: The Role of the Productivity Gap." *Journal of Development Economics*, 69(1), 1–21.

Williamson, O. E. 1985. *The Economic Institutions of Capitalism: Firms, Markets and History*. New York, Free Press.

The Commission on Growth and Development. 2008. The Growth Report: Strategies for Sustained Growth and Inclusive Development. New York: World Bank Publications.

The World Bank. 2001. *World Development Report 2002: Building Institutions for Markets*. Oxford: A World Bank Publication.

The World Bank. 1996. *World Development Report 1997: The State in a Changing World*. Oxford: A World Bank Publication.

6 Cementing neo-liberalism in the developing world

Ideational and institutional constraints on policy space[1]

Ilene Grabel

Introduction

During the debate over NAFTA in the early 1990s, Mead (1992) published an insightful paper, "Bushism Found," about that agreement, which was little noticed at the time, but has proven to be terribly prescient. He argued that the real significance of NAFTA lay in the mechanisms and commitments embedded within it that would lock in pro-corporate, neo-liberal economic reforms in Mexico. Additionally, and equally troubling to Mead, NAFTA allowed private corporate interests in the USA, Mexico, and Canada to gain new rights and protections which they could not possibly secure through ordinary domestic legislative avenues. Most prominent in this regard was the investment chapter of NAFTA (Chapter 11), which promised to protect corporations from strategies by which future governments might attempt to advance their national interest, but that would impose costs (actual or potential) on international investors. For Mead, not only did NAFTA represent an assault on the policy autonomy enjoyed by its signatories, but it even threatened to undermine democratic governance since it provided investors with the ability to sue national governments whenever they felt public policy infringed on corporate prerogatives.

Mead was not alone in locating the chief significance of NAFTA in its intended effect on policy autonomy. Advocating NAFTA, Krugman (1993) argued that the economic effects of the agreement on the US economy would be negligible. In his view, NAFTA was primarily a "political" agreement, the main import of which was to ensure that future Mexican governments could not easily reverse the liberal economic reforms of the Salinas administration. Like Mead, Krugman recognized that NAFTA was not about trade so much as it was about establishing an external constraint on the present and future governments of the signatory countries. While Mead worried about what this meant for democracy, Krugman celebrated the improved investment climate these restrictions would establish.

This chapter will examine ongoing intellectual and policy initiatives advanced by the economics profession and policy makers to lock in neo-liberal reform in developing countries by severely restricting the policy autonomy or policy space available to these countries. As NAFTA demonstrates, the profession has been wildly successful in achieving this objective. This is in part because it has advanced a two-pronged approach in the pursuit of neo-liberalism. The first operates on an ideological level and involves the recent theoretical advances purporting to show that neo-liberal reform is the only viable avenue forward for developing countries. In this context, I will examine the rise of the theory of "policy credibility" during the 1980s and 1990s and its more recent incarnation in the aggressive form of the concept of "policy coherence."

The second front operates on the level of institutional reform, and involves new means by which neo-liberalism can be achieved and secured against reversal in the (likely) case of opposition from those adversely affected, including any parties and leaders who seek alternative development paths. In this context, I will examine several institutional means by which neo-liberalism is being cemented. These include the creation of independent central banks; inflation targeting regimes; currency boards that prevent elected governments from using financial flows and policy in the service of developmental and social goals; and small-group trade and investment agreements (of which NAFTA is an exemplar) that not only augment the power of international investors but also mobilize this power to punish governments that waiver from the neo-liberal path. Obviously, there are other institutional means by which neo-liberalism is being cemented in developing countries, such as credit rating agencies and standards and codes (and the surveillance thereof). For reasons of space, we will not discuss these latter two channels.[2] Note that the other chapters in this section of the volume trace channels by which policy space in developing countries is constrained – Shapiro on ideology, Abugattas and Paus on fiscal space, and Van Harten on investment treaties. In addition, useful analyses of the constraints on policy space that come from bi- and multi-lateral agreements and institutions can be found in (Anderson 2009; Gallagher 2005; Shadlen 2005; and Wade 2003).

I contend that the institutional reforms discussed in this chapter draw their power not from a demonstrated record of developmental success,[3] but from the intellectual developments surveyed in the second section of the chapter. The net result of these two fronts is a substantial and dangerous loss of developmental policy space, which entails not only a higher likelihood of failure (e.g., in terms of the failure to industrialize and create employment), but also a much greater risk for those in developing countries who are least able to survive it. This loss of policy space increases the challenges faced by those seeking to create new opportunities for economic policies that are consistent with the new developmentalism (per many contributions to this volume).

Ideational constraints: from policy credibility to policy coherence

In the fight for development a new conceptual battle has arisen that, to date, has attracted very little attention from heterodox academic economists. It concerns the notion of policy coherence. Fortunately, the non-academic development community (namely, non-governmental organizations (NGOs) and the United

Nations Conference on Trade and Development [UNCTAD]) has recognized the significance of this issue, and is at present contesting the way in which this concept has been utilized in policy circles to legitimize an expansive neo-liberal vision of trade policy and investor rights, and to institute important constraints on national policy autonomy in developing countries.

Understanding the concept of coherence requires a look back at its powerful precursor, the theory of policy credibility that attracted so much attention in the mid-1980s and 1990s.

Credibility theory: paving the way for neo-liberalism by protecting the economy from the state[4]

The preoccupation of development economists with the idea of policy credibility emerged on the heels of two developments – one empirical and one theoretical. On the empirical level, the failure of the ambitious neo-liberal economic recon-struction of South America in the late 1970s and early 1980s prompted an anxious search for explanations. By the mid-1980s, a consensus had emerged among new-classical development economists that, despite the inherent correct-ness of the neo-liberal prescription for South America, the reform agenda never-theless failed to achieve its intended results because its architects had not taken into account the overall "policy environment" in which these programs were implemented.[5]

On the theoretical level, the current preoccupation with policy credibility stems directly from the precepts of new-classical economic theory. The seminal work of Kydland and Prescott (1977) was particularly important to the develop-ment of the theory of policy credibility. In this approach, rational agents use a *uniquely correct* economic model and take into account all available information to form expectations about the future. Among other things, agents must assess the credibility of an announced policy when forming expectations and making judgments about what actions to take. Unfortunately, however, assessing policy credibility is no simple matter. At issue are the perceptions of economic actors concerning the viability and effectiveness of announced policies, policymakers' commitment to sustain them, and hence, the likelihood of policy reversal or collapse.

In light of the importance of policy credibility, economists faced a challeng-ing question: How could economic policy be developed in this complex environ-ment, in which the success of policy depends critically on agents' perceptions of its viability? Two choices presented themselves: one could shade policy toward existing popular sentiments; or one could implement "correct" policy, policy that respects the fundamentals of new-classical economic theory. The former option is ruled out of court on the simple grounds that "incorrect" policy (no matter how popular) could not possibly retain credibility in the wake of the disruptions that would inevitably attend it. In the context of open capital markets, for instance, incorrect policy would precipitate capital flight. In contrast, correct policy (no matter how unpopular) would induce credibility over time as it proved

itself uniquely capable of promoting development and growth. A correctly specified policy would therefore impel rational agents to act "properly," at once
attracting international private capital inflows, achieving growth and stability,
and inducing the credibility necessary to sustain the policy regime.

In particular, the new-classical theory of policy credibility has come to
cement the intellectual case for the desirability and, indeed, inevitability of economic reconstruction along neo-liberal lines. The concept of policy credibility is
central to the broader task of elevating the market as the principal means of
directing economic affairs, and the effort to place severe constraints on state
manipulation of economic policy toward what are seen as particularistic aims. In
doing so, credibility theory has helped create an intellectual climate wherein
(contra the lessons of history) the state is cast as the chief obstacle to development and neo-liberal reform represents the sole means to secure development
objectives.[6]

The movement to insulate the market and the policy-making process from
politics has had many powerful and practical consequences in the developing
world, the most important of which is in the realm of monetary and exchange
rate reform, as we will see in the next section. For now, it will suffice to say that
the effort to "depoliticize" financial and exchange rate policy is reflected in the
creation of independent central banks (many of which utilize inflation targeting)
and currency boards that are beyond the reach of state representatives.[7]

Coherence: locking in the case for neo-liberalism[8]

> Harmonization and coherence have become the motherhood and apple pie
> of development-speak.
>
> (Bretton Woods Project 2002: 1)

Ideas about policy credibility have been carried forward and indeed amplified
into the new concept of policy coherence. I argue that the concept of coherence
today is code for another and altogether different goal: policy conformance.

Policy coherence is commonly used to refer to the need to harmonize the
liberal policies of the IMF, World Bank (WB), and WTO. On its face, the idea
that policies of the world's three most important multilateral institutions should
be coherent with one another is unobjectionable. After all, the inverse strategy of
"inconsistent" and "incoherent" policy seems simply absurd (as would the case
for in-credible policies). But, in practice, coherence has come to mean something very particular – that is, IMF–WB support for the WTO's efforts to
promote trade liberalization in the developing world. One analysis has described
coherence as "the streamlining of WB and IMF policies on trade to reflect provisions in WTO agreements" (BWP 2001).

The intuition behind the concept of policy coherence is simple: any individual
economic policy – such as free trade – will only yield beneficial outcomes if it is
nested in a broader policy environment that is conducive (that is, consistent or
coherent) with its objectives. From this perspective, the justification for

expanding the scope of trade reform and agreements to new areas over the last decade is that previous efforts to liberalize trade have failed to promote growth because of inconsistencies between trade and other economic and social policies.[9]

It is by now common knowledge that the IMF–WB have aggressively promoted trade liberalization for a quarter century. What is less well known is that these institutions intensified their promotion of trade liberalization by formalizing a policy of cooperation with the General Agreement on Tariffs and Trade (GATT) in 1993 and with the WTO via a series of agreements on "Policy Coherence" beginning in 1994.[10]

The first mention of policy coherence appears in the ministerial declarations preceeding the Uruguay Round of trade negotiations in 1993 (BWP 2003). These declarations articulated many goals, one of which was the "need to improve the 'coherence' of international policy making by establishing better linkage mechanisms between the GATT and the Bretton Woods institutions" (BWP 2003). This goal of policy coherence was embodied in the 1994 agreement that established the WTO. This agreement states that with the goal of "achieving greater coherence in global economic policy-making, the WTO shall cooperate, as appropriate, with the IMF and the WB..." (Article III.5 of the 1994 Agreement Establishing the WTO, cited in Caliari 2002: fn2).

These original coherence commitments have been reaffirmed and extended in different fora since the issue was first discussed. For instance, the WB and the IMF each signed separate agreements to cooperate with the WTO in 1996. At the 1999 Seattle WTO ministerial meeting, the WTO, WB, and IMF issued a "Joint Declaration on Coherence," which reflected a shared belief that trade liberalization was essential to the promotion of global growth and stability (BWP 2001). Following the Doha declaration of 2001, the WTO established a Working Group on Debt, Trade, and Finance charged with examining the potential of the organization to "strengthen the coherence of international trade and finance policies with a view to safeguarding the multilateral trading system from the effects of monetary and financial instability" (Nageer nd).

The concept of policy coherence is now percolating within other major multilateral institutions and organizations. For instance, in February 2001, the WB hosted a "Forum on Harmonization," which included representatives of the multilateral development banks and the Development Assistance Committee of the Organization for Economic Cooperation and Development (OECD). In April 2002, the WB created a forum for the annual review of progress on harmonization by donor organizations and countries. At its 2001 meeting, the Group of Seven (G7) called for the "harmonization of procedures, policies, and overlapping mandates of the multilateral development banks." At the United Nations (UN) conference on Financing for Development in Monterrey in March 2002, coherence, cooperation, and consistency of IMF–WB–UN policies was a centerpiece of the discussion. Coherence among the UN–IMF–WB–WTO figured prominently in discussions at the 2005 Copenhagen Social Summit. The UN Economic and Social Commission for Asia and Pacific (2007) has made a case for policy coherence in recent reports, by which they seem to imply the need for increased coordination among liberal international trade, investment, and domestic policies to enable countries in the region to reap the benefits of globalization.

In the hands of the IMF–WB–WTO, it is hardly surprising that coherence has come to mean the need for the simultaneous pursuit of complementary policies that further the neo-liberal agenda, and therefore preclude the use of development strategies involving the state in important ways. Today, the drive toward policy coherence has been entirely subsumed under this agenda.

One of the most visible manifestations of this drive has been the emphasis on trade liberalization and integration of developing countries into the WTO as critical components of WB–IMF work over the last decade. Indeed, UNCTAD notes that "the principle vehicle for trade liberalization are conditions attached to IMF–WB loans" (UNCTAD 1999: 87 in Rowden 2001). The WB's commitment to facilitate countries' accession to the WTO began in 1996 with the launch of the "Integrated Framework" program. In addition to the direct channel of formal conditionality and policy-based lending, the IMF–WB promote trade liberalization and the work of the WTO through technical assistance, training, and a variety of ex-ante instruments (such as the annual Country Policy and Institutional Assessments) (Caliari and Williams 2002). The technical assistance program aims, in the Bank's words, to "mainstream trade" in poverty reduction strategies.

Recent empirical studies trace the diverse channels by which IMF–WB work has promoted trade liberalization in the developing world and provided support to the WTO. For instance, a 1997 review of IMF programs by the NGO Oxfam finds that half of these programs targeted quantifiable reduction of trade restrictions as part of loan conditionality (Oxfam in Caliari 2002: fn. 3). The same study found that almost three-quarters of countries had restrictive trade regimes at the outset of their interaction with the IMF, but that four years later only one fifth of these same countries were classified as having restrictive trade regimes, and that the average number of trade-related conditions imposed on low-income countries increased three-fold between 1988–90 and 1997 (Oxfam in Caliari 2002: fn. 3).

A study by Rowden (2001: 11) shows that between 1997 and 2001, 36 countries agreed to bring their trade regimes in line with WTO accession requirements or committed to accelerate the implementation of WTO rules in official IMF documents. Rowden (2001) reports that between 1995 and 1999, 65 percent of all WB adjustment operations supported trade policy and exchange rate reforms (IBRD in Rowden 2001). Rowden also describes the case of Azerbaijan where, in 1997, conformity with WTO rules was an actual condition of IMF lending. A study by Khan (2007) demonstrates that the IMF has actually extended the reach of the WTO by demanding of developing countries a degree of trade liberalization that far exceeds the level promoted by the WTO.

Many factors explain IMF–WB decisions to promote trade liberalization and to cooperate with the WTO. Free trade ideology and the power of the US, the WTO and the interest groups that benefit from liberal trade reform must figure prominently in any account of WB–IMF trade advocacy. However, we must also consider that an intellectual foundation for the Bank's trade advocacy is provided by its own research that argues for the central role of trade in the promotion of growth and the reduction of poverty. The most important WB research output on this issue is the 2001 report, "Leveraging trade for development." Though it is outside the scope of this chapter, it warrants mention here that a large body of research calls into question the neo-liberal case for trade liberalization (especially of the "one-size-fits all" variety) in the developing world (Chang and Grabel 2004; Chang 2002; Rodrik 2007; and Rodríguez and Rodrik 2001).

It bears noting that up until now the discussion of coherence or harmonization among institutions other than the IMF–WB–WTO has not influenced policy in any clear way. It remains to be seen whether, in these various other venues, the concept of coherence will generate new policy initiatives or criteria for evaluating policy choices, or whether it is simply used as further justification for neo-liberal policies already on the table.

Institutional constraints on policy space: a selective examination

The neo-liberal agenda has not only been instantiated in the developing world through ideational means. A variety of complementary institutional constraints has also cemented this regime. These institutional constraints restrict the ability of developing country governments to pursue financial, exchange rate, trade, and industrialization policies that support new developmentist strategies. They also prevent them from responding to financial instability, while increasing the cost of policy experimentation through the establishment of mechanisms that internally and externally "lock-in" neo-liberal policies. In what follows, I consider two examples of these institutional constraints.

Credibility theory and the end of monetary and exchange rate policy for development

The theory of policy credibility has proven to be influential in the design and operation of the institutions that govern monetary and exchange rate policy in developing economies.[11] From the perspective of new-classical economic theory, the logic of extending the theory of policy credibility to the design of financial policy-making institutions is rather straightforward: to be credible, financial policy must be insulated from the vagaries of the political process, where short-sighted political goals often predominate. In the absence of this insulation, financial policy can be manipulated instrumentally by governments seeking to garner political support. Aware of this possibility, the (rational) public will know that announced financial policies "may lack credibility because they are economically inconsistent or politically unsustainable" (Schmieding 1992: 45–6).

Problems of financial policy credibility may also arise if policy makers have a history of strategically reneging on established policies in order to achieve a short-term political or economic objective. This is the problem of "time inconsistency" (Kydland and Prescott 1977). In this context, rational economic actors are likely to expect policy reversals and will act accordingly (such as by hedging against reversal). At best, the policy will fail to induce the intended results; at worst, it will be sabotaged. Financial policy credibility (and hence, success) may also be threatened if financial and fiscal policies are at cross purposes (such that one is expansionary and one is contractionary), an example of a phenomenon known as "Stackelberg warfare."[12]

From the perspective of new-classical economic theory, the task of gaining the public's confidence in the technical abilities and anti-inflationary resolve of financial authorities in developing economies is somewhat daunting. In such countries, it is reasonable to expect that the public will have limited confidence in both the personnel of financial policy-making institutions, and in the likelihood that the institution will be able to stay the course of politically unpopular policies. It is even reasonable for the public to question the longevity of new or reformed financial policy-making institutions. These uncertainties may stem from the immaturity of the institutions themselves, the legacy of high inflation, and/or from the rapid turnover of personnel in the government and financial institutions (Schmieding 1992: 45–6). In this context, new-classical economic theory maintains that it is necessary to staff politically insulated financial policy-making institutions with non-partisan technocrats in order to establish policy credibility.[13]

Central banks

The case for independent central banks in new-classical economic theory follows directly from this view on the prerequisites for credible policy. Central bank independence is seen to impart a degree of credibility to monetary policy that cannot be achieved when policy is developed by elected politicians. This credibility stems from the political insulation of the institution. Armed with respect for the precepts of new-classical economic theory and protected by institutional barriers from political contamination, the non-partisan technocrats who staff independent central banks are able to pursue credible (and time consistent) monetary policy in pursuit of an anti-inflationary course for the national economy.

A vast empirical literature seeks to substantiate the theoretical claims for the anti-inflationary performance of independent central banks. Initial studies focused on central banks in wealthy countries; these tended to confirm the hypothesis (Alesina and Summers 1993). More recently, efforts have been undertaken to substantiate these claims in the context of developing economies. An empirical study of twelve former communist countries finds that countries with independent central banks experience lower levels of inflation and greater macroeconomic stability than do countries with dependent central banks (Loungani and Sheets 1997). However, a substantial body of empirical research on developing economies presents mixed results (at best) on the relative performance of independent central banks (Bowles and White, 1994; Cardim de Carvahlo 1995; Cukierman *et al.* 1992; and Maxfield 1998). Indeed, Maxfield's

(1997) thorough survey of the empirical literature makes clear that the data supporting the case for central bank independence in developing countries is far from unambiguous, particularly in light of the sensitivity of the empirical results to diverse measures of independence. Grabel (2003, 2000) and Chang and Grabel (2004: Chapter 11) argue that the purported economic benefits of independent central banks (and currency boards) are not borne out by evidence (see studies by numerous economists cited therein); Epstein (2007) and Braunstein and Heintz (2006) argue that there are economic and social costs to the inflation obsession that drives these institutions; and Grabel (2000, 2003) argues that justification for independent central banks (and currency boards) derives from ideology that masquerades as economic theory and from the exercise of political power by the financial community.

Despite the ambiguous empirical basis for the case for central bank independence in developing economies, independence is nevertheless taken as a necessary (though not sufficient) step for achieving monetary policy credibility. Where central banks are new institutions (as in the former communist countries) or where the public has little confidence in these institutions, it may also be necessary to import central bank credibility by adopting the actual operating guidelines of credible Western central banks or even by importing central bank staff directly. Indeed, the German Bundesbank Law has been adopted by the Polish, Hungarian, Czechoslovak, and Bulgarian central banks. Credibility can also be created via externally imposed constraints on central bank operations. Such constraints are often embodied in IMF structural adjustment programs that tie financial and/or technical assistance to the central bank's adherence to certain operating practices, such as the refusal to finance government debt (Schmieding 1992).

The replacement of discretionary with rule-based monetary policy may also enhance central bank credibility. As before, this may involve importing credible rules from abroad. Increasingly, these rules are taking the form of quantitative inflation targets, about which there exists a gathering international consensus among new-classical and other mainstream economists. The IMF is also increasing pressure on the (independent) central banks of developing countries to adopt inflation targeting as part of their stabilization and/or technical assistance packages (Epstein and Yeldan 2008). As of 2006, 18 developing countries were committed to some form of inflation targeting (Epstein and Yeldan 2008) despite econometric results that indicate that there is no justification (in regards to economic growth benefits) for inflation targeting as it is currently being practiced throughout low- and middle-income countries (with targets set in a 3–5 percent band) (Pollin and Zhu 2006).[14]

But central bank credibility will only be enhanced by these constraints as long as the rules or targets themselves do not introduce time inconsistency or Stackelberg warfare, and as long as the public is confident that the rules will not be breached. This introduces a game-theoretic dilemma in which central banks must search for increasingly credible means by which rules can be enforced. If the public does not find the central bank's commitment to policy rules sufficiently credible, then the central bank may seek to have these rules incorporated into the legal system of the country. If mere laws are not sufficiently credible, then a constitutional amendment might be pursued (a "meta-rule") (Schmieding 1992: 50).

There is a tension between the strictures of monetary rules and considerations of policy credibility. Unforeseen exigencies may necessitate bending rules, which will yield them in-credible. Anticipation of such potential problems should undermine the attractiveness of rule-based policy in the uncertain global economic environment, let alone in the uncertain environment of many developing economies themselves. Perhaps because of these dilemmas, central bank reform efforts in the developing world initially focused on creating statutory and institutional independence, and then moved onto the establishment of inflation targets.[15]

The maintenance of central bank independence and inflation targeting means that central bank operations cannot support multiple economic and social goals, as they have in so many countries throughout their history. Historically, central banks have played critically important developmental roles. Their operations have promoted growth, employment creation, poverty reduction, investment, and financial stability. Central bank operations have also supported programs of industrial policy, credit allocation to economically or socially important sectors (such as housing, small business, and small agriculture), and export promotion through the maintenance of a competitive exchange rate and a variety of capital management techniques.[16]

Currency boards

Currency boards are seen by new-classical economists to enhance the credibility of the local currency (and the exchange rate) via the establishment of a direct link between it and the board's hard foreign currency holdings. Provided that the currency board maintains sufficient holdings of the foreign reserve currency, investors and the general public can be confident of the board's ability (not just its willingness) to maintain a fixed exchange rate. Moreover, the public is assured of protection against debasement of the local currency through inflation. This confidence in the fixed exchange rate may prevent the public from engaging in currency substitution, destabilizing speculation against the currency, and other actions that will undermine the stability of the domestic monetary system. Hence, even though currency boards do not render speculation against the currency impossible, they reduce the chances that speculators will lose confidence in the currency.

Currency boards epitomize the credibility advantages of rule-based financial policy; in all cases where currency boards have existed, they have operated in accordance with a strict set of simple, transparent rules.[17] As a consequence, they possess even less scope for discretion than do independent central banks – an important virtue for new-classical economists concerned about abuses of monetary discretion in developing economies. The legally/constitutionally binding rules that govern currency boards, coupled with institutional independence, preclude currency boards from ceding to political pressures for monetary expansion.

Several prominent new classical economists have endorsed currency boards on various grounds.[18] In the first instance, this support may seem surprising. After all, new classical economics preaches the virtues of unfettered markets, in which prices adjust instantly and without government interference in response to supply- or demand-side shocks. Currency boards prevent this adjustment by fixing the rate of exchange between the domestic and a foreign currency. But new classicals reconcile themselves to currency boards as an important "second best" alternative for developing economies, given the proclivity of governments to intervene in exchange markets and to print money to finance government expenditures. Insofar as these governments cannot be trusted to let foreign exchange markets operate freely or to exercise monetary discipline, currency boards provide a means for reducing government freedom while securing currency credibility. Moreover, the legal and institutional commitments under which currency boards operate renders the resulting currency values far more credible than those that arise under fixed exchange regimes lacking currency boards (Ghosh *et al.* 1998).[19]

As with independent central banks, the credibility of currency board rules may be enhanced by introducing credible external mechanisms to ensure compliance. This may involve efforts to import credibility by placing representatives of foreign central banks or multilateral institutions on currency boards, or by conditioning external financial or technical support on the compliance of the currency board with pre-determined rules.

Thus, independent central banks and currency boards are institutions that allow developing economies to fill the credibility deficit confronting economic policy. Currency boards and independent central banks that are either staffed or directly monitored by external actors or indirectly by foreign investors, allow developing economies to "import" or "borrow credibility" from abroad. These independent institutions act as a monitor and enforcer of monetary and exchange rate policies, which respectively constrain inflation and currency risks. These institutions act as agencies of restraint that minimize "investors' risk of policy reversal and therefore help to establish the credibility of the chosen policy options vis-à-vis market participants" (Dhonte 1997: 6–7). Independent central banks and currency boards assure investors that governments will not bend to popular pressures to abandon the "right" policies. The penalties for policy reversal include the loss of investor confidence and the withdrawal of private capital flows.

It bears noting that independent central banks and currency boards are posited as the institutional foundation for a more aggressive neo-liberal policy agenda (Kirshner 1998). Bowles and White (1994) describe the synergy between these institutions and neo-liberalism, arguing that: "Although the case for central bank independence is primarily based on providing lower inflationary outcomes, it also resonates with a wider agenda aimed at restoring 'discipline' and 'credibility' to economic decision-making in general" (Bowles and White 1994:

237). Maintaining central bank independence is one way that the public and (domestic and foreign) investors can be assured that the central bank will be able to pursue anti-inflationary monetary policy, and hence foster a favorable investment climate.

The operation of currency boards means that the exchange rate ceases to be a tool of development policy. This is unfortunate since maintenance of a competitive exchange rate plays a central role in export-led development, a strategy heralded even by the Bretton Woods institutions. Management of the exchange rate also plays an important role in influencing the allocation of investment to particular sectors in the economy.

The operation of currency boards also complements broader programs of neo-liberal economic reform. Currency boards enhance neo-liberal reform credibility by assuaging investor fears of policy reversal. Currency boards also promote reductions in government spending by precluding the printing of fiat money. This restriction also promotes privatization since central banks can not be used to provide aid to ailing state-owned enterprises. Currency board operations also complement neo-liberal reforms that promote external economic openness. Currency board rules stipulate that the local money supply can be increased only following an increase in foreign exchange holdings. An increase in foreign exchange holdings may result from improved net export performance or from private capital inflows. Expansion of the local money supply is predicated on the success of capital and current account liberalization, themselves important components of neo-liberal economic reform.

Policy coherence through small group agreements that lock-in neo-liberalism

Though the language of policy coherence does not appear as regularly in bi- or multi-lateral trade negotiations and agreements, a parallel movement is afoot in this domain to construct a coherent package of policies in developing countries. Most notably, we find here an embedding of complementary financial and investment policies nested into what are, ostensibly, bi- and multi-lateral trade agreements. This is particularly true of the trade agreements signed between the USA and individual or small groups of developing countries. In this context, what is most important about these agreements is the range of matters that they engage.

In 1994 NAFTA broke new ground insofar as it was as much – if not more – of an investment than it was a traditional trade agreement. It includes the controversial Chapter 11 provision that grants unprecedented rights to foreign investors vis-à-vis the state. Under Chapter 11, foreign investors have the right to seek damages for a range of governmental actions or policies that they can claim – even preemptively – are "tantamount to expropriation." These claims of loss (even potential loss) are adjudicated in unaccountable external arbitration bodies, such as the International Center for the Settlement of Investment Disputes (ICSID). NAFTA also de-legitimizes the right of governments to grant favored treatment to national investors, firms, or banks.

The US has used NAFTA, especially its Chapter 11 provision, as a prototype for the large number of bi- and multi-lateral trade and/or investment agreements it has been negotiating with developing countries over the last 15 years. Indeed, some agreements, such as the US-Chile and the US-Singapore trade agreements (effective 2003 and 2004, respectively) go much further in granting foreign investors the right to sue governments for losses associated with even the temporary imposition of capital controls during financial crises (Thirkell-White 2007: 35; Anderson 2009). The Central American–Dominican Free Trade agreement also includes these provisions on capital controls, as does the pending US–Colombia free trade agreement, along with 52 bilateral trade or investment agreements that the US has signed (Anderson 2009). These and other recent trade and investment agreements increase the cost of departing from neo-liberal policies by placing governments under the threat of lawsuits by foreign investors. The latter can bring legal action whenever certain state policies – those that target particular development, industrialization, social, or environmental goals or that protect an economy temporarily from financial instability – have interfered with their right to earn profits (see Van Harten, this volume). Anderson (2009) rightly identifies these strictures in trade and investment agreements as "policy handcuffs."

The justification for expanding the scope of trade agreements to these new areas is that previous efforts to liberalize trade have failed to promote growth because of inconsistencies between trade and other financial and social policies. What all of these agreements have in common is that they reinforce, and in many cases actually go much further than, the IMF–WB–WTO commitments to promote free trade and capital flows. As with IMF–WB–WTO policy, these agreements also redefine the appropriate role of the state, constrain state policy autonomy, and promote homogenous policies across developing countries. Thus, the US bi- and multi-lateral agreements support the drive toward what the WB–IMF–WTO views as coherence, but which we can more adequately describe as enforced conformance to the neo-liberal model.[20]

Conclusions

The concept of policy coherence has been invoked exclusively to legitimize ambitious and comprehensive liberalization schemes. This confirms many concerns about the abuse of the concept of coherence. The emphasis on policy coherence by the WB–IMF–WTO constrains the national policy space available to developing countries, locks in neo-liberal policies, and validates neo-liberal arguments about the limited (and perverse) role of the state in the development process. It is becoming far more difficult to pursue diverse types of national policies or for policy makers to engage in any type of (new developmentalist) policy experimentation because of the interlocking power of the IMF–WB–WTO and because of the formidable dispute settlement mechanisms in bi- and multi-lateral trade and investment agreements that threaten severe sanctions for any departures from the neo-liberal regime. It is used to validate the common, dangerous, and incorrect view that neo-liberal policies represent the only viable path to development for all countries. Like credibility then, it serves to close off consideration of any and all other paths to development. At present, there is a pressing need to separate the new emphasis on policy coherence from conformance with neo-liberal policies. This is necessary to protect developing countries' right to development and their right to policy experimentation. That policy coherence (and hence, success) must entail liberalization has been contradicted by historical and cross-country experience. Chang and Grabel (2004) (and many other scholars, such as Rodrik (2007), Chang (2002), and the work of many contributors to this volume) demonstrate that there exist multiple paths to development, and that high levels of feasible, sustainable, and stable economic growth can be achieved via an array of heterogeneous strategies. While any one country's policies must exhibit a degree of internal coherence in order to succeed, the evidence is clear that alternative policy regimes need not cohere around liberalization. Properly understood, policy coherence should entail an understanding of the uniqueness of diverse national contexts, path dependence, institutional embeddedness and stickiness, recognition that there exist multiple paths to development, and respect for national policy space.[21] There is also a need to rethink what is meant by the concept of policy coherence – the question is "coherence with what objectives and across what domains"? (See Winters 2001). Coherence can mean many different things. It can mean that economic policies within and across nations are consistent with development goals, as the OECD (2003) has suggested in its discussion of "policy coherence for development." Coherence might alternately involve consideration of the dynamic consistency between a nation's economic policies and its history, institutional structure, capacities, and prior policy choices. This implies that each country will have to discover its own set of available development schemes – schemes that are coherent in light of its own unique path. In concluding, it is imperative to recognize the importance of the concept of coherence while rescuing it from the straightjacket into which it has been fitted by the IMF–WB–WTO. Properly understood, coherence entails expanding, rather than diminishing, policy space. It implies heterogeneity of viable development paths across diverse national contexts. It is a concept that can be of tremendous use for those seeking to open development discourse to the myriad possibilities that exist. For these reasons academics must join the dialogue on coherence to rescue this concept from its corruption by the IMF–WB–WTO, and as part of the larger effort to evaluate the efficacy of global and national economic policies for development.

It may well be that the 2007–09 global financial and economic crisis, and the significant shifts in national power that will likely follow this, will create space for the kinds of policy diversity and policy experimentation that have long been called for by opponents of neo-liberal policy conformance. As of this writing, the IMF is being pressed by member countries to increase the representation and voice of countries (such as China) that have long rejected the idea that enforcing conformance to neo-liberal policy is a legitimate goal of the Fund (Landler 2009). Moreover, the momentum behind the movement to enforce neo-liberal conformance may have been dealt a fatal blow by the failures of this regime in its home, especially because US hubris is a casualty of the financial crisis. And finally, we may take heart from the fact that some developing countries are pushing back against the constraints on policy space associated with bilateral trade and investment agreements and ICSID. For example, Bolivia opted out of ICSID in 2007; Ecuador has limited its jurisdiction; Venezuela, Bolivia, and Argentina have publicly criticized the institution; and Australia, South Africa, Pakistan, and Brazil have pushed back against the terms of these bilateral agreements and investor dispute settlement mechanisms in serious ways.[22] While such sentiments in the developing world are not new, the current conjuncture may so weaken the case for neo-liberalism that they finally can be heard.

Notes

1 Paper prepared for Mount Holyoke College Conference, *Markets as means or master? Towards new developmentalism*. I thank participants at the conference (particularly, Shahrukh Rafi Khan) for incisive comments on the paper.
2 For critical analyses of credit rating agencies, see Sinclair 2005; on standards and codes, see Thirkell-White 2007 and Wade 2008.
3 Indeed, these reforms have had perverse effects on economic and social development.
4 The arguments in this subsection were advanced in Grabel (2000, 2003).
5 Two terms deserve clarification. The term "new-classical economic theory" refers to the extension of neoclassical theory that emerged in the 1970s and 1980s. It combines the "rational expectations" hypothesis with a presumption of instantaneous market adjustment. The term "neo-liberal economic policies" refers to the free-market economic policies that derive from new-classical theory.
6 See Shapiro, this volume, on rent seeking and the new-classical indictment of the role of elected officials in the policymaking process.
7 However, these institutional reforms fail on their own terms. Stated plainly: the effort to depoliticize financial policy via the creation of independent central banks and currency boards is ineluctably political (Grabel 2000, 2003).
8 The discussion of coherence draws on Grabel (2007).
9 This intuition is reminiscent of neoclassical theories of policy credibility and of Polanyi's (1967: 143) discussion of the rhetorical strategies employed by defenders of neo-liberalism (on both, see Grabel 2003). On the latter, Polanyi emphasized the propensity of advocates of free markets to explain their failure as stemming from insufficient liberalization rather than from the failure of markets themselves. He wrote:

> Its apologists [defenders of market liberalization] are repeating in endless variations that but for the policies advocated by its critics, liberalism would have delivered the goods; that not the competitive system and the self-regulating market, but interference with that system and interventions with that market are responsible for our ills.

10 The description of agreements and quotations from documents on coherence are drawn from reports generated by NGO researchers, especially Aldo Caliari at the Center of Concern, Jeff Powell at the Bretton Woods Project, and Rick Rowden at Action Aid.
11 Institutions and policy are treated herein as analytically distinct, but in practice they are thoroughly interdependent. For example, new-classical economists' support for an independent central bank is tied to the view that such an institution is uniquely qualified to pursue credible (read: anti-inflationary) monetary policy.

12 On Stackelberg warfare, see discussion in Sargent (1986). It refers to a game-theoretic dilemma wherein monetary and fiscal authorities engage in a non-cooperative game of "chicken" aimed at gaining dominance over one another.
13 Refer to Shapiro, Chapter 5 in this volume.
14 Roger and Stone (2005) is a wide-ranging review of international experiences with inflation targeting. They find that inflation targets are missed 40 percent of the time.
15 However, currency board operations are rule based. This emphasis on rule-based policy might strike some as odd in light of former Federal Reserve Chair Alan Greenspan's notable antipathy to rule-based policy in the US context. Most new-classicals, however, argue that such rule-based policies by independent institutions are necessary in developing countries because of the economic, political, and technical deficits that plague the policy process.
16 See Epstein (2006) for an extensive discussion of the historically important role of central banks as agents of development, Epstein *et al.* (2004) for a discussion of the role of central banks in supporting capital management techniques in a variety of national contexts, and Epstein and Grabel (2006) for a discussion of pro-poor central banking.
17 As Eichengreen (1999: 105) notes: "Closing off all avenues for discretionary monetary policy not just for a time but for the foreseeable future is something that few societies are prepared to do." This may account for the relatively small number of countries that today maintain currency boards as opposed to independent central banks.
18 The "arguments (of new classical economics) lend support to the case for currency boards, since currency boards are rule-bound and have no discretion in monetary policy" (Hanke *et al.* 1994: 39).
19 This is not to say that all currency board arrangements are intrinsically credible. For example, the IMF rejected an Indonesian plan to implement a currency board in February 1998 because the government's commitment to a fixed exchange rate lacked credibility due to low reserve holdings and political instability. The Argentine currency board was celebrated by mainstream economists as a model for other countries right up until it collapsed under the weight of speculation against the peso in 2002, after which time they revised their opinion of it and implicated it in the country's economic difficulties (Grabel 2002).
20 Future research on bilateral investment treaties might investigate how these agreements are ratified in developing countries, and how the lack of transparency of the ratification process creates space for governments to sign agreements to which civil society groups would otherwise object. For instance, it has been suggested that in one Latin American case, the government did not possess the full text of the agreement it signed and, in another, the treaty was ratified through an emergency measure in the constitution. I thank Luis Abugattas for this point.
21 See Wade's (2008]) discussion of "middleware" in connection with the right to policy experimentation and policy/institutional diversity across the developing world.
22 For details, see Anderson (2009) and Van Harten, this volume, for pathways out of bilateral investment treaties and investor dispute settlement mechanisms.

References

Alesina, A. and Summers, L. 1993. Central Bank Independence and Macroeconomic Performance: Some Comparative Evidence. *Journal of Money, Credit and Banking*, 25(2), 151–162.
Anderson, S. 2009. "Policy Handcuffs in the Financial Crisis: How US Trade and Investment Policies Limit Government Power to Control Capital Flows. Institute for Policy Studies, February, Washington. D.C. www.ips-dc.org/reports/policy_handcuffs_in_the_financial_crisis.

Bowles, P. and White, G. 1994. "Central Bank Independence: A Political Economy Approach." *Journal of Development Studes*, 32(2), 235–64.

Braunstein, E. and Heintz, J. 2006. "Gender Bias and Central Bank Policy: Employment and Inflation Reduction." Political Economy Research Institute, University of Massachusetts, Amherst, MA., Working Paper 06–1A. www.econ.utah.edu/genmac/WP/06–1A.pdf.

Bretton Woods Project. 2001. *More WTO–WB–IMF cooperation on trade* (Bretton Woods Update No. 25). Washington, D.C.: World Bank, http://brettonwoodsproject.org/art.shtml?x=16092.

Bretton Woods Project. 2003, July 30. Harmonisation and coherence: White knights or Trojan horses? *BWP: At Issue*. http://brettonwoodsproject.org/art.shtml?x=16735.

Cardim de Carvahlo, F. J. 1995. Financial Liberalization in Brazil and Argentina, www.ie.ufrj.br/moeda/pdfs/libebrasilargentina.pdf.

Caliari, A. 2002. "Coherence between trade and financial policies: Summary of current issues." Center of Concern. Washington, DC.

Caliari, A. and Williams, M. 2002. "Trade liberalisation and the role of international financial institutions." Commonwealth Foundation. Harrisburg, Pennsylvania.

Chang, H. 2002. *Kicking Away the Ladder: Development Strategy in Historical Perspective*. New York: Anthem Press.

Chang, H. and Grabel, I. 2004. *Reclaiming Development: An Economic Policy Handbook for Activists and Policymakers (Global Issues)*. London: Zed Books.

Cukierman, A., Webb, S. and Neyapti, B. 1992. "Measuring Independence of Central Banks and its Effect on Policy Outcomes." *World Bank Economic Review*, 6(3), 353–98.

Dhonte, P. 1997. "Conditionality as an Instrument of Borrower Credibility." IMF Working Paper on Policy Analysis and Assessment PPAA/97/2. International Monetary Fund. Washington, D.C.

Eichengreen, B. 1999. "Toward a New International Financial Architecture: a Practical Post-Asia Agenda." Institute for International Economics. Washington, D.C.

Epstein, G. 2006. "Central banks as agents of economic development." Working paper No. 54. UNU-WIDER, Helsinki, Finland.

Epstein, G. 2007. "Central banks, inflation targeting and employment creation." Political Economy Research Institute, University of Massachusetts, Amherst, MA, www.ilo.org/public/english/employment/download/elm/elm07–2.pdf.

Epstein, G. and Grabel, I. 2006. "Financial Policies for Pro-Poor Growth." Study prepared for the United Nations Development Programme. International Poverty Centre, Global Training Programme on Economic Policies for Growth, Employment and Poverty Reduction. Brasilia, Brazil.

Epstein, G. and Yeldan, E. 2008. "Inflation targeting, employment creation and economic development: Assessing the impacts and policy alternatives." International Review of Applied Economics, 22(2), 131–44.

Epstein, G., Grabel, I., and Jomo K. S. 2004. Capital management techniques in developing countries: An assessment of experiences from the 1990's and lessons for the future." G24 Discussion Paper No. 27, N.Y. and Geneva, www.unctad.org/en/docs/gdsmdpbg2420043_en.pdf.

Gallagher, K. (ed.). 2005. *Putting Development First: The Importance of Policy Space in the WTO and IFIs*. London: Zed Books.

Ghosh, A., Gulde, A.-M., and Wolf, H. 1998. "Currency boards: The ultimate fix?" IMF Policy Development and Review Department Working Paper No 98/8. Washington, D.C., www.imf.org/external/pubs/ft/wp/wp9808.pdf.

Grabel, I. 2007. "Policy Coherence or Conformance? The New WB–IMF–WTO Rhetoric on Trade and Investment in Developing Countries." *Review of Radical Political Economics*, 39(3), 335–41.

Grabel, I. 2003. "Ideology, power and the rise of independent monetary institutions in emerging economies." In: Kirshner, J. ed., *Monetary orders: Ambiguous economics, ubiquitous politics*. Ithaca: Cornell University Press, 25–52.

Grabel, I. 2002. "Neo-liberal Finance and Crisis in the Developing World." *Monthly Review*, 53 (11), 34–46.

Grabel, I. 2000. "The Political Economy of 'Policy Credibility': The New-Classical Economics and the Remaking of Emerging Economies." *Cambridge Journal of Economics* 24(1), 1–19.

Hanke, S., Joung, L., and Schuler, K. 1993. *Russian Currency and Finance: A Currency Board Approach to Reform*. New York: Routledge.

Khan, S. R. 2007. "WTO, IMF and the closing of development policy space for low-income countries: A call for new-developmentalism." *Third World Quarterly*, 28(6), 1073–90.

Kirshner, J. 1998. "Disinflation, Structural Change, and Distribution." *Review of Radical Political Economics*, 30(1), 53–89.

Krugman, P. 1993. "The uncomfortable truth about NAFTA: It's foreign policy, stupid." *Foreign Affairs*, (72)5, 13–19.

Kydland, F. and Prescott, E. 1977. "Rules rather than discretion: The inconsistency of optimal plans." *Journal of Political Economy*, 85(3), 473–91.

Landler, H. 2009, March 30. Rising powers challenge US on IMF role. *New York Times*, p. A12.

Loungani, P. and Sheets, N. 1997. "Central bank independence, inflation and growth in transition economies." *Journal of Money, Banking and Credit*, 29(3), 381–99.

Maxfield, S. 1998. *Gatekeepers of Growth*. Princeton: Princeton University Press.

Mead, R. W. 1992. "Bushism found: A second-term agenda hidden in trade agreements." *Harper's*, 285 (September), 37–45.

Nageer, F. (n.d.). *Fact sheet #4:* "What you need to know about trade-finance policy coherence." Center of Concern/US Gender and Trade Network, Washington, D.C.

Organization for Economic Cooperation and Development (OECD). 2003. "Policy coherence: Vital for global development (Policy brief), Paris. www.oecd.org/publications/Pol_brief.

Polanyi, K. 1967. *The Great Transformation*. Boston: Beacon Press.

Pollin, R. and Zhu, A. 2006. "Inflation and economic growth: A cross-country nonlinear analysis." *Journal of Post Keynesian Economics*, 28(4), 593–614.

Rodríguez, F. and Rodrik, D. 2001. "Trade policy and economic growth: a skeptic's guide to the cross-national evidence." In: Bernanke, B and Rogoff, K. eds., *NBER Macroeconomics Annual*. Cambridge: MIT Press.

Rodrik, D. 2007. *One Economics, Many Recipes: Globalization, Institutions & Economic Growth*. Princeton: Princeton University Press.

Roger, S. and Stone, M. 2005. "On target? The international experience with achieving inflation. targets." International Monetary Fund Working Paper No. 05/163. Washington, D.C., http://cdi.mecon.gov.ar/biblio/docelec/fmi/wp/wp05163.pdf.

Rowden, R. 2001. "IMF–WB–WTO synthesis report." Working Paper RESULTS Educational Fund. Washington, D.C.

Sargent, T. J. 1986. *Rational Expectations and Inflation (Harper Collins Series in Economics)*. New York: Harper Collins College Division.

Schmieding, H. 1992. *Lending stability to Europe's emerging market economies: On the potential importance of the EC and the ECU for Central and Eastern Europe (Kieler Studien)*. Tubingen: Mohr.

Shadlen, K. 2005. "Exchanging development for market access? Deep integration and industrial policy under multilateral and regional-bilateral trade agreements." *Review of International Political Economy*, 12(5), 750–75.

Sinclair, T. J. 2008. *The New Masters of Capital: American Bond Rating Agencies and the Politics of Creditworthiness (Cornell Studies in Political Economy)*. Ithaca: Cornell University Press.

Thirkell-White, B. 2007. "The international financial architecture and the limits to neo-liberal hegemony." *New Political Economy*, 12(1), 19–41.

UN Economic and Social Commission for Asia and Pacific. 2007. *Towards coherent policy frameworks: Understanding trade and investment linkages* (Studies in Trade and Investment No. 62). Thailand: UN.

UNCTAD. 1999. Trade and Development Report 1999. Geneva and NY: UNCTAD.

Wade, R. 2008. Financial regime change. *New Left Review*, 53 (September/October), 5–21.

Wade, R. 2003. "What Strategies are Viable for Developing Countries Today? The WTO and the Shrinking of 'Development Space.'" *Review of International Political Economy*, 10(4), 627–44.

Winters, L. 2001, July. "Coherence with no 'here' WTO co-operation with the WB and the IMF." Paper presented at CEPR/ECARES/WB conference on the world trading system post Seattle, Université Libre de Bruxelles, Brussels.

7 Mobilizing public resources for a new development strategy in the age of globalization

The fiscal space dilemma in Latin America

Luis Abugattas and Eva Paus

Introduction

At the beginning of the twenty-first century, Latin American countries are confronted with the development failure of the Washington Consensus and intensified competition in home and third markets. An expansion of knowledge-based assets has to be at the core of a new development strategy, with policies aimed at moving production up the value chain on a broad basis. Structural change towards higher value added activities is the only viable basis for a sustained increase in the standard of living for all. That is the high road to development. Inaction will put Latin America on the low road to development, with countries competing on the basis of falling wages, not rising productivity. Time is running short, as the rise of China and India is increasing competitive pressures dramatically in third markets and domestically.

The adoption of such a capability-focused strategy has to be coupled with the pursuit of the Millennium Development Goals (MDGs). Equating social development with economic development obliterates the necessary focus on structural change, as highlighted by Chang in this volume. But relegating social development to the back burner of development policies is equally unacceptable, as we cannot wait for the benefits of the new development strategy to trickle down to the poor in undue time.

In addition to the pursuit of knowledge-based assets and pro-poor policies, the new development strategy has to be based on development friendly macroeconomic management and an environmentally sensitive approach that does not seek short-term gain at the expense of long-term sustainability (Abugattas and Paus 2008). Here we focus on one aspect of the new strategy: development-oriented fiscal policies.

The government plays an activist role in the new developmentalist strategy, and it will need to increase public resources considerably to implement the requisite policies. However, governments in Latin America (and elsewhere) are caught in a fiscal space dilemma: their ability to raise resources (the actual fiscal space) stands in stark contrast to the resources needed for a new developmentalist strategy or with the potential policy space.

While there have always been constraints on fiscal space in developing countries, the current globalization process combined with the legacies of the Washington Consensus have significantly changed the intensity and nature of these constraints. An analysis of the factors constricting fiscal space in Latin America is the focus of this chapter.

We start by demonstrating that a capability-based development strategy cum MDG achievement requires a considerable increase in public resources in Latin America, and that an increase in public revenue has to be an important venue for raising these resources. We propose an analytical framework for assessing the fiscal space dilemma, which includes the sources of constraints – emanating from the globalization process on the one hand and the internal production structure and political economy on the other – as well as the channels through which they affect the available fiscal space. We apply this general framework to an analysis of the specific case of Latin America. We conclude with reflections on the changes needed to bring the actual fiscal space in Latin America closer to the potential fiscal space.

Resource needs for development: Latin America at the beginning of the twenty-first century

The development failure of the Washington Consensus in Latin America

Under the Washington Consensus, the role of the government declined dramatically – as producer, strategic planner of industrial priorities, and provider of public goods for development. The private sector and liberalized markets were to be the driving force behind economic growth, diversification, and poverty reduction. Many areas of public service provision were privatized, as advocates of free market policies argued that the private sector was in a better position to provide services to a larger share of the population and at lower prices.

After more than two decades of Washington Consensus policies in Latin America, it is clear that these expectations have not been met. The private sector compensated only partially for the decline in the public sector and in public investment. Furthermore, Latin America's investment ratio is a far cry from the 25 percent the Commission on Growth and Development (2008) identified as necessary for sustained economic growth.[1]

In 2006, the average investment ratio in Latin America and the Caribbean was only 20 percent, the same as in Sub-Saharan Africa, and below low-income countries (23 percent), middle-income countries (26 percent), and East Asia and Pacific (37 percent).[2]

Productivity growth in Latin America has been low (e.g., Paus 2004), and growth rates of per capita GDP have been disappointing, with the exception of the last few years where favorable external conditions have fueled economic growth (e.g., Ocampo 2008). But even the higher growth rates of close to 5 percent per year between 2003 and 2007 were lower than in any other region of the world (IADB 2008: 10).

Free market policies also did not lead to a reduction in poverty or a diversification of the productive structure in Latin America. On the contrary, most South American economies have returned to a comparative advantage based on primary products in agriculture and mining, while the exports of many Central American countries have come to be dominated by assembled labor intensive products (see, for example, Reinhardt and Wilson 2000).

The entry of China, India, and Central Europe into the global economy has led to a doubling of the global labor force (Freeman 2007) and intensified competitive pressures across a wide range of products. China, in particular, has developed capabilities and competitiveness in products across the whole range of technology-intensities. The legacy of the failed Washington Consensus coupled with the onslaught of competition from newcomers in international markets has left most of Latin America in a middle-income trap (Wade in this volume): wages are often too high to allow competitive production of unskilled labor intensive commodities, and productivity is often too low to allow producers to compete with more industrialized countries in the production of highly skill-intensive goods. The speed and breadth of China's penetration of global markets (and increasingly of Latin American domestic markets) greatly increases the urgency for Latin American countries to develop the skill base, or more broadly the knowledge-based assets, for new comparative advantages further up the value chain (e.g., Paus 2009).

A new development strategy requires more public resources

If China's high economic growth and impressive diversification in manufacturing turn up the heat for Latin American governments to find a way out of the middle-income trap, China's development strategy holds out valuable lessons in the conceptualization of such a way. In contrast to Latin America's free market policies of the last two decades, China has pursued a strategy of controlled liberalization of trade and foreign investment combined with strategic domestic investments in the expansion of the country's knowledge-based assets.

Most of the key tenets of the Chinese strategy are not new. With rare exceptions, latecomers in the development process have caught up with some form of protectionist measures and strategic government interventions aimed at developing national broad and targeted technological capabilities (e.g., Chang 2008 and this volume; Reinert 2007 and this volume; Rodrik 2007; Amsden 2001; Wade 1990 and this volume). What is arguably new in the Chinese model, compared to the earlier Asian Tigers, is the strong emphasis on promoting domestic R&D at an earlier stage in the development process.

The new development strategy in Latin America has to be a capability-centered strategy, where the expansion of domestic knowledge-based assets is at the core of achieving comparative advantages beyond primary products and unskilled labor-intensive goods. The particulars of such a strategy are country-specific, of course; after all, there are considerable differences among Latin American countries, even though they are all middle-income countries (with the exception of Haiti). But irrespective of the differences in the particulars, a capability-centered development strategy requires more pro-active government policies and more public resources.

Public support is needed to spearhead or complement capabilities in key areas of the private sector, to advance educational coverage and a technological-institutional infrastructure, and to expand physical infrastructure. Many of these interventions require additional public resources; whether it is infrastructure expansion, credit at preferential rates to help companies overcome market failures in increasing R&D, training and skill advancement, provision of technical and marketing knowledge, extension services in agriculture, etc. (e.g., Gallagher and Chudnovsky 2009; Paus and Shapiro 2007; Rodrik 2007a; Lall 2005).

The Commission on Growth and Development (2008: 35) points out that all successful development stories after WWII were based – in part – on high public investment in infrastructure, education, and health, and that public investment crowded in private investment rather than crowding it out. In the successful countries, public investment accounted for 5–7 percent of GDP.

Today, public investment ratios in Latin America fall way short of that benchmark. Though data on public investment is sketchy and comparisons across decades are fraught with difficulties, it is clear that – for most Latin American countries – public investment ratios have declined considerably since the 1970s. In Brazil, the public investment ratio fell from an average of 4 percent during 1960–80 to 2.2 percent in 2002 (Ferreira *et al.* 2005: 2).

In the seven largest Latin American countries, public investment as a share of primary government spending is lower today than it was 30 years ago, and it is only half of that of emerging Asia (IADB 2008: 16). The dramatic decline in investment ratios is a reflection of both the paradigmatic shift to the private sector under the Washington Consensus and of governments' attempts to reduce the fiscal deficit through a cut in public investment. The Brazilian case is particularly extreme as public investment in infrastructure fell by 174 percent of the total fiscal adjustment between 1980–84 and 1995–98 (OECD 2008: 37).

The pursuit of a capability-based development strategy to put countries on the high road to development is not the only reason for greater resource mobilization. There are other areas where increased funding is required as well; most importantly, for the achievement of the millennium development goals, environmental sustainability, and institutional capacity building.

Estimates of additional public resource needs for Latin American development

Country-specific assumptions and data are necessary to estimate the additional resource needs for a capability-based strategy, the millennium development goals, environmental sustainability and institutional capacity for any particular country. Such estimates are beyond the scope of this paper. Below we provide a brief overview of pertinent estimates of resource needs in these areas. The upshot is that the order of magnitude may well be around 5–7 percent of GDP.

Not all of these resources will have to come from the public sector, but governments will have to play a key role.

Infrastructure

Under the Washington Consensus, average infrastructure investment decreased from 3.7 percent of GDP in 1980–85 to 2.2 percent in 1996–2001, with public investment falling from 3.1 to 0.8 percent. Although private infrastructure investment increased, it made up for only one third of the decline in public investment (see Table 7.1).

In light of the drop in infrastructure investment, it is not surprising that Latin America's infrastructure coverage lags behind that of East Asia.[3] At the turn of the century, Latin America was considerably below the average for middle-income countries in road density, pavement rates, and fixed telephone lines, but above the average in mobile phone and sanitation coverage. Fay and Morrison (2005) estimate that an additional 1.3 percent of GDP is needed to meet consumer and business demand for infrastructure assuming modest growth rates ("the business as usual approach"), but that an additional two to four percentage points of GDP are necessary to keep up with China and catch up with South Korea.

Millennium development goals

At the UN Millennium Summit in New York in 2000, governments from around the world committed themselves to a quantum leap in reducing poverty and promoting basic human rights by 2015. A number of studies estimate the resource needs for the achievement of these millennium development goals (MDGs), though methodology, coverage, and assumptions vary widely. Some studies focus on the achievement of one particular MDG, while others estimate the cost of achieving several or all MDGs.

With respect to health, for example, Cepal (2008a: 102) estimates that, in 2015, Latin America will need \$3.6 billion (in 2006 prices) to attain the millennium development goals.[4] Regarding education, Cepal and UNESCO (2004: 8) calculate that \$149 billion (in 1995 prices) are needed to achieve four key education goals in Latin America by 2015: universal enrollment in preschool and primary school, secondary school enrollment rates of 75 percent, and eradication of adult illiteracy. That translates into an annual increase in education spending of 16.6 percent, considering that total public expenditures on education in Latin America were \$81.9 billion in 2000. Fan and Rosegrant (2008) project that an additional \$4.5 billion per year will be needed in Latin America to reduce poverty and hunger (MDG1) through investments in agriculture.

The Maquette for MDG simulation (MAMS), a dynamic computable equilibrium model, has been used to estimate the comprehensive resource requirements for achieving the MDGs in several Latin American countries.[5] For the case of Honduras, Bussolo and Medvedev (2007) find that, during 2001–15, government expenditures would have to increase at an average annual rate of 15.6 percent in

Table 7.1 Infrastructure investment in Latin America[1] 1980–2001 (as percent of GDP)

	1980–85			1996–2001			Change		
	Total	*Public*	*Private*	*Total*	*Public*	*Private*	*Total*	*Public*	*Private*
Telecommunications	0.45	0.30	0.15	0.94	0.17	0.77	0.50	-0.13	0.62
Power	1.95	1.64	0.31	0.71	0.31	0.37	-1.25	-1.33	0.06
Land transportation[2]	1.06	0.91	0.15	0.36	0.16	-1.25	0.69	-0.74	0.05
Total Infrastructure[3]	3.71	3.10	0.61	0.83	1.41	-1.46	-1.46	-2.27	0.80

Source: Calderón and Servén (2004: 30).

Notes
1 Weighted average based on Argentina, Brazil, Chile, Colombia, Mexico, Peru, Bolivia.
2 Investment in roads and railways.
3 Includes telecommunications, power, roads, railways, and water.

primary education, 11.7 percent in health, and 14.1 percent in water and sanitation to reach the millennium development goals. Vos *et al.* (2007: 16, 22) calculate that Costa Rica will need an additional 1.1 percent of GDP per year (2002–15) to achieve the MDGs and Ecuador will need an additional 1.3 percent. For Peru, the additional resource needs for MDGS are between 0.7 and 0.95 percentage points of GDP per year (Yamana 2007).

Other important resource needs

The MDG goals related to education focus on expanding education at the lower level. To escape from the middle-income trap, many Latin American countries also have to expand technological capabilities, and improvements in post-primary education need to support such efforts. For example, repetition and dropout rates at the secondary level are much higher in Latin American countries than in other countries at similar income levels, inequities in access to quality education are widespread, and there is often a mismatch between the skill needs of the market and educational offerings (e.g., Holm-Nielson *et al.* 2005: 40).

Additional resources are also required for the build-up of institutional capacity to improve the effectiveness of governance and policy implementation. Institution building entails the dismantling and/or reformation of institutions and organizations – legal, political, administrative, economic, and social – and the improvement of their efficiency and effectiveness. There is consensus on the centrality of institutional capacity building for development in Latin America, and wide recognition of the existing weaknesses (see contributions in Lora 2007). Programs for institutional capacity building involve high costs, including paying salaries high enough to attract capable individuals and to "professionalize" public administration. In this latter aspect, there is a significant public employment skill-penalty in most countries of the region.

Existing studies suggest that the financial resources required for institution-building are significant. Chile has already spent more than $1 billion in reforming its judicial system (Gobierno de Chile, cited in Addison 2008). Between 1994 and 2003, the Inter-American Development Bank (IADB) approved $358 million in loans for 22 reform projects of the judicial system in Latin America and the World Bank approved projects for eight countries (1998–2003) for $154.5 million (Pasara 2004).

Our brief survey of resource estimates highlights that, at the beginning of the twenty-first century, Latin American countries need significant additional resources to increase public investment, meet the MDGs, and promote a development strategy that aims at the expansion of knowledge-based assets and an increase of productivity.

Mobilizing public resources for development

Economists commonly distinguish four channels for the mobilization of public resources: foreign aid, deficit financing, efficiency improvements, and government revenues. While the relative importance of each of these channels will vary with country-specific characteristics, we argue here that for most Latin American countries an increase in government revenues will have to play a key role in raising the resources for the development needs discussed above.

Foreign aid

Since most Latin American countries are middle-income countries, external support – including grant aid and debt relief – will not play a significant role in the foreseeable future, with the exception perhaps of the poorest countries of the region.

Latin America's share in official development assistance (ODA) has been declining steadily, as ODA has become ever more focused on supporting the least developed countries, particularly in Africa. In 2007, Latin American countries received $6.9 billion of multilateral and bilateral ODA. That represents 6.6 percent of the total ODA flows to developing countries, and a decline from the 8.4 percent in 2002 (OECD 2007). Eighty percent of ODA to the region is bilateral, and total ODA makes up less than 0.4 percent of the region's GDP. In 2003, one third of total ODA to the region went to Bolivia, Honduras, and Nicaragua, mostly for debt relief (IADB 2005).[6]

Latin America also receives relatively little ODA in the context of Aid for Trade, which is aimed at enhancing the capabilities of developing countries to benefit from integration into the global economy. In 2005, the whole region received $1.4 billion of aid for trade, which is only 7 percent of the total global ODA made available for this purpose (OECD 2007).

Deficit financing

There is some room for increased deficit financing in Latin America, but – as in the case of foreign aid – it can only play a limited role in meeting the development needs of the sub continent. With higher growth after 2003, the public debt situation in Latin America improved considerably for most countries, until the onset of the global financial crisis in late 2007. Public debt as a percentage of GDP declined from 51 percent in 2003 to 35 percent in 2007 and, with the exception of Brazil, all major Latin American countries were projected to register a fiscal surplus in 2008, until the crisis hit. Nonetheless, even before the crisis, all countries – with the exception of Chile – had a structural deficit (IADB 2008: 13).[7] And structural debt as a share of GDP was still higher than it had been at the turn of the century (OECD 2008: 82).

Latin American governments have played a key role in the international debt market, with public debt accounting for over 50 percent of sovereign debt of all emerging market economies (OECD 2008: 81). Several Latin American governments have deliberately lowered their external debt exposure over the last few years, refinancing external bonds with internal debt in order to be less exposed to the vagaries of international financial markets. In case of sudden exchange rate changes, for example, the cost of foreign debt servicing increases considerably due to the currency mismatch problem. The value of external public bonds declined from 20.6 percent of GNP in 2003 to 11.1 percent in 2006 and relative to exports, the debt ratio fell from 71.4 percent to 35.8 percent (OECD 2008: 83).[8]

The global financial and economic crisis of 2007–09 underscores the wisdom of lower external debt exposure, as Latin American countries are in a much better position to face the crisis than they were, for example, during the crisis of the early 1980s. To sustain growth and development in the long run, governments need to keep prioritizing debt from domestic sources.

Governments can finance a deficit domestically through seignorage or increased borrowing. The former option is not possible to any significant extent because of its inflation-igniting potential. The latter option is limited by the underdeveloped capital markets in many Latin American countries. In 2003, the ratio of bonds outstanding to GDP was – on average – 37 percent for the seven largest Latin American countries, whereas it was 60 percent in East Asia and 141 percent in the G7 (Stallings and Studart 2006: 265).

Improved efficiency and reallocation of expenditures

A number of studies have argued that reducing inefficiencies in government expenditures can stretch existing government revenues a long way. Clements *et al.* (2007: 16, 18–19), for example, suggest that the quality of government services in Latin America is lower than in many fast-growing developing countries. They argue that it is important for countries to "tackle the institutional weaknesses that plague many countries in the region, including patronage in hiring and promotions, the absence of performance evaluation, and internal inequities in remuneration." While only country-specific analyses can identify actual sources of inefficiencies, eradication of inefficiency can only go so far. In a subcontinent where teachers and other public employees are often underpaid compared to the private sector, and where salaries constitute a high percentage of the national budgets, it is hard to see that eradication of inefficiencies will free up significant resources to address the financing needs highlighted in the previous section.

Reallocation of existing resources may be a more promising venue for raising resources for some Latin American countries. The most glaring example is a change in the military expenditure law in Chile. Under this law, which dates back to the late 1950s, 10 percent of the export revenues of the state-owned copper company CODELCO is automatically transferred to the military each year. From a development perspective, the military budget is an obvious target for expenditure reallocation. But the feasibility of any such reallocation is a political question. In the case of Chile, disclosures in 2008 of misused funds under the military expenditure law coupled with the global crisis may provide the necessary political momentum for a change in the law and a reallocation of funds for development.

Increasing government revenues

Economic theory can not tell us what the "right" level of taxation for a country is; a country's tax ratio (tax-to-GDP) evolves historically with the social preferences and development priorities of a country. Nonetheless, the data show that countries with a higher per capita GDP tend to have a higher tax ratio. That may be due to the fact that they have developed greater administrative capacity for tax collection and a broader tax base, as the structure of the economy has shifted away from agriculture (Burgess and Stern 1993).

Against the backdrop of such empirical regularity, many Latin American countries have a tax ratio that is lower than the "tax capacity" suggested by cross-country regression results. Thus there is room in a number of Latin American countries to increase tax revenue at a faster rate than income.

In 2006, the average tax ratio in Latin America was 14.9 percent (17.4, if we include social security contributions). South American countries have a higher tax ratio, on average, than Central American and Caribbean countries, 17 percent versus 12.9 (see Table 7.2), though there is considerable variation among the South American countries as well. In Brazil and Argentina, the tax ratios are way above the Latin American average, at 25.8 and 23.6 percent, respectively.

In international comparisons, Latin America's tax ratio, excluding social security contributions, is about the same as in South East Asia and about half of that in the OECD and the EU. But direct taxes play a much smaller role in Latin America than in the comparison regions (see Table 7.3), which imposes considerable constraints on Latin American governments' ability to expand tax revenue, as we will discuss in detail below.

How Latin America's actual tax ratio compares with a regression-based predicted tax ratio depends on the variables included in the empirical analysis. Lopez *et al.* (2006: 96) calculate that, controlling for per capita GDP, the median tax ratio in Latin America was 4.0 percent below its expected value in 2000. Honduras and Uruguay were the only two countries in their study where the tax ratio was larger than expected. Using a broader set of controls and a longer time period, Brun *et al.* (2006: 16) calculate a shortfall in Latin America's tax ratio of 3.7 percent for 1995–99 and 2.7 percent 2000–03.[9] And, controlling for per capita GDP and income inequality, Agosin *et al.* (2008) show a considerable gap between the expected and the observed tax ratio in Central American countries in the late 1990s. For Costa Rica, the gap is particularly large, with an actual tax ratio of 12.2 percent versus a predicted ratio of 20.6 percent.

In many Latin American countries, governments obtain considerable resources from non-tax sources, mainly by tapping the surplus of state-owned enterprises. In 2004, the average non-tax-revenue ratio was 5.6 percent, ranging from a low of zero in Haiti to a high of 17.6 percent in Chile (Villela *et al.* 2008: 24). Even though state-owned enterprises were privatized en masse under the Washington Consensus, there are still a number of large SOEs in the natural resource sector: for example, CODELCO in Chile, PEMEX in Mexico, Petrobas in Brazil, and PDVSA in Venezuela.

Table 7.2 Composition of tax revenue in Latin America, 2006

	Tax revenue as a share of GDP		Tax components as a share of total tax revenue excl. social security contributions				
	Total tax revenue	Excl. social security contr.	Taxes on income and profit	Property tax	Taxes on goods and services	Excise taxes	Trade taxes
South America							
Argentina	27.4	23.6	22.5	13.6	41.1	8.1	13.1
Bolivia	19.8	18.0	18.9	7.8	48.9	16.7	5.6
Brazil	34.2	25.8	27.1	10.9	50.4	6.2	1.6
Chile	19.5	18.1	38.7	3.3	40.9	11.0	2.2
Colombia	15.8	13.4	41.8	6.0	42.5	2.2	6.7
Ecuador	14.0	10.2	25.5	2.0	52.9	5.9	14.7
Paraguay	13.1	12.0	15.0	0.0	45.0	17.5	15.0
Peru	16.6	15.1	15.1	43.0	2.0	37.1	9.3
Uruguay	24.2	18.1	18.2	8.8	50.3	14.9	7.7
Venezuela	16.3	15.6	44.9	0.6	42.3	3.8	8.3
SAC (unw. av.)	**20.1**	**17.0**	**29.6**	**5.5**	**45.1**	**9.6**	**8.1**
Central America and Caribbean							
Costa Rica	14.0	13.7	24.8	3.6	39.4	22.6	8.0
Dominican Rep.	15.0	14.9	22.1	6.0	30.2	26.2	15.4
El Salvador	15.0	13.4	31.3	0.7	52.2	6.7	8.2
Guatemala	12.0	11.8	20.3	0.0	45.8	11.9	10.2
Haiti	10.2	10.2	17.6	0.0	28.4	5.9	33.3
Honduras	16.4	15.2	28.9	1.3	36.8	25.7	7.2
Mexico	9.8	8.7	49.4	2.3	42.5	0.0	3.4
Nicaragua	21.3	17.5	23.4	0.0	41.7	22.9	5.7
Panama	15.7	10.6	45.3	5.7	9.4	10.4	23.0
CACC (unw. av.)	**14.4**	**12.9**	**29.3**	**2.2**	**36.3**	**14.7**	**12.8**
LAC (unw. av.)	**17.4**	**14.9**	**29.4**	**3.9**	**40.9**	**12.0**	**10.3**

Source: Authors' calculations based on CEPAL (2008a: Table A-38).

Table 7.3 Latin American tax ratios in international comparison, 2005

	Direct tax burden	Indirect tax burden	Social security burden	Total tax burden
Latin America	5.0	9.8	3.1	18.0
SE Asia	7.0	7.2	0.8	15.0
OECD	14.9	11.8	9.5	36.3
EU	16.2	12.6	11.6	40.5

Source: Based on Aldunate and Martner (2006: Figure 2).

Conclusion

Which combination of the four channels for resource mobilization is most appropriate and possible for any particular country in Latin America and the Caribbean depends on the country-specifics. We have argued here that foreign aid is not an option for most countries, that improvements in efficiency can only make a limited contribution, that reallocation of expenditures may offer significant revenue opportunities for some countries, that high foreign debt financing is not desirable, and that domestic debt financing is limited in a number of countries by underdeveloped capital markets. In light of the magnitude of the public resources needed for a new developmentalist strategy, an increase in government revenues has to be a critical element for resource mobilization in many Latin American countries. The fact that tax ratios are relatively low makes an increase in government revenues a possible option. The key question is whether and how possibility can be turned into reality.

Fiscal policy space: analytical considerations

Over the last few years we have seen a growing literature on policy space for development; it focuses on the internal and external forces that circumscribe a government's ability to adopt new developmentalist policies in the current context of globalization. While there have always been internal and external constraints on policy adoption and implementation, the current globalization process has dramatically changed the nature and intensity of the external constraints. The proliferation of new rules for trade and investment, enshrined in multilateral and bilateral treaties, prohibit the adoption of development policies that have proven successful in the past; the growing importance of credit-rating agencies which define "good policies" with a focus on short-term financial stability clashes with the pursuit of "good" policies that focus on long-term development; and the intensification of international trade competition and of government competition to attract foreign investment may set off a race to the bottom in wage and tax competition.

This change in external constraints has reduced the degrees of freedom for the adoption of new development policies, and – together with the intensification of internal constraints – has led to the current discussion about the parameters shaping policy space in developing countries in the age of globalization. Much of the literature to date has focused on policy space for industrial policy (e.g., Abugattas and

Paus 2008; Thrasher and Gallagher 2008; and Muchhala 2007). Here we apply the concept of policy space to an analysis of a government's ability to increase public resources. We analyze the external and internal factors that circumscribe the *fiscal* policy space in the current globalization process; in other words, the forces that explain the gap between the potential fiscal policy space to achieve a desired outcome and the fiscal policy space actually available.[10]

Potential fiscal policy space is the amount of resources that an economy can mobilize towards a desired purpose – without prejudice to its fiscal sustainability – if it carried out all the necessary reforms to its expenditure, taxation and budgetary policies; including necessary changes in institutional and political arrangements. In contrast, available fiscal policy space is the amount of resources that an economy can mobilize for a desired development purpose subject to the constraints that are imposed by the structural, political, and institutional conditions, internally and externally.

The gap between the potential and available policy space is not fixed. The boundaries of available policy space vary over time and across countries, with differences in the nature and intensity of international constraints and internal constraints like the development-mindedness of a government and its willingness and ability to push the boundaries of available policy space.

To analyze the determinants of available fiscal policy space we propose a conceptual framework that includes the sources of constraints as well as the channels through which they affect the available space. Among the sources of constraints, we distinguish between constraints resulting from the globalization process on the one hand and from the internal productive structure and political economy on the other. On the globalization side, the key constraints are International Financial Institution (IFI) conditionality, global market constraints, tax competition for foreign direct investment (FDI), tax stabilization agreements, trade agreements, and investment agreements. On the internal side, the main constraints come from the productive structure, income distribution, and tax evasion. Both globalization and internal factors affect the available policy space through one or more of the four channels: an understanding of what constitutes an acceptable government deficit, the size of the tax base, the magnitude of the tax rate, and the ability to raise non-tax revenue. Table 7.4 summarizes our analytical framework of the constraints on available fiscal policy space.

The issue of fiscal space has come to the forefront in the recent literature on how to achieve the Millennium Development Goals. Most of the debate in that literature focuses on what constitutes fiscal solvency/sustainability. On the one hand, we have the approach promoted principally by the IFIs, which is mainly concerned with raising resources for development incrementally, and with the short-term consequences of an increase in public expenditures, in particular for fiscal stability (e.g., Development Committee 2006, Heller 2005). On the other hand, we have the approach, embraced primarily by the UNDP, which highlights the need for significant increases in public expenditures to achieve key development goals; it focuses on long term fiscal solvency and advocates a loosening of short-term fiscal requirements, if necessary (e.g., UNDP 2007; Roy *et al.* 2006).

The UNDP-based approach is in line with the new development strategy we advocate, and we incorporate it into our analysis. But it constitutes only one element in our broader framework for analyzing fiscal space (i.e., in terms of the matrix represented by Table 7.4). The proposed framework can be employed for the study of policy space in any country; we use it here for an analysis of available fiscal policy space in Latin America.

Available fiscal space in Latin America: constraints from the globalization process

At the beginning of the twenty-first century, available fiscal policy space in Latin America falls far short of potential fiscal space. In this section, we analyze the main external and internal factors that circumscribe the available fiscal space and that, at this juncture, tend to push the boundaries of the available space further away from the potential space rather than closer to it.

IFI conditionality

In the past, IMF conditionality in the framework of stabilization programs was one of the most stringent external constraints on expanding fiscal policy space in Latin America. The stabilization programs implemented in the region after the crisis of the 1980s were aimed at controlling inflationary pressures and consolidating fiscal solvency. One of the results was the dramatic drop in public investment documented earlier.

Over the last few years, this external constraint has been relaxed significantly, as most Latin America countries are no longer operating under programs with

Table 7.4 Framework for analyzing fiscal policy space

Fiscal space constraints	*Size of GB deficit*	*Tax base*	*Tax rate*	*Non-tax Revenue*
1.0 Globalization process				
1.1 IFI conditionality				
1.2 Global market constraints				
1.3 Tax competition for FDI				
1.4 Tax stabilization agreements				
1.5 Trade agreements				
1.6 Investment agreements				
2.0 Internal productive structure and political economy				
2.1 Economic structure				
2.2 Income distribution and political economy				
2.3 Tax evasion				

Source: Author conceptualization.

the IMF. Some countries chose to pay off loans from the IFIs in order to reduce their vulnerability to conditionality; e.g., Argentina, Bolivia, Brazil, Uruguay, and Venezuela.[11] In April 2007, Venezuela repaid all its loans from the World Bank – five years early. In 2008, Argentina, Venezuela, Bolivia, Brazil, Ecuador, and Paraguay agreed to create a "Bank of the South," envisioned as a South American alternative to the World Bank and IMF. To expand fiscal space Latin American countries have also proposed that borrowing for infrastructure should not be counted against debt targets.

Furthermore, international financial institutions themselves have started to reevaluate their position on what constitutes sound fiscal policy, acknowledging that fiscal policy can not only be concerned with short-term stabilization and fiscal solvency, but needs to identify and incorporate how public spending, taxation, aid, and borrowing may stimulate long-term growth and poverty reduction (Development Committee 2006). At the same time, the inflation targets have been relaxed. While the IMF used to press for a 1 or 2 percent inflation target, it has started to allow for rates up to 5 percent, and the World Bank tolerates inflation up to 12 percent (Verhoeven 2007). At the time of this writing, it is too early to know whether the apparent increased flexibility will, in effect, translate into practice during the current crisis or whether economic policy makers will be faced with conditionalities of the past.

Foreign capital market constraints

To the extent that governments want to borrow internationally, market responsiveness to domestic policies becomes a crucial element for policy-makers. The reaction of foreign capital to the perceived "risk" associated with a policy measure narrows the range of options within which countries in the region can effectively maneuver to expand fiscal space. Credit Rating Agencies (CRAs) play a central role in this context, as they follow rigid conventions for determining sovereign credit ratings and assessing the fiscal performance of countries (e.g., Elkoury 2008). Their exclusive focus on short-term solvency mirrors the traditional approach of the IFIs to fiscal sustainability, and it discourages the implementation of fiscal measures in Latin American countries that might be sound policy choices from a long-term development perspective.

There are other market forces that affect the foundations of the tax systems and the capacity of Latin American countries to mobilize additional resources. Increasing international integration, together with rapid technological progress, is likely to affect both the ability of countries to collect taxes and the distribution of the tax burden. Tanzi (2001) identifies eight different "fiscal termites" that undermine the capacity of countries to collect taxes: e-commerce and transactions, electronic money, intra-company trade, offshore financial centers, derivatives and hedge funds, the inability to tax financial capital, growing foreign activities, and foreign shopping. Besides eroding the tax base, these emerging trends diminish the capacity of the tax authorities to enforce taxes, with potentially significant negative effects on fiscal revenue.

Competition to attract foreign investment

IFI conditionality and market constraints affect the available policy space mainly through an understanding of fiscal sustainability that focuses on a small budget deficit and low inflation. The other constraints arising from the globalization process influence countries' ability to increase available fiscal space through their impact on the tax base, the tax rate, and the ability to tap non-tax resources.

In the current era of globalization, where productive capital is becoming ever more mobile internationally, it is increasingly difficult to tax capital, as it has considerable veto power by threatening to leave, by relocating, or by not investing in a potential host country. The constraints that capital mobility imposes on actual fiscal space are exacerbated by governments' aggressive competition for foreign investment through incentives and tax stabilization agreements, and through bilateral agreements which tie their fiscal hands.

Tax competition

The decision of where to invest by a transnational corporation (TNC) is influenced by the corporate income tax (CIT) in the home country and in the potential host country and by the rules of how taxes paid in the host country are treated at home. Empirical evidence suggests that taxes and incentives matter for investment decisions, both for FDI and for portfolio investment, at least at the margin. Hines (1999), for example, found that a one percentage point decrease in the CIT increases the flow of FDI by about 2 percent, while De Mooij and Ederveen (2003) concluded that the elasticity of FDI with respect to the host country tax rate is 3.3. Agostine and Jalile (2006) found a high foreign investment tax elasticity in Latin America for the period 1990–2002. Generally, empirical evidence tends to support the view that capital mobility puts downward pressure on CIT (e.g., Wilson and Wildasin 2004).

Tax competition happens through both changes in statutory tax rates and "incentive bidding" among countries, which affects the effective tax rates. The average CIT rate for Latin America declined from 34.5 percent in 1993 to 26.6 percent in January 2008, with a clear indication of cross-country convergence of CIT rates (KPMG 2007, 2008). The average CIT rate is now very close to that in the OECD (26.7 percent), Asia-Pacific (28.4), and the EU (23.2). The fact that there is still a wide dispersion in VAT rates among Latin American countries may be an indication that countries compensate differently for the revenue loss from declining CIT rates, and that the evolution of the CIT rate, in effect, reflects and responds to tax competition.

Like other developing countries, Latin American and Caribbean countries are relying increasingly on preferential tax regimes in the hope of attaining a variety of economic benefits. After a period of retrenchment these regimes are back on the scene, in many cases in the context of a renewal of industrial policy in the region (Melo and Rodriguez-Clare 2007). Preferential tax regimes target mainly the primary sector of the economy and export activities and provide investment incentives, particularly to FDI. Latin American countries tend to utilize tax expenditures, tax exemptions or tax deductions, differentiated tax rates, and accelerated depreciation (Bird 2006). These incentives lower the tax burden on business, but they constitute a fiscal cost for the state. Where these preferential regimes benefit foreign companies, which can deduct taxes paid in the host country from their total tax burden in the home country, developing countries are de facto transferring fiscal resources to the TNC's home country.

For any individual country the question is whether the benefits of the potential positive externalities from foreign direct investment are likely to be realized and whether they outweigh the loss of fiscal revenue. A growing number of studies have shown that the hoped for economic benefits from FDI do not necessarily materialize (e.g., Gallagher and Chudnovsky 2009; Paus 2005). Cost benefit analyses of FDI incentives have generated very mixed results (e.g., Hanson 2001). Nonetheless, incentives are widely used by governments in Latin America and elsewhere; the "bidding wars" make it difficult for any one government to act on its own and decide not to participate. The nature of the problem clearly requires a collective response at the regional, and probably global, level.

In addition to targeted fiscal incentives, Latin American countries have relied increasingly on Export Processing Zones (EPZs) as a means to promote export activities. EPZs offer significant tax incentives to companies operating under the regime, including in many cases zero CITs. There are 448 EPZs in Latin America and the Caribbean, employing more than six million workers (ILO 2007). In some countries, for example the Dominican Republic and other Caribbean states, EPZs constitute one of the major economic activities, besides tourism, which often offers significant tax benefits as well. In the Dominican Republic, EPZs account for more than 80 percent of total exports, which leads to a significant erosion of the tax base and an increasing divorce between the level of output growth and fiscal revenues. Bird (2006) suggests that the effective tax rate in EPZs in Latin America is 3 to 16 percentage points lower than that resulting from general tax incentives for export promotion. And the latter, in turn, is lower than the effective tax rate for other domestic economic activities.

What is particularly interesting in the Latin American context is that many governments have been eager to perpetuate the tax advantages of EPZs, even though WTO regulations provided a genuine opportunity for terminating them. The Agreement on Subsidies and Countervailing Measures of the WTO prohibits special incentives for exporting (and thus for EPZs) for developing countries with a per capita GDP of $1,000 and above. Article 27.4 of the agreement provided for a transition period of eight years for the abolition of export subsidies, until the end of 2003. However, at the request of developing countries, in 2002, the WTO extended the transition period until the end of 2007 for those countries whose exports did not account for more than 0.1 percent of world exports during 1998–2000, and whose GDP in 2000 did not exceed $20 billion. The 120 developing countries which met those criteria included Panama, Honduras, Guatemala, El Salvador, the Dominican Republic, Costa Rica, and Paraguay. Uruguay requested an extension, as its GDP was only slightly above the limit (Byrne 2003: 28).

Instead of phasing out the export subsidies by the end of 2007, the affected Latin American countries pushed for yet another extension of the transition period. In July 2007, the WTO approved yet another extension, until the end of 2015. The decision specifically includes 19 countries; 15 are in Latin America and the Caribbean (WTO 2007).

There are no comprehensive and reliable estimates of the fiscal cost of investment incentives and other preferential tax regimes in the region. Besides incentives extended in the form of favorable privatization prices, tax incentives, and the like, governments often set low service prices and compensate private investors with recurring operating subsidies. Such subsidies, moreover, are not always explicit, but often take the form of implicit guarantees. Villela *et al.* (2008: 17) calculate that the effective tax rates in the region are only about a third of the statutory value. Based on tax expenditure surveys in Latin America, estimates of the fiscal cost of incentives range from 7.4 percent of GDP in Colombia to 1.5 percent in Brazil (Martner and Tromben 2004). These estimates include all tax expenditures and not only those resulting from investment incentives.

Tax stabilization agreements

Another widely used instrument for attracting FDI is tax stabilization agreements (TSAs). The TSAs freeze the basic rules and regulations, including taxes, in force at the moment the agreement is entered into. Those rules and regulations then continue to apply to the investor during the term of the agreement, irrespective of legislative changes. TSAs are supposed to mitigate the political risk for a foreign investor and provide investment condition predictability. In some countries of the region, most large investments are protected by TSAs.

TSAs introduce rigidity into fiscal policy management. Considering the need for tax and other fiscal policies to adapt to changing circumstances, these agreements might result in the co-existence of different effective tax regimes in the same jurisdiction. This might discourage the implementation of tax changes aimed at increasing domestic resource mobilization, in particular when all major taxpayers are sheltered by stabilization agreements.[12]

This guarantee to investors also constrains the possibilities of taxing windfall profits that may result, for example, from exceptionally high commodity prices. In the case of Peru, the government negotiated a voluntary contribution from the mining companies, as it was unable to impose a tax on windfall profits. Tax stabilization agreements have emerged as a major source of dispute between governments and investors, imposing an additional constraint to fiscal policy, as we will discuss below.

Trade and investment agreements

Under the Washington Consensus, most Latin American countries have liberalized trade quite dramatically and unilaterally, while intra-regional economic integration schemes have deepened. At the same time, they have entered into trade and investment agreements with developed country partners aimed at establishing free trade areas within a decade. As a result, Latin American countries have forfeited the ability to use trade taxes to enhance fiscal resource mobilization, and through investment agreements they have seriously undermined other avenues that might have made it possible for the state to retain a larger share of the wealth generated in the domestic economy.

Trade agreements

Trade taxes which traditionally generated a significant share of tax revenue in Latin America have declined considerably since the mid eighties.[13] As a proportion of total tax revenues, they declined from 19.7 percent in the early 1990s to 13.6 percent in the early 2000s (Keen and Simone 2004: 341). By 2006–07, they had declined further to 9.1 percent. Unilateral tariff reductions have continued in recent years, both in terms of simple and trade-weighted tariff averages, as governments eliminated tariffs on capital goods and inputs to boost the competitiveness of domestic industry (see Table 7.5).

Recovering lost revenue through other taxes has proven to be a difficult task. Based on a study of 125 countries, Baunsgaard and Keen (2004) conclude that middle-income countries have been able to recover between 35 and 55 cents per dollar of lost trade income, whereas the lowest income countries have recovered very little. Latin America seems to have fared a little better. During the period from the early 1980s to the late 1990s, Haiti, El Salvador, Costa Rica, Chile, Trinidad and Tobago, and Panama recovered less than 70 percent of lost tariff revenue through other taxes, while Argentina, Bolivia, Guatemala, Ecuador, Uruguay, Barbados, Honduras, Colombia, and Peru had a recovery rate of more than 70 percent (IMF 2005: 26–7). Nevertheless, it may be difficult for the region to compensate for further trade tax losses.

By binding their trade liberalization in internationally enforceable commitments Latin American countries have relinquished the use of trade taxes as a means for resource mobilization. Fernandez de Cordoba and Vanzetti (2005) estimate the loss of revenues from the MFN tariff reductions considered in the current WTO negotiations at close to $11 billion for the Latin American region. For most countries of the region the estimated revenue losses exceed the expected welfare gains from trade liberalization (e.g., Wise and Gallagher 2006).

While trade agreements limit fiscal space on the one hand, they generate new expenditure demands on the other. There are the costs of compliance with customs valuation, Trade Related Intellectual Property Rights (TRIPS), Sanitary and Phytosanitary Measures (SPS) stipulated under the WTO Agreements, and compliance with stipulations in trade agreements between Latin American countries and the EU and the US (e.g., Finger and Schuler 2000).

Investment agreements

In their unabated quest for foreign direct investment, developing countries have increasingly resorted to investment agreements with developed countries, either

Table 7.5 Selected indicators of tariffs and revenues from trade taxes in Latin America

	MFN tariff simple average		MFN tariff trade-weighted average		MFN zero-duty imports/total imports		Effective tariff rate[c]		Trade taxes/ GDP average	Trade taxes/total tax revenue[d]
	1995–99	2005–06[a]	1995–99	2005–06[a]	1995–99	2005–06	1995–99	2005–06[a]	2006–07	2006
CACM										
Costa Rica	8.3	5.5	7.0	4.4	23.5	69.3	n.d	1.7	1.15	8.0
El Salvador	7.8	5.9	7.6	4.6	23.8	34.3	n.d	2.3	1.05	8.2
Guatemala	8.9	5.6	7.5	5.6	16.5	50.4	6.1	3.2	1.15	10.2
Honduras	8.7	5.6	8.3	7.9	23.0[b]	58.0	n.d	2.0	1.15	7.2
Nicaragua	8.7	5.6	6.1	4.9	14.6	51.9	3.5	1.8	1.00	5.7
ANCOM										
Bolivia	9.7	8.3	9.2	4.0	0.0	7.8	n.d	2.6	1.05	5.6
Colombia	12.5	12.5	11.3	8.0	3.1	5.1	n.d	6.5	0.95	6.7
Ecuador	12.5	12.5	11.3	8.0	3.1	5.1	n.d	6.5	0.95	14.7
Peru	14.2	10.2	13.4	6.8	0.0	19.9	8.8	5.3	0.80	6.0
MERCOSUR										
Argentina	13.6	11.9	12.5	5.4	7.7	18.3	n.d	3.7[b]	3.25[d]	13.1
Brazil	14.3	12.2	13.4	6.8	3.6	34.1	6.8	n.d	0.45	1.6
Paraguay	11.4	10.4	8.8	3.2	3.3	60.2	n.d	2.7	1.60	15.0
Uruguay	12.2	10.6	11.3	3.2	8.8	44.4	4.7	4.3	1.40	7.7

OTHER

Chile	10.7	6.0	10.6	5.7	0.2	0.4	n.d	3.2[b]	0.40	2.2
Mexico	15.1	12.7	10.0	2.5	8.8	31.8	1.9	1.8[b]	0.30	3.4
Venezuela	12.7	12.7	12.8	10.9	1.4	4.1	7.9	7.0[b]	1.40	8.3
Panama	10.3	7.2	9.6	9.5	7.3	41.1	n.d	3.3[b]	2.70	23.6
Dom Rep	14.8	8.5	12.3	9.7[b]	0.0	9.4[b]	n.d	4.1	2.00	15.4
Jamaica	20.0	7.3	17.3	10.5	5.5	49.2	4.8	4.3	n.d	n.d
Trinidad/Tobago	15.3	7.8	12.5	6.6	5.9	58.2	4.0	3.6	n.d	n.d
Haiti	n.d	2.8	n.d	2.9	n.d	n.d	n.d	n.d	3.20	33.3
Latin America									1.40	9.2

Sources: For headings 1–4, World Bank (2008: Trade At-A-Glance); For headings 5 and 6, CEPAL (2008a Table A-38).

Notes
a Or latest.
b Refers to 2000–04.
c Tariff revenue as a share of import value.
d Total tax revenue excluding Social security contributions.
e Includes export taxes.

through specific bilateral investment treaties (BITs) or through investment provisions included in the second generation free trade agreements. Like the special tax incentives and tax stabilization treaties, investment agreements create a very lopsided incentive structure in favor of foreign investors and to the disadvantage of national investors.

Under investment agreements, foreign investors can bring claims against the host country government about a change in regulations that allegedly violate their rights, i.e., profitability, and governments agree to abide by the results of compulsory investor-state arbitration outside of the host country's jurisdiction. The arbitration panels function with little transparency and accountability. Gus Van Harten (this volume) provides an excellent analysis of how these one-sided and non-reciprocal agreements operate to preclude a wide range of new development policies for developing countries.

Investment agreements do not address tax issues directly; signatory parties do not waive tax or regulatory sovereignty. The agreements Latin American countries have signed with the US, for example DR-CAFTA, Chile, and Peru, include taxation issues indirectly by means of an exception with regard to expropriation and compensation and submission of claims to arbitration under the agreements.

The potentially serious constraints that investment agreements impose on fiscal space stem from the broad definition of investment incorporated in the agreements. Since a tax measure is not defined, the definition is determined by case law and can be construed to include a variety of situations including laws, regulations, procedures, requirements, or practices. Since the agreements include only a diffuse notion of what constitutes an indirect expropriation, this is determined on a case-by-case basis by a fact-based inquiry, which needs to consider the extent to which the government action "interferes with reasonable investment-backed expectations" and what constitutes fair and equitable treatment.[14] A country can be sued, forced to pay compensation to a private investor or to reverse a tax administration resolution, when an arbitration panel decides that it is responsible for an indirect expropriation; i.e., when it subjects foreign investors to taxation, regulation, or other action that is deemed confiscatory.

Case law on international investment issues is still in the making, and we are witnessing awards that are inconsistent with other decisions rendered on similar issues, and also many dissenting opinions of individual arbitrators. That was the case in almost 40 percent of cases in 2007 (UNCTAD 2008a).

Although there is no comprehensive data on the total number of investor-state disputes that have been brought to arbitration under the different agreements, the available information clearly suggests a "litigation explosion." According to UNCTAD (2008), more than 80 percent of the 290 identified cases up to 2007 have been filed since 2002. In 35.2 percent of the 280 cases where the parties could be identified, a Latin American country is the defendant.

Recent disputes between foreign investors and the state in Ecuador provide good examples of the serious potential implications of these agreements for expanding fiscal space through enhanced domestic resource mobilization when foreign investors are involved. In 2006, Ecuador enacted Law 42 which levied a 50 percent tax on oil companies' wind fall profits in order to increase the state's participation in oil rents. Foreign oil companies operating in the country responded by initiating arbitration proceedings through the International Court for the Settlement of Investment Disputes (ICSID). The country is currently defending itself in nine arbitrations in ICSID from claims totaling $10 billion, which is a multiple of the country's annual development budget. The government recently settled with one company agreeing to pay $70 million; the company in turn agreed to leave the country and withdraw its $400 million claim (IISD 2008). Ecuador is also seeking a larger share of oil profits by modifying contracts with foreign companies; by turning them into service contracts the state will hold ownership of the operations. In the absence of an agreed solution with the foreign investors this change in contracts will certainly be taken to international arbitration and might imply significant claims.

With the boom in commodity prices, a few Latin American countries have re-nationalized some extractive activities (for example, Bolivia and Venezuela). Generally though, the trend has not been towards re-nationalization, but rather toward renegotiation of contracts with transnational corporations in extractive industries with the goal of appropriating a larger percentage of the rents.

These examples illustrate that tax and other measures aimed at increasing domestic resource mobilization could rise to the level of investment disputes where formerly they would have been dealt with in domestic tax courts. This adds an additional layer of complexity to the attempts of Latin American countries to expand actual fiscal space. In the context of the current "litigation explosion," the possibility is real that governments will be accused of breaching treaty obligations (not to expropriate and to afford the investors fair and equitable treatment) when enacting measures aimed at raising the fiscal resources needed for development.

Available fiscal space: constraints from the internal production structure and political economy

Efforts to increase domestic resource mobilization in Latin America also confront significant internal constraints. We saw already that direct taxes constitute only a relatively small share of total tax revenue (Table 7.2), which is the result of high income inequality in the region, the development model of past decades, the power constellations that have shaped the tax structure, and the high degree of tax evasion.

While a small personal income tax base has always imposed constraints on broadening actual fiscal space in Latin America, the structural changes which resulted from Washington Consensus policies have tightened these constraints further. The change in economic structure away from manufacturing, the shrinking of the middle class, the rise of the informal sector, and the continued decline in fiscal legitimacy have significantly raised the challenge of increasing the direct tax burden.

There are fewer political constraints on increasing indirect taxes, which currently constitute the bulk of tax revenue in Latin America. But any move to increase the value added tax (VAT) rates will worsen the income distribution after taxes, unless it is designed with a focus on greater progressivity.

Small personal income tax base

In many Latin American countries the personal income tax base is small and taxation on wealth is very limited. The development pattern under the Washington Consensus has not been conducive to expanding the income tax base. Rather, it has generally exacerbated the structural characteristics of the economy which constrain the tax base. In addition, the high income inequality in the region has resulted in an unusually small middle class and a rich class that pays little taxes on income and wealth.

Economic structure

A significant percentage of the people in Latin America does not have to pay personal income taxes; either because their income is too low and so they are not required to pay taxes or they are in the informal sector and thus outside the reach of tax authorities.

In most Latin American countries, the tradable sector has provided little new employment since the economic reforms, while employment has expanded faster in non-tradable goods-producing sectors and in services. But even though these latter sectors have demonstrated a greater capacity to generate employment, they have done so at the cost of low or negative productivity growth, which has translated into low, non-taxable salaries and wages (Sainz 2007). As a result, the tax base for personal income taxes is small as a proportion of all formally employed wage earners. A study of seven Latin American countries found that nearly two thirds of employees do not pay personal income taxes because their income is below the minimum income threshold for paying income taxes (OECD 2008: 133).[15]

The economic reforms have failed to modernize the traditional agricultural sector in the region. This sector still accounts for a significant proportion of employment and GDP in some countries, particularly in Central America, Bolivia, Ecuador, Paraguay, and Peru. Traditional agriculture is, for the most part, totally absent from the income tax base. In a regression analysis of the determinants of the tax ratio in Latin America, Cetrángolo and Gómez-Sabaini (2007: 27) included the share of agricultural value added in GDP as an independent variable. The coefficient on the variable was sizable, negative, and statistically significant, lending support to the role of the agricultural sector in the low tax base and tax burden in Latin America.

The size of the informal economy is another characteristic of the economic structure which constrains the income tax base and which has increased significantly in a number of countries. During the 1990s, 66 percent of all new jobs in the region were generated in this sector. In the early 2000s, the informal economy in Latin America accounted, on average, for 38.3 percent of GDP, ranging from a low of 28.2 percent in Mexico to a high of 68.2 percent in Paraguay (Vuletin 2008). Employment in the informal sector ranges from a high of 73 percent in Bolivia to a low of 37 percent in Chile (see Table 7.6).

Income distribution and political economy

Latin America has long had the most unequal income distribution in the world. After the economic reforms, income inequality has become even worse. In most countries of the region poverty levels have not declined significantly, and in some countries they have worsened (ECLAC 2004). The tax system does very little to reduce inequality. In the European OECD countries, the Gini coefficient drops from 47.6 before taxes and transfers to 28.2 after they are taken into account. In Latin America, in contrast, it falls only slightly, from 51.6 to 49.6 (OECD 2008: 122).

Part of the story of high income inequality in Latin America is the small middle class. The region has not been successful in developing a robust middle class, which forms the core of the base for personal income tax revenue in developed countries. The income of the middle class makes up only 13.2 percent of total income in Latin America, well below the 31.6 percent in OECD countries (Solimano 2006: Figure 2).[16] Even in Chile, which has the highest income per capita in the region measured in purchasing power parity, the share of middle-class income in national income is low – even by Latin American standards. Two of the main sources for jobs providing a middle-class income are the

Table 7.6 Size of the informal sector in Latin America

	Labor informality (productive definition) % of workers	*Year*
Bolivia	73.4	2004
Paraguay	70.4	2005
Guatemala	69.0	2004
Peru	65.6	2006
Nicaragua	64.7	2005
Ecuador	62.6	2006
El Salvador	55.2	2004
Brazil	53.9	2005
Dominican Republic	51.6	2006
Mexico	49.2	2005
Venezuela	48.6	2005
Panama	48.0	2004
Uruguay	41.6	2005
Argentina	41.5	2006
Costa Rica	40.5	2006
Chile	37.0	2003

Source: OECD (2008: 169).

civil service and the more entrepreneurial part of the private sector. In Latin America, the downsizing of the state, the compression of public sector salaries, and a stagnant sector of small and medium-sized enterprises have weakened these socioeconomic strata.

The fact that income taxes and taxes on property constitute a small share of total fiscal revenues cannot solely be attributed to the reduced tax base or weaknesses in tax administration. Tax systems, as any other public policy, respond in the last instance to power and political conditions. Political economy factors are important in explaining the prevailing situation in Latin America. The power coalition that dominates the state in most countries of the region represents domestic economic elites and their foreign partners. The tax system reflects the interests of those in power who legitimize it on the basis of "trickle down" economics and by claiming that lower taxes will eventually increase the tax base leading to higher revenues. But this has not happened in the region.

On the one hand, while non-wage income as a proportion of total income has been increasing in most countries of the region, income such as interest, dividends, and capital gains are in most cases tax exempt. On the other hand, the maximum statutory personal income tax rate has been progressively lowered, while the minimum rate has been increased. For the region as a whole, the maximum tax rate has declined from an average of 35.2 percent in 1992 to 28.8 percent in 2004 (ECLAC 2004). Only in Peru does personal income tax revenue reach 1 percent of GDP; in all other countries it is well below that (Cetrángolo and Gómez-Sabaini 2007: 38). In the same vein, property taxes contribute only marginally to fiscal revenue; 4 percent of tax revenue excluding social security contributions.

The richest population segment in the region is paying a very low share of income taxes and very low property taxes as well. The top decile of income earners faced an effective tax rate of a mere 8 percent of their income (Birdsall and de la Torre 2001: 36). In Colombia, the effective tax rate for the richest 10 percent is only 3 percent, and in Peru, it is 1.7 percent. When households that control more than 40 percent of income and the bulk of the wealth pay little taxes, the impact on revenue collection is obvious. Schmitt (2003) simulated what would happen to the revenue in Latin America if countries adopted a tax system with the levels and the progressivity of the US tax system, taking into account the income distribution prevailing in the region. He found that revenues would increase substantially, ranging from 1.9 to 20.5 percent of GDP, depending on the country.

The main obstacles to increasing fiscal revenues by taxing the rich are political. Securing the fiscal resources needed for development demands the emergence of a different political coalition with enough power to influence public policies, putting the interests of the majority above the interest of the few.

Tax evasion: the deficit of fiscal legitimacy

Attempts to increase the tax effort in Latin American countries confront the lack of "fiscal legitimacy." There is a close link between tax collection and social cohesion and between social cohesion and democratic governance (OECD 2008). Fiscal policy is at the core of the social contract that glues a society together, and it is crucial for assuring democratic legitimacy. Democratic legitimacy motivates people to pay taxes; it emerges from the state performing its role efficiently by providing public goods and social services.

In Latin America, tax morale is quite low, and a significant proportion of the population finds tax evasion acceptable (Torgler 2003). This is a reaction to a perceived failure of the state. Taxpayers do not think that their money is well utilized, and in particular the middle class has to fund out-of-pocket many of the services that should be provided by the state, including citizens' security. At this point, the state is caught in a "catch 22." It needs resources to provide public goods and services, and at the same time the lack of resources makes it extremely difficult to provide them in such a way as to enhance democratic and fiscal legitimacy. This in turn limits the state's possibilities to secure the resources that would be needed.

Vuletin (2008) found that the tax burden is a robust explanatory variable of the size of the informal economy, and that there is strong link between informality and general tax evasion. But the OECD (2008: 157) argues that informality is not the driving force behind tax evasion. In the case of Mexico, small firms – which constitute most of the informal employment – accounted for only a tiny fraction of tax evasion in 2004, 0.07 percent of GDP compared to an overall estimated tax evasion of 3 percent of GDP. The main reason is that the wages in the informal sector are so low that most employees would not have to pay income taxes if they were in the formal sector. The same is not true, however, for the tax revenue lost from the non-application of a value added tax in the informal sector.

Increasing the tax effort in Latin America will depend to a large extent on the progress achieved in improving overall democratic governance in the countries of the region. And, as the OECD (2008: 38) argues: "A key to raising fiscal legitimacy is to improve the social impact of fiscal policy."

Conclusions

In this chapter we analyzed the fiscal space dilemma in Latin America, examining how internal and globalization factors are constricting the actual fiscal space for Latin American governments and thus their ability to pursue a new development strategy. We focused on the big picture and overall trends; a detailed analysis of which combination of all the potentially constraining factors is the actual constraining set in any particular country is an important subject for future research.

There is no one magic bullet for the expansion of fiscal space, given the multitude of constraining factors. Many constraints will have to be addressed concomitantly, some at the global level, some at the regional level, and some at the national level. Here we offer some general observations for relaxing the fiscal space constraints.

First, some of the constraints can only be relaxed through action at the supra-national level, sometimes at the global level and other times at the regional level. Besides the need to review the conditionalities imposed by the IFIs, collective action is needed to address constraints emerging from tax competition and competition for investments. In the first case, governments have to aim for a progressive harmonization of taxes at the regional level to secure the needed fiscal space for development and establish a level playing field for investments in the region.

In the case of investment incentives, action at the sub-regional or regional level might not be enough to address the perverse fiscal effects of individual countries' practices. Multilateral action might be the only way to avoid a pernicious race to the bottom that would only benefit TNCs in a globalized world with increasing capital mobility. It is necessary to establish multilateral rules governing investment incentives, an issue that has been absent so far from all bilateral trade and investment agreements. Developed countries are already seeking some action in this direction to avoid the effects of harmful tax practices being pursued in the OECD. A similar approach needs to be taken at the multilateral level.

There is also an urgent need to regulate CRAs. This was clearly recognized in the meeting of the G20 in the spring of 2009. Due to their significant effect on the markets these private firms should not act without the required regulation that would hold them accountable for their actions. Finally, collective action at the international level is needed to address the restrictions imposed by "fiscal termites."

Second, countries need to regain domestic policy space. Trade and investment agreements should be renegotiated with the goal of achieving a more balanced set of rights and obligations between the state and foreign investors. In particular, the provision governing investor-state disputes should be reviewed to avoid its interference with the sovereign right of states to tax economic undertakings under their jurisdiction.

An alternative path would be to renounce those agreements as some countries in the region are already proposing. Some Latin American countries are moving away from investment treaty arbitration, such as Ecuador, Bolivia and Venezuela.[17] Australia concluded an agreement with the US that did not adopt investment treaty arbitration as a means of dispute settlement.

Third, for the new economic development strategy to be successful, the playing field has to be leveled between foreign and domestic producers. In many countries, the incentive structure is now biased in favor of foreign producers (for example investment incentives and tax exemptions). That is not warranted because (a) expected benefits from FDI will not necessarily materialize, and (b) a strategy focused on the expansion of knowledge-based assets will only be successful if domestic producers play a key role. Governments have to recognize the importance of a level playing field before they will be motivated to address some of the factors constraining fiscal space. In the Latin American case, that means – among other things – that governments should then request a termination of the extension of special benefits for exporters under Article 27.4 of the Agreement on Subsidies and Countervailing Measures (SCM).

Fourth, while the political challenges of increasing tax revenues are daunting, they are clearly not insurmountable. The case of Brazil provides a powerful example. The country that today has a tax ratio comparable to OECD countries had a tax ratio of 17.4 percent in 1960 (Serra and Alfonso 2007: 32). Making the rich shoulder a greater share of the tax burden – through property taxes, reduction of exemptions, and increase in tax collection effort – will first require a change in the power coalition dominating the government in a number of Latin American countries.

But there are also other possibilities of increasing the tax burden. The introduction of progressive VAT taxes is an important option, if governments have the administrative ability to enforce them. Ffrench-Davis (2009) revived the interesting idea of taxing cross-border financial transactions. Such a policy would kill two birds with one stone, as it could generate considerable fiscal revenue, while also reducing the likelihood of erratic short-term capital flows with their damaging impact on macro stability.

Finally, some of the fiscal constraints imposed by the current structure of production will be loosened as governments adopt the new developmentalist strategy we have discussed in this chapter and in this volume. The challenges for escaping the fiscal space dilemma are considerable. And overcoming the fiscal space dilemma is only one of the necessary conditions for the success of a new developmentalist strategy. Nonetheless, there is hope. The development failure of the Washington Consensus combined with the global economic crisis provides a propitious conjuncture for changing the rules that govern the globalization process and for pursuing a new developmentalist strategy.

Notes

1 The Report distills lessons from successful development stories since 1950. It focuses on the 13 countries which have grown at an annual rate of 7 percent for more than 25 years: Botswana, Brazil, China, Hong Kong, Indonesia, Japan, the Republic of Korea, Malaysia, Malta, Oman, Singapore, Taiwan, and Thailand.
2 World Bank. World Development Indicators. Accessed April 1, 2009.
3 Vos *et al.* (2007: 3) suggest that "lagging infrastructure development could account for as much as one third of the difference in economic growth performance between East Asia and Latin American countries during the 1980s and 1990s."
4 The estimate is based on an extrapolation of detailed cost calculations in three areas of intervention in ten countries to all of Latin America and the Caribbean. The study focuses on the cost of reducing child mortality rates, improving maternal health, and combating malaria and tuberculosis in Haiti, Bolivia, the Dominican Republic, Nicaragua, Ecuador, Jamaica, Guatemala, El Salvador, and Peru. The country estimates of needed expenditures in 2015 range from a low of $12 million for Jamaica to a high of about $168 million in Peru and Guatemala.
5 MAMS incorporate MDG 2, 4, 5, and part of 7. For an excellent discussion of MAMs and the challenges in MDG modeling see Bussolo and Medvedev (2007).
6 Some studies suggest that even for these countries additional ODA flows may well decline in the future (Heller *et al.* 2006).
7 The IADB study focuses on Argentina, Brazil, Chile, Colombia, Peru, Mexico, and Venezuela, which together account for over 90 percent of Latin American GDP. It

arrives at the structural fiscal balance by looking at potential output and the long run prices of major export products, e.g., copper in the case of Chile.

8 The data presents the average for Argentina, Brazil, Chile, Colombia, Mexico, Peru, Uruguay, and Venezuela.

9 Brun *et al.* (2006) control for initial per capita GDP, the import ratio, mining and oil exports as a share of total exports, and the share of agricultural value added in GDP.

10 We follow here the conceptual distinction by Moreno and Rodriguez (2005), who use the terms "objective" and "effective" policy space.

11 Peru is the odd one out in this context, as it entered voluntarily into an agreement with the IMF.

12 In the case of Peru, tax stabilization agreements generally lapse after ten years. However, in the case of concessions regarding public works in infrastructure and utilities, the term is subject to the life of the agreement with a maximum of 60 years.

13 In this sub-section we focus on trade in goods. However, services trade liberalization could have important fiscal effects as it will promote off shoring, diverting economic activity outside the jurisdiction, enhance capital mobility, and provide the grounds for more services being supplied by the temporary movement of natural persons' services providers. Also, it may be in the area of services, however, where the greatest problems to prevent transfer pricing are observed. The complexity of services transactions, the relative novelty and innovation they present, and the difficulty to value and price the different components, may be an insurmountable difficulty for the controlling public agencies.

14 The scope of indirect expropriation is presented in an Annex to the Investment chapter of the Agreements. In the case of the Peru-US Agreement, for example, it is in Annex 10-b.

15 The countries included in the study are Argentina, Brazil, Chile, Colombia, Costa Rica, El Salvador, and Mexico.

16 The "middle class" is defined as households with a per capita income between 75 and 125 percent of the median income.

17 The new Ecuadorian Constitution makes it illegal for the country to enter into international treaties that could lead to investor-state arbitration unless disputes are settled in Latin American forums. Bolivia withdrew from the ICSID in May 2007. On February 2008, the National Assembly passed a Resolution approving Venezuela's withdrawal from ICSID; no action has been taken to date.

References

Abugattas, L. and Paus, E. 2008. "Policy Space for a Capability-Centered Development Strategy for Latin America." In: K. Shadlen and D. Sanchez-Ancochea, eds., *Responding to Globalization in the Americas: The Political Economy of Hemispheric Integration.* New York and London: Palgrave Macmillan, 113–143.

Addison, K. 2008. "Latin American Free Trade Agreements with the EU: Agenda for Dominatio," www.grain.org/briefings/?id=211.

Agosín, M., Machado, R., and Schneider, A. 2008. "The Struggle for Tax Reform in Central America." In: D. Sánchez-Ancochea and I. Morgan, eds., *The Political Economy of the Public Budget in the Americas.* London: Institute for the Study of the Americas, University of London.

Agostini, C. and Jalile, I. 2006. "Efecto del Impuesto a las utilidades en la Inversion Extranjera en America Latina," http//ssrn.com/abstract=968079.

Amsden, A. 2001. *The Rise of "The Rest:" Challenges to the West from Late-Industrializing Economies.* Oxford, New York: Oxford University Press.

Baunsgaard, T. and Keen, M. 2004. "Tax Revenue and (or) Trade iberalization," IMF Working Paper WP/05/112, Washington D.C.

Bird, R. 2006. "Tax Incentives for Foreign Direct Investment in Latin America and the Caribbean: Do They need to be harmonized?" ITP Paper 0601, International Tax Program, Institute for international Business, University of Toronto, Toronto.

Birdsall, N. and Augusto de la Torre with Menezes, R. 2001. "Washington Contentious: Economic Policies for Social Equity in Latin America. Findings of the Commission on Economic Reform in Unequal Latin America," Sponsored by the Carnegie Endowment for international Peace and Inter-American Dialogue. Carnegie Endowment, Washington, D.C. www.cgdev.org/content/publications/detail/2923.

Brun, J.-F., Chambas, G., Combes, J.-L., Dulbecco, P., Gastambide, D. A., Guérineau, S., Guillaumont, S., and Gratiosi, G. R. 2006. "Fiscal Space in Developing Countries," Concept Paper. UNDP, New York.

Burgess, R. and Stern, N. 1993. "Taxation and Development," *Journal of Economic Literature* 31(2), 762–830.

Bussolo, M. and Medvedev, D. 2007. "Challenges to MDG Achievement in Low-Income Countries: Lessons from Ghana and Honduras," World Bank, Policy Research Working Paper 4383, Washington. D.C.

Byrne, P. 2003. "Regimenes tributarios especiales en la region Mercosur: implicancias de politicas tributarias y de comercio para la integracion regional," TalleTecnico: Impacto Fiscal de la Integracion Economica, INTAL, June 11–12, Buenos Aires, draft.

Calderón, C. and Servén, L. 2004. "Trends in Infrastructure in Latin America, 1980–2001," Policy Research Working Paper series No. 3401, World Bank, Washington D.C.

Cepal. 2008. "Estudio Económico de America Latina y el Caribe, 2007–2008," Santiago, Chile: UN-Cepal.

Cepal. 2008a. "Millenium Development Goals. Progress towards the Right to Health in Latin America and the Caribbean," Santiago: United Nations.

Cepal and UNESCO. 2004. "Financiamiento y gestión de la educación en América Latina y el Caribe," Síntesis. LC/G.2253 (SES.30/15).

Cetrángolo, O. and Gómez-Sabaini, J. 2007. "La Tributación Directa en América Latina y los Desafios a la Imposición sobre la Renta," Serie Macroeconomía del Desarrollo No 60. CEPAL, Santiago de Chile, Chile.

Clements, B., Faircloth, C., and Verhoeven, M. 2007. "Public Spending in Latin America: Trends and Key Policy Issues," prepared for the 19th regional seminar on fiscal policy, January 29–February1. ECLAC, Chile.

Commission on Growth and Development. 2008. "The Growth Report: Strategies for Sustained Growth and Inclusive Development," Washington D.C.: World Bank.

Delgado C. 2007. "Peru Tax Incentives/Disincentives to Investment in Utilities," Payet, Rey & Cauvi Law Firm, February, 14.

De Mooij, R. A and Ederveen, S. 2003. "Taxation and Foreign Direct Investment: A Synthesis of Empirical Research," *International Tax and Public Finance*, 10(6), 673–694.

Development Committee. 2006. "Fiscal Policy for Growth and Development: An Interim Report," http://siteresources.worldbank.org/DEVCOMMINT/Documentation/20890698/DC2006-0003(E)-FiscalPolicy.pdf.

ECLAC. 2004. "A Decade of Social Development in Latin America," LG/G.2212; April. ECLAC, Santiago, Chile.

Elkouri, M. 2008. "Credit Rating Agencies and Their Potential Impact on Developing Countries," UNCTAD Discussion Papers, No 186, Geneva.

Fan, S. and Rosegrant, M. W. 2008. "Investing in Agriculture to Overcome the World Food Crisis and Reduce Poverty and Hunger," *International Food Policy Research Institute Policy Brief 3*, Washington D.C.

Fay, M. and Morrison, M. 2005. "Infrastructure in Latin America & the Caribbean," World Bank, Finance, Private Sector and Infrastructure Unit, Latin America & the Caribbean Region, Washington D.C.

Ferreira, C., Gonçalvez, P., and Gonçalvez, L. 2005. *Welfare and Growth Effects of Alternative Fiscal Rules for Infrastructure Investment in Brazil*. Rio de Janeiro: Fundação Getulio Vargas.

Fernandez de Cordoba, S. and Vanzetti, D. 2005. "Coping with Trade Reforms," UNCTAD, mimeo, Geneva.

Ffrench-Davis, R. 2009. "Crisis global, flujos especulativos y financiación innovadora para el desarrollo," *Revista CEPAL*, 97, 57–75.

Finger, J. M. and Schuler, P. 2000. "Implementation of Uruguay Round Commitments: The Development Challenge," The *World Economy*, 23(4), 511–525.

Freeman, R. B. 2007. "The Challenge of the Growing Globalization of Labor Markets to Economic and Social Policy." In: Paus, E. ed., Global Capitalism Unbound: Winners and Losers from Offshore Outsourcing. New York: Palgrave Macmillan.

Gallagher, K. and Chudnovsky, D. eds. 2009. *Rethinking Foreign Investment for Sustainable Development*. Anthem Press.

Hanson, G. 2001. "Should Countries Promote Foreign Direct Investment?" G24 Discussion Paper series, No. 9, UNCTAD/Center for International Development, Harvard University, Geneva/Cambridge, Massachusetts.

Heller, P. S. 2005. "Understanding Fiscal Space," IMF Policy Discussion Paper, PDP/05/4,Washington.DC., www.perjacobsson.org/external/pubs/ft/pdp/2005/pdp04.pdf.

Heller, P., Menachem, K., Debrum, X., Thomas, T., Koranchelian, T., and Adenauer, I. 2006. "Making Fiscal Space Happen: Managing Fiscal Policy in a World of Scaled-Up Aid," UNU-Wider, Research Paper No 2006/125.

Hines, J. R. Jr. 1999. "Lessons from Behavioural Responses to International Taxation," *National Tax Journal*, 52(2), 305–22.

Holm-Nielsen, L. B., Thorn, K., Brunner, J. J., and Balán, J. 2005. "Regional and International Challenges to Higher Education in Latin America." In de Wit, H., Jaramillo, I. C., Gacel-Ávila, J., and Knight, J. eds., *Higher Education in Latin America. The International Dimension*. Washington: The World Bank, 39–69.

IADB. 2008. "All That Glitters May Not Be Gold. Assessing Latin America's Recent Macroeconomic Performance," Research Department. http://idbdocs.iadb.org/wsdocs/getdocument.aspx?docnum=1385301.

IADB. 2005. "The Millennium Development Goals in Latin America and the Caribbean: Progress, Priorities and IDB Support for Their Implementation," Washington, D.C.: Inter-American Development Bank.

ILO. 2007. "ILO Database on Export Processing Zones (revised)," Working Paper 251. Geneva.

IISD (International Intitute for Sustainable Development). 2008. Investment Treaty News. September 1, Winnipeg, Canada.

IMF (International Monetary Fund). Fiscal Affairs Department. 2005. "Dealing with the Revenue Consequences of Trade Reform," www.imf.org/external/np/pp/eng/2005/021505.htm.

Keen, M. and Simone, A. 2004. "Tax Policy in Developing Countries: Some Lessons from the 1990s and Some Challenges Ahead." In: Gupta, S., Clements, B., and G.

Inchauste, G. eds., *Helping Countries Develop the Role of Fiscal Policy*. Washington, D.C.: IMF, 302–352.

KPMG. 2008. KPMG's Corporate and Indirect Tax Rate Survey. KPMG International, www.in.kpmg.com/TL_Files/Pictures//CorpTaxRateSurvey2007.

KPMG. 2007. "Corporate Taxes in Latin America: A Competitive Comparison with Other Emerging Markets from 1997 to 2007," www.kpmg.fi/page.aspx?Section=174.

Lall, S. 2005. "Rethinking Industrial Strategy: The Role of the State in the Face of Globalization." In: K. Gallager, ed. *Putting Development First*, London and New York: Zed Books, pp. 33–68.

Lopez, H. J., Perry, G. E., Arias, O. C., Maloney, W. F., and Serven, L. 2006. "Poverty Reduction and Growth: Virtuous and Vicious Circles," Washington, D.C.: World Bank.

Lora, E. 2007. ed. *The State of State Reform in Latin America*. Washington, D.C.: Inter-American Development Bank.

Martner, R. and Tromben, V. 2004. "Tax Reform and Fiscal Stabilization in Latin American Countries," Serie Gestion Publica, CEPAL, Santiago, Chile.

Melo, A. and Rodriguez-Clare, A. 2007. "Políticas e Instituciones de Desarrollo Productivo." In: Lora, Eduardo, ed., *El Estado de las Reformas del Estado en America Latina*. Washington, D.C and Bogotá: IADB, World Bank and Mayol Ediciones.

Moreno, M. A. and Rodriguez, F. 2009. "Plenty of Room? Fiscal Space in a Resource-Abundant Economy: The case of Venezuela." In: Roy, R., and Heuty, A. eds., *Fiscal Space: Policy Options for Financing Human Development*, New York/London: UNDP-Earthscan Publishers, 399–482.

Muchhala, B. 2007 "The Policy Space Debate: Does a Globalized and Multilateral Economy Constrain Development Options?" *Asia Program* Woodrow Wilson International Center for Scholars, No. 136, April, Washington. D.C.

Ocampo, J. A. 2008. "El Auge Económico Latinoamericano," *Revista de Ciencia Política*. 28(1), 7–33.

OECD. 2008. *Latin American Economic Outlook, 2009*. OECD Development Centre, Paris.

OECD. 2007. *OECD Journal on Development: Development Co-operation – 2007 Report*, Paris.

Pasara, L. 2004. "Reformas del Sistema de Justicia en America Latina: cuenta y balance," www.juridicas.unam.mx/inst/evacad/eventos/2004/0902/mesa11/2785.pdf.

Paus, E. 2009. "The Rise of China: Implications for Latin American Development," *Development Policy Review*. 27(4), 419–56.

Paus, E. 2005. *Foreign Investment, Development, and Globalization. Can Costa Rica Become Ireland?* New York and London: Palgrave Macmillan.

Paus, E. 2004. "Productivity Growth in Latin America. The Limits of Neo-liberal Reforms," *World Development*, 32(3), 427–445.

Paus, E. and Shapiro, H. 2007. "Capturing the Benefits from Offshore Outsourcing in Developing Countries: The Case for Active Policies." In: E. Paus, ed., *Global Capitalism Unbound. Winners and Losers from Offshore Outsourcing*. New York and London: Palgrave Macmillan, 215–228.

Reinhardt, Nola and Peres, Wilson. 2000. "Latin America's New Economic Model: Micro Responses and Economic Restructuring." *World Development*. 28(9), 1543–1566.

Reinert, E. 2007. *How Rich Countries Got Rich and Why Poor Countries Stay Poor*. New York: Public Affairs.

Rodrik, D. 2007. *One Economics, Many Recipes: Globalization, Institutions and Economic Growth*. Princeton: Princeton University Press.

Rodrik, D. 2007a. "Industrial Development: Stylized Facts and Policies." In: United Nations, *Industrial Development for the 21st Century*, New York: United Nations.

Roy, R., Heuty, A., and Letouzé, E. 2006. "Fiscal Space for Public Investment: Towards a Human Development Approach," Paper prepared for the G24 Technical Meeting, Singapore, September 13–14, 2006.

Sainz, P. 2007. "Equity in Latin America in the 1990s." In: Jumo, K. S. and Jackes, B. eds., *Flat World, Big Gaps: Economic Liberalization, Globalization Poverty and Inequality*. New York, Pennang, New Dehli: Orient Longman, Zed Books, TWN. Published in association with the United Nations, pp. 242–272.

Schmitt, J. 2003. "Is It Time to Export the US Tax Model to Latin America?" Center for Economic and Policy Research, Washington, D.C. www.cepr.net/index.php/publications/reports/is-it-time-to-export-the-us-tax-model-to-latin-america.

Serra, J. and Afonso, J. R. R. 2007. "Fiscal Federalism in Brazil: An Overview," *Cepal Review*. April, 29–51.

Solimano, A. 2006. "Asset Accumulation by the Middle Class and the Poor in Latin America: Political Economy and Governance Dimensions," Serie Macroeconomía de Desarrollo, No 55, ECLAC. Santiago de Chile Santiago.

Stallings, B. with Studart, R. 2006. *Finance for Development. Latin America in Comparative Perspective.* Washington, D.C.: Brookings Institution.

Tanzi, V. 2001. "Globalization and the Work of Fiscal Termites," *Finance and Development*, 38(1), 34–37. www.imf.org/external/pubs/ft/fandd/2001/03/tanzi.htm.

Torgler, B. 2003. "Tax Morale in Latin America," Prepared for the 3rd Conference on Responsible Regulation: International Perspectives on Taxation, ctsi.anu.edu.au/publications/taxpres/Torgler.pdf.

Thrasher, R. D. and Gallagher, K. P. 2008. "21st Century Trade Agreements: Implications for the Long-Run Development Policy," Frederick S. Pardee Center for the Study of the Longer-Range Future, Paper No. 2. Boston University, Boston.

UNCTAD. 2008. *World Investment Report 2008.* New York and Geneva: United Nations.

UNCTAD. 2008a. "Latest Developments in Investor-State Dispute Settlement," HA MONITOR N0 1, 2008, UNCTAD/WEB/ITE/IIA/2008/3.

UNDP. 2007. "Primer: Fiscal Space for MDGs," www.undp.org/poverty/e-discussions/fiscalspace/docs/Primer%20Fiscal%20Space_06–03%20UG.doc.

Verhoeven, M. 2007." Fiscal Space and Fiscal Priorities: Infrastructure, Trade and Poverty," CSO–WB–IMF Dialogue, www.brettonwoodsproject.org/art-552709.

Villela, L., Roca, J., and Barreix, A. 2008. "The Fiscal Impact of Trade Liberalization." In: Tanzi, V., Barreix, A., and Villela, L. eds., *Taxation and Latin American Integration*. Washington: Inter American Development Bank.

Vos, R., Sánchez, M. V., and Inoue, K. 2007. "Constraints to achieving the MDGs through domestic resource mobilization," United Nations. DESA Working Paper No. 36, ST/ESA/2007/DWP/36, New York.

Vuletin, G. 2008. "Measuring the Informal Economy in Latin America and the Caribbean," IMF Working Paper, WP/08/12, Washington, D.C.

Wade, R. 1990. *Governing the Market. Economic Theory and the Role of the Government in East Asian Industrialization.* Princeton: Princeton University Press.

Wilson, J. and Wildasin, D. 2004. "Capital Tax Competition: Bane or Boon," *Journal of Public Economics*, 88(6), 1065–1091.

Wise, T. and Gallagher, K. 2006. "Doha Round and Developing Countries: Will the Doha Deal Do More Harm than Good?" RIS (Research and Information System for Developing Countries), Policy Brief, No 22., New Delhi.

World Bank. 2008. *World Trade Indicators 2008*. Washington, D.C.: World Bank.

WTO. 2007. "Article 27.4 of the Agreement on Subsidies and Countervailing Measures," G/SCM/120, Geneva.

Yamana, G. 2007. "Costing MDG Achievement in Peru and Policy Implications: A Play in Three Acts," Reaching the Millennium Development Goals [MDGs]: An International Perspective, A Researchers-Stakeholder Forum. Policy Conference, June 12 2007.

8 Investment treaties as a constraining framework

Gus Van Harten

Introduction

What do we mean by "the market" from a legal perspective? Economic relationships that are enforceable by law and that undergird markets vary from state to state. Property rights are subject to various forms of regulation (Cohen 1933: 41–9). Contracts may not be enforceable when they are found to contradict community values or frustrate core aims of the state. Cultural norms shape and restrain economic choices of firms and other actors (Hall and Soskice 2001: 9–14). Coercive power, when it emerges in markets, may be wielded by state or non-state actors, or both (Collins 1997: 72). Within government, authority may be allocated differently in different states based on their arrangements for federalism or the separation of powers. Underlying all market economies, then, are diverse sets of norms and institutions that affect the form of the market and the manner in which the goals of efficiency and productivity are positioned in relation to other objectives such as national security, political stability, social justice, or environmental sustainability (Ruggie 2003; Okun 1975: Ch 1; Hirsch 2005).

Since the 1990s, a host of rules and processes have been established at the international level to restrict the regulatory activities of states and to shape the balance struck between competing priorities in the market. These rules are typically subject to interpretation, application, and enforcement by institutions very different from conventional courts. In the case of investment treaties,[1] a set of rules and adjudicative processes have been established to advance and protect the economic demands of foreign investors by constraining the policy choices of states (Swedberg 2003: 196–7). There are now well over 2,000 bilateral investment treaties (BITs), of which roughly two-thirds are in force, as well as numerous regional economic agreements that contain an investment chapter (UNCTAD 2006: 26). These treaties establish a general constraining framework premised on broadly framed standards that protect investors from state regulation, backed by the use of compulsory arbitration to resolve investor claims against states.[2] The aim of this chapter is to provide a legal analysis of investment treaty law and arbitration as a constraining framework that applies (primarily, at least in its effect) to governments of developing or transition states. The analysis seeks to complement an overarching new developmentalist[3] perspective, as advanced in this volume, although that wider perspective is more forward-looking than the present reactive analysis. Nevertheless, it is important to understand how investment treaty arbitration impacts regulatory decision-making in order to formulate effective state responses.

There are three components to this analysis. It first involves questions of scope. To what institutions does the framework apply? Does it apply to state entities, non-state entities, or certain states only? To what activities of these entities does the framework apply? Does it apply to a limited class of activities or economic sectors? Or, if the framework applies generally, is its application limited by exceptions? Second, the analysis addresses the substantive standards that govern conduct under investment treaties. What primary rules constrain and influence the behavior of regulated entities? What sort of language is used to define the rules? Does it have a specific and identifiable meaning or is it ambiguous and open to varied interpretation by those authorized to resolve disputes? Third, the framework's mechanism for dispute settlement and enforcement is examined. Who is authorized to interpret and apply the rules? What are the consequences of a finding of noncompliance? Is the framework a self-regulatory mechanism or is it subject to binding adjudication? What conditions must be exhausted before the resort to adjudication? And what consequences follow from the adjudicator's finding of unlawful conduct? An examination of these questions allows one to dissect the constraining framework and, in turn, to characterize it as an instrument that generates market rules and so shapes underlying economic relationships.

The core argument is that investment treaties provide an extraordinarily robust, though far from immutable or impregnable, framework to constrain state policy making. This is also in relation to policies that are well established in advanced industrialized economies as means to advance the economic position of the state and to balance competing priorities in business regulation. This is especially true for investment-related policies of the state that support domestic capital or employees in targeted sectors, that put conditions on foreign investors to encourage export production or linkages with the domestic economy, that revise the terms of investment contracts to account for changing market conditions, or that apply quality- or access-related standards to privatized service providers and utilities. Moreover, the constraints under investment treaties apply broadly to virtually any state measure that may substantially reduce the value of foreign-owned assets. The scope of the framework is broad; it relies on vague and open-ended standards to regulate states; and it allows for compulsory arbitration in a manner that appears to be structurally biased in favor of investors and against host governments. There are options within this constraining framework for states to pursue industrial policies that involve a pragmatic weighing of costs and benefits, as well as regulation, of foreign investment. However, this may require a state to reject the legitimacy of investment treaty arbitration, take steps to protect its assets from seizure abroad, and resist pressure from other states and international financial institutions to pay awards regardless of how dubiously the treaties have been interpreted by arbitrators.

The dispute settlement mechanism

As a constraining framework, investment treaties have three main elements. First, they apply broadly to regulatory activity that affects foreign investors. Second, they lay out ambiguous standards to protect investors from regulation. Third, they establish a uniquely powerful form of dispute settlement and enforcement based on the use of compulsory arbitration and state liability in public law. We begin by examining this third aspect.

The elements of investment treaty arbitration

Investment treaty arbitration is an especially powerful means to regulate and discipline states because (a) it allows direct claims by investors, usually absent the customary requirement to exhaust legal remedies that are reasonably available in the host state itself; (b) it allows for a retrospective and internationally-enforceable damages award against the state for virtually any regulatory measure including legislative and judicial acts, and; (c) it relies on private arbitration to resolve questions of public law in a manner that appears structurally biased in favor of claimants and against respondent states.

Since the late 1960s, states have taken the rather drastic step of consenting generally under investment treaties to the compulsory arbitration of all future disputes with any individual or company that qualifies as an investor under the treaty. These consents have expanded rapidly among developing and transition countries, especially since the early 1990s (Van Harten 2008: 93). Unlike the consent to compulsory arbitration in a contract, a treaty-based consent by a state opens the door to claims by any business that can establish itself as foreign, including by pointing to a holding company abroad through which ownership of domestic assets has been channeled. Thus, the door is opened to claims by business entities that are unknown to the host state, that have not themselves committed productive capital to the host state, or that are owned ultimately by nationals of the host state (e.g., Tokios 2004). In the case of a treaty-based consent, then, the state loses its relative ability under investment contracts to predict and manage liabilities arising from the use of investor-state arbitration to determine the state's regulatory authority and policy space. Arbitrators are given wide-ranging and comprehensive jurisdiction to discipline states for past regulatory acts. This introduces significant uncertainties and liabilities into public budgeting and, more broadly, for state policies consistent with a variety of development strategies. Notably, the treaties authorize investors to bring claims against governments to discipline them; they do not provide for states to bring claims against investors for activities of investors that harm the public interest (Johns 1994: 903–11).

In terms of the apparent bias in investment treaty arbitration, BITs allow arbitrators who are appointed on a case-by-case basis (rather than having secure tenure as do judges) to resolve regulatory disputes between business and state and to delineate the policy space available to governments. This final resolution of disputes and definition of law and policy takes place in a context where only one class of parties (the investors) brings the claims. Thus, a one-sided structure has been established in which arbitrators have an apparent incentive to decide cases and interpret the law in favor of investors to encourage more claims to be brought and, in turn, more business for the arbitration industry. Further, under most of the treaties, the ultimate authority to appoint arbitrators (when the disputing parties do not agree) is given to organizations at which majority voting power is exercised by appointees of the major capital-exporting states (as at the International Centre for Settlement of Investment Disputes – ICSID) or of business organizations themselves (as at the International Chamber of Commerce). Put differently, in the resolution of core questions of public law on the appropriate role of the state, and thus the appropriate construction of markets, arbitrators lack the objective guarantees of independence present in domestic and international courts (Van Harten 2007: Ch. 7; Van Harten 2008a).

The dynamic of state liability

The core disciplinary power of investment treaty arbitration is the authority of arbitrators to award damages (involving "state liability") against the state, and the ability of investors to seek enforcement of awards against assets of the state within and outside its territory. Such awards differ from those in private or commercial law because they are used to discipline sovereign acts of legislatures, courts, or executive agencies. It is rare even in advanced industrialized economies to allow state liability for legislative or judicial acts, and for general policy or discretionary decisions of the executive, where the state's conduct has been found retrospectively to have been unlawful. State liability raises concerns about its fiscal impact and the possible deterrence of regulatory measures that states might otherwise pursue as part of a wider development strategy. Indeed, outside of investment arbitration, it is unheard of to allow such questions to be resolved finally by arbitrators rather than judges.

Many awards to date under investment treaties have disciplined states for general regulatory measures that affect foreign investors only indirectly and in unintended ways. It is likely that at least some of these awards have been based on interpretations that were more expansive than what was anticipated by states when the treaties were negotiated. The prospect of tribunals adopting expansive pro-investor approaches to ambiguous treaty language, as have numerous tribunals to date, exacerbates the wider implications of state liability. First, states face the high costs of defending claims in circumstances where the rules are uncertain and malleable, or where they have been subject to conflicting interpretations by past tribunals. Second, because of this uncertainty, the state faces greater pressure to settle cases than if the law was reasonably clear and balanced. In the words of one US lawyer, the ability to sue under an investment treaty is:

an open invitation to unhappy investors, tempted to complain that a financial or business failure was due to improper regulation, misguided macroeconomic policy, or discriminatory treatment by the host government and delighted by the opportunity to threaten the national government with a tedious expensive arbitration.

(Rogers 2000)

Second, states face the cost of awards. To date, there have been 32 known awards against states[4] with an average value of $98 million, usually against mid-sized developing or transition states.[5] Awards have followed primarily from regulatory disputes in the following sectors, each of which has led to an award (or awards) of at least $100 million: banking and financial services; energy; media and information technology; water and sewage services; and telecommunications. Other sectors in which disputes have arisen include: resource extraction – oil; production of goods; waste disposal concessions; construction; tourism; import/export of goods; shipping; and security services. The majority of awards have been for under $10 million (although an award of even a few million dollars may be significant for a state's budget). However, at least 12 awards have been for over $50 million including one for over $1 billion (although the latter award was granted by a tribunal that assumed jurisdiction, arguably creatively, based on an investment contract that incorporated the compulsory arbitration clause in a BIT even though the BIT itself was not shown by the claimant to be in force). These large awards send a strong signal to states that a wide range of regulatory measures could trigger an investor claim, with potentially devastating fiscal consequences for the state.

Third, the threat of a claim and an award may cause the state to withdraw a legitimate measure that it would otherwise pursue in the public interest. In the Ethyl case under NAFTA's investment chapter (Chapter 11), the Canadian government had banned a gasoline additive that was manufactured by a US firm (Ethyl 1998). The ban was justified by Canada on environmental and public health grounds. In response, the US firm brought a NAFTA claim, arguing that the ban amounted to an expropriation. After the tribunal decided that it had jurisdiction over the claim, Canada settled the case by agreeing to remove the ban, declare publicly that the gasoline additive was not an environmental or a health risk, and pay $19 million in compensation to the US firm.

An example of a pro-investor award: Occidental No. 1

As mentioned, there are numerous awards in which tribunals have adopted an expansive pro-investor approach when interpreting silence or ambiguity in an investment treaty. An example is the decision of the tribunal in Occidental No. 1. The award is reviewed here both to highlight some of its expansive approaches to the US–Ecuador BIT (1997) and as a prelude to the detailed discussion below on the scope and standards of investor protection under investment treaties.

In Occidental No. 1 (2004) the tribunal made an award of approximately US$75 million against Ecuador in favor of the US firm Occidental, in a dispute involving Occidental's eligibility for value-added tax (VAT) refunds in the oil sector. The tribunal's interpretations of the US–Ecuador BIT (1997) were expansive in a number of ways. First, the tribunal adopted an apparently contradictory position on whether or not the underlying dispute arose from a contract, an issue that had significance for certain aspects of the operation of the treaty. On the one hand, the tribunal concluded that Occidental's claim arose under the BIT and was thus distinct from claims arising under Occidental's oil contract with Petroecuador; this had the implication that the BIT's "fork in the road" clause (requiring the investor to choose to pursue either a treaty claim or available domestic remedies, but not both) did not bar Occidental from bringing a BIT claim even though Occidental had already pursued domestic remedies under the oil contract. On the other hand, the tribunal also concluded that the dispute concerned "the observance and enforcement" of an investment contract, which had the implication that the BIT's exception for tax measures would not apply to Ecuador's decision to deny VAT refunds to Occidental because that exception included a further exception for contractual disputes. Thus, the tribunal approached the dispute in separate instances as one that arose only under the treaty, but also as one that related to a contract. In both cases, these disparate approaches had the effect of resolving the relevant issue in favor of the foreign investor, thus facilitating the claim and the eventual award.

Also troubling is that the tribunal, in its decision on the merits of the dispute, adopted an expansive reading of various standards of investor protection in the BIT, including the concepts of arbitrariness, national treatment, and fair and equitable treatment, as the basis for its finding that Ecuador violated the treaty. Regarding "arbitrariness," the tribunal concluded that Ecuador's conduct (by way of its Servicio de Rentas Internas – SRI) was not motivated by any "prejudice or preference" and was rather based on "reason and fact." Yet, the tribunal concluded, based on a liberal framing of the concept of arbitrariness, that the "very confusion and lack of clarity" arising from the SRI's practices "resulted in some form of arbitrariness, even if not intended." Regarding the standard of national treatment, the tribunal resorted to the BIT's most-favored-nation (MFN) obligation in order to remove the BIT's requirement that national treatment is only required where foreign and domestic investors are found to be "in like circumstances." Instead, the tribunal found that national treatment was not limited in this way because Ecuador had concluded other BITs that did not attach this limiting phrase to their phrasing of the national treatment standard (although it would be reasonable to conclude that all BITs implicitly limit the standard of national treatment to comparisons between domestic and foreign investors who are in like circumstances, unless the BIT provides expressly to the contrary) and that Ecuador was therefore required to provide the same treatment on VAT refunds to oil "producers" like Occidental as it did to other "exporters" (of, for example, flowers) who, unlike "producers," were eligible for VAT refunds under Ecuadorian law.

Lastly, the tribunal adopted a broad reading of the standard of fair and equitable treatment. It adopted the (controversial) expansive view of some earlier tribunals that this broad and malleable standard obliges a state, onerously, to "ensure a transparent and predictable framework for [investors'] business planning and investment" and to "act in a consistent manner, free from ambiguity and totally transparently in its relations with the foreign investor." The tribunal concluded further that the state has a duty of transparency and predictability as a component of fair and equitable treatment and that this "is an objective requirement that does not depend on whether the Respondent [state] has proceeded in good faith or not." Finally, with little discussion and with no reference to outside authority, the tribunal concluded dubiously that this expansive reading of fair and equitable treatment "is not different from that required under [customary] international law." This conclusion contradicted not only the submissions of Ecuador but also those made by other states, including the US and Canada, in other investment arbitrations. By subjecting capital-importing states to this expansive version of the fair and equitable standard, tribunals like that in Occidental No. 1 (2004) arguably apply much more intensive constraints on regulatory decision-makers in developing and transition states than are applied to governments in North America and Europe under their domestic law.

On these issues, the tribunal in Occidental No. 1 (2004) adopted expansive readings of various components of the BIT, found that Ecuador had violated these expansive versions of the treaty standards, and issued a large award in favor of Occidental.[6] Although they do not establish actual bias on the part of arbitrators, awards like Occidental No. 1 (2004) may further the perception that investment treaty arbitration is structurally biased in favor of investor interest.

The scope of the rules

Investment treaties apply to virtually any regulatory activity because they define key concepts like "investor," "investment," and state "measures" in broad, flexible terms. The implications of this are discussed below.

Democratic choice, governmental flexibility, and the definition of "state measures"

Investment treaties apply explicitly or presumptively to any measure of a state party to the treaty. This is important because it means that a state's obligations and liabilities under the treaties affect not only regulatory acts that isolate or target specific investors in an intentionally abusive way, but also general measures of the legislature, judiciary, or executive that apply to all investors, whether domestic or foreign, for reasons of public interest. This includes measures that are consistent with or even mandated by the domestic constitution or other sources of international law, such as international human rights law. Although this fettering of policy choice and regulatory flexibility also takes place under other international regimes, the constraints imposed by investment treaties are intensified greatly by their unique remedial and enforcement structure, as discussed above (Kumm 2006).

Regulatory activity and the definition of "investment"

The definition of "investment" in the treaties is also typically broad and flexible, extending beyond tangible assets, for example, to include intangibles such as market share, goodwill, intellectual property rights, or "any asset." As a result, the obligations imposed on states typically apply to any act of the state in virtually any sector in which assets are open to foreign ownership, unless the act in question is expressly exempted from the treaty.

Some treaties are one-sided in that its exceptions apply to one state party (usually the developed state) and not the other. This is apparent in the case specific exceptions from commitments, typically in investment treaties concluded by the US or Canada, to remove foreign ownership restrictions across a state's economy (so-called "pre-establishment national treatment," see below). In treaties containing such commitments, the states' parties usually exclude certain regulatory activities or economic sectors from the broad commitment to liberalize foreign investment, in order to exempt those activities and sectors from foreign ownership and penetration. Thus, in the four BITs concluded to date between either the US or Canada and an Andean Community state (Bolivia, Colombia, Ecuador, and Peru), the following sectors are subject to specific exceptions *for the US or Canada* in at least one of the BITs:

- oil and gas
- mining
- fishing
- air and maritime transport
- shipping
- banking, securities, and other financial services
- government insurance, subsidies or grants
- state enterprises
- broadcasting
- telephone services
- social services (e.g., public law enforcement, income security, public education, health and child care), and
- foreign investment screening.

In contrast, of these sectors, only the following are subject to specific exceptions *for the relevant Andean Community state* in at least one of the BITs:

- leasing of minerals and pipeline rights of way on government lands
- traditional fishing (not including fish processing or aquaculture)
- air and maritime transport
- subsidies or grants, and
- broadcasting.

As a result, the developing state party to the treaty faces much wider obligations to allow foreign entry into its economy – free from screening requirements or other conditions of access – and to refrain from privileging domestic capital in its industrial strategy.[7] The treaties are non-reciprocal.[8] Naturally, it is counter-intuitive from a development perspective for a developing state to expose itself to more extensive obligations to allow access and ensure non-discrimination for foreign capital than does the industrialized capital-exporting state.

Forum-shopping and the definition of "investor"

Under investment treaties, an "investor" typically includes not only natural persons or companies owned directly by natural persons of a state party to the treaty, but also holding companies that are set up in the opposite state party under the treaty, yet owned and controlled by investors from a third state (for example, Netherlands-Bolivia BIT (1994): Art. 1(b)). Based on such provisions, many treaties adopt a liberal approach to forum-shopping[9] such that a state, after consenting to compulsory investor-state arbitration, must assume that any investor with a significant presence in its economy may have access to arbitration even where the host state has not concluded an investment treaty with the state of origin of the ultimate owner of the investment in question. A liberal approach to forum-shopping, furthered in the treaties themselves but also in the interpretations of BITs by numerous tribunals (e.g., Aguas del Tunari 2005; Tokios 2004), invites investors to design their corporate structure so as to maximize opportunities to bring treaty claims on the most favorable terms against a state in which they own assets.

The standards of investor protection

Investment treaties lay out broad and flexible standards by which state conduct is evaluated in the arbitration of investor claims. Arbitrators, by their interpretation and application of these standards, determine matters of law that have wider implications for how regulatory authority is construed in relation to private interests and demands. The standards typically and most prominently include:

- national treatment
- most-favored nation (MFN) treatment
- fair and equitable treatment
- limitations on expropriation
- specific prohibitions on performance requirements, and
- a duty to observe other obligations to investors (so-called "umbrella clauses").

Each of these standards is discussed below. Notably, in 30 known awards under investment treaties to date, a tribunal has based its finding that the state violated the treaty on the fair and equitable treatment standard in 23 cases (in one case, via an MFN clause); on limitations against expropriation in ten cases; on national treatment in seven cases; on an umbrella clause in five cases; and on prohibitions on performance requirements in one case. In a number of awards, multiple standards were found to have been violated by the state.

National treatment

Although the treaty language may vary, "national treatment" generally requires a state to treat foreign investors from the opposite state no less favorably than it treats domestic firms or persons who are in like circumstances. Although the state is also typically permitted to treat foreign investors more favorably than their domestic counterparts, as in the provision of special tax holidays or regulatory exemptions (e.g., US–Ecuador BIT (1997: Art. II(1); Switzerland–Philippines BIT (1999): Art. IV (2) and (3)). National treatment always applies at the post-establishment stage of an investment. However, it may also be extended to the pre-establishment stage, as in BITs concluded by the US or Canada and in both NAFTA and CAFTA. Where a treaty extends national treatment to the pre-establishment stage of an investment, any restrictions on foreign ownership or control for that sector of investment are also barred unless the treaty specifically exempts the relevant sector or regulatory activity from the obligation.[10] Under an absolute rule of pre-establishment national treatment, the state would have to allow 100 percent foreign access and ownership in every sector of its economy.

A prudential approach to national treatment might limit the concept to situations in which a state appeared to have specifically and intentionally targeted a foreign investor for harmful treatment because the investor was foreign. This approach is prudential in that it creates relatively predictable implications for states and arguably coincides with the intentions of states when most of the treaties were negotiated. However, the interpretative approach of most tribunals to date has not been limited in this way. Rather, national treatment is usually taken to go beyond intended discrimination to include so-called de facto discrimination. A violation may thus occur when a state measure, although neutral on its face, has some discriminatory effect on foreign investors relative to the category of domestic investors selected for comparison (in Occidental No. 1, as discussed above, the tribunal chose a very broad category for comparison to Occidental's oil activities – i.e., all "exporters"). Indeed, the meaning of national treatment can be expanded by a tribunal to encompass, in the extreme, any exercise of authority that differentiates in any way between a foreign and domestic investor, where the differentiation is less favorable to the foreigner (e.g., Pope and Talbot Inc 2001: para. 78–9).

Most-favored-nation treatment

Similar to national treatment, MFN treatment requires a state to treat foreign investors from the opposite state party no less favorably than it treats investors from third states. Thus, the protection available to foreign investors in one investment treaty may be extended to the state's other investment treaties that contain an MFN clause. An implication of MFN clauses, as interpreted by numerous tribunals, is that investors can shop around and collect for themselves the best set of legal protections available from all investment treaties concluded by the host state. In Occidental No. 1, the tribunal relied on the US-Ecuador

BIT's (1997) MFN clause to remove the express requirement that national treatment was limited to situations in which foreign and domestic investors were both "in like circumstances." The tribunal did so by referring to another Ecuadorian BIT that did not explicitly use the term "in like circumstances." The tribunal opted for the MFN-based interpretation that favored the investor (and claimants generally) by expanding the situations in which a measure may be found to discriminate against a foreign investor.

MFN treatment has also been used by tribunals to extend not only substantive obligations in the treaty, but also procedural aspects of a state's consent to arbitration. Thus, some investment treaties contain limitations on the investor's right to bring an arbitration claim (such as a fork in the road clause, as mentioned above). In some arbitration awards (e.g., Maffezini 2000: para. 65; Azurix 2003: para. 60; Sempra 2005: para. 92–4; Continental Casualty 2006: para. 77–8 and 86), these limitations have been discarded by the tribunal on the basis that the state's MFN commitment in a BIT required it to extend more advantageous procedural elements of its consent to arbitration in any other investment treaty to the BIT under which the investor brought a claim. However, other tribunals have adopted a conflicting approach by concluding that an MFN clause does not extend beyond the substantive protections in another treaty unless the MFN clause states clearly that it extends to procedures. Of course, the existence of this conflict itself poses significant difficulties for states faced with possible state liability under the treaties, as well as investors faced with the costs of claims.

Fair and equitable treatment (including full protection and security)

Typically, investment treaties require states to afford foreign investors "fair and equitable" treatment (of which, for present purposes, "full protection and security" is treated as a component) (e.g., Spain–Bolivia BIT (2001): Art. 3 (1); US–Romania BIT (1994): Art. II (2) (a)). Different investment treaties phrase the obligation in different ways, of course, but all provide for a minimum level of treatment states must provide to foreign investors. Perhaps unsurprisingly, given its breadth and flexibility, the standard has been relied on more frequently than other standards as a basis for awarding damages against the state.

The broad discretion assigned to arbitrators in interpreting this standard, in particular, is demonstrated by the CMS (2005) award against Argentina. Here, the tribunal concluded that the fair and equitable treatment standard, although "somewhat vague," should be read to require Argentina to maintain a stable legal and business environment in the midst of its financial crisis, and that this was "an objective requirement unrelated to whether [Argentina] has had any deliberate intention or bad faith" (CMS 2005: para. 274 and 280). On this reading, the tribunal decided that Argentina's devaluation of the peso violated its BIT with the US, requiring payment of a large award to a US firm that had invested in the privatized gas sector, and heightening the prospect of further awards (which have indeed followed) against the country. The CMS (2005) tribunal, along with other tribunals, rejected Argentina's submission (echoed by other states in other arbitrations) that fair and equitable treatment is merely a component of, and thus limited by, the "minimum standard of treatment" as understood in customary international law. In response, tribunals have tended either to reject the argument outright or to adopt an expansive view of the customary standard itself, sometimes with little or no discussion of relevant sources of international law (CMS 2005: para. 284).

Expropriation, including "regulatory" expropriation

A historical motivation for the conclusion of investment treaties by major capital-exporting states was to protect assets of their multinational firms from expropriation or nationalization in the developing world (e.g., US–Argentina BIT (1994): Art. IV (1); Spain–Peru BIT (1996): Art. 5), even where major assets were acquired during and retained after the colonial period. What was probably not anticipated was the degree to which these limits on expropriation would be open to wide-ranging interpretations, beyond the concept of direct expropriation, to include so-called indirect, "creeping," or regulatory expropriations by a state. Under these wider meanings of the concept, general measures of a state that leave an investor's ownership intact but that otherwise cause it economic harm (even incidentally to general regulation for legitimate purposes) may be classified as expropriation requiring payment of full market compensation to the investor. Such an expansive reading was adopted in the Metalclad (2000) award against Mexico under NAFTA, where the tribunal concluded that expropriation included:

> not only open, deliberate and acknowledged takings of property, such as outright seizure or formal or obligatory transfer of title in favour of the host State, but also covert or incidental interference with the use of property which has the effect of depriving the owner, in whole or in significant part, of the use or reasonably-to-be-expected economic benefit of property even if not necessarily to the obvious benefit of the host State.
>
> (Metalclad 2000: para.103)

A similarly expansive approach was adopted under the Spain–Mexico BIT (1996) by the tribunal in Tecmed, which declined to consider the public benefits of government acts that reduce the value of an investment as a basis for differentiating compensable expropriation from non-compensable regulation. The tribunal stated: "we find no principle stating that regulatory administrative actions are per se excluded from the scope of the [BIT], even if they are beneficial to society as a whole – such as environmental protection" (Tecnicas Medioambientales Tecmed 2003: para. 121).

Prohibitions on performance requirements

Investment treaties concluded by the US and Canada, modeled after NAFTA, prohibit specific performance requirements, not only at the post-establishment stage of an investment, but also at the pre-establishment stage. These prohibitions apply to a wide range of measures that have been used historically by governments to condition the entry and operation of foreign investors in their domestic economy. Many states, including Western and Asian industrialized states, have used such tools to promote export-oriented development, domestic employment, or linkages between foreign investment and the domestic economy (Wade 2003; UNDP 2005: 134; World Commission 2004: 80–1).

Typically, in the relevant investment treaties, a prohibition on performance requirements lays out a list of specific measures that are barred. The prohibited measures may include, for example, those requiring foreign investors to achieve local content; carry out research and development; transfer technology or pro-duction processes; restrict imports or domestic sales as a proportion of produc-tion; or export a certain level of products or services (e.g., US–Bolivia BIT (2001): Art. VI). Thus, the treaties read like a shopping list of policies used suc-cessfully in the past by industrialized countries to screen or channel foreign investment as part of a wider development strategy.

Umbrella clauses and BIT arbitration of disputes arising from an investment contract

Many investment treaties contain an "umbrella clause" that obligates the state parties to observe or respect their "obligations" to foreign investors, beyond the obligations contained in the treaty itself. Thus, the state assumes a potentially wide-ranging duty under the treaty to respect the obligations it has entered into by way of contracts, administrative orders, or other legal instruments separate from the treaty. A consequence is that investment treaties may establish two (or more) parallel systems of interpretation and enforcement (one under the treaty and another under the dispute settlement arrangement(s) provided for in the con-tract or other legal instrument containing obligations to investors) in relation to the same underlying dispute between an investor and the state. It is indeed common for disputes arising from investment contracts to be submitted by an investor to arbitration under an investment treaty instead of (or in addition to) the dispute settlement process that was agreed to by the investor under the con-tract. In this respect, umbrella clauses have been interpreted by tribunals to allow the investor to avoid its contractual commitment to accept a particular forum (often domestic courts or domestic arbitration) for the settlement of contractual disputes, and litigate that dispute instead (or again) under the BIT (e.g., Duke Energy 2008). This reveals how investors can use investment treaties to avoid or limit their contractual undertakings on dispute settlement. In this manner, BITs may expand state liability significantly beyond what it was believed to encom-pass at the time a privatization program was adopted.

The constraining framework for industrial policy

Consistent with a new developmentalist perspective, legal analysis of investment treaties should examine whether treaty-based rules and processes tend to facilitate or hamper a state's ability to use markets to further an industrial strategy by, for example, supporting key sectors in furtherance of higher-end comparative advantage (Abugattas and Paus 2008: 116, 130). The answer offered by this chapter is that investment treaties seriously constrain such options for developing and transition states. Broad standards, backed by a uniquely powerful arbitration mechanism, protect foreign firms whose primary interest will be to further their business strategies where those strategies may conflict with the development priorities of a host government. Bargaining power shifts in favor of multinational firms and against groups that benefit from the regulation of foreign investors or the attachment of conditions to their entry into the domestic economy.

Thus, in pursuing new developmentalist strategies, states confront a costly process of adjudication that appears to be biased against them and that may trigger (if the state loses) significant diplomatic and economic pressure – whether levied by the World Bank, other international financial institutions, the investing community, or by major capital-exporting states – to comply with awards. By relying on an ostensibly fair adjudicative process, the system presents strong claims of legitimacy for pro-investor constructions of the market arrived at by arbitration tribunals, and for a consequently limited role of the state in developing and transition economies.

Even so, developing and transition states are not without options in the face of the constraining framework, even if options are greatly restricted. States with a strong electoral mandate or public interest commitment to a particular measure should not be deterred from pursuing it, although they should consider how best to structure the measure in the face of possible investor claims. States also retain opportunities to negotiate the settlement of disputes both before and during arbitration, in which case the state's bargaining position will reflect the context of the dispute and, especially, the investor's interest in avoiding adverse publicity[11] or maintaining positive relations with the host government. An investor has an interest to avoid the high cost of arbitration, especially when it is not a large firm and when it appears the state will contest the claim vigorously.

The ability of investors to collect on awards by tribunals is also open to doubt. States can refuse to pay an award on various grounds, such as violation of domestic law or the lack of legitimacy of the award or adjudicative process. When a state refuses to pay, the investor may be forced to pursue assets of the state in the territory of other states pursuant to the relevant arbitration treaties that provide for extra-territorial enforcement of awards. This chasing of assets is fraught with uncertainty about the value, location, and vulnerability of assets abroad.[12] As such, the state retains bargaining power even after an award is issued, and it seems prudent for a state threatened with or involved in a claim to identify its assets abroad and ensure that they are not left exposed, for example in states that adopt a liberal approach to enforcement of foreign arbitration awards (such as France) (Turck 2001; Schwartz 1997).

Further, the pro-investor character of the system is not written in stone. Investment treaties are often silent or ambiguous on important questions and thus open to interpretations that offer a degree of flexibility and policy space to states. Some tribunals have indeed interpreted investment treaties in a relatively state-friendly way, as customary international law was once presumptively interpreted to favor sovereign autonomy. But the thrust of the system – and the interpretations arrived at by many tribunals – is to prioritize the promotion and protection of foreign investment as the ultimate aim of the system and, by extension, the state itself. The orientation remains a preference for construction of markets that favors the established centers of capital and that constrains domestic strategies aimed at industrialization and technological capacity-building by developing and transition states.

How should states respond? I will begin with some defensive strategies. States should first be prepared to vigorously bargain and litigate claims against them, and consider the option of refusal to pay an award where it is based on dubious reasoning and an unfair process. It is legitimate for the unsuccessful party in arbitration, whether or not it is a state, to bargain over the amount that should be paid even after an award has been issued, in light of the challenges surrounding award enforcement by the successful party. Over the longer-term, states should work to improve their autonomous legal capacity by developing a small nucleus of in-house lawyers with expertise in international investment law (and related subjects), around whom additional capacity can be hired or retained as necessary. This nucleus of legal capacity must be employed directly by the host government and accountable to its senior decision makers so that it will be seen as providing reliable and fully confidential advice. It should be responsible for identifying and evaluating the state's liabilities, identifying options for negotiation (or re-negotiation) of investment treaties and contracts, and conducting/managing litigation to defend against claims. The team should be supported by a tracking and monitoring capacity on the foreign ownership of significant assets within the state and on state assets located abroad (where such assets may be vulnerable to seizure).

Let us now turn to more forward-looking responses. As mentioned, states should not abandon or dilute policies central to their development strategy, and they should not be deterred by threatened claims. Such threats are a serious matter, but the costs and risks to investors must not be discounted, and this operates in favor of the host state. States should also be prepared to challenge the authority and legitimacy of institutions that occupy a prominent place within the system, where the institution is not adequately representative of the diverse interests at play in investor-state disputes. More strategically, states should consider renegotiating or abrogating existing treaties and, toward this end, should collect information on allowable timelines for abrogation under their treaties. Treaties that are targeted in this way might include those concluded with capital-exporting states that have weaker bargaining power or whose treaties have allowed a disproportionate number of claims (relative to productive capital flows). Other systemic reforms – such as multilateral efforts to narrow the key jurisdictional concepts or standards of investor protection – are also important, but require more complex strategies to re-negotiate or abrogate hundreds of treaties.

Lastly, states may wish to replace the current system with an international investment court or appellate body that reflects principles of openness, representation, and independence in judicial decision-making. An international court could be mandated to interpret and apply the treaties afresh from the troubling jurisprudence that has emerged from some arbitration tribunals.[13] It would also be likely to provide a more credible balancing of the regulatory position of states and the business demands of investors. It would thus afford more space, free from the threat of a catastrophic damages award, for policies that utilize markets as a means rather than the master.

Conclusion

The definition and evolution of "the market" under investment treaties depends on the allocation of adjudicative power to constrain the role of state in developing and transition states. Under investment treaties, this power was assigned to arbitrators, rather than judges, who may reasonably be perceived to favor investors, and who are subject to the appointing authority of executive officials at international organizations where voting power is concentrated in the major capital-exporting states or directly in business organizations. The adjudicative power of arbitrators is also backed by major states' commitments to enforce awards against assets of a developing or transition state within their territory. The terms of the treaties themselves often belie the claim that investment treaties entail reciprocal legal rights and obligations of states; a treaty may be one-sided, not only in its actual effects (where capital flows are overwhelming into and not out of the developing state) but also in its legal terms (where, for instance, the developed state enjoys exceptions from foreign ownership and entry that are denied to the developing state). It is indicative that, other than under NAFTA, major capital-exporting countries have wisely not consented to investor-state arbitration in treaties with each other.

To date, the operation of investment treaty arbitration is more consistent with an attempt to consolidate wealth in favor of existing concentrations of capital in major states as opposed to the realization of efficient and productive markets based on transparent rules subject to interpretation by an independent process of adjudication (Harvey 2005: 161). The message of this chapter is not that states should adopt a parochial or hostile stance to foreign investment, or that they should favor domestic capital and other domestic interests in all cases. It calls not for ideological struggle, but for careful attention to the bargaining processes whereby governments may wish to attract, condition, and regulate foreign capital on terms that are agreeable to the host state (Mortimore 2008: 45–6). Foreign investment, like the market, is a means to the end of improving the state's economic position and the welfare of its population. As one component of planning toward new developmentalism, then, governments should assess their legal exposure to investment treaty arbitration and the degree to which this exposure may frustrate or preclude strategies that approach markets and foreign investment pragmatically.

Notes

1 "Investment treaties" include any treaty – whether a bilateral investment treaty (BITs) or a bilateral or regional trade agreement containing an investment chapter – that provides for compulsory investor-state arbitration.

2 Although precise data is difficult to compile in light of the practice of, among other reasons, forum-shopping (explained later in the chapter), it appears that the majority of FDI flows into developing and transition economies is subject to an investment treaty providing for compulsory arbitration of investor-state disputes. In contrast, because the major developed states have not concluded investment treaties with each other (other than in the case of Canada and the US under NAFTA), the majority of FDI flows into the major capital-exporting states is unlikely to be governed by the investment treaty arbitration regime.

3 See in Part I of this volume the contributions by R. Wade; H.-J. Chang; and E.S. Reinhart, Y.E. Amaïzo, and R. Kattel; as well as the concluding chapter by S. R. Khan.

4 This includes the following: CSOB (against the Czech Republic, $1.05 billion); CME (Czech Republic, $351 million); Siemens (Argentina, $298 million); BG Group (Argentina, $235 million); Azurix (Argentina, $182 million); Sempra (Argentina, $160 million); Rumeli Telekom (Kazahkstan, $150 million); CMS (Argentina, $149 million); Aguas Aconquija (Argentina, $142 million); Enron (Argentina, $128 million); Occidental Petroleum (Ecuador, $75 million); LG&E (Argentina, $57 million); Archer Daniels Midland (Mexico, $35 million); Desert Line Projects (Yemen, $21 million); Wena Hotels (Egypt, $21 million); Metalclad (Mexico, $17 million); Victor Pey Casado (Chile, $13 million); American Manufacturing (Congo, $9 million); MTD (Chile, $7 million); Tecnicas Medioambientales Tecmed (Mexico, $7 million); Duke Energy Electroquil (Ecuador, $6 million); S.D. Myers (Canada, $6 million); Middle East Cement (Egypt, $4 million); Continental Casualty (Argentina, $3 million); Swembalt (Latvia, $3 million); Sedelmayer (Russia, $3 million); Feldman (Mexico, $2 million); Nykomb (Latvia, $2 million); Petrobart (Kyrgyz Republic, $1 million); AAPL (Sri Lanka, $600,000); Pope & Talbot (Canada, $500,000); Maffezini (Spain, $300,000). Award amounts have been rounded and approximated where interest and foreign exchange rates were not clear from the award. Some awards may be subject to annulment or set aside proceedings. The award in CSOB is included because the origins of the respondent state's consent are connected to a BIT; in that case, the tribunal based its jurisdiction on the incorporation into a contract of the compulsory arbitration clause in a BIT which the claimant had not shown to be in force.

5 There have been 9 awards against Argentina; 4 against Mexico; 2 each against Ecuador, Egypt, Chile, Canada, and Latvia; and one each against the Slovak Republic, the Czech Republic, Kazahkstan, Yemen, Congo, Russia, the Kyrgyz Republic, Sri Lanka, and Spain.

6 A related BIT arbitration is ongoing in Occidental No. 2 in which Occidental is reportedly seeking $3 billion in compensation (Peterson 2008).

7 Even in the case of the US and Canada, significant gaps are apparent where sectoral exceptions included in one BIT are omitted from another BIT (particularly where the BIT in question permits forum-shopping).

8 Although there are, again, important variations; for example, Bolivia's BIT with the US is less one-sided in this respect than are Ecuador's BITs with the US and Canada.

9 BITs concluded by Canada, the Netherlands, Switzerland, the U.K., and the US usually contain a liberal approach to forum-shopping whereas those concluded by Belgium, France, Germany, and Spain, for example, adopt a more restrictive approach by requiring the investor to have its administrative seat in the opposite state's territory or to be substantially owned or controlled by natural persons of the opposite state.

10 Pre-establishment national treatment is sometimes referred to as "market access" or as a "right of establishment."
11 Claims against developing states have reportedly been abandoned or settled by major firms such as Nestlé (against Ethiopia) and Bechtel (against Bolivia) in the face of concerted public pressure.
12 For instance, many states exempt central bank reserves from enforcement actions arising from an arbitration award (Lee 2002).
13 Like-minded states could achieve institutional reform of this sort by concluding a new treaty, subsequent to their existing investment treaties, that creates a judicial body modeled after the conventional courts that, in all other contexts, are charged with the final resolution of regulatory disputes between business and state.

References

Abugattas, L. and Paus, E. 2008. "Policy Space for a Capability-Centered Development Strategy for Latin America." In: D. Sánchez-Ancochea and K. C. Shadlen, eds., *The Political Economy of Hemispheric Integration*. New York: Palgrave Macmillan.

Aguas del Tunari SA v. *Republic of Bolivia*. 2005. Award on jurisdiction, October 21, 2005.

Azurix Corp v. *Argentine Republic*. 2003. Award on jurisdiction, December 8, 2003.

Cohen, M.R. 1933. *Law and the Social Order*. New York: Harcourt, Brace and Co.

Collins, H. 1997. "The Sanctimony of Contract." In: R. Rawlings, ed., *Law, Society, and Economy*. Oxford: Clarendon Press.

Continental Casualty Company v. *Argentine Republic*. 2006. Award on jurisdiction, February 22, 2006.

CMS Gas Transmission Company v. *Argentine Republic*. 2005. Award on the merits, 12 May 2005.

Duke Energy Electroquil Partners & Electroquil S.A. v. *Republic of Ecuador*. 2008. Award on the merits, August 18, 2008.

Ethyl Corporation v. *Government of Canada*. 1998. Award on jurisdiction, June 24, 1998.

Hall, P. A. and Soskice, D. 2001. "An Introduction to Varieties of Capitalism." In: P.A. Hall and D. Soskice, eds., *Varieties of Capitalism*. Oxford: Oxford University Press.

Harvey, D. 2005. *A Brief History of Neoliberalism*. Oxford: Oxford University Press.

Hirsch, M. 2005 "The Sociology of International Law: Invitation to Study International Rules in their Social Context." *University of Toronto Law Journal* 55(4): 891–939.

Johns, F. 1994. "The Invisibility of the Transnational Corporation: An Analysis of International Law and Legal Theory." *Melbourne University Law Review* 19(4): 893–923.

Klein, N. 2007. *The Shock Doctrine*, New York: Macmillan.

Kumm, M. 2006. "Constitutional Democracy Encounters International Law: Terms of Engagement." *New York University Law School Working Paper* No. 47, New York.

Lee, P. L. 2002. "Central Banks and Sovereign Immunity." *Columbia Journal of Transnational Law* 41(2): 327–96.

Maffezini (Emilio Agustin) v. Kingdom of Spain. 2000. Award on jurisdiction, January 25, 2000.

Metalclad Corporation v. *United Mexican States*. 2000. Award on the merits, August 30, 2000.

Mortimore, M. 2008. "The Transnationalization of Developing America: Trends, Challenges, and (Missed Opportunities)." In: D. Sánchez-Ancochea and K. C. Shadlen, eds., *The Political Economy of Hemispheric Integration*. New York: Palgrave Macmillan.

Netherlands–Bolivia BIT. 1994. Agreement on encouragement and reciprocal protection of investments between the Kingdom of the Netherlands and the Republic of Bolivia (entered into force November 1, 1994).

Occidental Exploration and Production Company v. *Republic of Ecuador* (2004), Award on the merits, July 1, 2004.

Okun, A. M. 1975. *Equality and Efficiency: The Big Tradeoff.* Washington: The Brookings Institution.

Peterson, L. E. 2008. "Path cleared for examination of the merits in Occidental v. Ecuador arbitration at ICSID..." *Investment Arbitration Reporter* 1(10) (September 17, 2008).

Pope & Talbot Inc v. *Government of Canada* 2001. Award on the merits, phase 2, April 10, 2001.

Rogers, W. 2000. "Emergence of the International Centre for Settlement of Investment Disputes (ICSID) as the Most Significant Forum for Submission of Bilateral Investment Treaty Disputes," Presentation to the Inter-American Development Bank Conference of October 26–27, 2000.

Ruggie, J. G. 2003. "Taking Embedded Liberalism Global: The Corporate Connection." In: D. Held and M. Koenig-Archibugi, eds., *Taming Globalization: Frontiers of Governance.* Cambridge: Polity Press.

Schwartz, E.A. 1997. "A Comment on Chromalloy Hilmartin, à l'américaine." *Journal of International Arbitration* 14(2): 125–35.

Sempra Energy International v. *Argentine Republic.* 2005. Award on jurisdiction, 11 May 2005.

Spain–Bolivia BIT. 2001. Acuerdo para la promoción y la protección recíproca de inversiones entre el Reino de España y la República de Bolivia (signed October 24, 2001; had not entered into force as at June 1, 2006).

Spain–Mexico BIT. 1996. Acuerdo para la promoción y la protección recíproca de inversiones entre los Estados Unidos Mexicanos y el Reino de España (entered into force December 18, 1996).

Spain–Peru BIT. 1996. Acuerdo para la promoción y la protección recíproca de inversiones entre la República de Perú y el Reino de España (entered into force February 17, 1996).

Swedberg, R. 2003. *Principles of Economic Sociology,* Princeton: Princeton University Press.

Switzerland–Philippines BIT. 1999. Accord entre la Confédération suisse et la République de Philippines concernant la promotion et la protection réciproques des investissements (entered into force April 23, 1999).

Tecnicas Medioambientales Tecmed, SA v. *United Mexican States.* 2003. Award on the merits, 29 May 2003.

Tokios Tokelès v. *Ukraine.* 2004. Award on jurisdiction, April 29, 2004.

Turck, N. B. (2001) "French and US Courts Define Limits of Sovereign Immunity in Execution and Enforcement of Arbitral Awards." *Arbitration International* 17(3): 327–342.

United Nations Conference on Trade and Development (UNCTAD). 2006. *World Investment Report 2006.* New York: United Nations.

United Nations Development Programme (UNDP). 2005. *Human Development Report 2005.* New York: United Nations.

US–Argentina BIT. 1994. Treaty between United States of America and the Argentine Republic concerning the Reciprocal Encouragement and Protection of Investment (entered into force October 20, 1994).

US–Bolivia BIT. 2001. Treaty between the Government of the United States and the Government of the Republic of Bolivia concerning the Encouragement and Reciprocal Protection of Investment (entered into force June 6, 2001).

US–Ecuador BIT. 1997. Treaty between the United States of America and the Republic of Ecuador concerning the Encouragement and Reciprocal Protection of Investment (entered into force May 11, 1997).

US–Romania BIT. 1994. Treaty between the Government of the United States of America and the Government of Romania concerning the Reciprocal Encouragement and Protection of Investments (entered into force January 15, 1994).

Van Harten, G. 2008. "Investment Treaty Arbitration and Its Policy Implications for Capital-Importing States." In: D. Sánchez-Ancochea and K. C. Shadlen, eds., *The Political Economy of Hemispheric Integration*. New York: Palgrave Macmillan.

Van Harten, G. 2008a. "A Case for an International Investment Court," Paper presented to the Inaugural Conference of the Society for International Economic Law, Geneva, July 16, 2008.

Van Harten, G. 2007. *Investment Treaty Arbitration and Public Law*. Oxford: Oxford University Press.

Wade, R. 2003. *Governing the Market: Theory and the Role of Government in East Asian Industrialization*. Princeton: Princeton University Press.

World Commission on the Social Dimension of Globalization. 2004. *A Fair Globalization: Creating Opportunities for All*. Geneva: International Labour Organization.

Part IV

Case studies in pro-active government

9 Government reform and industrial development in China and Mexico

Kevin P. Gallagher and M. Shafaeddin[1]

Introduction

There are striking similarities between China and Mexico's economic development over the last quarter century. There are also significant differences. Like Mexico, China's economic model was not performing well and needed reforms, including export promotion. Like Mexico, China was a one-party state during the period of reform (Mexico democratized in 2000). Like Mexico, China has sought to attract foreign direct investment (FDI) into manufacturing and high technology sectors to gain access to technology.

As we will see, this is where the similarities end. China's annual average per capita growth rate has topped 8 percent over the last three decades, while Mexico's has been barely about 1 percent. China's annual average growth rate in manufacturing value added has been well over 10 percent since 1980, whereas Mexico has been closer to 3 percent. China is becoming the manufacturing powerhouse of the world economy and an increasing source of innovation, moving up the technology ladder from assembly-based manufacturing activity. In Mexico, manufacturing remains at the low end of the technology ladder and is losing its competitiveness relative to China (Gallagher and Porzecanski 2008; Gallagher *et al.* 2008; Pizarro and Shafaeddin 2007; Dussel Peters 2005, 2007). We show that, on the one hand, Mexico's performance is in part a function of a neo-liberal mindset that sees a very limited role for the state while integrating into the world economy. China, on the other hand, followed a pro-active globalization strategy. Mexico's route to international integration has come at the expense of industrialization and learning; China's pro-active approach has made it the manufacturing powerhouse of the world economy.

The purpose of this chapter is to examine the extent to which government policies toward industrial learning, which enhances value added in exports, and subsequent development have differed in the two countries over the past quarter century. The chapter is divided into four sections following this introduction. The first section is a short literature review on industrial learning. The second section examines the case of Mexico; the third section analyzes China. The last section summarizes our main findings and draws lessons for research and policy.

The role of learning in industrialization

Regardless of the theoretical framework deployed, the role of learning in capacity building is paramount for industrial development. Yet, the literature has two poles. On one end, the proponents of governments playing a strong role in industrialization stress "learning-by-doing." At the other end, those in favor of market-led industrialization believe in the contribution of "learning through trading."

A neo-developmentalist approach argues that learning contributes to industrialization through "learning-by-doing" and experience. In contrast, neo-classical or neo-liberal approaches argue that industrialization comes from "learning through trading." The essential difference between the two is that the first group favors government intervention and the second argues for the operation of market forces without government interference.

In the neo-classical theory of international trade, technological knowledge and information is freely available; diffusion of knowledge is costless, instantaneous, and automatic; there is no significant learning process; and technological development is without risk. All markets are competitive and comparative advantage is determined by factor cost. As the existence of increasing return and barriers to entry are assumed away, there is no need for latecomers to invest in human capital or intervene in the market to promote knowledge intensive products manufactured by established firms. Further, there are no static or dynamic externalities. Production costs in different products are not interdependent; there are no spill-over effects. Similarly, there are no inter-temporal relations between present income/costs and future income/costs, as experience has no place in cost/income determination. In a nutshell, as there is no market or institutional failure, there is no need for any policy intervention.

The importance of learning and knowledge accumulation has been emphasized in the post-war and modern theoretical and empirical literature since the publication of the pioneering article on learning-by-doing by Arrow (1962). To him, the acquisition of knowledge is a product of experience which grows with time. The need for government intervention in learning by doing is articulated in "capability building theory." The theory of capability building (TCB) is based on the infant industry argument of Friedrich List, according to which "mental capital," or the accumulation of knowledge and experience, is regarded as the main element of "productive power" [development] and industrialization. Industrialization in newcomer countries would not take place according "to the natural course of things" (through the operation of market forces alone) and government policies should aim, *inter alia*, at facilitating learning at both the industry and country levels (see Shafaeddin 2005a for details). The importance of learning and experience in industrialization has also been emphasized by many other scholars (Linder 1961; Krugman 1984; Nelson and Winter 1982).

The theoretical and empirical literature on TCB theory is vast.[2] One strand, the evolutionary theory of TCB, is most relevant for developing countries. The evolutionary version of TCB draws not only on the infant industry argument but also on the evolutionary theory of change (Nelson and Winter 1982) and new growth theory (see Lucas 1988; Romer 1986, 1987). Scholars of this version of TCB regard technological capabilities (learning) and technology absorption and diffusion, as the backbone of industrialization and international competitiveness (e.g., Teubal 1987).[3] They define technological capabilities (TCs) in a very broad sense at all levels of firm activities (i.e., beyond the technique of production) "as *the information and skills – technical, organizational and institutional – that allow productive enterprises to utilize equipment and information efficiently"* throughout the value chain (Lall 1993: 7) [italics added]. Evolutionary theory also considers the interaction of a firm with other firms and the external environment in obtaining inputs in the sale and marketing of its products, and particularly in the innovation of new products and processes.

In contrast to neo-classical theory, under TCB, technology is not freely available; the market fails to develop technological capabilities automatically due to dynamic externalities and linkages, lack of information, uncertainties, risks, and missing and malfunctioning markets. Technological learning involves costs and takes time. It does not take place instantaneously because the required learning is a long, costly, and evolutionary process. It requires purposeful efforts by enterprises as well as government to pursue policies for capability building through R&D, development of knowledge, and organizational change, particularly at early stages of industrialization (Schmitz and Hewitt 1991: 190; Teubal 1996: 449; Moore 1997: 516). Government policies should be both functional and selective. Selective and targeted intervention is especially necessary because learning is technology specific, firm specific, and activity specific, and technologies differ in their tacit features and externalities (Lall 2005). Further, all activities and industries can not be developed at the same time because of the scarcity of skills and other resources (Shafaeddin 2005a).

R&D for the development of domestic technological capabilities and upgrading is the backbone of TCB. R&D is seen as so important even some neoclassical economists advocate it (Baldwin 1969). The experience of many developing countries with traditional import substitution indicate that learning from experience alone is insufficient to amass necessary technological capabilities; appropriate policies are required to overcome market failures constraining the development of technological capabilities (Bell *et al.* 1984).[4] In fact, in the case of Asian NICs (newly industrialized countries), government policies and close cooperation between the government and the private sector were crucial in promoting technological capabilities for industrialization and upgrading and for remedying the related obstacles (see, for example, Lall 2005).

In the age of globalization, government action to enhance a firm's competitive advantage becomes more important than before because the minimum entry barriers and skill requirements have become higher and the risks involved in entering new activities has increased (Archibugi and Michi 1997: 121; Shafaeddin 2005a; Lall 2005). FDI may provide certain skill and marketing channels for exports. Further, it is argued that when an economy opens to trade and FDI, an initial period of imitation will lead to large catch-up opportunities and a shift towards innovation "as the knowledge gap is reduced and the economy's technical maturity rises" (Van Elkan 1996). However, a test of FDI's impact on the industrialization of a developing country is its impact on the development of local capabilities through spillover channels of demonstration effects, training effects, and linkages effects (Paus 2005). Such capabilities can be influenced, *inter alia*, by learning, experience, skill development, and the accumulation of knowledge by the host country's labor force. Generally speaking, the findings of the literature on FDI's spillover effects in the host country is mixed (for a comprehensive review of this literature see: Görg and Greenaway 2004).

While learning and technological development are firm specific, they are also activity specific. For example, "the learning curve differs across quite similar products such as distinct types of memory chips" (Gruber 1992: 885). IT industries, which began at the assembly operation stage in Mexico and China, are both supply dynamic and demand dynamic. They are supply dynamic because they provide important linkages with other industries and have learning effects in the economy via production. They are demand dynamic because international trade in these products has been expanding rapidly during recent decades. While examining the processing industries in Mexico and China, we will, in particular, focus on the development of these industries.

Our aim is to investigate how policies have contributed to the success of China in accumulating the knowledge necessary to enhance local value added in exports, which Mexico has failed to do. Our main focus will be on R&D and its role in the process of industrialization, although other contributing factors to the development of local firm capability will be discussed as well.

From learning to hoping: Mexican industrial strategy under NAFTA

Mexico's industrial strategy has radically transformed over the past quarter century. The goal has remained the same: "catch-up" with the industrialized world in industrial technologies and capabilities. However, the means have changed. Until 1984, meeting the nation's development objectives centered on a government-led model of learning. Since that time, however, the core means to industrialization has been market led. This section shows that, whereas before 1984 Mexico actively pursued the development of technological capabilities through government policy (though not very successfully), in more recent decades government policy has been restricted to creating an FDI friendly environment in the hopes that it would bring technological know-how that would automatically spill over into the broader economy. Mexico has had an advantage over China because it has had privileged market access to the USA through NAFTA since 1995.

Over both periods Mexico has certainly aimed at becoming an industrialized country. Mexico has diversified away from an economy mainly based on primary products, has received unprecedented amounts of FDI, and has significantly boosted exports. However, these inroads have come at considerable cost. Mexico has become plagued by a lack of linkages between foreign firms and the domestic economy, painfully low levels of technological capacity building, low valued added in exports of the maquiladora sector, an overdependence on the United States as a chief export market, and a lack of competitiveness vis-à-vis China.

ISI and industrial learning

In Mexico and elsewhere, the tools of ISI are a number of key policies, including major public investment in infrastructure; import tariffs, licenses, and quotas to buffer domestic firms and enhance their technological capabilities; exchange rate controls; and direct government investment in key sectors (Fernández 2000). Through this process, Mexico attempted to create "national leaders" in the form of key state owned enterprises (SOEs) in the petroleum and steel industries, among others. These sectors were linked to chemical, machinery, transport, and textile industries that also received government patronage (Baer 1971; Amsden 2001). Indeed, in the first decades after the Second World War, these sectors received over 60 percent of all investment, public and private (Aguayo Ayala 2000).

In addition to SOEs and state patronized private industries, Mexico established export-processing zones called maquiladoras in the mid-1960s. Maquiladoras are "in-bond" assembly factories where imports of unfinished goods enter Mexico duty-free provided the importer posts a bond guaranteeing the export of the finished good. Many maquiladoras are located in the US–Mexico border region and include electronics and non-electrical machinery, much of the automotive industry, and apparel. The SOEs, state patronized private enterprises, and maquiladoras supplied growing internal and external markets. From the beginning of the Second World War until the early 1980s, this strategy had mixed results in Mexico. In terms of income growth, this period is often referred to as Mexico's "Golden Age." During this time, the economy grew at an annual rate of over 6 percent, or over 3 percent in per capita terms (Cypher 1990). What's more, public investment appeared to crowd-in private investment. According to one study examining the period of 1950 to 1990, for every 10 percent increase in public investment there was a corresponding bump in gross private capital formation of 2–3 percent (Ramírez 1994).

To some extent, policies geared toward buttressing domestic firms from foreign competition resulted in the learning of complex manufacturing capabilities and the creation of some industries and firms that still exist today. However, because policies were not geared toward the penetration of foreign markets, the learning that occurred was not at the technological frontier and firms could not benefit from the process of learning by competing. Finally, the protective support for industrial learning was not given a well-defined end date and therefore did not provide an incentive for firms to prepare for global competition without support (Fernández 2000). The results were therefore uneven, as reflected in Figure 9.1.

Market-led industrialization

During the late 1970s and early 1980s, much of the industrial development strategy was financed through oil revenue (or borrowing against expectations of future oil revenue). As a result, the Mexican government and private sector embarked upon a period of gluttonous borrowing and public spending. The borrowing binge, coupled with a fixed nominal exchange rate, generated a large external debt and caused rising inflation, growing real exchange rate appreciation, and renewed current account deficits (Kehoe 1995). From 1970 to the early 1980s, Mexico's foreign debt rose from $3.2 billion to more than $100 billion (Otero 1996). When oil prices suddenly dropped in 1982, a time of high world interest rates, Mexico announced that it was unable to meet its debt obligations – a "watershed event" for developing countries (Rodrik 1999). A major devaluation plunged Mexico into economic crisis.

In response to the crisis, Mexico abandoned its state-led industrialization strategy to pursue a market-led strategy. Influenced by international institutions and a rising level of domestic constituents frustrated with past policy, Mexico completely re-oriented its development strategy after the 1982 crisis. The most decisive changes came under President Carlos Salinas de Gortari (1988 to 1994). Salinas articulated three over-arching goals: achieve macroeconomic stability, increase foreign investment, and modernize the economy (Lustig 1998). As in the past, the heart of the plan lay in the manufacturing sector. By opening the economy and reducing the role of the state in economic affairs, Mexico hoped to build a strong and internationally competitive manufacturing sector.

Meeting these goals required a top-to-bottom revamping of Mexico's foreign and domestic economic policies. From 1985 to 2009 Mexico signed over 25 trade or investment deals, with the NAFTA as the capstone (ed. Wise 1998). To make investments less cumbersome for foreign firms, Mexico also reformed its technology transfer requirements. During the ISI period, Mexico's "Technology Transfer Law," was geared toward strengthening the bargaining positions of the recipients of foreign technology. All technology transfers had to be approved by the Ministry of Trade and Industrial Promotion, which monitored the extent to which technology transfer could be assimilated, generated employment, promoted research and development, increased energy efficiency, controlled pollution, and enhanced local spillovers. In 1990, this was dismantled with a new technology transfer law which relinquished all government interference in the technology process to the parties involved in FDI. Government-enforced conditions on technology transfer were phased out and technology agreements no longer needed government approval (although they must be registered). Moreover, the law now contains strict confidentiality clauses (UNCTC 1992).

These trade and investment policies set the stage for FDI in the manufacturing sector to be the engine of Mexican development. There were also changes in domestic policies in order to align the manufacturing sector with the new, neoliberal macroeconomic, trade, and investment policies. In a marked split from the past, Mexico's overarching approach to industrial policy became "horizontal" in nature. Rather than targeting a handful of firms and industries as it had done under ISI, the state was to treat all firms and sectors equally, without preference or subsidy. In a horizontal fashion, the state liberalized imports along with exports, phased out subsidies and price controls, and privatized all but a handful of SOEs (Dussel Peters 1999, 2003).

Performance of the new strategy

The performance of industrial development in Mexico has been uneven, at best. On the one hand, Mexico has structurally diversified away from primary products, technologically upgraded some of its manufacturing export sectors, and increased the level of exports and investment. On the other hand, there has neither been much technological learning for the majority of domestic firms nor has there been linkage between the maquiladora manufacturing enclaves and the rest of the economy. Furthermore, Mexican manufacturing has become dangerously linked to the US economy and is losing competitiveness to China.

Indeed, Mexico has transformed itself from a primary products-based economy to one that is more diversified. In 1940, agriculture accounted for 22 percent of total output. By the early 1970s, agriculture had shrunk to less than 10 percent and in 2005 was just 4 percent of GDP. In 1940, manufacturing was 17 percent of GDP. It reached a peak of 26 percent in 1987 and fell to 18 percent in 2005. The services industry accounted for 50 percent of GDP in the 1960s and close to 70 percent in 2005 (Reynolds 1970; World Bank 2008).

There has also been significant diversity within manufacturing and industrial upgrading in many sectors. Table 9.1 exhibits the top ten Mexican Exports in 1980, 1990 and 2005. Although petroleum is the lead export in each period, the composition of the rest of the top ten is quite different in 2005 than it was in

Table 9.1 Mexico's top ten exports to the world

Rank	Product		
	1980	*1990*	*2005*
1	Petroleum	Petroleum	Petroleum
2	Natural gas	Motor vehicles	Motor vehicles
3	Fruit and vegetables	Power generating machinery	Telecommunications equipments
4	Nonferrous metals	Fruits and vegetables	Television receivers
5	Coffee, tea	Nonferrous metals	Motor vehicle parts
6	Fish	Iron and steel	Office machines
7	Motor vehicles	Electrical machinery	Electricity distribution equipment
8	Textile fibers	Organic chemicals	Lorries
9	Inorganic chemicals	Office machines	Electrical machineries
10	Metalliferrous ores	Miscellaneous manufactures	Electrical circuits

Source: UNCTAD (2008).

1980. By 2005, all of the top ten exports (which comprise approximately 75 percent of total exports) except petroleum are manufactured goods.

The volume of trade and investment has been significant as well. Real exports between 1980 and 2007 increased by a factor of ten and FDI as a percentage of GDP has increased by a factor of three and is close to $20 billion each year (third only to China and Brazil in terms of FDI inflows to developing countries) (World Bank 2008; UNCTAD 2008). The majority of exports and FDI has been in manufacturing, with electronics and auto as the leading sectors.

Finally, there has been some scattered use of advanced technology and processes within the manufacturing sector, chiefly in the *maquiladoras*. Researchers drawing on the experiences of Delphi and General Motors depict two other "generations" of maquiladoras in these firms following the first generation described above. From 1982 until NAFTA, MNCs in the *maquila* industry developed a higher level of technological sophistication and automation, a somewhat more autonomous level of decision making relative to corporate headquarters, and a relative increase in the number of Mexicans in MNC management tiers. In terms of work organization, the gender mix became a bit more balanced and work was performed in a team atmosphere rather than in traditional assembly production. These firms experienced a "third generation" of innovation in the post-NAFTA period, characterized by clusters which are formed around technical centers, assembly plants, suppliers of components, and suppliers of services. There was also a greater level of technological development, with an increasing amount of higher skilled work and engineering capabilities (Carrillo and Hualde 2002).

The increased diversification and rise in the volume of exports and FDI have come at considerable cost. Rather than spurring technological transfer and R&D activities, such transfers have shrunk considerably. FDI has been heavily concentrated by industry and region, is characterized by a growing gap between productivity and wage growth, and has limited linkages with the rest of the Mexican economy (Shafaeddin and Pizarro 2007; Puyana and Romero 2006; Dussel Peters 2008). In a large study covering 52 Mexican industries, Romo Murillo (2002) finds that foreign presence is negatively correlated with backward linkages. Other econometric analyses that looked broadly at the effects of FDI on the Mexican economy between 1970 and 2000 found that investment liberalization was significantly correlated with increases in FDI and subsequent exports, but also led to a higher incidence of imports, the displacement of local firms (Dussel Peters *et al.* 2003), and crowding-out of domestic investment (Agosin and Machado 2005).

Rather than increasing the amount of R&D, FDI has been negatively correlated with R&D; such expenditures by the top 20 foreign firms fell from 0.39 percent of output in 1994 to 0.07 percent in 2002 (Dussel Peters 2008). Technological decisions for MNCs operating in Mexico are largely made in company headquarters far from Mexico, where technological developments occur and often remain (Unger and Oloriz 2000). A major assessment of FDI and R&D and innovation systems in Mexico concluded that

Technological developments occur mainly in the home bases of MNCs and only a small portion is transferred to Mexico. This process ensures, on the one hand, that Mexico participates actively in the globalization of production, and on the other hand, that its participation in the globalization of scientific and technological activities is very poor. As companies transfer only some of their R&D to Mexico ... the present concentration of corporate R&D will by and large lead to an even stronger international divergence of technological development.

(Cimoli 2000: 280)

The assessment attributes the poor performance of Mexico's FDI and trade-led learning strategy to a very weak institutional response by Mexico's fledgling innovation system; low levels of interaction between manufacturing sectors and local institutions (finding that public sector or universities were not collaborating with firms); and low levels of technological capacity and coordination among universities.

The assessment characterizes Mexico as having a "maquila innovation system." This is a system that imports technology and equipment and hosts networking activities by MNCs in a manner divorced from the broader economy. The result has been that knowledge and technological advances are kept in developed economies. Imported inputs lead to replacement of the learning capabilities that could be built in to domestic suppliers of equipment and a virtual wipe out of many of the firms that had capabilities before reforms. Additionally, the personnel working on limited amounts of R&D are doing so solely within a global MNC network largely divorced from interaction with domestic universities and research centers (Cimoli 2000).

These findings are depicted in the two graphs in Figure 9.1. The top graph exhibits production capacity, competitiveness, and sectoral linkages. During the ISI period there was considerable growth in firms' sectoral domestic linkages and an upward trend in the international competitiveness and production capacities of larger exporting firms. During the transition period out of ISI the international competitiveness and production capacities of large firms skyrocketed while the linkages between these exporters and local firms began to diminish in favor of imported inputs. In the post-NAFTA period, the level of competitiveness and capacity reached a plateau (albeit at a high level).

Cimoli's assessment reaches a similar conclusion in terms of technological capabilities, as seen in the second graph. Here, during the ISI period there was a great deal of domestic firm imitation and innovation of technologies, but these capabilities diminished throughout the reform period as larger foreign export firms (namely maquiladoras) increasingly imported technology. The imported technology did lead to an improvement of production processes and the product quality of exporting firms, which is now at the world technological frontier – though largely due to MNC decisions outside of Mexico.

More recently, the gains in trade and investment flows have been jeopardized. Throughout this transition, Mexico has become increasingly reliant on the US

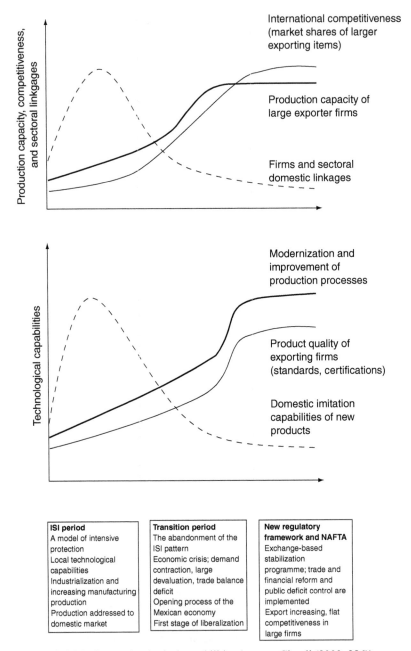

Figure 9.1 Mexican technological capabilities (source: Cimoli (2000: 286)).

economy. By 2005, 86 percent of all Mexican exports were destined to the US and 54 percent of all Mexican imports originated in the US. Thus, when the US economy slows down, the Mexican economy does so as well, as revealed by the 2007–09 global financial and economic crisis.

Perhaps of greater concern is the fact that Mexico is losing its competitive foothold in the US economy despite its close proximity and favorable tariff access. Two separate studies examined the extent to which Mexican exports were under "threat" in the US economy. Threat was defined as whether a sector was losing market share in the US while China was gaining or gaining market share in the US while China gained faster. In 2005, more than 53 percent of all Mexican exports were under some kind of threat and 97 percent of all Mexico's high technology exports (representing 24 percent of all Mexican exports) were under threat (Gallagher *et al.* 2008; Gallagher and Porzecanski 2008). Indeed, many MNCs moved from Mexico to China. A study shows that Mexico has become "proximity dependent." In other words, Mexico is not attracting any new foreign investment in sectors or regions that are not strategic for re-export to the United States (Sargent and Matthews 2007, 2008).

Crossing the river by touching each stone: technological learning in China

Like Mexico, China embarked on a process of economic reform over a quarter of a century ago. Like Mexico, it has sought to attract FDI into manufacturing and high technology sectors in order to gain access to technology and marketing channels for exports. Nevertheless, China's industrial development is very different from Mexico's in two important ways. First, in contrast to Mexico's rapid opening of markets and integration into the world economy, China has taken a more gradual and experimental approach to integration, upgrading, and industrial development. Secondly, alongside reforms, China continued a parallel set of targeted government policies to support and nurture industrial development. These policies have been geared toward learning through R&D and training to develop the capabilities of domestic firms in order to increase value added in exports.

From Mao to the market: economic reform in context

In a somewhat similar fashion to Mexico, China underwent a period of state-led industrialization from the late 1940s until 1978. This period has been referred to as the period of "Big Push Industrialization." As in Mexico, during the Big Push the Government's goal was to move towards rapid industrialization through import substitution. The basic strategy was to invest in strategic industries identified by government decision-makers. The industries selected included those with the largest potential for backward linkages. Integration with the global economy was extraordinarily low (Naugthon 2007).

Eighty percent of the targeted industries were "heavy" industries, such as steel, which were linked with coal, iron ore, machinery, and other sectors. A number of other industries such as chemical fertilizers, motor vehicles, and electric generating equipment were also among those created by the government. Almost all of these industries were dominated by a State Owned Enterprise (SOEs) and the planners assigned them production targets and prices. The government also allocated labor force to industrial firms. Through one lens this effort was successful as the industrial base of the country was created. From 1952 to 1978, industrial output grew at an annual rate of 11.5 percent and the share of industrial sector in GDP increased from 14 to 44 percent while the share of agriculture fell from 51 to 28 percent (Naugthon 2007).

However, these policies also involved some shortcomings. First and foremost, the focus on industrialization neglected the growth of household consumption and the development of the countryside. Whereas capital formation grew at more than 10 percent per year from 1952 to 1978, private consumption grew only 4.3 annually. Employment generation was also low, given the capital-intensive nature of the main targeted industries. Perhaps the gravest shortcoming was the lack of technological capabilities of the targeted firms. Further, human capital formation did not expand enough for these sectors to become efficient and competitive internationally (Naugthon 2007).

Chinese economic reforms started in 1978, two years after the death of Mao Zedong. In this year, China embarked on a program of economic reform aimed at strategic integration into the world economy by following a "dual track" policy. The policy consisted of liberalizing FDI and the inflow of imported inputs to selected industries, while buttressing these sectors to the point of maturity and nurturing other sectors until they were ready to face competition with imports. Since then, according to the literature, China's industrial strategy has been three-pronged. First, government policy aimed at creating endogenous productive capacity, in the form of targeting specific industries through state ownership (SOEs) or government support; paying increasing attention to science and technology policy; and linking the SOEs with the private sector and research institutes. Second, and very importantly, Chinese support for domestic industry has always had an eye on markets outside of China. China has also gradually and strategically integrated into world markets in order to gain access to technology, finance, and world markets. Third, in undertaking economic reform, China's new leaders followed an experimental approach and a much less certain attitude toward reform than in Mexico. The Mexican Government was ideologically committed to reforming towards a market economy and free trade. In a sense, free trade and a market based economy was seen as an end in and of itself in the case of Mexico; it was taken for granted that such a transition would enhance learning through trade and lead to the deepening of industrialization and promotion of growth. By contrast, Chinese policy used the market and trade as a means to development. Hence, for Chinese policy makers, market and government policies were to supplement each other while the weight of each would change as the economy would develop.

It was never conceivable to Chinese policy-makers that their economy would postpone economic development until after an interlude of system transformation. It was always assumed that system transformation would have to take place concurrently with economic development, and indeed that the process of economic development would drive market transition forward and guarantee its eventual success. Individual reform policies were frequently judged on the basis of their contribution to economic growth (rather than to transition as such). In the beginning the approach was followed because reformers literally did not know where they were going: they were reforming "without a blueprint" and merely seeking ways to ameliorate the obvious serious problems of the planned economy. But even after the goal of a market economy gradually gained ascendance in the minds of reformers, it was not anticipated that market transition would be completed until the economy reached at least middle-income status. And in fact, that is exactly what eventually happened.

(Naugthon 2007: 86).

Deng Xiaoping referred to this strategy as "crossing the river by feeling each stone," (Naugthon 2007). This approach stands in stark contrast to the Washington Consensus approach adopted in Latin America and Mexico, which advocated swift "shock" transitions to a market economy (Williamson 1990).

China's gradual and experimental approach to reform allowed for the development of domestic firms and industries before liberalizing fully. More importantly, it also created an environment in which the potential "losers" from liberalization would be less numerous (Naugthon 2007). Components of market and planned economies coexisted in this dual track policy, which has been referred to as a socialist market economy in the literature (see, for example, Singh 1993).

The role of R&D

Unlike in Mexico, where it was assumed technology would be transferred through trade and FDI, conscious attention to science and technology (S&T) policy and research and development (R&D) has been a cornerstone of China's industrial development and integration into the world economy. The Chinese government learned in practice that technology acquisition from abroad through MNCs alone will not necessarily lead to the transfer and development of technology; there was a need for increasing the absorptive capacity of domestic firms and the development of indigenous technological capacity building. To accomplish this, the strategy of the Chinese government included government support; indigenous R&D and innovation investment within individual firms; and creation of R&D institutions. It also included alliance among firms in a strategic industry and their cooperation with research institutes and universities, as well as foreign firms (Qian 2003).

Government policy included direct investment; provision of guidance; institutional and financial support; creating a favorable environment for innovation; the introduction of competition into the domestic market for the strategic industries (e.g., telecommunication); and development of national standards and patents for main IT products (Wang *et al.* 2007; Fan *et al.* 2007: 359). The S&T strategy of the Government also aimed to upgrade the industrial base of the country. It was selective, targeted, and responsive to the market dynamic with growing emphasis on the private sector (including MNCs). Beginning in the early 1980s, China implemented a number of policies that not only aimed at conducting basic research but also put equal emphasis on the deployment and diffusion of technology. Table 9.2 provides a snapshot of China's key S&T policies between 1982 and 2000 (see also the case of Mobile communication industry and high-definition disc player industry below).

The government apparatus for guiding S&T consisted of six different entities: the Chinese academy of Science together with five relevant Ministries, including the Ministry of Information Technology, which was specifically created for supporting IT industries (Xiwei and Xiangdong 2007: 318). The national system of innovation was geared to basic research as well as R&D in selective activities. The 863 Programme (1986) aimed at high basic and applied research in seven areas and 15 topics with the cooperation of private enterprises. The seven areas included, in order of priority given by the planners, information technology, laser, automation, biotechnology, new material technology, astro-technology and energy technology (Fan and Watanabe 2006: 311). The "climbing program" of 1992 was oriented towards the acceleration of basic research. By contrast, from its inception in 1988, the Torch program was market-oriented and geared mainly towards the commercialization of R&D results. Its objectives ranged from enabling an environment for high-tech industries to creation of high-tech zones, executing projects in the aforementioned selected areas, and training and facilitating international cooperation (Fan and Watanabe 2006: 312). In 1995 the government passed the "Decision on Accelerating Scientific and Technological Progress" in order to intensify technological development (Walsh 2003: 105).

The Ninth Five-Year Plan (1996–2000) specifically emphasized the development of capabilities to increase domestic value added in assembly operations in the computer industry and its peripherals. This was followed by an emphasis on innovation in integrated circuits and software technology in the Tenth Five Year Plan (2001–05) under the so-called "Golden Projects" (Xiwei and Xiangdong 2007: 321).

The National System of Innovation (NIS) was dynamic in terms of both institutional development and the change in the relative role of government and private enterprises. The S&T system in China consisted of universities, research institutes, and public and private enterprises, including foreign firms. The interrelationship between universities/research institutes and industry is unique (Chen and Kenney 2008). Furthermore, the system went through continuous reforms in terms of policies and the involvement of actors in R&D. To benefit from "collective efficiency" through clustering, a number of high-tech zones (technology parks) were established (by 1992, 52 high-tech zones had been established) (Xiwei and Xiangdong 2007: 319).[5]

Table 9.2 Development of China's national innovation system

Policy	Dominant feature	Year
Key technology R&D program	Encouraging efforts in key technologies	1982
Resolution of the reform of S&T system (CCCP)	Adopting flexible system on R&D management	1985
Sparkle system 5	Promoting basic research in agriculture	1985
863 program	High-tech promotion	1986
Torch program	High-tech commercialization, high-tech zones	1988
National S&T achievements spreading program	Promoting product commercialization	1990
National engineering technology research centre program	Technology transfer and commercialization of research	1991
Climbing program	Promoting basic research	1992
Endorsement of UAEs by SSTCC	Promoting university and industry linkage	1992
S&T progress law	Technology transfer, S&T system reform	1993
Decision on accelerating S&T progress (CCCP)	Promoting URI-industry linkage	1995
Law for promoting commercialization of S&T achievement	Regulating the commercialization of S&T achievement	1996
Super 863 program	Commercialization, break-through in key areas	1996
Decision on developing high-tech industrialization	Encouraging technology innovation and commercialization	1999
Guidelines for developing national university science parks	Accelerating the development of university science parks	2000

Source: Xiwei and Xiandong (2007).

Close links were also developed among enterprises, universities, and research institutes. Further, commercialization of R&D was encouraged. In particular, the role of private enterprises in R&D increased significantly over time. Table 9.3 shows the evolution of R&D in China from 1987 to 2003 where the number of R&D institutes increased by 67 percent. By 2003, however, the number of public institutes decreased while the private sector (enterprise)-led institutes more than doubled. This trend is mimicked in terms of spending. In 1987, 60.7 percent of R&D expenditure was undertaken by public institutes. By 2003, the share of the private sector was 62.4 percent and that of research institutes and universities was 36 percent (Table 9.3). The distinction between private and public entities involved in R&D is, however, blurred as some state universities and research institutes own enterprises engaged in research (Chen and Kenney 2008).

Expenditure and policy has not been horizontal, but has been targeted to specific sectors and industries as outlined above. In allocating R&D expenditures, China has targeted a handful of sectors, namely the electronics, semiconductor, and automotive sectors, to eventually serve as "national champions" (Xiwei and Xiangdong 2007).

The results of the implementation of S&T policy for China are striking when compared with Mexico's experience. Table 9.4 shows that, on average, more patents are filed in China each year than in all of the Latin American countries (LACs) combined, let alone Mexico. Furthermore, whereas in LACs only 13 percent of all patents are held by residents, in China that figure is above 75 percent. Similar results are also evident when comparing the number of scientific articles published by Chinese scholars with the number published by Latin American scholars.

Moreover, the relative importance of inventions has increased sharply over time (Table 9.5). It is true that the share of domestic firms in total patents and in patents granted for invention has decreased since China's accession to the WTO in 2000 because of the increasing involvement of foreign companies in China. Nevertheless, the number of invention patents granted to domestic firms has accelerated sharply during the period from 2000 to 2005. The annual average growth rate of invention patents granted to domestic firms was 27.3 percent

Table 9.3 Evolution of R&D in China, 1987 to 2003

	Number of R&D institutes		R&D expenditure (in 100 million yuan, %)	
	1987	2003	1987	2003
Public Research Institutes	5,222	4,169	106.8 (60.7)	399 (25.9)
University R&D Units	934	3,200	7 (4)	162.3 (10.5)
Enterprise R&D Units	5,021	11,300	62.1 (35.3)	960.2 (62.4)
				1,521.5
Total	11,177	18,669	175.9 (100)	521.5 (100)

Source: Xiwei and Xiandong (2007).

Table 9.4 Selected science and technology indicators

	1980–2005	*2000–05*
East Asia and Pacific		
Patent applications, nonresidents	27,119	64,234
Patent applications, residents	17,387	44,106
Patent applications, resident share	**64.12%**	**68.66%**
Research and development expenditure (% of GDP)	0.89	1.09
Scientific and technical journal articles	11,505	24,804
China		
Patent applications, nonresidents	24,236	58,876
Patent applications, residents	18,785	43,509
Patent applications, resident share	**77.51%**	**73.90%**
Research and development expenditure (% of GDP)	0.98	1.21
Scientific and technical journal articles	10,386	22,979
Latin America and the Caribbean		
Patent applications, nonresidents	19,044	29,850
Patent applications, residents	3,792	4,056
Patent applications, resident share	**19.91%**	**13.59%**
Research and development expenditure (% of GDP)	0.57	0.57
Scientific and technical journal articles	9,666	16,472
Mexico		
Patent applications, nonresidents	7,051	12,745
Patent applications, residents	540	498
Patent applications, resident share	**7.65%**	**3.91%**
Research and development expenditure (% of GDP)	0.39	0.41
Scientific and technical journal articles	2,026	3,488

Source: World Bank (2008).

during 2005 as compared with 18.3 percent during 1990–2000. As a result, the share of invention in total patents granted to domestic firms has almost doubled from 2000 to 2005.

Training

In tandem with R&D, China has a high level of support for tertiary education and training. Over 20,000 scientists and engineers graduate from Chinese universities each year (MOST 2006). The high level of education in science and technology, as well as the existence of facilities for vocational education, facilitates the training of skilled manpower for technological development. In 2005, the number of graduates in the fields of science and technology from universities and junior colleges was 1,256,000, or over 1,000 per million people. In the same year the corresponding number of graduates from postgraduate courses was 95,000, or over 90 per million.[6] Continuous attention to education was a characteristic of the overall Chinese development strategy before, as well as after, the reform period. According to the World Bank, government expenditure on tertiary

Table 9.5 The share of invention in granted patents (1990–2005)

	1990	2000	2005
Share of invention in total granted patent	16.9	12	24.9
Share of domestic invention in total invention	29.9	48.7	38.8
Share of invention in total domestic patent	5.9	6.5	12.1

Source: People's Republic of China (2006).

education per student was 90 percent of GDP per capita in 1999 (in Mexico that figure was 48 percent for the same year) (World Bank 2008).

Comprehensive information on the training program of the government is lacking. Nevertheless, there are indications that the government focussed on enhancing high-tech skills and education by establishing state funded training centers (Walsh 2003: 71). Some universities were also involved in training, with a number of them benefiting from partnership with MNCs for training in addition to R&D (Walsh 2003: 83). The Beijing University of Post and Communication is one example of cooperation with MNCs in training. Foreign investors also independently provided some training to local staff (Walsh 2003: 96).

The government created a large number of vocational schools. In 2005, there were 198,566 vocational schools in China, out of which 11,611 were secondary schools and 4,230 were technical training. The number of graduates for vocational secondary schools increased over 21 times between 1978 and 2005. Furthermore, the government policy to send students abroad helped the development of domestic skills in research and development even though some of them never returned to China. The combination of these factors allowed rapid expansion of persons engaged in scientific and technical activities in more recent years, resulting in an increase by over 21 percent during 2001–05 when 3,810,000 people were engaged in this area. There remains, however, a lack of upper management staff despite the fact that some Chinese who have studied and worked abroad have returned to the country.

Other measures to build-up capabilities of national enterprises

In contrast to Mexico, the main motivation to develop domestic firm capabilities was the realization by the government and national enterprises that the transfer of technology from MNCs did not occur automatically (Fan *et al.* 2007: 360). Under joint ventures there was a limit to the transfer of technology to Chinese partners (Walsh 2003: 113). The effort to develop capabilities of domestic firms, in turn, simulated the rivalry among MNCs to be involved in the R&D programs of domestic firms in order not to be denied access to the large Chinese market.

The Chinese Government has followed a gradual and dual policy in developing the capabilities of domestic enterprises. It has gradually increased the role of private firms in the process of industrialization and export expansion. For example, the share of private enterprises in exports increased to 18 percent in 1985 and to 60 percent in 2005 (Naugthon 2007). At the same time, it has implicitly, or explicitly, established a division of labor between SOEs and private enterprises. Private enterprises have focused, as expected, on short-term opportunities, low-cost production, and high profitability. By contrast, SOEs concentrated on long-term goals through investment to develop new products rather than profitability per se (Li and Xia 2008). In their efforts, SOEs benefited little from the spill-over effects of MNCs (Girma, Gong, and Gorg 2008). SOEs were privileged to have better access to government funds and loans from the banking system (Li and Xia 2008).

In their applied R&D, SOEs benefited from a program called "National Science and Technology Diffusion" which was specifically designed for, and devoted to, them. This strategy is criticized for not having market oriented goals in the case of SOEs. In our view, however, it has been plausible to reform SOEs gradually in order to prevent the long-term objectives of the government from being undermined; SOEs had social objectives and responsibilities in addition to their long-term technological goals.

To provide sources of investment for domestic firms, China established two funds: the Export Development Fund for the larger firms and the Fund for Small and Medium Enterprise Incursions into International Markets for suppliers. The government also offered value-added tax refunds to exporting firms, and the Chinese Export–Import Bank provided loans with preferential interest rates.

Chinese domestic firms enjoyed the advantage of familiarity with the domestic market as well as allocation of a significant part of the domestic market to them by the government (e.g., in the telecom equipment industries) (Fan *et al.* 2007: 358). Still, the newcomer domestic firms in China, like enterprises in other developing countries, suffered from two main disadvantages, as compared with MNCs, in the development of capabilities for and commercialization of new technology: resource disadvantages and reputation disadvantages, particularly in the IT sector where the technology is complicated and changes rapidly (Gao *et al.* 2007). A number of firms were given incentives as well as support by the government that, coupled with some capabilities developed during the import substitution period, allowed them to break into the market by developing frontier technologies (see below). In addition to support from the government, the leading domestic firms collaborated with customers and cooperated with MNCs (Gao *et al.* 2007).

The role of FDI

The contribution of MNCs to the financial resources needed for R&D has been small. Nevertheless, they have become increasingly involved in R&D in China. Foreign high-tech R&D in China has gone through three phases: explanatory and strategic partnership (early-mid 1990s), expansion (mid-late 1990s), and consolidation (late 1990s to the present) (Walsh 2003: 86–91). During the 1990s, MNCs role in R&D represented more of a "show" than genuine action since engaging in R&D was a pre-condition for obtaining approval to establish joint ventures. During the second phase, MNCs started to expand training centers. It was only during the third phase that the MNCs became interested in moving up the value-added production chain to upgrade their products and thus needed to invest in local R&D (Walsh 2003: 86–91).

Meanwhile, the Chinese government also provided MNCs "a range of preferential policies, including tax rebates, construction loans, access to modern facilities and other incentives," particularly in the case of IT industries (Walsh 2003: xiii and 56). While encouraging foreign firms to undertake R&D in China, the authorities initially entered into partnerships with a number of foreign firms to create inter-firm rivalry and to accelerate technological development (Walsh 2003: 77–8 and 80–2). As a result, wholly foreign-owned firms established R&D facilities in the country (Walsh 2003: 79). Attracting multiple foreign partners was particularly successful in the IT industry. It is estimated that around 120 to 400 foreign R&D centers were operational in 2003 (Walsh 2003: xiv). All main MNCs involved in the IT industry have established R&D centers in China. In Beijing alone, 18 main centers were established between 1993 and 2003.[7] Domestic firms also benefited, to some extent, from partnerships with MNCs. For example, Legend, Stone, Founder and Great Wall learned a great deal about modern manufacturing in addition to technology development (Walsh 2003: 79). Nevertheless, the Chinese authorities realized that joint ventures with MNCs alone would not be sufficient for technology transfer.

Generally speaking, in China, unlike Mexico, FDI has crowded in domestic investment as government efforts aimed at building the capabilities of domestic firms. As predicted by The Theory of Capability Building (TCB), enabling domestic capabilities in turn motivated MNCs to invest in R&D. As domestic firms were involved in the development of technological capabilities, many MNCs were motivated to join them in their R&D in order to access the domestic market, particularly since the government also provided them with other incentives.

In China, efforts to indigenously develop technological capabilities and bring such technologies to market have been coupled with the targeted but aggressive acquisition of foreign technologies through foreign direct investment. The strategy has been to either develop a sector or technology nationally, or to "import" the technology through FDI. Initially, licensing FDI was conditional to arrangements for the transfer of technology and provision of linkages to local firms, joint ventures, and partnership. In 2001, such conditions have been dropped, however the government encourages MNCs to invest in R&D, particularly in information technology, "by offering a range of preferential policies" that include tax rebates, construction loans, access to modern facilities, and other incentives" (Walsh 2003: xiii and 56). Whereas national Mexican firms only capture approximately 5 percent of the inputs of foreign firms, in China that number is well over 20 percent (Gallagher and Zarsky 2007).

Summary and implications for development policy

It is clear from this analysis that Mexico and China have followed very different paths for acquiring technological capabilities. Mexico was the "champion of liberalization" but China may be described as new-developmental – evocative, but not a clean replication, of the NIC developmental states (see: ECLAC 2001). Alongside reform, China put in place functional and targeted government policies.

Perhaps more importantly, we have shown how Mexico's strategy was to dismantle a past set of policies and China's strategy was to build new policies for the future. Mexico knew where it wanted to be and thought it had an easy way to get there: dismantle the old policies and learning and growth would follow. China also had the same goal but was more modest about how to achieve it. China has implemented a two pronged policy. While reforming the economy, it has taken a more gradual and experimental approach to liberalization and integration into the world economy. Meanwhile, it has continued a parallel set of targeted policies in support of the development of indigenous capabilities for technological learning.

As early as 1990, the Mexican Government relinquished all interference in the technology process, leaving it entirely to the parties involved in FDI. MNCs were also provided various incentives, particularly in export processing zones, without having to meet performance commitments. Economic liberalism also led to a reduction in government investment in R&D, education, and training. The assumption was that the market forces would take care of these issues.

Through trial and error, China has learned that reliance on market forces and FDI alone will not automatically lead to the transfer of technology and increase value added in exports. There was a need to develop the capabilities of domestic firms. While formulating and implementing a comprehensive but selective and targeted strategy aimed in particular at IT industries, the government developed an institutional framework for S&T development and a dynamic national system of innovation. It consisted of the Chinese Academy of Science, relevant ministries, private enterprises, universities, and research institutes. Close links were established among these entities in the public and private sectors. Both basic research and the application and diffusion of technology have been emphasized from the early 1980s.

A shortcoming of this analysis is that it lacks a full examination of the independent effect that these government policies have on learning and industrialization relative to other facts – such an undertaking is an impossible one given the limits of current data and methods. Nevertheless, the results of our study are consistent with those of a number of other empirical studies in the TCB literature of capability building theory and other new developmentalist literature (Wade 1990; Paus 2005; Puyana and Romero 2006; Amsden 2001; Paus and Gallagher 2008; Singh 1993; Chang 2005; Shafaeddin 2005b; Lall 2005). This body of literature makes a strong case for the need of government support in the pursuit of industrialization to nurture domestic firms in a globalizing world. The contrast between the economic philosophy and policies of Mexico and China decisively confirms this general finding.

Notes

1 The authors email contacts are Shafaeddin@gmail.com and kpg@bu.edu respectively. This chapter draws from an article by the same authors that appeared in *Technology and Society*.
2 See for example the reference in (Bruton 1998: 930). There are at least two versions of TCB. Lazonick's (1991) theory is concerned basically with large firms of developed countries and thus not discussed here.
3 For a good presentation and development of the theory see (Lall 1993).
4 For more details see (Pizarro and Shafaeddin 2007).
5 They were mainly located in Beijing, Shanghai, and Shenzhen. Sixty-seven percent of 33,392 high-tech enterprises were located in high-tech parks (Fan *et al.* 2007: 356).
6 Based on (People's Republic of China 2006), Tables 21–13 and 21–9.
7 They include Intel, SAP, Motorola, Lucent, Turbolinux, Nokia, IBM, Ericson, Agilent, Mirosoft, Matsushita, NEC, and Samsung (Chen 2008: Table A1).

References

Agosin, M. R. and Machado, R. 2005. "Foreign investment in developing countries: Does it crowd in domestic investment?" *Oxford Development Studies*, 33(2), 149–62.
Aguayo Ayala, F. 2000. "La estructura industrial en el modelo de economia abierta en Mexico." Mexico: John D. and Catherine T. MacArthur Foundations.
Amsden, A. H. 2001. *The Rise of the Rest: Challenges to the West from Late-Industrialization Economies*. Oxford: Oxford University Press.
Archibugi, D. and Michie, J. 1997. "Technological globalisation or national systems of innovation?" *Futures*, 29(2), 121–37.
Arrow, K. J. 1962. The Economic Implications of Learning by Doing. *The Review of Economic Studies*, 29(3), 155–73.
Baer, W. 1971. "The role of government enterprises in Latin America's industrialization." In: D. T. Deithman, ed., *Fiscal Policy for Industrialization and Development in Latin America.* Gainesville: University of Florida, 263–92.
Baldwin, R. E. 1969. "The Case against Infant-Industry Tariff Protection." *The Journal of Political Economy*, 77(3), 295–305.
Bell, M., Ross-Larsen, B., and Westphal, L. 1984. "Assessing the Performance of Infant Industries." *Journal of Development Economics*, 16(1/2), 101–28.
Bruton, H. J. 1998. "A Reconsideration of Import Substitution." *Journal of Economic Literature*, 36(2), 903–36.
Carrillo, J. and Hualde. A. 2002. "La maquiladora electronica en Tijuana: hacia un cluster fronterizo (Electronic Maquiladoras in Tijuana: Towards a Border Cluster)." *Revista Mexicana de Sociología,*64(3), 125–71.
Chang, H.-J. 2005. *Why Developing Countries Need Tariffs: How WTO NAMA Negotiations Could Deny Countries' Right to a Future*. Geneva: South Centre.
Chen, K. and Kenney, M. 2007. "Universities/research institutes and regional innovation systems: the cases of Beijing and Shenzhen." *World Development*, 35(6), 1056–74.
Chen, Y. C. 2008. "Why Do Multinational Corporations Locate Their Advanced R&D Centres in Beijing?" *Journal of Development Studies*, 44(5), 622–44.
Cimoli, M. 2000. *Developing innovation systems: Mexico in a global context*. New York and London: Continuum.
Cypher, J. M. 1990. *State and capital in Mexico: Development Policy Since 1940*. Boulder, Colorado.; Oxford: Westview Press.

Dussel Peters, E. 2008. *Invesion extranjera directa en Mexico: desempeño y potencial.* Mexico City: Siglo XXI.

Dussel Peters, E. 2007. "Opportunidades en la relacion economica y commercial entre China y Mexico." CEPAL-UNAM, Santiago.

Dussel Peters, E. 2005. "Economic opportunities and challenges posed by China for Mexico and Central America," Deutsches Institut für Entwicklungspolitik, Bonn, www. die-gdi.de/CMS-Homepage/openwebcms3.nsf/%28ynDK_contentByKey%29/ENTR-7BMJL2/$FILE/Studies%208.pdf.

Dussel Peters, E. 2003. "Industrial Policy, Regional Trends, and Structural Change in Mexico's Manufacturing Sector." In: Middlebrook, K.J. and Eduardo Zepeda, eds., *Confronting Developing, Assessing Mexico's Economic and Social Policy Challenges.* Stanford: Stanford University Press.

Dussel Peters, E. 1999. "Reflexiones sobre conceptos y experiencias internacionales de industrializacion regional." In: CRD and E. D. Peters, eds., *Dinamica Regional y Competitividad Industrial.* Mexico City: Editorial JUS.

Dussel Peters, E., Lara, J. J. P., and Gomez, G. W. 2003. *La industria Electronica en Mexico: Problematica, Perspectivas y Propuestas.* Guadalajara: Universidad de Guadalajara.

ECLAC. 2001. *Economic survey of Latin America and the Caribbean.* Santiago: United Nations.

ECLAC. 1999. *Foreign Direct Investment in Latin America, 1999.* Santiago: United Nations.

Fan, P., Gao, X., and Watanabe, K. N. 2007. "Technology strategies of innovative Chinese domestic companies." *International Journal of Technology and Globalisation,* 3(4), 344–63.

Fan, P. and Watanabe, C. 2006. "Promoting industrial development through technology policy: Lessons from Japan and China." *Technology in Society,* 28(3), 303–320.

Fernández, J. 2000. "The Macroeconomic Setting for Innovation." In: Cimoli, M. ed., *Developing Innovation Systems: Mexico in Global Perspective.* New York and London: Continuum Books.

Gallagher, K. P. and Porzecanski, R. 2008. *Climbing up the Technology Ladder? High Technology Exports in China and Latin America.* Berkeley: Center for Latin American Studies, University of California Berkeley.

Gallagher, K. P. and Zarksy, L. 2007. *The Enclave Economy: Investment and Sustainable Development in Mexico's Silicon Valley.* Cambridge, Mass.: The MIT Press.

Gallagher, K. P., Moreno-Brid, J. C., and Porzecanski, R. 2008. "The Dynamism of Mexican Exports: Lost in (Chinese) Translation?" *World Development* 36(8): 1265–80.

Gao, G., Hin Chai, K., Liu, J., and Li, J. 2007. "Overcoming 'Latecomers Disadvantages' in Small and Medium-sized Firms: Evidence from China." *International Journal of Technology and Globalization,* 3(4): 364–83.

Girma, S., Gong, Y., and Gorg, H. 2008. "Foreign Direct Investment, Access to Finance, and Innovation Activity in Chinese enterprises." *World Bank Economic Review,* 22(2): 367–82.

Görg, H. and Greenaway, D. 2004. "Much ado about nothing? Do domestic firms really benefit from foreign direct investment?" *The World Bank Research Observer,* 19(2), 171–197.

Gruber, H. 1992. "The learning curve in the production of semiconductor memory chips." *Applied Economics,"* 24(8), 885–94.

Kehoe, T. J. 1995. "A Review of Mexico's Trade Policy from 1982 to 1994." *The World Economy,* 18(4), 135.

Krugman, P. 1984. "Import protection as Export Promotion: International Competition in the Presence of Oligopoly and Economics of Scale." In H. Kierzkowzki, ed., *Monopolistic Competition and International Trade*. Oxford: Clarendon Press, 180–93.

Lall, S. 2005. Rethinking Industrial Strategy: The Role of the State in the Face of Globalization. In: K. P. Gallagher, ed., *Putting Development First: The Importance of Policy Space in the WTO and IFIs*. London: Zed Books.

Lall, S. 1993. "Policies for building technological capabilities: lessons from Asian experience." *Asian Development Review*, 11(2), 72–103.

Lazonick, W. 1991. *Business organization and the myth of the market economy*. Cambridge: Cambridge University Press.

Li, S. and Xia, J. 2008. "The roles and performance of state firms and non-state firms in China's economic transition." *World Development*, 36(1), 39–54.

Linder, S. B. 1961. *An essay on trade and transformation*. New York: John Wiley.

Lucas, R. E. 1988. "On the Mechanics of Economic development." *Journal of Monetary Economics*, 22(1), 3–42.

Lustig, N. 1998. *Mexico: the remaking of an economy*. 2nd edn. Washington, D.C.: Brookings Institution.

Moore, R. E. 1997. "Learning-by-Doing and Trade Policy in a Developing Economy." *The Journal of Developing Areas*, 31(4), 515–28.

MOST. 2006. *National High Tech R&D Program*. Beijing: Ministry of Science and Technology of the People's Republic of China.

Naugthon, B. 2007. *The Chinese Economy: Transitions and Growth*. Cambridge, Mass.: MIT Press.

Nelson, R. R. and Winter, S. G. 1982. *An Evolutionary Theory of Economic Change*. Cambridge, Mass.; London: Belknap Press.

Otero, G. 1996. Neo-liberal Reform and Politics in Mexico. In: G. Otero, ed., *Neo-Liberalism Revisited: Economic Restructuring and Mexico's Political Future*. Boulder, Colorado: Westview.

Paus, E. A. and Gallagher, K. P. 2008. "Missing Links: Foreign Investment and Industrial Development in Costa Rica and Mexico." *Studies in Comparative International Development (SCID)*, 43(1), 53–80.

Paus, E. 2005. *Foreign Investment, Development, and Globalization: can Costa Rica become Ireland?* Basingstoke: Palgrave Macmillan.

People's Republic of China. 2006. *Statistical Yearbook*: Beijing.

Pizarro, J. and Shafaeddin, M. 2007. From Export Promotion to Import Substitution; Comparative Experience of China and Mexico, "International Conference on Policy Perspectives on Growth, Economic Structures and Poverty Reduction," Beijing, June 2007, UNCTAD, 3–9.

Puyana, A. and Romero, J. 2006. "Trade liberalization in Mexico: some Macroeconomic and Sectoral Impacts and Implications for Macroeconomic Policy." *International Development association (IDEAS) and UNDP conference on Post Liberalization constraints on Macroeconomic policies*, January 27–29, 2006.

Qian, Y. 2003. "China's Transition to a Market Economy: How Far Across the River?" In: N. C. Hope, M. Yang Li, and T. Yang, eds., *Chinese Policy Reform at the Millennium*. Stanford, Calif.: Stanford University Press.

Ramírez, M. 1994. Public and Private Investment in Mexico, 1950–1990: An Empirical Analysis. *Southern Economic Journal*. 61(1), 1–17.

Reynolds, C. W. 1970. *The Mexican economy: Twentieth century structure and growth*. New Haven & London: Yale University Press.

Rodrik, D. 1999. *The new global economy and developing countries: making openness work.* Washington, D.C.: Overseas Development Council.

Romer, P. M. 1987. "Growth Based on Increasing Returns Due to Specialization." *The American Economic Review*, Papers and Proceedings of the Ninety-Ninth Annual Meeting of the American Economic Association, 77(2), 56–62.

Romer, P. M. 1986. "Increasing Returns and Long-Run Growth." *The Journal of Political Economy*, 94(5), 1002–37.

Romo Murillo, D. 2002. "Derramas Tecnologicas de la Inversion Extranhera en la Industria Mexicana." *Comercio Exterior* 53(3): 230–43.

Sargent, J. and Matthews, L 2009. "China vs. Mexico in the Global EPZ Industry: Maquiladoras, FDI Quality, and Plant Mortality." *World Development*, 37(6), 1069–82.

Sargent, J. and Matthews, L. 2008. "Capital Intensity, Technology Intensity, and Skill Development in Post China/WTO Maquiladoras." *World Development*, 36(4), 541–59.

Sargent, J. and Matthews, L. 2007. "China vs. Mexico in the Global EPZ Industry: Maqiladoras, FDI Quality and Plant Mortality." University of Texas Pan American Center for Border Economic Studies, Austin, Texas.

Schmitz, H. and Hewitt, T. 1991. "Learning to Raise Infants: A Case Study in Industrial Policy." In C. Colclough and J. Manor, eds., *States or Markets? Neo-liberalism and the Development Policy Debate.* Oxford: Clarendon Press.

Shafaeddin, M. 2005. "Friedrich List and the Infant Industry Argument." In K. S. Jomo, ed., *The Pioneers of Development Economics, Great Economists on Development.* London and New York: Zed Books.

Shafaeddin, M. 2005a. "Towards an Alternative Perspective on Trade and Industrial Policies." *Development and Change*, 36(6), 1143–62.

Shafaeddin, M. 2005b. *Trade policy at the crossroads: the recent experience of developing countries.* Basingstoke: Palgrave Macmillan.

Shafaeddin, M. and Pizarro, J. 2007. "From Export Promotion to Import Substitution: Comparative Experience of China and Mexico." University Library of Munich, Germany.

Singh, A. 1993. *The Plan, the Market and Evolutionary Economic Reform in China.* Geneva: UNCTAD.

Teubal, M. 1996. "R&D and technology policy in NICs as learning processes." *World Development*, 24(3), 449–60.

Teubal, M. 1987. *Innovation performance, learning, and government policy: selected essays.* Madison, Wisconsin: University of Wisconsin Press.

UNCTAD. 2008. *World Investment Report.* Geneva: United Nations.

UNCTC. 1992. *Foreign Direct Investment and Industrial Restructuring in Mexico.* New York: United Nations Centre on Transnational Corporations.

Unger, K. and Oloriz, M. 2000. "Globalization of Production and Technology." In: M. Cimoli, ed., *Developing Innovation Systems: Mexico in Global Perspective.* New York: Continuum Books.

Van Elkan, R. 1996. Catching up and slowing down: Learning and growth patterns in an open economy. *Journal of International Economics*, 41(1–2), 95–111.

Wade, R. 1990. Governing the market: economic theory and the role of government in East Asian industrialization. Princeton, N.J.; Oxford: Princeton University Press.

Walsh, K. 2003. *Foreign High-Tech R&D in China; Risks, Rewards, and Implications for US–China Relations.* Washington, D.C.: The Henry L. Stimson Centre.

Wang, Q., Wang, H., and Li, M. 2007. "Industrial standard based competition and Chinese firm strategic choices." *International Journal of Technology and Globalisation*, 3(4), 422–36.

Williams, J. 1990. *Latin American Adjustment: How Much Has Happened?* Washington, D.C.: Institute of International Economics.

Wise, C. ed. 1998. *The Post-NAFTA Political Economy: Mexico and the Western Hemisphere.* University Park, Pennsylvania: The Pennsylvania State University Press.

World Bank. 2008. *World Development Indicators.* World Bank.

Xiwei, Z. and Xiangdong, Y. 2007. "Science and technology policy reform and its impact on China's national innovation system." *Technology in Society*, 29(3), 317–25.

10 Growth and development in Africa

Challenges and opportunities

Leonce Ndikumana

Introduction

The history of African economic development in the post-independence era teaches us a number of lessons that are of great relevance for the continent's growth prospects in the post-2007–09 global financial and economic crisis (global crisis) era. A number of growth dilemmas are worth highlighting in this context. First, while African countries have been able to achieve high levels of growth, they have been unable to sustain them for an extended period. Indeed, growth has been characterized by booms and busts; volatility and instability have been the key characteristics of post-independence development in Africa. It is estimated that the average African country has experienced at least two episodes of such cycles since the 1960s (Ndulu *et al.* 2008; Arbache and Page 2007). One important contributing factor to growth instability is the high dependence on primary commodities trade, exposing economies to terms of trade shocks. Indeed, most growth spurts and collapses have been driven by terms of trade shocks.

The second dilemma is that growth has remained "elusive" – to borrow Easterly's (2002) expression – in the sense that even when growth was achieved, it remained a mirage for the majority of the population. The gains from growth in terms of social development have remained limited, uneven, and very slow to materialize. A key reason is that the foundations of growth have remained narrow, as a result of the failure of structural transformation in most African economies. A related reason is that growth has typically been jobless, hence the slow improvement in living standards.

Third, Africa's growth has been a story of chronic and widening financing gaps. The gap between domestic saving and demand for private and public investment has forced African countries to rely heavily on external financing. However, until recently, African countries have remained below the radar screen of international private investors, hence relying primarily on official loans and grants. The growth collapses of the 1980s and 1990s were to a large extent the result of a financing crisis, as African countries were suffocated by ballooning external debts. Africa's inability to mobilize domestic resources is an important reason for its inability to reach and sustain high levels of growth.

The dependence of African countries on external financing is partly the cause of the heated debate over the gains from official development aid. The story of aid and African development can be summarized as simply "not enough": not enough aid to close the resource gap; not enough results to show for the volume of aid received. Today, Africa is receiving much more aid than it received in the 1970s. Aid has allowed countries to finance important development programs, especially in the social sector; it has supported countries in post-conflict reconstruction, in addition to emergency aid during crises. Countries that have been able to establish a supportive policy environment and developed appropriate leadership have and will continue to reap substantial gains from aid in terms of social development. Yet, for the majority of African countries, the gains from aid have simply not been enough.

The quest for globalization has brought a number of dilemmas of its own. Africa has engaged with globalization, embarking on sustained reforms aimed at opening its markets for trade and investment. However, globalization has increasingly marginalized the continent in the world economy. While African trade has increased substantially, its share in global trade remains small, both in absolute value and relative to its population share. Africa's exports represent only 3 percent of global exports (Figure 10.1).

Similarly, the continent remains on the sideline of financial globalization. While the continent has been able to attract a rising volume of private capital

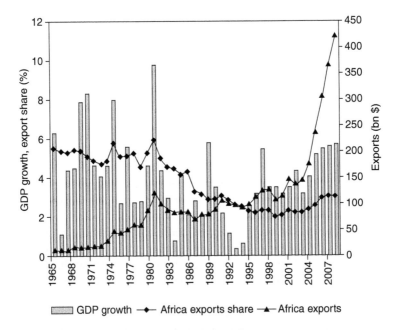

Figure 10.1 Africa's growth and exports (total and share in world trade), 1965–2007 (source: African Development Bank and UNCTAD databases; 2009(f) = forecast from AfDB/OECD/UNECA (2009) *African Economic Outlook* (2009)).

over the past decades, its share in total capital flows remains small. The continent accounts for about 10 percent of total foreign direct investment (FDI) to
low- income countries (Figure 10.2).

It is true that limited integration in global financial markets has helped shield
Africa from the first-round effects of the global crisis. However, this is of little
comfort as limited integration also undermines the continent's ability to raise
private capital to fill the widening resource gaps caused by the global crisis as
shown in Figure 10.2.

The global crisis highlighted more than ever before the growth and development dilemmas faced by African countries. It has made these dilemmas even
more prominent and the need for a policy response more urgent. This global
crisis is different from earlier crises that hit the continent in that it is not of
Africa's own making. It is not due to financial distress arising from excessive
borrowing as in the 1980s and 1990s; it is not a result of social conflict and
political instability, which has been the origin of growth collapses in several
countries. Yet, it has been just as, if not more, devastating as the earlier crises.
However, this global crisis has also provided a platform for a systematic reex-
amination of the growth and development models African countries have followed since independence. The global crisis has demonstrated that African
countries have indeed based their growth on weak foundations. The continent
must seize this opportunity to rethink its growth strategies and its position in
the global economy. It is critically important that the continent not let a major
crisis go to waste.

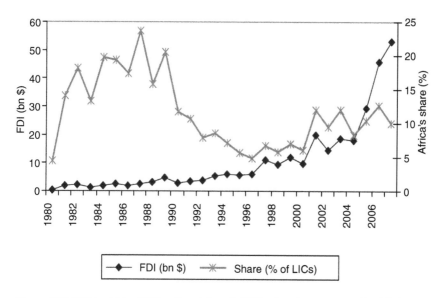

Figure 10.2 FDI to Africa (billion $) and share in FDI to low-income countries (%) (source:
African Development Bank and UNCTAD databases; 2009(f) = forecast from
AfDB/OECD/UNECA (2009) *African Economic Outlook* (2009)).

African recent economic performance

Trade-led growth

Since the turn of the century, and before the global crisis, African countries have recorded higher growth, prompting observers to talk of a turn from the stagnation of the 1980s and 1990s (Figure 10.3). This higher growth was attributed to internal as well as external favorable factors. Internal factors include improved macroeconomic conditions and strong performance of key sectors, including services. External factors include strong global demand for, and high prices of, African commodity exports, increased resource inflows (including debt relief and more aid), as well as private capital flows.

However, by and large, the key factor for growth in Africa has been trade. In fact, in recent years, African trade has increased faster than global trade. As a result, Africa's share in global trade is increasing, although it remains small relative to the size of the continent in terms of population. The share of African trade increased steadily from 1998 (1.9 percent) to 2007 (3 percent). Episodes of export growth tend to also be characterized by high growth (Figure 10.1). Commodity price booms drive export booms, as natural resources represent a large share of Africa's exports. Oil exports alone account for more than half of the continent's GDP growth.

Growth: good but not good enough

Despite the substantial growth recovery since the turn of the century and before the global crisis, recorded growth is good but not good enough. Two main reasons account for this skepticism. First, while growth rates are higher, they are still below thresholds needed to substantially reduce poverty. Second, and relatedly, high growth has not yet generated substantial gains in terms of poverty reduction.

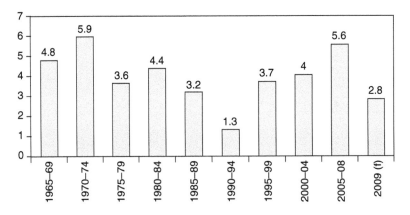

Figure 10.3 Africa's real GDP growth rate (%), 1965–2009 (source: AfDB, OECD, UNECA, 2009. African Economic Outlook 2009. Tunis, Paris, and Addis Ababa).

Given the high levels of poverty in many African countries, growth rates of 5–6 percent are good, but simply not good enough. In 1999, the United National Economic Commission for Africa estimated that African countries needed to grow by at least 7 percent per annum to reach the Millennium Development Goals (MDGs) by 2015. Very few countries have been able to record such growth rates on a consistent basis. There are several reasons why growth has not been high enough and that the gains in poverty reduction have been limited. First, growth has been driven by sectors with little employment creation potential. This is especially the case for the capital-intensive oil sector. Second, high growth rates have not lasted long enough to establish a sustained rise in per capita incomes or to stimulate savings and domestic investment. Sustained high growth rates are also necessary to attract foreign capital, an important ingredient of capital formation and private sector development. In addition, the lack of accompanying redistributive policies perpetuates inequality. In the context of high inequality, growth may even increase poverty levels.

So Africa has not really turned the corner!

The foregoing analysis raises three important questions:

> Question 1: If current growth is not enough, how can growth rates be raised?
> Question 2: Africa has been here before; how is high growth sustained?
> Question 3: The "people" have not seen the growth dividends; how can gains from growth be enhanced by equitable distribution?

Question 1: how to increase growth rates?

A key reason for African countries' inability to reach high growth rates is an inadequate increase in productivity. Historical evidence indicates that productivity growth is a primary driver of long-term growth in developed and emerging market economies. Africa has failed to initiate a productivity growth take-off and this is the main reason for the low levels of growth recorded throughout the post-independence period.

Low productivity is prevalent in all sectors and raising it will require targeted and systematic strategies to alleviate sector-specific constraints to productivity growth. In the case of agriculture, the focus must be on increasing agricultural infrastructure such as irrigation infrastructure, rural roads to connect producers to input and output markets, electrification, and drinking water systems to reduce water-born diseases so as to increase labor productivity. In addition, African countries have lagged behind other developing regions in technological innovation in agriculture. The green revolution has bypassed Africa, and the continent has not benefited from other agriculture productivity enhancing technological breakthroughs. Farmers in today's African villages are still utilizing the same techniques as their grandparents, on land that has deteriorated in fertility. It is not surprising that yields have not increased, implying that the capacity of the land to feed people is much lower today than in the 1960s. As seen in Table 10.1, net agricultural production in Africa is lower in 2007 compared to 1970 (with an index of 99 in 2007 compared 110 at the 1999–2001 base).

In the manufacturing sector, a key constraint to productivity growth is high production costs, both direct and indirect. Direct costs are high mainly due to poor infrastructure. Africa lags behind other regions in most areas of infrastructure in both quality and quantity. The percentage of paved roads in sub-Saharan Africa is half the average of low-income countries (Table 10.2). The continent also suffers from locational disadvantage relative to input markets, both of which raise transport costs and production costs. Indirect costs primarily arise from the administrative and regulatory environment. In many African countries the cost of doing business is so high that it discourages investment and trade. These high costs explain to a large extent Africa's struggle in developing its manufacturing sector. Growth of manufacturing was the main cause of Asian countries growth over the past decades. Africa largely remained on the sidelines. In fact, Africa's share in global manufacturing value added fell over the past decades, from 0.4 percent of total in 1980 to 0.3 percent in 2005. Its share of manufactured exports also declined during the same period (Page 2009).

Increasing growth rates will require substantial change on various margins, including policy framework, better sectoral policies, harnessing natural resources, and investing in natural resource "discovery." Macroeconomic policy frameworks in African countries have typically been conservative, focusing on establishing and sustaining macroeconomic stability by controlling inflation and preserving exchange rate stability. The underlying assumption is that achievement of macroeconomic stability unlocks trade and investment, thereby providing a basis for raising growth. The evidence on African countries does partly support that precept, as illustrated by rising growth rates in the 2000s following episodes of painful economic reforms. However, macroeconomic stability is

Table 10.1 Net agricultural production per capita, 1970–2005 (index base 1999–2001 = 100)

	1970	1980	1990	2000	2007
Africa	110	95	95	99	99
East Africa	135	116	107	98	100
Central Africa	150	126	116	99	89
North Africa	85	81	84	98	106
Southern Africa	124	129	112	105	100
West Africa	97	74	83	99	98
Caribbean	148	125	123	102	93
South America	72	78	82	99	114
Asia	60	64	81	100	113
Eastern Europe	132	132	144	97	113
LDCs	117	104	97	99	105

Source: FAO, FAOSTAT (http://faostat.fao.org).

Table 10.2 Some indicators of infrastructure availability, Africa compared to other regions

	Improved water source (% of population with access), 2004	Fixed line and mobile phone subscribers (per 100 people), 2006	Paved roads (% of total roads), 2000
Sub-Saharan Africa	56.1	14.5	11.9
Low and middle income	79.9	44.4	26.8
Middle East and North Africa	89.5	52.6	62.8
World	82.7	59.5	35.9

Source: African Infrastructure Country Diagnostic database.

only part of the story. While it does provide incentives for investment from a risk perspective, it does not overcome other structural constraints to investment and trade, notably the shortage of finance. In fact, when macroeconomic stability is achieved via tight monetary policy, this discourages trade and investment due to high credit costs. Hence, the policy makers in Africa will continue to face this policy dilemma associated with the trade-off between gains from tight monetary and fiscal policy in terms of macroeconomic stability and losses in terms of depressed domestic demand. The global crisis has already led policy makers to initiate expansionary policies, notably through a reduction of bank lending rates to boost consumption and investment. There is definitely a need for a shift in policy orientation towards a more flexible and growth oriented macroeconomic framework.

A shift toward a growth oriented macroeconomic framework presents important challenges itself, most notably a lack of adequate policy instruments to reach growth targets. The advantage of the narrow policy frameworks currently followed by African countries is that they require a limited number of instruments to achieve inflation targets, namely monetary tools (money supply and the interest rate). Once the set of goals is expanded to include real targets such as growth and employment, then more instruments need to be activated to reach those goals. Credit policies are among such instruments which have been used successfully in the case of Asian countries. A detailed discussion of the application of these policies in the case of African countries is provided in Pollin *et al.* (2006) in the case of South Africa; Pollin *et al.* (2007) in the Case of Kenya; and Epstein and Heinz (2006) in the case of Ghana. The key is to design mechanisms to increase access to credit for the private sector in general, but especially for sectors and activities which have been identified as having the highest potential for employment creation in addition to large output multipliers. The mechanisms include three important complementary strategies: (1) credit subsidies for targeted sectors/activities; (2) loan guarantee schemes to encourage lending to these targeted sectors/activities; (3) an increased role of development finance institutions. In the case of the latter strategy, the key is to fill the financing gaps faced by the primary drivers of growth and employment creation, namely agriculture, non-agriculture rural activities, and small and medium enterprises (Ndikumana 2009).

Many African countries can still grow much faster by better harnessing their natural resource endowment. Resource-rich African countries have grown faster than their resource scarce counterparts, but it is believed that these growth rates are still below their true potential. A more efficient exploitation of the natural resource endowment can allow African countries to grow faster. This involves negotiating better rents with international extraction companies in terms of taxes and royalties. It also involves more investment in discovery. It is indeed believed that a substantial amount of underground resources have yet to be discovered. However, both discovery and management of resources are "government intensive," in the sense that they require adequate management capacity to deal with the complexities of the sector specific technology and business model.

Unfortunately in many cases such capacity is still lacking. African countries could gain much by committing to invest a share of the revenue from natural resources into building capacity in these areas. This is an investment whose returns are certain and large.

Question 2: sustaining high growth

Almost all African countries have been able to record a high GDP growth rate some times, but very few have been able to do so on a consistent basis. In other words, growth volatility has been a perennial feature in the economic history of the continent (see eds. Ndulu *et al.* 2008). The challenge then is how to sustain high growth so that it can have the expected impact on social development. This chapter emphasizes three pillars of any national strategy for sustaining growth: (1) rethinking comparative advantage: from "God-made" to "man-made" comparative advantage; (2) increasing the resilience of the economy to shocks; (3) preserving macroeconomic stability while raising growth.

(1) RETHINKING COMPARATIVE ADVANTAGE: FROM "GOD-MADE" TO "MAN-MADE" COMPARATIVE ADVANTAGE

African countries have been too comfortable following an ill-advised strategy for too long: selling their natural resources for cheap in exchange for expensive imported intermediate and consumption goods as well as physical capital (equipment). In other words, they have allowed nature to dictate their relationship with the rest of the world. As a result, the continent has experienced growth spurts and growth busts, driven primarily by terms of trade shocks. As can be seen in Figure 10.4, terms of trade deteriorated throughout the 1980s and 1990s as growth also deteriorated, and improved since the turn of the twenty-first century when growth also recovered.

Breaking away from this pattern requires breaking away from resource dependence by developing other areas of comparative advantage that utilize other resources and take advantage of technological advances. The continent needs to exploit opportunities in technological innovation, thus "leap frogging" in the development path towards integration into the global economy. The continent could thereby overcome its structural impediments to growth such as geography and distance from the centers of global trade.

(2) INCREASING THE RESILIENCE TO SHOCKS THROUGH DIVERSIFICATION

Sustaining high growth rates requires building more resilient economies. As discussed above, this requires moving away from dependence on natural resources. Resource-rich countries in fact have a better chance of achieving this goal by utilizing resource revenues to finance new activities, targeting those with the highest value addition and greatest potential for growth and employment creation. Thus these economies can stimulate a steady process of economic transformation by moving up the value chain and developing market niches regionally and globally.

The continent must design a solid industrial policy that promotes manufacturing and key areas of the service sector. At the moment, Africa trails other continents in manufacturing production (Page 2009). The focus must be on strategies to alleviate structural and regulatory constraints on expansion of the manufacturing and service sectors. These include investments in key hard and soft infrastructure (electricity, transport infrastructure, water, information and communication technology, and trade logistics) and strengthening and streamlining regulation. These strategies will help reduce the cost of production and improve the general business environment – another area where Africa is still lagging behind.

(3) PRESERVING MACROECONOMIC STABILITY WHILE RAISING GROWTH

Macroeconomic stability remains an important pre-requisite for raising and sustaining high growth rates. This is important for stimulating investment, saving (efficiency in portfolio decisions), consumption, and trade. It is also important for attracting foreign capital. It serves as a seal of approval from the public that the government is in control of the economy, thus establishing the needed credibility to encourage private activity. However, it must be understood that macr-

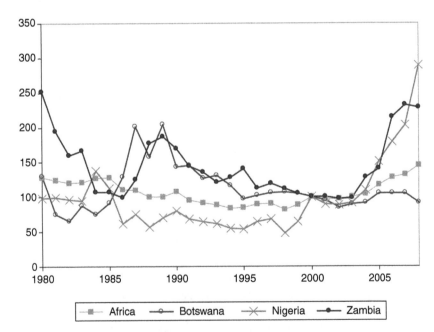

Figure 10.4 Terms of trade (annual percentage change) (source: AfDB database).

oeconomic stability is not an end in and of itself; it is, and must be seen as, a means to the end of achieving higher growth and eventually higher living standards. In a growth/employment oriented macroeconomic framework, two important qualifications are worth emphasizing with respect to macroeconomic policy. With regard to inflation control, it is important to emphasize that effective inflation control must combine policies that manage aggregate demand with those aimed at stimulating the supply side of the economy. Indeed, in many African countries, spurts in inflation often originate from supply shortages, especially food. So in these cases, inflation control is not just controlling money supply, it is ensuring adequate food supply.

With regard to public finance, the focus is too often on containing an unqualified public expenditure aggregate as a component of domestic demand. Rather, the goal should be efficient expenditure management aimed at promoting the most productive public expenditures, such as infrastructure and human capital investments. Through appropriate allocation of public spending, any short run effect of expansionary fiscal policy is likely to be offset by the positive impact on supply through expanded productive capacity. Hence fiscal policy can be an effective and potent instrument for a growth oriented macroeconomic program; a dividend sacrificed in a narrow view of fiscal policy that only considers the impact of public spending on aggregate demand. For these positive supply side effects to materialize, public spending must be efficient. That means a careful selection of public investment programs with adequate provision for the maintenance of infrastructure to preserve its quality.

Ultimately creating macroeconomic stability is a way to achieve two other goals: the diversification of the economy and the building of a more resilient economy. Hence, strategies at the macroeconomic and sectoral level must be seen as complementary.

Question 3: increasing the impact of growth on poverty reduction

In most African countries poverty remains high despite improvements in the growth performance before the global crisis. The evidence suggests that poverty tends to respond very slowly to growth acceleration (Arbache and Page 2007). Asymmetrically, growth decelerations cause disproportionate increases in poverty. This may be due primarily to three factors. First, a large number of Africans are just barely above the poverty line, so that even a marginal loss in income causes a slide back into poverty. Second, growth is often accompanied with less than proportional increases in employment. Yet, access to employment remains the most reliable means for allowing the poor to overcome poverty. Third, high levels of inequality still prevail in many African countries. As a result, growth dividends are unequally distributed, and the poor typically get excluded. In fact, growth may even increase income inequality, in which case growth can coexist with rising levels of poverty. A typical example is the ballooning numbers of poor people in African urban centers amid increasing aggregate prosperity.

These facts call for "mainstreaming" poverty reduction into national development policies, as it has been embedded into the Poverty Reduction Strategy
Papers (PRSPs). Three particular points need to be emphasized here. First, to
substantially increase the gains from growth in terms of poverty reduction, the
priority must not be on poverty reduction per se, but on income creation. Before
one can redistribute income, income must be created in the first place. Hence,
the starting place is a pro-growth national strategy.

Second, employment creation must feature prominently as an objective of
major national policy frameworks, notably macroeconomic policy framework,
sectoral policies, PRSPs, rural development policies, financial development policies, trade policies, policies guiding relationships with trade partners (including
new trade partners), and globalization policies in general, among others.

Sectoral policies can play a critical role in achieving the poverty reduction
objective through employment creation. This requires mechanisms for encouraging and supporting activities with the highest employment creation potential, both
directly and indirectly through upstream and downstream linkages. This holds for
government interventions as well as those of donors. In particular, agriculture must
return to the center stage of poverty reduction strategies. Despite widespread
acknowledgement of the critical role of this sector for African economies, it has
received relatively less financial support than would be dictated by its share in
output and employment. Aid for agriculture has declined systematically over the
years, from an already low 5 percent in 2000 to only 2.8 percent in 2006 (Figure
10.5). This is less than one third of the share going to humanitarian aid.

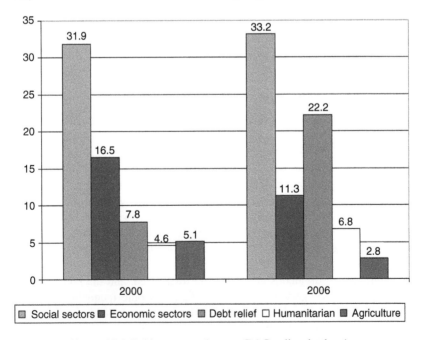

Figure 10.5 Share of DAC aid per sector (source: DAC online database).

Third, policies for raising the impact of growth must address the critical problem of inequality: "No citizen must be left behind." African countries exhibit high levels of inequality compared to countries in other regions with comparable income levels. Within Africa, middle-income Sub Saharan African (SSA) countries exhibit higher levels of inequality compared to low-income countries.[1] North African countries enjoy both low levels of poverty and low level of inequality.

At the aggregate level, beyond income inequality per se, inequalities arise in the areas of access to public services, access to assets, and access to finance. These inequalities have a direct impact on poverty. Limited access to these services worsens living standards by exposing the poor to health risks and limiting social mobility, which is typically achieved through education. Unequal access to public services also perpetuates inequities in opportunities for integration into the mainstream economy, thus trapping the poor in the informal sector where returns to labor are low.

The causes of inequalities at the aggregate level and across segments of the population are often political, arising from the structure of the polity and the dynamics of power. This generates what is often termed "horizontal inequality," between social groups and regions. Hence in some countries large inequalities in access to public services are observed along regions, the same way power is demarcated along regional lines. Thus, Ngaruko and Nkurunziza (2000, 2005) observe that access to education was higher in Southern Burundi under the military regimes because it was the region of origin of the military rulers. Similarly, the imbalance of power in Uganda to the advantage of the Center and the South is also reflected in the imbalance of access to public services between the two regions compared to the North, which scores much worse in all areas of human and social development (Ndikumana and Nnanyonjo 2005). Therefore, strategies for increasing gains from growth must include measures to redress inequality across population groups and regions. This requires the deliberate decision to focus investment in historically disadvantaged regions, areas, or social groups.

Going from here to there: we need a model

The foregoing discussion reveals that the challenges facing African countries are immense and that an urgent response to these challenges is required, despite the magnitude of the task at hand. It is also clear that business as usual won't do. African countries need to do things differently, capitalizing on successful experiences while designing strategies to address failures. In addition, the global crisis has made imperative the need to revisit the growth model pursued by African countries thus far.

However, in doing so policy makers must resist the temptation of easy dichotomization, which is typically counterproductive. It is not a matter of choice between markets and the government, between market fundamentalism and state fundamentalism, or between export-led growth and inward oriented growth. African countries have made those and similar choices before with poor results, and often damaging effects. The appropriate growth model will need to combine the relevant elements of each approach to address a country's particular circumstances, unlocking its potential while alleviating its structural constraints.

What African countries need then is an exercise in "balancing" policy choices. In particular, they must find a balance between (1) government and markets, (2) export-led growth and strong domestic and regional markets, (3) short-term crisis response mechanisms and strategies for addressing structural constraints to long-term growth. The difficulty is that there is no pre-assembled model or framework for each African country to utilize to advance its national development agenda. Each country will need to design its own while attempting to reach the three levels of balancing. In doing so, policy makers must engage in three-dimensional thinking:[2] (i) think back/again; (ii) think across; (iii) think ahead.

Thinking back/again

African policy makers need to carefully review their country's past experiences with development policy to identify what worked and what did not. This would then allow them to avoid past mistakes and bank on acquired positive experiences. As indicated earlier, most African countries have been able to record high growth rates at some point. In cases where these growth rates were driven by commodity booms, they typically evaporated as soon as the booms ended. Countries failed to take advantage of booms to build assets as a source of future income and as a cushion for the impact of negative shocks on commodity exports and prices. Unfortunately, this has happened repeatedly. Now policy makers know that commodity booms do not last forever. They also must know that commodity booms need not be a curse. The challenge is to design strategies to make resources a true asset for building the foundations for sustained growth.

In many cases high growth rates were not necessarily attributed to commodity booms. For example, the growth performance at the turn of the twentieth century in many countries has been attributed to successful implementation of stabilization policies. Good reformers generally scored well in increasing their growth rates, demonstrating that consistency in policy reforms does pay off. This is an important lesson for African countries going forward. And now the challenge is to resist any temptation of policy reversal as a result of pressure from the negative effects of the global crisis.

Thinking across

Some countries in Africa and elsewhere have been successful in reaching and sustaining high rates of growth for extended periods. These countries must have been doing something right that others can emulate. The idea is to identify best practices in Africa, and in other developing countries, that can inspire a national strategy for stimulating a growth take-off and sustaining it over time. However, care must be exercised to adapt strategies to country-specific circumstances.

They also must be adapted to era-specific conditions. Indeed the world has changed, and with globalization and innovations in all areas, what was once possible may no longer be feasible today. What was allowable then may no longer be allowable today given current global conventions, agreements, and market conditions. The reality is also that in some cases, African countries may not have the opportunity to climb the same ladder that others used to reach the top of the development hill, as those on the top often engage in "kicking away the ladder" as Chang (2003) so eloquently put it. It is up to each African country to identify strategic partners that are willing to lend a helping hand in its search for a viable growth plan. This means that African countries will have to not only strengthen existing alliances but also build new ones to better position themselves in the globalized and more competitive world.

The African landscape also offers good examples of successful growth models. Despite the negative impact of the global crisis, classic African success stories still have much to offer others in terms of growth strategies. On the one hand, Mauritius and Tunisia are good examples of successful export diversification; the two countries have been able not only to generate good growth rates, but also to weather the storm of the global crisis much better than others. Botswana, on the other hand, teaches us that good political and economic governance needs to be supported by a good diversification policy to sustain high levels of growth. The country has the governance capacity and credibility it takes to design and implement strategies for building a more resilient economy through diversification. In that context, the global crisis could be a good opportunity for a major rethinking of the country's growth strategy. Also, success in doing so could serve as an inspiration for other resource-rich countries.

Think ahead

Good development strategy must always stay ahead of the curve. Sound development policy cannot be limited to managing chaos and responding to crises. In fact, many crises happen exactly because development policy has not been forward looking enough. Many agree that the current global crisis originated from a financial crisis caused by myopic, lax regulatory policy that allowed undisciplined finance to grow unchecked, to the point where risk became unsustainable. The real economy took a back stage to financial exuberance, only to be crushed by the financial meltdown. Similarly, many agree that the food crisis in Africa was a result of a long period of policy amnesia in which agriculture was abandoned. Declining investments and inadequate technological innovation in the sector lead to lower production and stagnation in productivity. As a result, supply continued to lag behind demand and food security was eroded. Yet another example is climate change shocks, which are a result of utilization systems of natural resources and manufacturing technologies that are only focused on short-term benefits and pay little attention to long-term costs. A final example, which applies to developing countries in general and African countries in particular, is poor infrastructure quality, which is generally the result of poor planning/budgeting of maintenance infrastructure. Hence, more often than not, the focus is on new roads when maintenance would be much cheaper.

The focus on short-term results is often a result of the urgent need to solve real developmental problems. Unfortunately, a myopic approach to the resolution of urgent development problems can ultimately create more problems in the future than it solves. It may put down a small fire today while leaving the society exposed to chaos of a bigger proportion in the future. Myopic policymaking is also often due to political interests dominating economic interests. The time horizon of policy making becomes constrained by the political term in office. Thus the policy maker discounts heavily the costs of resolving the big future chaos while weighing heavily the gains from putting down the small fires today.

The question then is what environment generates forward looking policy making. This raises the issue of leadership: we do need good leadership to operate whatever growth/development model is envisioned to get African countries to higher levels of growth.

A model needs leadership for implementation

Designing and implementing a development strategy is "government intensive." It requires credibility, accountability, and security (broadly defined). Two useful scenarios arise. The first is that of a benevolent authoritarian leader, who sees the welfare of the future generations as a positive function of his/her own welfare. We call this the "visionary authoritarian leader." This leader enjoys the benefits of full control over the polity and economy so that once an agenda is decided upon, he/she faces no political constraints to implementation. The second is that of a leader who is bound by institutional mechanisms accountable to the people, more commonly referred to as "democratic governance." Both models will definitely generate superior results to those under autocratic regimes. The challenge for African countries is how to generate these kinds of leadership.

What can Africa expect from the development partners?

In rethinking its growth model, Africa also needs to re-examine its relationships with its development partners. In particular, it is important to assess the gains from aid in relation to its trends, its allocation, and its effectiveness. Much has been written and said on the impact of aid on growth in Africa and other developing countries. Thus far, the evidence is quite mixed. Sachs *et al.* (2004) consider aid an indispensable part of a solution to Africa's growth/poverty traps by initiating a "big-push," launching the continent on a high growth path. Others posit that aid can help stimulate growth only if the right institutional conditions are fulfilled (see Collier and Dollar 2002). Others are critical of the very idea that aid could have an impact on growth at all (Easterly 2006).

In the case of Africa, the reality is that the continent has received a considerable amount of aid over the past decades. However aid remains largely below the actual financing needs of the continent. The perennial gap between investment demand and savings on the one hand, and export revenues and import demand on the other, constitute a structural constraint to an investment-led growth take off. Because of the inability of the continent to mobilize sufficient domestic resources and attract sufficient private capital flows, it has constantly relied on official development aid. But it is clear that, once again, the continent is confronted with another dilemma of "not enough": not enough development aid to meet the need; aid has not been predictable enough to allow adequate planning of development programs; and not enough development outcomes to show for all the aid received. So one may legitimately wonder: "where has all the aid gone"? Rethinking the relationship between Africa and its development partners for the purpose of putting the continent on a high growth path will require addressing all three dilemmas.

Not enough aid to meet demand: scaling up aid pledges and honoring commitments

The recent years have seen a renewed commitment to increasing aid to Africa, starting with the 2005 Gleneagles Summit where G8 countries committed to doubling aid to Africa. This commitment has also been expressed through specific initiatives such as the Global Fund for the fight against malaria and TB and the US Millennium Challenge Account in favor of the African continent. However, the delivery has remained much below expectations. For example, less than half of the pledges made at the Gleneagles Summit have thus far been delivered. Activities under the Global Fund remain chronically under funded. The global crisis made matters worse. On the African side, financing gaps widened; on the donor side the ability and willingness to disburse more aid diminished. While the April 2009 G20 Summit committed to scaling up financing for development through restocking the coffers of the Breton Woods Institutions, the real challenge remains the ability to deliver timely and sizable resources to the continent in times of exploding needs. The global crisis raises the urgency of scaling up aid delivery to Africa. At the same time, it offers a great opportunity for investing in African development and making Africa a part of the solution to the global economic problem. The credibility of the continent's development partners is at stake; it is time for action, not just new pledges.

Not enough predictability of aid: harmonization of aid processes with national planning cycles

The current aid delivery processes have been plagued by lack of harmonization and unpredictability of aid, making it difficult for African countries to adequately plan and implement their development programs. Donor preferences have predominantly dictated the allocation of aid resources across sectors. Aid disbursements have been slow due to, among other things, rigid and often antiquated procedures. As a result, aid is not there when it is needed, and when it does arrive, it is often not at the place where it is needed the most.

The various high level forums between donors and the continent have called for more aid harmonization and alignment with national development strategies. Such a call was made in September 2008 in Accra, Ghana at the High Level Forum on Aid Effectiveness and reiterated in Doha in November 2008. Nonetheless, the results on the ground remain disappointing.

Harnessing new development partnerships

The emergence of Africa's new trade and aid partnerships is likely to have a major impact on aid architecture. China, in particular has become a major trading partner with Africa. From 2001 to 2007, Africa's exports to China increased from $4.7 billion to $34.5 billion.

Imports experienced a similar increase over the same period (Figure 10.6). The rise of China, India, and other countries (Korea, Brazil, etc.) as economic partners has already ignited heated debates about the implications for aid coordination, aid effectiveness, and aid conditionalities. The new partners, especially China, bring a new vision to aid and trade relationships. Whereas traditional partners have emphasized donor's national interests and, at least in principle, institutional considerations (including human rights and democratic governance), the new players advocate for business relationships aimed at advancing the interests of both partners. This has made Africa's traditional partners visibly uncomfortable, arguably because of the risk of aid condoning, or even supporting, regimes with a poor governance record. But equally important is the stiff competition the new players have brought in the quest for investment and markets in the continent.

It is evident that the new players, especially China, have a clear agenda for their relationship with Africa. The new model has blurred the lines between aid

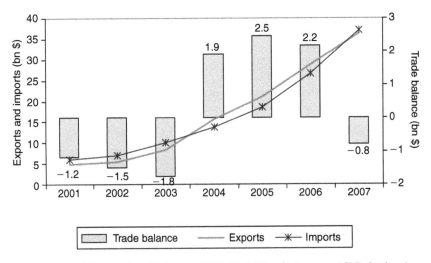

Figure 10.6 Africa's trade with China, 2001–07 (billion $) (source: AfDB database).

and investment, where the two are often a package deal between the host country and China. Such deals ultimately amount to barter trade, whereby China provides infrastructure investment in exchange for the rights to resource exploitation. The West has cried foul, arguing that African countries are being shortchanged in the process. A classic case is the multi-billion dollar deal with the Democratic Republic of Congo (DRC), where the country is to get major infrastructure assets in exchange for mineral resource extraction rights. While it is possible that the deal favors China on a net basis, it is undeniably true that the DRC will receive real assets in exchange for its mineral resources. For decades, starting from the colonial era, the West has exploited the country's mineral resources, and the country has not seen much in exchange in terms of real assets. At least in the new model, it can claim roads, railways, hospitals, and schools that will benefit its people.

The emergence of new development partners offers Africa an important opportunity to diversify its sources of financing – including aid and FDI – as well as its export markets. However, to take full advantage of such new opportunities, African countries must develop a clear strategy of engagement with the new trade and development partners. This strategy must be designed to advance the national development agenda. In doing so, African countries may want to consider a regional approach to dealing with the new development partners, both to increase their bargaining power and to advance the regional integration agenda. It is important to identify areas of investment and trade where the interests of China and Africa converge. Infrastructure investment at the national and regional level is one such area. Engagement with China, India, Korea, and other new partners can help alleviate the severe shortage of funding that constrains the development of national and regional infrastructure.

For increased African voice and representation in the global arena

Thus far, Africa has been on the sidelines of the global debates on development policy, regulation and governance of finance, trade, and institutions. Yet these debates shape the continent's prospects for growth and development as well as its access to global markets and finance. This marginalization is a result of inadequate representation of the continent in key global regulatory bodies, such as the Breton Woods Institutions, the G20, and other forums. Even when the continent is represented, its effective influence on the processes is very limited.

The global crisis has provided an opportunity to reiterate the call for greater empowerment of African countries to effectively influence the debate on international financial affairs, articulate their interests, and be an integral part of global standards setting and monitoring mechanisms. In particular, African membership in the G20 needs to be formalized and its membership in critical global regulatory bodies such as the Financial Stability Forum (FSF) needs to be increased (only South Africa is currently a member of the FSF and G20).

Moreover, voting rights at international financial institutions, which are currently based on shareholdings, must be revised to remove the bias in favor of rich countries and to recognize the importance of the IFIs to the achievement of the development plans of its members. It is time that the world considers a stronger Africa as an asset to the world economy. Africa is, and must remain, part of the solution to the global crisis.

Summing up

African economies have experienced hard times before. Crises have come and gone, and unfortunately the continent has failed to learn the lessons from earlier crises on how to avoid new ones. This global crisis is different, to a certain extent, most importantly because it is not of Africa's own making. Yet it is similar to prior crises in that it too has exposed the weak foundations of the continent's growth. It took African countries decades of painful reforms to record several consecutive years of GDP growth rates above 5 percent, but it took only a few months to cut growth prospects by half. With its excessive dependence on trade and a narrow range of activities as engines of growth, the continent remains severely exposed to the vagaries of global demand for primary commodities. With a weak domestic resource base, the continent is further exposed to shocks to international financial markets. The global crisis demonstrated once again that as the global demand for commodities plummets so does African growth. Further, when international liquidity dries up, African countries have serious trouble bridging their financing gaps, which brings private sector activity and major public investment programs to a halt.

More than ever before, African countries need to rethink their development model. They especially need to design strategies to build more resilient economies that can withstand external shocks and minimize the damage caused by such shocks on living standards. They need to increase their competitiveness and move up the value chain in their production systems to benefit from integration into the global economy. This chapter has outlined some elements of a strategy that can help achieve these goals. The strategy involves more than tinkering at the margins of the existing policy frameworks; rather it will require some creative innovations in policy orientation and an expansion of the policy tool kit at the disposal of policy makers. In particular, policy frameworks need to be broadened to include real goals, especially growth and employment creation. Countries need to move beyond stabilization and embark on pro-growth, pro-employment policy making. Macroeconomic policies and sector policies should be seen as tools for providing incentives and influencing the allocation of resources towards sectors and activities with the most growth and employment creation potential. An emphasis on employment creation is a central element of a strategy for achieving shared growth and a viable route towards sustainable poverty reduction.

While globalization offers important opportunities for African countries, it also presents substantial challenges. Yet, the continent cannot and should not disengage; rather the way forward is to forge strong alliances within the continent and engage in South-South partnerships to increase its bargaining power in the global economy. Africa cannot afford to remain on the sidelines of globalization; for while it may benefit from the globalization bonanza during prosperous times, we now know that the fallout of a global crash spares no one, not even the bystanders. Also, Africa needs to engage in global development and regulation debates and be part of the solution to global economic problems.

Notes

1 The Gini coefficients for Botswana, Namibia, South Africa, and Cape Verde are 61, 60, 57.8, 80.7, and 50 respectively. Except for Comoros, all other SSA countries have Gini coefficients below 50.
2 An analogy borrowed from an intervention by Dr Mouhtar Mansur, then Executive Director at the African Development Bank, during a meeting of the Korea Africa Forum on Economic Cooperation (KOAFEC), in October 2008.

References

AfDB/OECD/UNECA. 2009. *African Economic Outlook* 2009. Paris and Tunis: OECD and AfDB.

Arbache, J. S. and Page, J. 2007. "More growth or fewer collapses ? a new look at long run growth in Sub-Saharan Africa." World Bank Policy Research Working Paper 4384, Washington DC.

Chang, H.-J. 2003. *Kicking Away the Ladder: How the Economic and Intellectual Histories of Capitalism Have Been Re-Written to Justify Neo-Liberal Capitalism*. London, Anthem Press.

Collier, P. and Dollar, D. 2002. "Aid allocation and poverty reduction." *European Economic Review* 46 (8), 1475–500.

Easterly, W. 2006. "The Big-Push Déjà Vu." *Journal of Economic Literature* 44 (1), 96–105.

Easterly, W. 2002. *The Elusive Quest for Growth: Economists' Adventures and Misadventures in the Tropics*. Cambridge, MIT Press.

Epstein, G. and Heinz, J. 2006. "Monetary Policy and Financial Sector Reform For Employment Creation and Poverty Reduction in Ghana," University of Massachusetts, Amherst, Political Economy Research Institute, Working paper 113, Amherst, Massachusetts.

Ndikumana, L. and Nnanyonjo, J. 2005. "From Failed State to Success Story?" In J. K. Boyce and O'Donnell, M. eds., *Peace and the Public Purse: Economic Policies for Postwar Statebuilding*. Boulder Colorado: Lynne Rinner, 15–54.

Ndikumana, L. 2009. "Revisiting Development Finance Institutions to Accelerate African Economic Development." In: *Accelerating Africa's Development Five Years into the 21st Century*. African Development Bank, Tunis.

Ndulu, B., O'Connell, S., Bates, R., Collier, P., Soludo, C. C., Azam, J.-P. Fosu, A., and Njinkeu, D. eds. 2008. *The Political Economy of Economic Growth in Africa, 1960–2000*. Cambridge: Cambridge University Press.

Ngaruko, F. and Nkurunziza, J. D. 2005. "War and its duration in Burundi." In: Sambanis, N. and Collier, P. eds., *Understanding Civil War: Evidence and Analysis*. Washington, DC: World Bank Publications, Volume 1, Chapter 2.

Ngaruko, F. and Nkurunziza, J. D. 2000. "An economic interpretation of conflict in Burundi." *Journal of African Economies* 9 (3), 370–409.

Page, J. 2009. "Seizing The Day? The Global Economic Crisis and African Manufacturing." Paper prepared for the African Development Bank experts meeting on the impact of the global economic crisis, Tunis, April 10, 2009.

Pollin, R., Epstein, G., Heintz, J., and Ndikumana, L. 2006. *An Employment-Targeted Economic Program for South Africa.* Northampton, MA: Edward Elgar Publishing.

Pollin, R., Heintz, J., and Wa Ginthinji, M. 2007. *An Employment-Targeted Economic Program for Kenya.* New York: UNDP.

Sachs, J. D., McArthur, W. W., Schmidt-Traub, G., Hruk, M., Bahadur, C., Faye, M., and McCord, G. 2004. "Ending Poverty Traps." draft.

Part V

Conclusion

Moving to alternatives

11 Climate-resilient industrial development paths

Design principles and alternative models

Lyuba Zarsky

Introduction

The unfolding drama of global climate change has paradigm-shifting implications for development theory and policy. Despite recent findings that the Washington Consensus is adrift (Rodrik 2008), development practice remains largely wedded to global, market-driven, neo-liberal policies based on maximizing GNP growth and high-energy consumption, by maximizing inflows of foreign investment, integrating with global supply chains, and eschewing pro-active industry policies.

The climate change imperative – the urgent need to both mitigate and adapt to climate change – has arisen at a time when many medium-income developing nations are on the threshold of major investments in industry and energy infrastructure. It is also a time of deep global economic inequity, spurring efforts by the global community – such as the Millennium Development Goals – to alleviate poverty and promote social development, including via new business models.[1] Finally, the climate change imperative has emerged at a historical moment when development theory has been shaken loose by the economic, social, and environmental shortcomings of neo-liberal orthodoxy. These three factors combine to create an opportune moment to consider how industrial transformation and economic development could – and indeed, must – evolve along new "climate resilient" paths.

This chapter considers the broad contours of climate resilient industrial development paths and evaluates climate-resilience in three development models. In keeping with the other chapters of this volume, it defines development as an increase in local capacities for production and innovation. However, it argues that the central objective of development strategies in a climate-constrained world is not industrialization *per se*, but the generation of sustainable livelihoods.

The chapter is in five sections. Section two reviews the recent science about global climate instability and outlines links between climate change and economic development. Section three broadly defines climate resilient development. Section four outlines five design features of climate resilient industry polices. Section five evaluates three economic development models against the design features: (1) neo-liberal globalization; (2) sustainable globalization; and (3) new developmentalism. The final section concludes, and suggests directions for further research.

Climate change imperative

Global warming is here. According to the Fourth Assessment of the Intergovern-mental Panel on Climate Change (IPCC 2007: 2), "warming of the climate system is unequivocal, as is now evident from observations of increases in average global air and ocean temperatures, widespread melting of snow and ice and rising global average sea level."

Scientific reports since the Fourth Assessment have found that the signs of global warming are accelerating faster than predicted, including melting of Arctic sea-ice, glaciers, and ice sheets. Sea level rise in 2009 was 80 percent greater than predicted by the IPCC just two years before. Over the past 25 years, temperatures have increased at an average rate of 0.19 degrees centigrade per decade (UNSW 2009). A September 2009 conference of climate scientists found that "since the late 1990s, greenhouse gas emissions have increased at close to the most extreme IPCC scenarios" and there is a significant possibility of 4 degrees warming before the end of the century (*Science Daily* 2009).

The scientific consensus, and the assumption of the Kyoto Protocol, is that the avoidance of dangerous climate instability requires that warming be kept below 1.5 degrees centigrade. A higher level of warming portends major regional and local impacts on eco-systems, human settlements, food production, and bio-diversity. A revised target of 2 degrees put forth by the US at the December 2009 climate negotiations in Copenhagen triggered intense protests by African NGOs who chanted "Two degrees is suicide!" (COP 15 (2009).

The primary anthropogenic contribution to global climate change is the emis-sion of carbon dioxide from the burning of fossil fuels and deforestation. As indicated above, under a business-as-usual scenario with no mitigation of emis-sions, the IPCC's Fourth Assessment in 2007 projected an increase of 3.5 degrees centigrade by the end of the century (IPCC 2007). Despite more than a decade of global climate diplomacy, global carbon emissions were 40 percent higher in 2008 than in 1990. Even if emissions were stabilized at the current rate and brought to zero by 2030, just 20 more years of emissions would result in a 25 percent probability that warming will exceed 2 degrees (IPCC 2007). In a 2009 review of the science since the IPCC's Fourth Assessment (UNSW 2009), an Australian team of climate scientists concluded:

> If global warming is to be limited to a maximum of 2 degrees C above pre-industrial values, global emissions need to peak between 2015 and 2020 and then decline rapidly. To stabilize climate, a decarbonized global society – with near-zero emissions of CO_2 and other long-lived greenhouse gases – needs to be reached well within this century.... [E]very year of delayed action increases the chances of exceeding 2°C warming.
>
> (UNSW 2009: 7)

Even with mitigation efforts, climate models predict that the planet will continue to warm as a result of past carbon emissions, necessitating human adaptation.

The impacts of climate change on humans are defined by the interface between bio-physical and socio-economic systems. The primary expected changes in bio-physical systems are first, increased temperature and changes in rainfall patterns; and second, sea-level rise and an increase in the incidence and severity of disasters (fire, storms). There is also increasing evidence of the possibility of ocean acidification with attendant loss of biological productivity of marine life. The bio-physical impacts will vary greatly by region and locale.

Bio-physical impacts will have a variety of secondary effects on socio-economic systems, including severe stresses on water availability (drought and flooding) and damage to existing assets and infrastructure. These stresses in turn, are likely to trigger a high degree of social stress and conflict, not least due to impacts on agriculture (Table 11.1).

The impacts of climate change will be felt most acutely by people in developing countries for two reasons. The first is bio-physical risk. Besides the poles, climate models show warming trends to be greatest in sub-Saharan and northern Africa, as well as parts of south, central, and east Asia (IPCC 2007: Figure SPM2). Second, developing countries, especially least-developed countries, lack the capacity to adapt to climate stress. Adaptive capacity is a broad-ranging concept that spans basic socio-economic resilience stemming from wealth (income, technology, knowledge) to abilities to mitigate specific climate-related threats, such as climate monitoring and disaster planning.

Together, bio-physical risk and lack of adaptive capacity comprise the vulnerability of individuals, economies, communities, or nations to adapt to global climate change. In an effort to provide guidance on climate risk for global investors, the Canadian consulting group Maplecroft calculated a composite "climate change vulnerability index" based on bio-physical risk and adaptive capacity. Unsurprisingly, but worrisome nonetheless, the most vulnerable regions are the poorest (Figure 11.1).[2]

To date, official development assistance and global adaptation finance have sought to reduce vulnerability primarily by increasing local capacities to undertake discrete climate adaptation efforts, such as climate monitoring and disaster response. It is clear, however, that to significantly increase climate resilience, developing countries must increase local economic productivity, in both agriculture and industry, generating higher incomes, as well as revenues for infrastructure investment, and better health.

Ironically, for many of the poorest people in developing countries, vulnerability to climate change is exacerbated by lack of access to reliable and affordable energy. While the earth is dangerously warming as a result of the historical emissions of fossil fuel-driven industrialization in OECD countries, some 2.4 billion people in developing countries still use traditional biomass fuels for cooking and heating; around 1.6 billion lack access to electricity (UNDP 2005a). Beyond enhancing human welfare, energy is a key input for industrial development, at both micro and macro levels.

Large developing countries like China, India, Brazil, and South Africa have built dynamic industrial sectors driven largely by fossil fuels and, as a result,

Table 11.1 Expected impacts of climate change

Bio-physical impact	Social impact	Economic impact
Increased temperature and changes in rainfall patterns	Reduced agricultural productivity (drought) Reduced marine productivity Water stress and scarcity Increased prevalence of disease Forced migration	Reduced supplies and higher prices for food Changes in arability and cropping patterns Reduced availability and higher prices for water Change in distribution of labor supply
Sea level rise and increased incidence or intensity of disasters (storms, fires)	Damage to assets and infrastructure Population displacement Conflict	High cost of insurance Disruption of supply inputs Disruption of final markets Sudden labor scarcity or influx
Cumulative bio-physical impacts	Carbon regulation Conflict	Rising fossil fuel prices Governance breakdown

Source: Adapted from Tanner and Mitchell (2008).

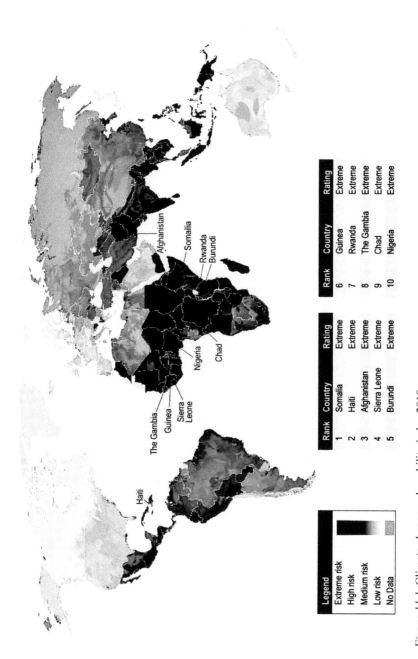

Figure 11.1 Climate change vulnerability index 2010.

have emerged as the largest current source of carbon emissions. Defining the obligations of developing and developed countries for mitigating carbon emissions has become the pivot – and the stumbling block – of attempts to craft a global climate regime.

The climate imperative requires developing countries to integrate mitigation and adaptation as central features of development strategy, considering not only threats to lives and livelihoods but also new opportunities for industrial transformation. A global effort to regulate carbon and replace carbon-based energy infrastructure, for example, will spur dramatic growth of low carbon and renewable energy technology industries, including off-grid technologies. Developing countries may be able to leapfrog fossil fuel-based growth and create competitive advantages in low and no carbon energy and industrial technologies and processes. Given the large stakes, it is little wonder that the Human Development Report called climate change "the defining human development issue of our generation" (UNDP 2007).

Defining climate resilient development

The first step in defining climate resilient paths of industrial development is to define development itself. Rather than growth or poverty alleviation, this chapter defines (economic) development as the building of local capacities for economic production and innovation. Such endogenous capacities are the foundation for both economic growth and poverty alleviation. Numerous studies, including by this author, have found that, in a global economy, promoting GNP growth without strengthening underlying local productive capacities generates economic enclaves dependent on foreign investment and export markets (Gallagher and Zarsky 2007). Also, attempts to alleviate poverty without enhancing local productive capacity founder when external assistance is withdrawn (Easterly 2002).

Local capacities for production and innovation embrace knowledge, skills, technology, infrastructure, human solidarity, and governing institutions. Such capacities not only create or enable the grasp of current opportunities to enhance productivity and social welfare, they also enable adaptation to changing conditions – economic, social, or climactic. The capacity to adapt is a central feature of climate resilience.

The overarching objective of productive and innovative capacities is to provide and sustain livelihoods. In climate resilient development models, sustainability is a foundational principle for all economic activity. To be sustainable, livelihoods must be derived from productive activities that are:

1   Ecologically sound: they must maintain the health of terrestrial, marine, air, and atmospheric eco-systems and bio-diversity, at local and global levels.
2   Economically viable: they must enhance local productive capacities and allocate them efficiently.
3   Socially resilient: they must promote equity and social solidarity.

The ability to sustain livelihoods may be highly compromised under rapidly changing and uncertain climactic conditions, as well as a rapidly evolving climate regime which drives rapidly changing fuel prices. To maintain livelihoods, development strategies must explicitly incorporate knowledge of existing and projected local and regional climactic conditions and build in industrial and resource diversification and other strategies to enhance resilience.

The overarching goal of climate resilient industrial development should thus be to generate local capacities to sustain livelihoods for all people under a range of climatic conditions in ways that do not exacerbate global warming. Another way to say this is that the goal is to reduce vulnerability stemming from lack of an adequate livelihood. Many people in developing countries are already highly vulnerable to seasonal climate change and other risks.

The goal of promoting sustainable livelihoods conflates what are today often approached as separate objectives – poverty alleviation and industrial transformation. A focus on reducing vulnerability could invigorate current development efforts. As two leading climate and development researchers argue: "climate change may actually be an opportunity to create pathways out of chronic poverty through targeted efforts to enhance vulnerability reduction and adaptation" (Tanner and Mitchell 2008: 6).

Moreover, a focus on sustainable livelihoods removes the focus of development away from "growth for growth's sake," enabling a redirection away from wasteful, high-energy, water-intensive consumption patterns. Finally, it embraces both wage and non-wage forms of livelihood and livelihoods derived from both agriculture and manufacturing.

Development strategies aimed at creating sustainable livelihoods thus have as their starting point three integrated objectives: (1) increasing income (and equity) by increasing the productivity of economic activities; (2) promoting growth in local capacities for production and innovation; and (3) increasing resilience of economic activity by incorporating knowledge about climate uncertainty and other environmental information.

With this starting point in mind, climate resilient development can be conceptualized as a socio-economic trajectory that generates and sustains human livelihoods in ways that both mitigate and adapt to global climate change. Central to mitigation is the transition to non-carbon energy sources. At the global level, it means developing along a path that stabilizes atmospheric concentrations within the range of 350–450 ppms, a level that is understood to be consistent with warming 1.5–2 degrees C. For developing countries, mitigation will primarily consist of ensuring that new investment in industry, transport, and infrastructure is based on low-carbon and/or renewable energy.

Climate resilient industrial development paths must be strongly focused on adaptation; that is, on reducing vulnerability to global climate change. A central aspect of adaptation is that both the change in global average temperature and local and regional impacts of global climate change are highly uncertain (Figure 11.1). One reason is that climate scientists poorly understand how local and global feedback loops interact. In some parts of Africa, for example, it is not clear if rainfall will be greater or less or both. Moreover, models predict greater climate variability.

The subject of a burgeoning literature, adaptation requires the mobilization of investment in activities along a continuum. On one end are discrete actions that respond to particular emerging or expected climate changes; for example building or reinforcing sea walls in coastal cities or relocating populations of soon-to-be-submerged islands. On the other end are investments that promote adaptive capacity by targeting the drivers of vulnerability; like poverty, unsustainable industry, lack of sustainable livelihoods, poor health, lack of education, good governance, etc. In other words, reducing vulnerability to global climate change entails reinvigorating traditional development goals (Table 11.2). Also critical to climate resilient development is investment in problem-solving and response capacities. There is great uncertainty as to how climate change will unfold and with what impacts. As stated above, capacities for social learning, deliberation, and innovation will be at a premium.

Policy design principles

Climate-resilient development paths entail a high level of social planning and integration of knowledge, both scientific and traditional. They also require a high level of social solidarity, given the potentially catastrophic disruption to existing livelihoods. Implied is a central role for public policy, in terms of both content – policy objectives and tools – and the process of designing and implementing policy. Gleaned from a review of "traditional" development case studies, as well as a burgeoning literature on climate and development, this section outlines five principles as starting points for the design of climate resilient development policy.

Pro-active industry policy

Over the past two decades, neo-liberal approaches to development have eschewed pro-active industry policies aimed at nurturing targeted industry sectors in favor of industry-neutral, "market-driven" integration into global supply chains. The performance, however, has been mixed at best. Latin American countries that rigorously followed the neo-liberal prescription, for example, have fared poorly in terms of growth and employment compared to China and other East Asian countries (Gallagher and Chudnovsky 2010 and Chapter 12 this volume).

Industrial policy has two objectives in terms of linking climate and development. First, it aims to reduce vulnerability by promoting financially sustainable livelihoods. Second, as outlined by UNCTAD (2009: xiii), it seeks to "shift production and consumption patterns towards the use of those primary commodities, means of production, and consumer goods that place a lower burden on the earth's atmosphere than the current GHG [greenhouse gas] intensive ones." Linking climate change mitigation policies with traditional development goals,

Table 11.2 Adaptation and development: A continuum of investment activities

Address the drivers of vulnerability	Build response capacity	Manage climate risk	Confront specific climate changes
Enhance underlying factors to reduce vulnerability to poverty and harm; increase local capacities for production and innovation; mobilize investment for low or non-carbon energy; promote solidarity and social problem-solving	Build robust systems for innovation and problem solving for both climate and non-climate related activities; e.g. communications and planning processes	Integrate climate information into decisions to reduce negative directs effects on resources and livelihoods; e.g. disaster management, 'climate proofing infrastructure'; build infrastructure to manage flood-drought cycles	Confront and respond to direct climate changes; e.g. sea level rise, melting glaciers, drought
Climate-resilient development			Discrete adaptive

← ... →

Source: Adapted from McGray *et al.* (2007) and Tanner and Mitchell (2008).

argues UNCTAD, "requires industrial policies that foster the creation of capabilities to produce or participate in the production of such goods and their subsequent upgrading" (UNCTAD 2009: xv).

Pro-active, climate-resilient industry policy need not privilege import protection policies as in older ISI models. The goal, rather, is to identify efficient, climate-friendly, high employment industries and to nurture them by overcoming local market failures. A wide range of policy tools is available, including public support for research and development, science and technology policy, finance and credit, support for training and education, technology partnerships with multinational corporations, reforms in domestic patent law, etc. An Overseas Development Institute review of comprehensive policies for low carbon growth already employed by nine developed and developing countries concluded that "there is a role for government leadership to identify low carbon growth sectors which may provide competitive advantage and employment growth" (Ellis *et al.* 2009: ix).

There is ample evidence that pro-active industry policies can be effective in promoting climate-friendly industrial growth. Rock and Angel (2005) show that pro-active industry policies in East Asia are enabling a "sustainability transition." China's industry support policies have propelled its emergence as a leader in solar photovoltaic and wind technology, as well as "clean coal" technologies such as direct coal liquefaction (UN-DESA 2009). Brazil's support for the development and deployment of a domestic sugar-based ethanol industry allowed it to capture a vibrant export market in the burgeoning global bio-fuels sector (UN-DESA 2009). In India, local government support enabled the emergence of a major domestic supplier of solar energy systems for households and industry (Box 11.1).

Box 11.1 Tata BP Solar: The role of industry policy

Based in Bangalore, India, Tata BP Solar produces domestic and industrial solar water heating systems, solar lanterns, home lighting systems, water pumping systems, integrated PV systems for buildings, and solar streetlights. In addition to 30% of the domestic Indian market, Tata BP Solar also has a 67% share of the Bangladeshi market, 25% in Nepal, 35% in Sri Lanka, and over 90% in Bhutan. Company profits rose from 16 million rupees in 1991–92 to 4,690 million rupees (106 million USD) in 2004–05.

Tata BP Solar's commercial success is attributable to the interaction of global market forces and domestic policy. The joint venture partnership is a collaboration between BP and Tata Power Company, a member of India's renowned Tata business family. The government of India provided a supportive, enabling policy environment. India's large-scale solar PV programmes are driven by government subsidies, with tax incentives and other financial incentives. In many cases, it is government agencies who take the lead on developing rural energy initiatives in India, by making a policy decision and bringing in an appropriate company (such as Tata BP Solar) with the required knowledge and capabilities to serve local markets.

Not all of Tata BP Solar's markets are located at the base of the pyramid. However, the company has demonstrated an ability to reach some of the poorest and most isolated communities. In the Himalayan region of Ladakh, Tata BP Solar worked with the Ladakh Renewable Energy Development Agency (LREDA) and the Indian Ministry of Non-Conventional Energy Sources to provide solar home systems to 80 remote mountainous villages, as the first phase of an initiative aimed at providing electricity to the whole Ladakh region.

In Punjab, the Tata BP Solar collaborated with the Punjab Energy Development Agency on a programme to deliver 225 solar water-pumping systems to farmers for irrigation purposes. Much of the success of Tata BP Solar's business model is the provision of a complete service to their customers. This long-term commitment is underpinned by the contractual relations established between the company and the local government. In Ladakh, end-users were charged for installation and maintenance, thus ensuring their commitment. Training was provided not only in technical skills, but also in educating and working with the end-users to ensure proper operation and maintenance of the systems.

Source: Wilson *et al.* (2008)

Industrial diversification

Providing sustainable livelihoods in developing countries is largely a function of creating employment-generating enterprises (or agricultural operations) that are interlinked in productive industry sectors. Climate constrained industrial development thus has significant overlap with a development emphasis on industrial transformation and diversification. Many economists argue that diversification, rather than specialization, is the central driver of economic growth (Rodrik 2007).

Many developing countries have based their industrial development strategy on one or a handful of export sectors, either primary or manufacturing, integrated into global supply chains. Such a strategy makes livelihoods highly vulnerable to exogenous shifts, including rapid changes in exchange rates, emergence of lower cost competitors, global market collapse due to over-inflated expectations, etc. In the Mexican city of Guadalajara, for example, some 22,000 workers lost their jobs between 2001–03 due to a combination of global market contraction in the IT industry and the entry of China into the WTO (Dussel 2005).

For two reasons, industrial diversification is likely to become more central to sustaining livelihoods as climate change unfolds. First, fossil fuel prices will rise due to climate action and/or scarcity. As a result, long global supply chains will be more expensive, especially those based on air and truck freight. Local companies will become more competitive in servicing local markets. Moreover, MNCs (multinational corporations) will increasingly seek local supply inputs for products aimed at both export and domestic markets. Secondly, climate events may make global supply chains more vulnerable to disruption. Insurance costs are likely to rise, further reducing the competitiveness of global input sourcing. A corollary to the renewed emphasis on industrial diversification is the rising importance of producing for domestic markets (Working Group 2009).

Investment

At the heart of climate resilient industrial development paths is the mobilization, leveraging, and strategic targeting of investment. Private and public, domestic and international sources of capital and finance are required to rapidly ratchet up industries that promote sustainable livelihoods and transform production and consumption structures towards low or no carbon growth. "Countries that identify, target, and secure new green investment and growth opportunities," concludes the Overseas Development Institute, "stand to benefit more from the transition to a low carbon economy" (Ellis *et al.* 2009: ix).

Where will investment funds come from? At the international level, efforts to mobilize climate-related finance have focused on official development assistance, such as the Global Adaptation Fund, and emissions trading and offset schemes such as the Clean Development Mechanism (CDM) and the burgeoning Reducing Emissions from Deforestation and Forest Degradation (REDD) fund. To date, however, adaptation financing has been very meager, while CDM projects are concentrated in China and India, largely in hydro-electric dams and reducing emissions in dirty industries, such as cement and chemicals (International Rivers 2008). Indeed, the CDM has been widely criticized for its failure to promote sustainable development (Schneider 2007). Nonetheless, within the context of a strategic, pro-active approach for industrial development, developing countries might find opportunities to gain or leverage investment through international climate-related funding mechanisms.

A much greater source of investment is private capital, including domestic savings and foreign direct investment (FDI). Policies that improve the overall functioning of domestic financial markets and the quality of FDI are key to climate resilient industry growth. In parallel with a pro-active approach to industry policy is a pro-active approach to investment, in both form and function. In terms of form, governments need to look towards new types of collaborations with investors, including via public-private partnerships and social entrepreneurship.

A pro-active approach to investment entails the creation and incorporation of decision-making frameworks to allocate investment in both industry and infra-structure in ways that optimize dual goals of increasing economic productivity while reducing climate risk, both local and global. Without such a framework, investment could be maladaptive. For example, massive investment in palm oil plantations in Indonesia to service global demand for bio-fuels exacerbates *global* climate risk because it increases net carbon emissions due to native forest clearing; and increases *local* climate risk because it undermines forest liveli-hoods and bio-diversity resources (Block 2009).

New decision-making frameworks are emerging that seek to evaluate returns on alternative investment options according to integrated indicators of economic pro-ductivity and climate risk (ECA 2009). Obviously, these frameworks entail first an assessment of climate risk based on scientific and local knowledge. Given the high level of uncertainty, assessments are based on a range of scenarios linking local and regional climate-weather interactions to potential economic losses to existing productive assets, as well as potential economic gains from adaptation investment.

The Economics of Climate Adaptation Working Group applied such a framework to project the economic costs of climate risk and identify a portfolio of investment options to reduce risk in test cases in eight different regions of the world, including North and North East China (drought risk to agriculture); the Mopti region in Mali (risk to agriculture from climate zone shift); and Georgetown, Guyana (risk from flash floods). The study's findings are sobering i.e., that a "significant economic value is at risk" from climate change. Encouragingly, however, the test cases revealed that "rational measures to improve climate resilience are in many cases also effective steps to strengthen economic development" (ECA 2009: 56). In Mali, for example, "the implementation of climate-resilient agricultural development could potentially bring in billions of dollars a year in additional revenue" (ECA 2009: 12).

Knowledge-intensive local adaptive management

Climate resilient development policies, including industry policies, will have to be regularly re-evaluated and re-designed to adapt to anticipated and unanticipated local climactic conditions, as well as to new climate knowledge. Indeed, knowledge about local and regional bio-physical conditions and their socio-economic impacts will need to be foundational in shaping industrial development.

A new field of policy research is exploring principles for adaptive management and, led by the International Institute of Sustainable Development and The Energy Research Institute, applying them to climate change adaptation (Figure 11.2). Adaptive management is based on creating avenues for new information and changing conditions to be incorporated in policy redesign and implementation. It allows institutions to continually gain knowledge, make assessments, monitor, and change course or procedure.

Adaptation to anticipated conditions is based on developing a comprehensive understanding of cause and effects (as much as possible); adaptation to unanticipated conditions requires a comprehensive understanding of overall system dynamics and complexity – in this case, the global climate system and its socio-economic interactions.

Four types of policies can be identified as adaptive:

- No regrets: policies that achieve desired objectives under a range of circumstances. In the climate change world, these policies have often been considered to be cost-effective investments in climate change mitigation.
- Triggers: policies that adjust automatically to changing circumstances. An example might be water pricing policies that change according to water supply (e.g., drought).
- Complex system: policies that derive from complexity theory, and which point towards effective intervention in multi-dimensional systems. An understanding of such policies will require investment in education and R & D.
- Review: policies that build-in review of prior policies and investment decisions.

Partnerships

Climate-resilient industry policy has a challenging agenda, demanding a high degree of knowledge, flexibility, and social solidarity. While government must provide leadership, the primary form of governance and collective action should be partnerships between government, the private sector and civil society. All sectors are needed both to provide information and to undertake action, including the design and implementation of effective policy.

Tri-sector collaboration can take a variety of forms and have a variety of functions. At the macro level, an overarching "industry council" could be tasked with developing a comprehensive approach to investment and industry policy. One policy might be to promote micro-level "social business" partnerships that integrate environmental/climate and financial returns via credit, tax relief, business training, etc.

Climate resilience in three development models

The previous section sketched overarching objectives and policy design principles as foundational criteria for climate resilient industrial development paths. This section considers climate resilience in three actual development models: (1) neo-liberal globalization; (2) sustainable globalization; and (3) new developmental.

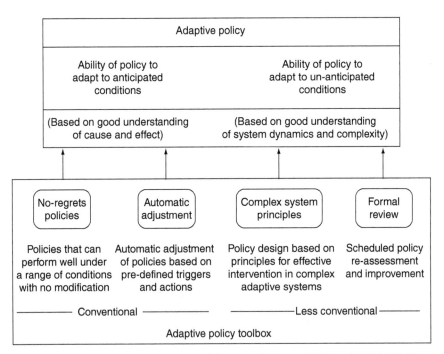

Figure 11.2 Adaptive policy: a conceptual framework (source: IISD and TERI (2006)).

Neo-liberal globalization

The over-arching objective of the neo-liberal globalization development model is to increase the rate of economic growth measured as GNP (or GDP) per capita by market-based integration into the global economy. The primary policy prescriptions are to maximize inflows of foreign direct investment (FDI) and integrate into global supply chains in which final products are generally exported to OECD countries. Economic growth promotes livelihoods directly by generating employment and indirectly by generating fiscal revenues for public goods such as education and health (Easterly 2002).

The fundamental design principle for industrial development in the neo-liberal model is to promote market forces. Pro-active industry policies are actively eschewed. The primary policy tools are liberalization, privatization and deregulation, as well as investment incentives aimed broadly at increasing the quantity of FDI inflows. Though apparently "neutral," neo-liberal industry policies tend to favor foreign investors and multinational corporations over local producers. They also give foreign investors maximum freedom over all aspects of business management (Rodrik 2007). Benefits to local productive capacities are assumed to come from knowledge and technology spillovers by MNCs, who also diffuse "best practice" environmental management standards to local producers (OECD, 2002).[3]

Rather than industrial diversification, the pursuit of comparative advantage is the primary route to economic and industrial growth in the neo-liberal globalization model. Developing countries are urged, for example, to specialize in low-wage manufacturing industries, monoculture primary commodities, and/or extractive industries. Investment plays a central role and the emphasis is on mobilizing private foreign capital. Indeed, the model could be renamed "FDI-led growth."

Finally, the neo-liberal globalization model treats the natural environment as exogenous to economic modeling and external to core industrial development goals. Generally, the environmental impacts of industry are conceived as externalities that can be ignored until incomes are higher. Rather than incorporating scientific knowledge and utilizing adaptive management to integrate and balance the twin objectives of economic growth and bio-physical resilience, the neo-liberal model emphasizes a singular policy tool-kit that aims to maximize efficiency and yield of commercial output.

The neo-liberal globalization model poses severe shortcomings for climate resilient development in terms of both mitigation and adaptation. First, a focus on GNP growth makes livelihoods secondary; an indirect outcome rather than the central objective of development. Moreover, the model virtually ignores bio-physical sustainability, creating a high level of livelihood vulnerability. Many studies have documented the reality of "jobless growth" and growth in commercial value at the expense of long-term resource productivity. Brooks et al. (2009) provide a "dramatic example" from the Sahel:

> [D]evelopment policies in the 1950s and 1960s sought to achieve a shift from subsistence to commercial agriculture ... to ensure that countries

which were soon to be independent were capable of maintaining stable, functional national economies that were integrated into the world economy. The result was the intensification of agriculture, agricultural expansion into areas viewed as underutilized, the undermining of traditional risk-management measures and the marginalization of pastoralists. This all occurred during an usually wet period. When rainfall declined in the late 1960s, culminating in severe drought in the early 1970s, agriculture and pastoralism collapsed, resulting in a famine that killed hundreds of thousands of people and millions of animals, precipitating severe social disruption.

(Brooks *et al.* (2009: 745))

The second shortcoming of the neo-liberal model lies in its "neutral" industry policies. A host of studies have shown that, in the absence of pro-active industry policy, FDI-led growth tends to promote industrial enclaves, rather than broad-based growth. The primary reason is that hoped-for knowledge, technology, and human capital spillovers from MNCs have not materialized (Cordero and Paus 2008; Gallagher and Zarsky 2007; Hanson 2001; Jenkins 2006). Rather than seek local suppliers, MNCs source inputs globally, reducing potential contributions to sustainable livelihoods directly through employment and indirectly by inhibiting the growth of local enterprises with increased capacities for production and innovation. Besides creating livelihoods, such capacities are needed to promote a low-carbon transition rapid enough to stave off catastrophic climate change while simultaneously promoting sustainable livelihoods.

A third shortcoming is the neo-liberal model's emphasis on FDI as the primary source of investment in domestic industry. In addition to increasing vulnerability to exogenous disruption, FDI-led growth can retard the domestic financial reforms needed to mobilize domestic savings. Even in the poorest countries, pools of domestic savings are much bigger than foreign funds. In addition, tax "holidays" and other incentives minimize the contribution of MNCs to public funds. Both domestic savings and public funds are needed to mobilize the massive amounts of investment required for both climate mitigation and adaptation.

Another weakness of FDI-led growth is that it generates a competitive global bargaining context in which developing (and developed) countries are reluctant to raise and enforce local environmental standards or demand environmental conditionalities of MNCs, a phenomenon which I have elsewhere described as "stuck in the mud" (Zarsky 2004). The problem can be overcome only by global environmental standards that seek to internalize environmental externalities, such as carbon emissions. However, proponents of neo-liberal development – including many developing country governments – argue that global environmental standards, such as might be imposed in a global climate treaty aimed at reducing carbon emissions, obstruct development (i.e., growth) goals.

Citing the principles of state sovereignty and the right to development, as well as the purported environmental benefits of higher income as expounded in the "environmental Kuznets curve," they argue that developing countries should be free to set their own environmental standards. Combined with the reality that current atmospheric carbon concentrations are the historical responsibility of developed nations, this logic resulted in the distinction in the Kyoto Protocol between Annex I (developed) countries with obligations to reduce carbon emissions and Annex II (developing) countries with no specific mitigation obligations.

A final shortcoming of the neo-liberal model for climate resilience is that it puts MNCs singularly at the heart of industrial investment decisions that are likely to greatly affect the ability of local enterprises and communities to adapt to climate change. The actual impacts of global climate change are highly uncertain and will unfold at local and regional levels. Collaborative governance is needed to determine climate-response actions, including potential trade-offs between reducing climate risk and increasing or maintaining economic growth.

The strength of the neo-liberal model lies in the potential role that foreign finance and FDI could play in promoting climate resilient industrial development. MNCs have significant financial, technological, and management knowhow that could, given the right policy framework, be harnessed to promote bio-physically and socio-economically sustainable livelihoods. Mobilizing global capital markets for industry and infrastructure projects that reduce climate risk while promoting economic growth would help to fill the large need for adaptation financing.

Sustainable globalization

Building on the "corporate social responsibility" movement, progressive business leaders and Robert Zoellick, head of the World Bank, have recently called for a model of "inclusive and sustainable globalization" (WBCSD 2007; Zoellick 2007). This model shares many features of the neo-liberal model. The overarching objective remains increasing GNP growth by promoting FDI inflows through liberalization, deregulation, and privatization policies, albeit with a more nuanced emphasis on integrating local producers into global supply chains (Moran 2006).

The sustainable globalization model has two distinctive features, both of which potentially contribute to climate resilience. The first is the call for environmental standards and objectives, including mitigation of carbon emissions, to be integrated into industry and business management. Two policy tools are recommended. First, global business firms are encouraged to voluntarily adopt "best practice" in all their production, distribution, and marketing activities, wherever they are based. Second, the model explicitly recognizes the need for a global climate framework in which all states, developed and developing, shoulder obligations to reduce carbon emissions.

The second distinctive feature is the emphasis on the role of private-public partnerships (PPPs) to promote specific sustainable development objectives. Heavily promoted at the 2002 World Summit on Sustainable Development

(WSSD) in Johannesburg, PPPs are emerging as a vehicle whereby global companies collaborate in specific capacity-building and infrastructure projects with local governments, international institutions, development groups, and other "development actors." The overwhelming number of WSSD Partnerships target water and sustainable energy projects (Biermann *et al.* 2007).

In addition to helping deliver public goods, MNCs are also working in partnerships with governments and/or NGOs to promote enterprises for sustainable development, targeting especially the poorest income groups in developing countries (UNDP 2005b). The contribution of MNCs is either philanthropic, more recently called "social investment," or via core business activities through "social business" (Yunus 2007). Aimed at creating enterprises that are financially sustainable while serving the poor, such an approach can potentially achieve more in terms of climate resilient development than purely aid-driven initiatives. Off-grid sustainable energy and water enterprises, for example, are fast growing sectors of MNC partnerships in social business (Box 11.2). To date, however, social business has remained marginal to total MNC core business activity and to national development strategies.

Box 11.2 **Energiebau: Partnering for off-grid energy**

Energiebau is a mid-size German company providing and wholesaling solar electrification systems. In addition to serving customers in Germany and Europe, it delivers off-grid solar systems to remote communities, mostly in Africa. Energiebau partnered with the German capacity building development organisation InWEnt in a 1.1 million Euro public-private partnership to provide off-grid energy to rural communities. Local religious and community groups helped design and implement the project. The concept involves a village-level solar powered system supplemented by a generator in times of peak usage and bad weather. The generator is powered by locally cultivated jatropha oil, which provides income for local cultivators as well as energy fuel independence.

Source: Wilson *et al.* (2008)

Despite its strengths, the sustainable globalization model has major weaknesses in terms of promoting climate resilient development. The primary weakness is that, despite innovations at the margin, it is based on the assumption that the combination of global environmental regulation, business goodwill, and global market forces can deliver sustainable development. Like the neo-liberal model, it promotes "neutral" industry policies that inhibit more muscular environmental commitments to channel paths of industry evolution (needed to mitigate climate change) and that have had limited results in nurturing local broad-based sustainable growth (needed to reduce vulnerability). Successful project-based PPPs that enhance local productive capacities provide pointers toward a new developmental model but remain sidelined until they are scaled up and incorporated into core thinking and policy about industrial development.

New developmentalism

A new developmentalist model has a different starting point than either neo-liberal or sustainable globalization models. While it aims to achieve GNP growth, the overarching objective is to promote endogenous productive and technological capacity, incorporated in the concepts of industrial transformation and diversification (Rodrik (2007, p. 245) and this book, Part I). Moreover, unlike the neo-liberal and sustainable globalization models, which are rooted in a belief in the power of global market forces, new developmentalist models emphasize the centrality of local socio-economic and institutional landscapes in driving development outcomes. Countries which have adopted new developmentalist models, such as China, Singapore, and Brazil, generally have a better track record in terms of both GNP and job growth than those like Mexico and the Philippines, which have adopted a neo-liberal model (Amsden 2003; Evans 1995; Agosin and Meyer 2000).

Industry policy in new developmental models is based on the idea that governments must be pro-active to capture the benefits of global market forces, including spillovers from FDI, for industrial upgrading, transformation, and diversification. It is not the specific tools of industry policy – which span from performance requirements and credit subsidies to support for targeted research and development and investment in education and training – which make up the essence of new developmentalism. Rather, it is the commitment to determine what blend of industry-promotion policies are likely to work in a specific national context.

New developmentalism shares some features with "old" developmentalism based on import protection and export promotion. Both pro-actively use industry policy tools to nurture growth of targeted industries. However, the new developmental "broad-gauged" approach focuses more on overcoming market failures – including information and coordination – which inhibit industrial development (Stiglitz 2005). It also aims to work in partnership with MNCs to promote "quality" FDI; that is, investment in strategic industries and technologies. Finally, it looks to both domestic and export markets for possible industrial growth.

A new developmental framework offers several advantages over globalization-based models for climate resilient development. A strong and strategic role for government leadership in promoting industry could channel FDI, R&D, and public investment towards low-carbon and zero-carbon energy and industry growth. Moreover, the "embedded autonomy" framework of collaboration between government and the private sector provides partnership-based flexibility in adapting to changing climatic, as well as market, conditions (Evans 1995).

At the center of the new developmental model is the mobilization of domestic savings rather than foreign capital to promote industrial transformation (Bresser-Pereira 2009). Nonetheless, foreign investment can play a strategic role in new developmental models, including by explicitly targeting low-carbon and other sustainable industries and technologies. For example, in December, 2007, China announced a "dramatic revision" of its foreign investment strategy, the "keystone" of which is an "emphasis on quality over quantity." The second of five new policies is:

> ...encouragement of investment in sustainable resources and environmental protection. Foreign investors are encouraged to support the newly implemented Circular Economy (i.e. sustainable development) and Cleaner Production policies, as well as invest in the area of environmental protection, sustainable resources and anti-pollution. The 2007 catalog greatly expands the list of encouraged investments in this area. On the other hand, foreign investment in high resource-use, high-energy-use and high-pollution enterprises is restricted or prohibited.
>
> (quoted in Dickinson 2007)

Despite its strengths, new development theory has three shortcomings in promoting climate resilience. The first is a blindness to the natural environment. New developmental theorists generally have not integrated bio-physical constraints into development strategy and have ignored the potential interaction of industry and environmental, including climate policy. A large literature on "sustainable development" remains un-integrated into much new developmental thinking.

One exception is the work of "sustainability transition" researchers studying the interaction of global market forces and local institutions in promoting socio-technological innovations which point towards a more sustainable industrialization. In a study of cement and electronics industries, Rock *et al.* (2009: 241) found that the

> capitalist developmental states in East and Southeast Asia have been better able [than countries with neo-liberal policies] to harness global economic forces for technological and sustainability transitions through an openness to trade and investment and effective public–private institutions able to link cleaner technologies and environmental standards to production activities in firms.

The second shortcoming of the new developmental framework is that it does not explicitly target pro-poor growth, although it does focus on promoting employment. In all societies, poorer people, both urban and rural, are more vulnerable to risk in general and will be more vulnerable to climate risk. Moreover, the model is gender-blind, not differentiating between men and women in terms of capacities and constraints. Recent studies have shown that women are differentially and particularly vulnerable to climate change impacts, food shortages due to drought or flooding, and higher incidence of disease (Aguilar *et al.* 2007). Women are also key agents of enterprise and resource management. To promote broad-based climate resilience, new development models will need to conceive of the poor as agents of enterprise and specifically adopt gender inclusive, pro-poor industry development policies.

The third shortcoming of the new developmental model for climate resilience is that its focus on social collaboration typically encompasses only (national) government and the private sector. A wider range of actors will be needed to chart a climate resilient of industrial development, including municipal governments, labor and community groups, international development organizations, and others. A summary of the conceptualization of climate resilience in the three development models is presented in Table 11.3.

Conclusion: from models to paths?

This chapter has presented a theoretical framework to conceptualize the purpose and the practice of development given the imperative to mitigate and adapt to global change. It defined the objective of climate resilient development as the generation of local, broad-based productive capacities that can provide livelihoods that are environmentally and economically sustainable and that promote social solidarity. It outlined five principles for the design of industry policies that could nurture climate-resilient, sustainable livelihoods and evaluated climate resilience in three current development models.

The chapter has two central findings. First, aspects of climate resilience are embodied in each of the three models. The neo-liberal globalization model emphasizes the importance of mobilizing global capital for development, especially FDI. The sustainable globalization model highlights the importance of global carbon regulation, the potential role of business in reducing poverty, and the benefits of multi-stakeholder, tri-sector partnerships in designing and implementing industrial development projects and governance (Table 11.3).

The second finding is that two elements of the new developmentalist model – the overarching objective to build endogenous productive capacity and its embrace of a strong role for government in industrial development – make it the most robust of the three models as a starting point for the design of climate resilient development paths. Without these two elements, it is highly unlikely that developing economies will develop on a low-carbon trajectory or that they will significantly reduce their vulnerability to intensifying climate instability.

A strong role for government in industrial development will require institutional reform and capacity-building, at both national and global levels. World trade rules have been built to facilitate the neo-liberal globalization model. WTO reform is urgently needed to define "policy space" for climate resilient industrial development, not least to avoid global trade wars. Nationally, governments need to invest in building the state managerial capacities of pro-active industry policies, especially in countries that have adopted the neo-liberal globalization model.

These two elements, however, are merely starting points. None of the models puts climate risk into the center of development planning. Global climate instability will have highly differential impacts, both spatially and temporally. Industrial development policies will need to be flexible and adaptive to local natural and institutional conditions. Climate-resilient development, in short, points not towards a singular "model" but a plurality of development paths. The work of understanding the theory and praxis of such paths has only just begun.

Table 11.3 Climate resilience in three development models

	Development objectives	Industry policy	Diversification	Investment	Adaptive management	Partnerships
Climate resilience	Sustainable livelihoods Reduce climate risk (mitigation and adaptation)	Pro-active, targeted Promote local capacities for sustainable production and innovation Low/no carbon	Promote industry diversification Produce for local and export markets	Targeted, strategic Mobilizes domestic and foreign, public and private sources	Incorporates knowledge about local climactic conditions Principles of adaptive management	Promotes collaborative governance Private public partnerships Social business
Neo-liberal globalization	GNP growth Global economic integration	Neutral Promote FDI (spillovers)	Promote specialization Produce for export markets	Maximize FDI inflows Official aid		
Sustainable globalization	"Green" GNP growth Poverty alleviation Global economic integration	Neutral Promote FDI (spillovers; local supply linkages) Integrate in global supply chains	Promote specialization Produce for export markets	Maximize FDI inflows Social investment		Private public partnerships
New developmental	Industrialization Build-up of globally competitive domestic core manufacturing industries	Pro-active; targeted Promote local capacities for production and innovation Cleaner production technology	Promote industrial diversification Produce for export and local markets	Targeted Strategic Mobilize domestic savings		Strategic collaboration with business

Source: Author conceptualization.

Notes

1 Refer to Chang Chapter 3 of this volume on the MDGs.
2 Maplecroft Climate Change Vulnerability Index (CCVI) rates 166 countries on their capacity to mitigate risks to society and the business environment posed by changing patterns in natural hazards, such as droughts, flooding, storms, and sea level rises, and the resulting effects on ecosystems. The climate change vulnerability factors are divided into six groups: economy; natural resource security; ecosystems; poverty, development, and health; population, settlement, and infrastructure; and institutions, governance, and social capital; and comprises of 33 indicators. The CCVI was calculated using a Geographical Information System (GIS) model. Each cell represents an area of approximately 25 km². For more information see www.maplecroft.com.
3 A large literature has found little evidence that FDI generates "horizontal" knowledge spillovers, that is, to firms in the same industry, and mixed evidence that it generates "vertical," that is local supply chain, spill-overs (for a review, see Gallagher and Zarsky 2007: Chapter 1). Pointing towards a more nuanced approach, a number of studies have found that local "absorptive capacities" are needed to capture FDI spillovers, including well-developed financial markets (Alfaro *et al.* 2003), and technological capabilities in local supplier firms (Chudnovsky and Lopez 2010).

References

Alfaro, L., Chanda, A., Kalemli-Ozcan, S., and Sayek, S. 2003. "FDI spillovers, financial markets and economic development," IMF Working Paper WP/03/186, www.imf.org/external/pubs/ft/wp/2003/wp03186.pdf.

Agosin, M. and Mayer, R. 2000. "Foreign investment in developing countries: Does it crowd in domestic investment?" Discussion Paper 146, UNCTAD, Geneva, www.unctad.org/en/docs/dp_146.en.pdf.

Aguilar, L., Araujo, A., and Quesada-Aguilar, A. 2007. "Gender and climate change," IUCN (International Union for the Conservation of Nature) Fact Sheet, www.genderandenvironment.org/admin/admin_biblioteca/documentos/Factsheet%20Climate-Change.pdf.

Amsden, A. 2003. The Rise of the Rest, Challenges to the West from Late-Industrializing Economies. New York, Oxford University Press.

Biermann, F., Chan, M.-S., Mert, A., and Pattberg, P. 2007. "Multi-stakeholder partnerships for sustainable development: does the promise hold?" In: P. Glasbergen, F. Biermann and A. P. J. Mol, eds., Partnerships, Governance and Sustainable Development, Reflections on Theory and Practice. Cheltenham: Edward Elgar, 239–60.

Block, B. 2009. "Global palm oil demand fueling deforestation." World Watch Institute: Eye on Earth, April 10, Washington D.C. www.worldwatch.org/node/6059.

Bresser-Peereira, L.-C. 2009. "From old to new developmentalism in Latin America." Escola de Economia de São Paulo, Getulio Vargas Foundation, No. 193, June 26: 2–37, http://virtualbib.fgv.br/dspace/bitstream/handle/10438/2682/TD%20193%20-%20Luiz%20Carlos%20Bresser%20Pereira.pdf?sequence=1.

Brooks, N., Grist, N., and Brown, K. 2009. "Development futures in the context of climate change: challenging the present and learning from the past." Development Policy Review 27(6), 741–65.

Chudnovsky, D. and Lopez, A. 2010. "A missed opportunity: foreign investment and sustainable development in Argentina." In: Gallagher and Chudnovsky, eds., Rethinking Foreign Investment for Sustainable Development, Lessons for Latin America. London: Anthem Press, 77–98.

COP 15 (2009). African Civil Society Demonstration at COP 15, www.youtube.com/watch?v=ajTozq7xQWk&NR=1.

Cordero, J. and Paus, E. 2008. "The unrealized potential of FDI for development." In: Working Group on Development and the Environment in the Americas, Foreign Investment and Sustainable Development: Lessons from the Americas. Washington: Heinrich Boell Foundation, 21–4.

Dickinson, S. M. 2007. "Quality over quantity," China International Business, December 7, www.danwei.org/danwei_fm/china_businesscast_2007_fdi_ca.php.

Dussel, E. 2005. *Economic Opportunities and Challenges Posed by China for Mexico and Central America*, Bonn: German Development Institute.

Easterly, W. 2002. *The Elusive Quest for Growth, Economists' Adventures and Misadventures in the Tropics*, Cambridge: MIT Press.

ECA (Economics of Climate Change Working Group). 2009. "Shaping Climate Resilient Development, A Framework for Decision-Making," Climate Works Foundation, Global Environment Facility, European Commission, McKinsey & Company, The Rockefeller Foundation, Standard Chartered Bank and Swiss Re, available at the website of the European Commission at www.ec.europa.edu.

Ellis, K., Baker, B., and Lemma, A. 2009. Policies for Low Carbon Growth. Overseas Development Institute (UK), November 27.

Evans, P. 1995. Embedded Autonomy, States and Industrial Transformations. Princeton, Princeton University Press.

Gallagher, K. and Chudnovsky, D. 2010. Rethinking Foreign Investment for Sustainable Development, Lessons for Latin America. London, Anthem Press.

Gallagher, K. and Zarsky, L. 2007. Enclave Economy, Foreign Investment and Sustainable Development in Mexico's Silicon Valley. Cambridge, MIT Press.

Hanson, G. 2001. "Should countries promote foreign direct investment?" G24 discussion paper No 9, www.unctad.org/en/docs/pogdsmdpbg24d9.en.pdf.

IISD (International Institute of Sustainable Development) and TERI (The Energy and Research Institute). 2006. "Designing policies in a world of uncertainty, change and surprise," www.iisd.org.

International Rivers. 2008. "Rip-Offsets: The failure of the Kyoto Protocol's Clean Development Mechanism," November 2008, www.internationalrivers.org/en/node/4614.

IPCC (Intergovernmental Panel on Climate Change). 2007. *Fourth Assessment: Climate Change 2007 Synthesis Report*, Contribution of Working Groups I, II and III to the Fourth Assessment Report of the Intergovernmental Panel on Climate Change, Core Writing Team, eds. Pachauri, R. K. and Reisinger, A. IPCC, Geneva, Switzerland.

Jenkins, R. 2006. "Globalization, FDI and employment in Vietnam," UNCTAD, www.unctad.org/en/docs/iteiit20061a5_en.pdf.

Maplecroft. 2010. Climate Change Vulnerability Index, www.maplecroft.com.

McGray, H., Hammill, A., and Bradley, R. 2007. Weathering the Storm, Options for Framing Adaptation and Development. Washington: World Resources Institute.

Moran, T. 2006. Harnessing Foreign Direct Investment for Development. Washington DC, Center for Global Development.

OECD. 2002. Foreign Direct Investment for Development: Maximizing Benefits, Minimizing Costs. Paris, OECD.

Rock, M., Murphy, J. T., Raiah, R., van Seters, P., and Managi, S. 2009. "A hard slog, not a leap frog: Globalization and sustainability transitions in developing Asia." Technological Forecasting and Social Change 76 (2), 241–54.

Rock, M. T. and Angel, D. P. 2005. Industrial Transformation in the Developing World. New York: Oxford University Press.

Rodrik, D. 2008. "Is There a New Washington Consensus?" www.project-syndicate.org/commentary/rodrik20.

Rodrik, D. 2007. One Economics, Many Recipes. Princeton: Princeton University Press.

Science Daily. 2009. "What could 4 degree warming mean for the world?" October 1, available on www.sciencedaily.com.

Schneider, L. 2007. "Is the CDM fulfilling its environmental and sustainable development objectives? An evaluation of the CDM and options for improvement." Oko-Institut Report for World Wildlife Fund (WWF), November 5, www.oeko.de/oekodoc/622/2007–162-en.pdf.

Stiglitz, Joseph. 2005. "Development policies in a world of globalization." In: K. Gallagher ed., Putting Development First. London: Zed Press, 15–32.

Tanner, T. and Mitchell, T. 2008. "Entrenchment or enhancement: could climate change adaptation help to reduce chronic poverty?" IDS Bulletin 39(4): 6–15.

UNCTAD (United Nations Conference on Trade and Development). 2009. *Trade and Development Report, 2009* (Geneva: UNCTAD).

UN-DESA (UN Department of Economic and Social Affairs). 2009. "Stronger industrial policies needed to face climate and development challenges," Policy Brief No. 23, August, New York, www.un.org/esa/policy/policybriefs/policybrief23.pdf.

UNDP. 2007. Human Development Report 2007/08: Fighting Climate Change: Human Solidarity in a Divided World. New York: Palgrave MacMillan.

UNDP. 2005a. Energy Services for the Millennium Development Goals. Washington DC: World Bank/UNDP.

UNDP. 2005b. *Unleashing Entrepreneurship: Making Business Work for the Poor*, New York: UNDP.

UNSW (University of New South Wales). 2009. The Copenhagen Diagnosis: Updating the World on the Latest Climate Science, UNSW Climate Change Research Centre, Sydney, Australia.

WBCSD. 2008. "From challenge to opportunity: the role of business in tomorrow's society," www.wbcsd.org/DocRoot/CZ2dt8wQCfZKX2S0wxMP/tomorrows-leaders.pdf.

Wilson, E., Zarsky, L., Shaad, B., and Bundock, B. 2008. "Lights on or trade off? Can 'base of the pyramid' approaches deliver solutions to energy poverty?" In P. Khandachar and M. Halme, eds., Sustainability Challenges and Solutions at the Base of the Pyramid: Business, Technology and the Poor. Sheffield: Greenleaf Publishing.

Working Group (Working Group on Climate Change and Development). 2009. Other Worlds Are Possible, Human Progress in an Age of Climate Change. London: New Economics Foundation.

Yunus, M. 2007. Creating a World Without Poverty, Social Business and the Future of Capitalism. Philadelphia, Perseus Books.

Zarsky, L. 2004. "Stuck in the mud? Nation-States, globalization and environment." In: K. Conca and G. D. Debelko eds., *Green Planet Blues, Environmental Politics from Stockholm to Johannesburg*, Boulder: Westview Press, 82–93.

Zoellick, R. 2007. "An inclusive and sustainable globalization," speech given October 10, www.polity.org.za/article.php?a_id=118901.

12 Towards new developmentalism

Context, program, and constraints[1]

Shahrukh Rafi Khan

Introduction

We make a case for new developmentalism as an alternative to neo-liberalism, which has been resoundingly critiqued in this volume and elsewhere. The essence of new developmentalism, explored in the various chapters of this volume, particularly Chapters 2–4, was defined briefly in Chapter 1 as enabling the acquisition of an indigenous technology capacity in the move to high productivity activities.[2] Why does neo-liberalism continue to dominate development discourse despite being so effectively challenged?[3] First, the political support of high-income country (HIC) administrations results in its continued dominance in influential international organizations and donor agencies that set the operational agenda. Thus, intellectual battles may be won without necessarily changing the operational canvas. A wise scholar, referring to the capital theory debate in the 1970s, suggested in dramatic terms that even though the head of the octopus had been smashed, its tentacles (represented by economics departments) continued to teach as before, oblivious to the generals' concession.[4] When people hold on to "truths" with ideological passion, it is difficult to change perspectives.

Second, in the development economics field, neo-liberalism continues to be influential for the aforementioned reason, but also because of a lack of a recognized alternative. Indeed, the debate need not be characterized as ideological. While neo-liberals do hold to their prescriptions with ideological conviction, developmentalist critics for the most part have been pragmatists. For them, the principle concern has been with what works.[5]

Thus, this is no longer the old Hayek-Lange debate on the efficiency of decentralized markets, based on the more effective use of information relative to centralized planning, based in theory on better co-ordination.[6] The potential efficiency of markets has been conceded and, in broad strokes, the economic development debate can now be cast in terms of whether the market is the master (an ideological neo-liberal perspective)[7] or merely the means. The latter position is implicitly part of a pragmatic "new developmentalism" perspective.

This chapter contends that, in varying forms, "new developmentalism" is the agenda of developmental states. While there are considerable variations in detail in the writings of heterodox economic development scholars, there appear to be sufficient commonalities to make a case for this assertion. This chapter explores the economic development debate, since the justification for the use of the term new developmentalism and the assertion that this represents a coherent alternative requires at least a cursory diversion into the history of development economics thought to provide context. I then distinguish new developmentalism from developmentalism, following which a brief conceptualization of industrial policy and its institutional underpinnings in the context of limited state capacity is proffered as a key element of new developmentalism. Next, I review the state of manufacturing in low- and middle-income economies and the current global economic context which may constrain the implementation of industrial and support policies. The chapter ends with a discussion of "getting there."

The development economics debate[8]

If we loosely think of the evolution of development economics in terms of a series of crises that the established paradigm cannot resolve, the most significant shift in the last century was the Keynesian contribution to resolving the unemployment, and associated poverty, problem in the 1930s.[9] For development economics, this was instrumental in establishing a case for intervention.

The developmentalists and Latin structuralists theorized and presented prescriptions for rapid economic development based on industrialization. As indicated in the introduction, among others, the developmentalist pioneers included Rosenstein-Rodan (1943), Nurkse (1953), Lewis (1954), and Hirschman (1959).[10] Prebish (1962) is prominent among the Latin American structuralists in making the case for import substitution industrialization based on the inherent advantages of manufacturing relative to problems associated with specializing in the export of primary commodities.

The early development economics literature did not make the distinction between economic growth and development that has now become common-place after the critiques and contributions of Seers (1969), Haq (1976), Sen (2000), and others suggesting that economic growth is not a sufficient condition for social or human development or poverty alleviation. We support this view, but the reference in this chapter is to the narrower concept of economic development.

Notwithstanding the optimism of the developmentalists, mass poverty persisted. A neo-Marxist approach was initiated by Baran (1952) based on class analysis and asymmetrical power in a neo-colonial context. Following in this vein, dependency theory in the 1960s posited the impossibility of economic development in the "periphery" so long as there were links to the "core" or "center."[11] Radical development theory, with its prescription of social revolution, did not gain traction in a cold war environment and neither did the "de-linking" prescription of dependency theory.

The political climate in the 1980s, with conservative politicians in ascendancy in the US, UK, and Germany, as well as concomitant leadership changes in international financial organizations and aid agencies, set the stage for the neo-liberal counter revolution with structural adjustment at the core of its operational program. Little *et al.* (1970), among others, initiated the conceptual tools and empirical case against developmentalism, or what was scathingly referred to as "dirigisme" by Lal (2000), who posited that government failure was more damaging than market failure.[12] The debt crisis of the early 1980s caused many countries to turn to the IMF for support, and this enabled the latter to implement a neo-liberal economic program.[13]

However, neo-liberalism was unable to resolve the crisis of mass poverty, and in fact empirical evidence accumulated to demonstrate that structural adjustment programs increased mass poverty and inequality.[14] A report commissioned in 2000 by the US Congress, led by a prominent conservative economist Alan Meltzer of Carnegie Mellon University, concluded that despite its stated mission, the World Bank achieved little in the way of poverty reduction.[15]

For developmentalists, inspiration was first provided by Japan's success, but this was viewed as an isolated miracle. The East Asian Tigers then appeared on the horizon, but initially their progress was classified either as cases of special strategic partnerships (Korea and Taiwan with the US) or of non-representative city-states (Singapore and Hong Kong). Warren (1980) sparked a debate in the political economy of development literature by suggesting the possibility of industrialization in low-income countries (LICs) despite neo-colonialism.[16]

Industrialization in the newly industrialized countries (NICs) was not a fly by night phenomenon and a new tier of countries including Malaysia, Thailand, and Indonesia appeared on the scene with robust economic growth rates. This new group of countries took over light manufacturing markets as unit labor costs rose for the older tigers and they diversified into higher value added manufacturing.[17] Other countries, including China and India, have gathered momentum[18] and still others like Vietnam are in the "take-off" stage.[19] In all cases, competing approaches lay claim to economic successes.

Scholars like Amsden (1989, 2001, 2008), Chang (2002, 2005), Johnson (1982), and Wade (2004) have argued that interventionist approaches incorporating strategic industrial policy (with some nuance and variation) explained the success of the East Asian newly industrialized countries.[20] Reinert (2007) used a historical perspective to make a similar point. The World Bank (1993) contended that this success had more to do with markets, stable macroeconomic policies, and good governance delivering a sound education (i.e., with neo-liberalism).[21] While the role of state intervention was conceded to be important, the probability of replicating this experience was not viewed as generally feasible given the prevalence of government failure. Rodrik (1994) and others challenged the implicit contention that the East Asian economic development experience was a "miracle," as evident from the title of the World Bank volume.

The concession that the "one size fits all" approach "exaggerated the gains from improved resource allocation and their dynamic repercussions, and proved to be both theoretically incomplete and contradicted by evidence" was a prevalent theme in the World Bank's (2005: 11) reassessment of the 1990s reforms. The World Bank's reassessment suggests a move towards pragmatism. On page 83, the reader gets the impression that the institution is agnostic on industrial policy, yet on pages 143–4 the report adopts Rodrik's (2007) industrial policy recommendations. Even so, the continuing endorsement of the Washington Consensus or neo-liberal policies, albeit applied differently in different contexts, suggests no fundamental change in thinking at the World Bank as of yet. The new creed represents a move from "getting prices right" or "getting policies right" to "getting institutions right." However, Reinert (2007) convincingly argues that the right institutions can be a by product of adopting the right activities. In any case, this is likely to be an interactive process.[22]

The debate between new developmentalists and neo liberal scholars is likely to intensify. As earlier indicated, the debate has been extended to explain the success of China and India. Thus, while Panagariya (2004) claims market driven "pro-entry" (neo-liberal) reforms explain the Indian take-off, Rodrik and Subramanian (2004) claim it is based on pro-business and pro-incumbent (industrial) policies. A similar debate extends to explaining China's astounding economic take-off.[23]

One could argue that the agenda of "developmentalist states" – a term widely used in the economic development literature – is represented by new developmentalism.[24] The neo-liberal approach is more ideologically driven, and espouses what Stiglitz (2004) calls, "market fundamentalism."[25] Thus, this debate could be viewed as one between fundamentalists and pragmatists.[26]

Two issues are of particular concern in this debate. First, is there reason to proffer a new-term for a well specified alternative to neo-liberalism, when an older one like "developmentalism" may fit just as well? One could argue that there are rapidly diminishing returns to the proliferation of terms, so a strong case needs to be made to use the term new developmentalism rather than just sticking with developmentalism. Such a justification would at least in part have to be based on spelling out and clarifying what the new term encompasses and on making a substantive distinction between developmentalism and new developmentalism. Second, even if an alternative agenda in the form of new developmentalism could reasonably be specified, there remains the issue of whether LICs can implement such an agenda. This refers to both the internal ability of states and the external environment in the early part of the twenty-first century.

Developmentalism and "new developmentalism"[27]

Just as Latin American structuralism drew inspiration from developmentalism, neo-structuralism, now common in Latin America scholarship, draws inspiration from what could be termed new developmentalism.[28] As in the case of developmentalism and structuralism, the conceptual underpinnings for new developmentalism are market failures and an important component of the policy agenda is industrial policy.[29]

Industrial policy is defined as the ability of the state to strategically influence targeted industries that exhibit increasing returns, among other dynamic efficiencies, and meet export objectives by creating comparative advantage.[30] More broadly, effective industrial policy requires supportive policies addressing trade, technology, employment, finance, infrastructure, competition, and institutions, and is a core element of new developmentalism just as structural adjustment was, and arguably still is, the core element of neo-liberalism.[31]

The trade theory underpinning of this approach is that of dynamic comparative advantage resulting inter alia from high potential for technological development, learning by doing, training, labor productivity, income-elasticity, economies of scale, energy efficiency, externalities (including diffusing managerial and marketing skills) which justify product selection, and specialization regardless of "inherent" comparative advantage. This goes back to the thinking of the early developmentalists who advocated industrialization premised on the dynamic efficiencies forthcoming from the industrial sector, as indicated above, as opposed to other sectors.[32]

New developmentalist scholars have established the role of the state as important, premised on a reasonably efficient economic bureaucracy, which came as an important challenge to the neo-liberal agenda of rolling back the state based on an assumption of "government failure."[33] These scholars also pointed out that the implementation of the neo-liberal program of structural adjustment is actually no less reliant on "good government" than the implementation of the industrial policy program. However, that notwithstanding, the commonality among new developmentalist scholars is their eclecticism, pragmatism, and support of institutional development with the market harnessed as a mere means for development.[34]

So far, one could argue that little has been said to distinguish developmentalism from new developmentalism. It would be difficult to make the case that the pioneering developmentalists were not pragmatic and eclectic. Indeed, Lewis (1954) was agnostic about whether industrialization should be engineered by public or private enterprises. I suspect his response, if questioned on this issue, would be "whatever works," and this is fairly evident from his writings. In this regard, the vision of the developmentalists and new developmentalism is the same. Both argue for sustained economic development and believe that industrialization based on the simultaneous development of indigenous technological capacity is likely to deliver just that. The underlying vision of the developmentalist import substitution industrialization (ISI) program was incorrectly confuted by critics that focused on the tools used by governments. Thus, developmentalism in this critique was not understood to be a vision, but rather heavy handed intervention, centralized planning, and corrupt and inefficient bureaucracy.[35]

The body of scholarship that I refer to as new developmentalism represents a careful and painstaking empirical demonstration that the developmentalist vision has been realized by several states in the race for global survival.[36] While there are differences among these countries, the commonality was their coherent, nuanced, and well implemented industrial and support policies. This came as a challenge to the mainstream view attributing developmental success to free market policies. Establishing an alternative explanation has been a breakthrough in the economic development literature, particularly since a bastion of neo-liberalism like the World Bank has acknowledged it, even if it did not acknowledge the works of some of the key authors responsible for the breakthrough.[37]

Many additions and conceptual refinements have been made to developmentalist thinking based on case studies of East and South East Asian NICs. The operational design principles identified by Robert Wade in Chapter 2 of this volume include the following. First, incentives to businesses in the East Asian NICs were premised on delivery, and performance criteria were used to achieve success. Thus, continued incentives were based on a firm's ability to show productivity growth, local content use, profit growth, or all of the above by breaking into export markets.[38] Further, the state needs to be able to sanction non-delivery.[39] Second, the government ensured the discipline of internal market competition, even as firms were protected from premature external competition, by determining an optimal number of players in an industry (preserving both competition and economies of scale). Without such competitive discipline, import-substitution industrialization can degenerate into crony capitalism, as was the case in many low-income countries under ISI policies. Third, to create the rents necessary to induce activity, the state needs to try to get the incentives right, which is not the same as getting prices right.[40] Finally, ISI and export promotion (EP) have a symbiotic association and are not alternative strategies. Thus, while some industries may be going through an ISI phase, others may have graduated to EP. ISI is viewed here as necessary to build a base for EP, which in turn provides resources, particularly foreign exchange, to further ISI in other industries propelling the economy up the value chain.[41]

New developmentalism represents as much a theory of government as a set of economic development policies.[42] Since it has been distilled from what worked, using an inductive method, it embodies eclectic and pragmatic industrial policy in a coordinated set of support policies. But as Robert Wade, Ha-Joon Chang, and Reinert *et al.* point out in Chapters 2–4 of this volume, the essence of new developmentalism is changing the focus of attention to building indigenous technological capacity in the context of shifting resources to increasing returns, higher productivity activities.

There is another important reason to distinguish new developmentalism from developmentalism: to distance it from what developmentalism has become associated with, such as the use of heavy handed and incompetent bureaucracies, misguided policies that backfired, rent seeking, inefficiency, and ineffectual support policies by planning agencies. More recently, the waters have been muddied by Easterly (2007) who refers to developmentalism as an ideology on par with communism, socialism, and fascism and as prone to "dangerous and deadly failure." Interestingly, the half-century of developmentalism that he refers to has, he claims, been led by the intelligentsia of the IMF, World Bank, and the UN, with the core component being structural adjustment.[43]

The early developmentalists should also not be faulted for failing to have the kind of environmental consciousness that is so widespread today. Since the well-being of the poor is central to economic development and since environmental degradation has the most devastating consequences for the poor, new developmentalism must embrace environmental safeguards that did not have political salience in the mid-twentieth century.[44] The case for sustainable industrial development now needs to be a central element in industrial policy and is summarized here.[45]

As painfully discovered by HICs, much of the environmental damage from industrialization without safeguards is irreversible.[46] As with other things, common sense suggests that prevention is much cheaper than finding a cure. This is especially so given our limited knowledge of the actual extent and nature of the damage to eco-systems. It is better to use the precautionary principle and initiate protections, than expect to deal with future consequences. Not doing so will result in immense human and economic costs, in terms of lost lives, working days, and productivity (from illnesses) and health care. Thus, there is a win-win case in preventing environmental degradation.

Since much of the burden falls on the poor, there is also a strong social justice argument for avoiding environmental degradation. Finally, given the cumulative degradation that has occurred to the global commons, particularly after the industrial revolution, the world has reached a tipping point on climate change, and business as usual is simply not possible. That said, industrial revolutions – premised on strategic industrial policy, encompassing environmental and social safeguards, technological systems, institutional development, and agricultural revolutions – are central and necessary, though not sufficient conditions, for addressing mass poverty.

New developmentalism views poverty as a symptom and the real issue as the ability to generate sustainable high quality jobs in increasing returns industrial activities. Thus the approach to poverty alleviation could be viewed as trickle down. However, there is a self-conscious distancing from the compartmentalization of neo-liberalism, whereby structural adjustment is viewed as creating the poverty, and poverty alleviation programs as addressing the fall out. Hence the variant of structural adjustment programs called PRGF (poverty reduction growth facility), which continue to have the same debilitating conditionalities as earlier facilities is viewed as an oxymoron. For this reason, both Ha-Joon Chang and Rienert *et al.* in Chapters 3 and 4 of this volume view the exclusive focus on MDG (Millennium Development Goals) as band aid and false development and argue for a change of focus to the required nature of production as the central aspect of development.

The state of manufacturing in middle- and low-income countries

While industrial policy is the core agenda of new developmentalism, manufacturing carries the most importance because of its great potential for structural transformation, externalities, increasing returns, product diversification, and moving up the value chain (elaborated above as dynamic efficiencies).[47] We review the state of manufacturing drawing on The World Bank's World Development Indicators, which reported data from 1960 to 2007 in August 2009. This half-century of data has been split into three periods; up to 1980, from 1981–94, and 1994 onwards. The post-War period up to 1980 has been referred to by Amsden (2008: 118) as the Golden Age for policy due to the benign neglect of the US, the only force capable of projecting imperial power. The period from

1980s onwards is referred to as the Dark Ages; the structural adjustment era that represented much greater US policy interest in low- and middle-income countries and hence much greater policy constraints for them. This period has been bifurcated into 1990–94 and 1994–2007 because the latter period represents greater trade policy restrictions with the conclusion of the Uruguay Round of trade talks and the formation of the WTO as an implementing agency.

Transition economies (ex-socialist countries) are included if they secured loans from the IMF and were thus subject to policy advice. Countries with populations of less than five million are viewed as special cases vis-à-vis the realization of dynamic efficiencies and are not included in the sample. After these exclusions, we were left with a sample of 80 countries. When data were available, means were computed within periods and t-tests conducted to see if differences were significant across periods (reported in Appendix Table 12.1). For most transition countries, data were only available for the third period and we calculated the percentage change from the first to the last year for which data were available, since in all cases a trend was evident.

Data were only available for three-fifths of the 80 countries in the sample for the first two periods. For almost half of these countries (46.8 percent), mean manufacturing increased across the periods. For 34 percent there was no change and it was negative 19.1 percent for the remaining fifth. In the post-WTO period, the trend virtually reversed. Of the 79 countries for which data were available, 48 percent showed a decline in manufacturing as a percentage of GDP, 32 percent an increase, and for a fifth there was no change. Thus it appears that the post-WTO period represents the real dark-age, whereby two thirds of the countries reveal a decrease or no change in manufacturing activity. Differences are evident, as reported in Table 12.1, when the sample is disaggregated by income classification and region, and the percentage change in means is computed for countries for which a more or less complete data set is available from 1960–2007.

There was an increase in manufacturing activity for LICs and for LMCs (low middle-income countries) in the 1981–94 period as compared to the 1960–80 period. However, this is reversed for LICs and for LMCs the percentage increase is halved in the post-WTO period compared to the 1981–94 period. There is a consistent decline for UMCs (upper middle-income countries). The regional disaggregation shows a consistent increase for East Asia and the Pacific region, for Middle East and North Africa, and less so for South Asia. There is a consistent decrease for Latin America and the Caribbean and a reversal post-WTO for Sub Saharan Africa. We also estimated the means for the whole sample for which adequate data were available between 1960 and 2007 and it confirmed an average increase in manufacturing as a percentage of GDP: 8.9 percent for the 1981–94 period and a decline of 5.3 percent in the post-WTO period. Data for Europe and Central Asia were only available for the third period and so a comparison of means was not possible. Excluding The Russian Federation, for which only six years of data were available, the other 11 countries revealed a consistent downward trend that averaged 34 percent, a loss of a third of their manufacturing activity in the process of transition to market economies.

Table 12.1 Change in mean size of manufacturing as a percentage of GDP by income classification and region

Country classification and region	1960–80	1918–14	1995–2007	% change in mean SOM across first two periods	% change in mean SOM across second two periods
LIC	9.78 (21)	12.45 (31)	11.24 (30)	27.30	–9.72
LMC	14.95 (19)	16.02 (21)	17.02 (21)	11.47	6.11
UMC	23.17 (7)	22.74 (7)	19.75 (7)	–18.56	–13.15
EA&P	13.78 (6)	17.25 (8)	20.44 (8)	25.18	18.49
LA&C	20.50 (12)	19.80 (12)	18.18 (12)	–3.4	–8.18
ME&NA	11.56 (5)	15.56 (6)	18.06 (6)	25.71	16.07
SA	12.87 (4)	13.61 (5)	14.91 (5)	5.75	9.55

SSA	10.34 (20)	11.44 (26)	10.20 (25)	10.64	–10.84
Total	13.72 (47)	14.94 (59)	14.15 (58)	8.89	–5.29

Source: World Development Indicators; Country classification based on World Bank (2009: 351).

Notes

Appendix Table 1 has been used for the computations of means. The numbers in the parenthesis in columns 3–5 indicate sub sample sizes. Since E&CA countries are included in the country classification but not as a disaggregated region for the second two periods, the total sample exceeds the regional total by two. The last two columns report percentage changes in the means.

LIC = Low income country ($935 or less).

LMC = Lower middle income country ($936–$3,705).

UMC = Upper middle income country ($3,706–11,455).

SOM = Manufacturing value added as a % of GDP.

EE&P = East Asia and the Pacific.

E&CA = Europe and Central Asia.

LA&C = Latin America and the Caribbean.

ME&NA = Middle East and North Africa.

SA = South Asia.

SSA = Sub-Saharan Africa.

Conceptualizing industrial policy and its implementation[48]

Currently, Rodrik (2007) is among the most influential writers on industrial policy for the developmental state; so much so, that many of his design principles (Rodrik 2007: 114–17) have been adopted by the World Bank (2005: 144). Given this broader acceptance, some of his ideas are considered here.[49]

Rodrik views the case for industrial policy as premised on market failures: in particular information and co-ordination.[50]The assumption of information failure is premised on the state and businesses not knowing, but needing to discover, underlying cost structures, opportunities, and constraints. The co-ordination failure harkens back to Rosenstein-Rodan (1943), whereby there is a simultaneous need for upstream and downstream investments for the activity in question to be effectively pursued. Rodrik lays emphasis on the policy process as strategic public-private collaboration, rather than on instruments, whereby the state is learning from and assisting the private sector and the two mutually share responsibilities and evaluate outcomes. If the process is right, the instruments will follow and Rodrik suggests half a dozen by way of illustration (Rodrik 2007: 117–19). One of Rodrik's concerns is support only for first movers who otherwise see their profits dissipated with imitation.[51]

Rodrik (2008) points out that many, if not most, LICs are already engaged in some form of industrial policy. In fact, he reasons that industrial policy is no more subject to capture and government failure than state intervention in health, education, or for macro stabilization. However, while the latter interventions are taken for granted, there is unreasonable mainstream intellectual resistance to the former. He indicates that with simple design principles like "embeddedness," a carrot and stick policy, and transparency and accountability, industrial policy can and has contributed much to economic development.

Our approach is complementary to Rodrik's and our emphasis is on the public sector discovering and nurturing "successes." If the state has the capacity, then creating "successes" should be central to industrial policy. However, we are assuming minimal state capacity to indicate that even that does not rule out industrial policy.

While the lack of information, coordination failures, and other market failures may curb some kinds of activities, we start with the presumption that in most low-income countries entrepreneurship and the urge to profit continues notwithstanding and is manifested in individuals exploring different activities.[52] While imitation in the Schumpeterian sense does reduce rents, this is part of the market system and there are always other entrepreneurs exploring other activities.[53] The point is that the state needs to discover what has the best potential to generate dynamic efficiencies, including scale economies (exports for small states), and to nurture those businesses. It is unlikely that the state can or needs to concern itself only with the first mover. In fact, imitation is important and an indicator that the activity has promise.

A possible tool for identifying "successes" could be the scrutiny of foreign trade statistics or disaggregated manufacturing sector data. Those identified as successful could be urged on to other higher value products or activities by relaxing credit, information, or infrastructural constraints. Thus an important component of industrial policy could be nurturing such successes by understanding and relaxing constraints. Here, Rodrik's advice on open channels of communication between the public and private sector are highly relevant.[54]

Rodrik (2007: 111–12) suggests the possibility of using pockets of excellence in the bureaucracy as a mechanism of support.[55] An alternative is to restructure planning agencies, which have increasingly become redundant and wasteful. For example, in Pakistan, the planning commission contains a large section for primary education, as does the federal ministry of education. Concurrently, education delivery is constitutionally a provincial subject and was devolved to the district level in 2000 to be closer to the grassroots clientele. While redundancies can be addressed as part of public sector reform, converting the planning commission into a Bureau of Economic Activity with a one point mandate of nurturing promising activities is advisable, as it entails inter-ministerial supportive roles to ensure upstream and downstream activities are in place.[56]

While one might anticipate most dynamic efficiencies to be in the manufacturing sector, as the name Bureau of Economic Activity suggests and as Rodrik points out, there may be promising non-industrial activities, like information technology, which qualify for support. More importantly, much of the Bureau's work would be interfacing with other agencies and ministries to ensure that support systems are in place. All advocates of industrial policy now acknowledge the importance of the ability of such an agency to set and monitor performance criteria (e.g., exports or employment growth) and to have the political strength to sanction or withdraw support if need be.[57]

Planning Commissions used to have prestige and draw the best and brightest but, over time, particularly with the sway of neo-liberalism, have lost their sheen. A revamped and relevant Bureau could change that.[58] As Chang (2006: 98) points out, such a bureau needs to have power over other related ministries, be immune from the funding veto of the finance ministry, and be answerable directly to the chief executive, but with a cabinet level check on economic practice.

Economic globalization and industrial policy

Industrial policy can be both facilitated and deterred by economic globalization, which is defined as various forms of global economic interactions among nations, including among high-income and lower-income countries. Such interactions include the freer movement of capital (direct investment and capital flows), goods, services, technology, and labor. Economic globalization is driven by institutions like the WTO and IMF that are supposed to further the economic globalization agenda but that have also been viewed as responsible for closing the policy space for a new-developmentalist agenda.[59]

There are several important contributions to the literature on this issue of diminishing policy space. The Human Development Report 2005 of the UNDP

(2005: 133–9) laments the closing of space for economic development policies. Based on the "single undertaking," post-Uruguay Round members have to comply with all agreements as a package. This includes accepting the jurisdiction of a strengthened resolution procedure that in turn enforces compliance. The UNDP (2005) argues that the agreements as a package have severely restricted the scope for industrial and technology policy. It points out that even as late as the early 1990s, India continued to successfully build its domestic automobile components industry with high tariffs, local content requirements, and training clauses that are now ruled out by TRIMs (Trade Related Investment Measures).

The Agreement on Subsidies and Countervailing Measures (SCM) prohibits a wide range of input, export, and credit subsidies to support domestic industrialization. Copying and reverse engineering for technology acquisition are blocked by TRIPS (Trade Related Intellectual Property Rights) and TRIPS plus (the more stringent version pushed in regional and bi-lateral agreements). Thus, it argues that a path that was open to and followed by the currently high- and middle-income countries has been closed.

An edited volume by Gallagher (2005) contains several chapters that address this issue including a chapter by Wade (2005), who also argues that the WTO via the Uruguay Round Agreements (URA) has blocked access to technology with TRIPS by prohibiting the practice of compulsory licensing in negotiations with MNCs (multinational companies).[60] Similarly, TRIMs has ruled out specifying performance requirements (local content, trade balancing, export clauses, joint-ventures, R&D, training) in such negotiations. The SDT (Special and Differential Treatment) for low-income countries merely allows more time for compliance, but the date of reckoning inevitably approaches and many requests for extensions have been turned down by the WTO.[61] Gallagher (2007) estimated that "more than 25 percent of total WTO cases between 1995 and 2005 dealt with dismantling policy space in developing countries." Further, he reported that "in all cases the final ruling upheld the demand." In the same volume, Chang (2005a) argues that high-income countries extensively used industrial and technology policies to promote domestic industrialization, and that once productivity gaps are accounted for, current LICs have not been as protectionist in the equivalent phase of industrialization.

Amsden (2005) is more sanguine about policy space. First, she argues that various articles of the WTO still allow for tariffs: Article XVIII, to counter balance of payments destabilization; Article XIX, to counter import surges; and Article VI, to counter unfair trade practices.[62] Second, she asserts (Amsden 2005: 220) that "as a consequence of limited agreement in the area of TRIMs, LICs are able to maintain or even strengthen..." various performance requirements including local content, trade balancing, and exports. Third, the WTO continues to permit subsidies to promote R&D, regional development, and environmentalism. In particular, countries with a per capita income of less than $1,000 are permitted to use export subsidies via science parks and EPZs (Export Processing Zones) based on SDT. Thus, she argues that much scope still exists to support science and technology for industrial policy.[63]

Similarly, while recognizing that much policy space has been conceded by LICs in the Uruguay Rounds, Rodrik (2007), UNCTAD (2006), Chang and Grabel (2004: 69), and Chang (2006, 2009) argue that there is still room for creative industrial policy and suggest methods and policy tools for attaining it. For example, tariff rebates and the provision of production and marketing information is still possible. Import controls are still possible for countries facing balance of payment problems. Local hiring, technology transfer clauses, targeted subsidies, and directed credit, training, and infrastructure leave plenty of wiggle room. The above measures could be used strategically as part of economic development and industrial policy rather than in an ad hoc fashion. Cimoli *et al.* (2009: 555) suggest that TRIPS "contains a series of loopholes, safeguard clauses, and exceptional provisions" that could be exploited.

LICs may therefore still have mechanisms to negotiate policy space and offset its closing. However, while this may be the case in theory, for most LICs there is very little leeway in practice. They may lack the necessary resources, not have enough leverage when negotiating with MNCs, or lack the knowledge, technical, and negotiating skills to take advantage of the leverage they do have. Also, even the existing policy space is threatened by the powerful aid and trade leverage of HICs and the policy leverage mediated through International Financial Institutions (IFIs).

Getting there

The practical relevance of the debate on economic development approaches in general, and on the nature of and space for industrial policy in particular, is how best to address the issue of economic growth and poverty alleviation in low-income countries.[64] New developmentalists view an industrial revolution, supported by an agricultural revolution, as central to this process. One viewpoint, as indicated above, suggests that there is still considerable wiggle room for low-income countries. If so, policy should address how best this space could be exploited because recent evidence suggests that deindustrialization is setting in on a massive scale in low- and middle-income countries (A12.1).

Drawing on the literature and the other chapters of this volume, this chapter distinguishes new developmentalism from developmentalism and identifies industrial policy, embedded in supportive policies pertaining for example to institutions, trade, technology, finance, and fiscal incentives, as the core element of a new developmentalist program. It identifies key design principles for industrial policies that could even be implemented with a minimal level of bureaucratic competence. However, ultimately what counts is not what to do and how to do it but the conditions under which such structural transformation takes place.

It seems that what drives nations' development efforts is the consciousness of being left behind at a collective and policy level.[65] Nations are conscious of being in a race and hence the constant references by politicians to getting left behind and the need to get to the twenty-first century. Researchers from low-income countries immediately flip to the relevant tables in the Human Development Report and World Development Report to see how their country fared on the score cards, even if they are expatriates. This is not much different from following how the national teams are faring in sports. The drivers for catch up are both individual and collective, as is the pride felt by accomplishments in this regard.[66]

Leaders often share this collective desire and are certainly judged by this yardstick, whether the form of government is democracy or not. Much is ignored or forgiven those that are perceived to have made strides.[67] Political leaders are also subject to enormous pressures that result from dealing with internal security, power struggles, ethnic and regional conflicts, disasters, and external pressures while confronted with the temptations of maximizing their own objective functions. Sometimes things do fall into place. Some of this may be a result of good statecraft and good economic policies, but luck and positive cumulative causation from fortuitous past investments (such as social and physical infrastructure in China or higher education in India) can play a role. Perhaps a potent mix of patriotism and bureaucratic competence makes the difference. What this speculation suggests is that we may know more about what works than how it comes about or how to "get there."[68]

High-income countries (HICs) are now also in a complex position. While a rising tide lifts all boats, they are nonetheless also in a race and one in which they may want to maintain if not increase their lead.[69] The old argument, now rephrased due to terrorism, is that world security will require prosperity and it is in the HICs enlightened self-interest to allow it to emerge.[70]

As indicated above, there are many pressures internally and externally that prevent political leaders from pursuing economic development. Internal pressures are unique to each country and understanding and addressing these constraints has to be the starting point.[71] Externally, high-income countries should reverse what they are currently engaged in: using international organizations to squeeze the policy space for economic development or, to borrow the term well utilized by Ha-Joon Chang, from "kicking away the ladder." Realistically, in terms of the relationship between states, the world has been and will remain Darwinian for a while yet. One could take some comfort from the view that the manifestation of this reality, in the move from colonialism to neo-colonialism, is now less harsh. Nonetheless, LICs have to make progress despite their internal and external constraints. Low-income states confront a collective action problem, and as the largest player, assuming good intentions, their task will be much easier and short term sacrifices more easily solicited if other agents in society perceive that they are engaged in delivering economic and social development.[72]

Appendix

A12.1 Average size of manufacturing value added as a percentage of GDP over time for low and middle income countries

	Status	Region	Income	1960–80	1981–94	1995–2007	% change
Algeria	LMC	ME&NA	13.25 (16)	12.82 (14)	7.78 (13)	ns	−39.31* (1.14E-07)
Angola	LMC	SSA	na	6.91 (10)	4.04 (13)	na	−41.35* (0.00174)
Argentina	UMC	LA&C	35.94 (16)	26.83 (14)	20.33 (13)	−25.34* (5.47E-07)	−24.23* (5.47E-07)
Bangladesh	LIC	SA	na	13.88 (14)	16.02 (13)	na	15.42* (9.72E-08)
Belarus	UMC	E&CA	na	na	(18)	na	−17.74
Benin	LIC	SSA	10.45 (10)	7.94 (14)	8.48 (11)	−24.02* (0.0006)	6.80** (0.03)
Bolivia	LMC	LA&C	13.44 (11)	17.03 (14)	15.71 (13)	26.71* (0.003)	ns
Brazil	UMC	LA&C	29.29 (21)	30.18 (14)	17.43 (13)	ns	−43.43* (4.14E-08)
Bulgaria	UMC	E&CA	na	na	(12)	na	−29.34
Burkina Faso	LIC	SSA	15.57 (21)	14.88 (14)	14.77 (12)	ns	ns
Burundi	LIC	SSA	8.96 (11)	10.27 (14)	8.32 (11)	14.62* (0.054)	−18.99* (0.004)
Cambodia	LIC	EA&P	na	na	(15)	na	110.28
Cameroon	LMC	SSA	9.67 (16)	14.17 (14)	19.69 (13)	46.53* (0.0003)	28.03* (4.36E-05)
Chad	LIC	SSA	9.84 (19)	11.52 (12)	8.67 (13)	17.07*** (0.025)	−32.87* (0.003)
Chile	UMC	LA&C	23.88 (21)	19.62 (14)	17.89 (13)	−17.84* (3.77E-08)	−0.09** (0.043)
Columbia	UMC	LA&C	21.78 (16)	21.11 (14)	16.00 (13)	ns	−24.20* (3.26E-09)
Congo, Dem. Rep. of	LIC	SSA	na	10.63 (12)	6.05 (12)	na	−43.09* (0.0002)
Côte d'Ivoire	LIC	SSA	9.91 (16)	16.69 (14)	19.08 (13)	68.42* (1.33E-07)	14.32** (0.015)
Dominican Republic	LMC	LA&C	18.13 (16)	16.33 (14)	16.07 (13)	−9.93** (0.038)	ns
Ecuador	LMC	LA&C	na	na	(3)	na	−3.4
Egypt, Arab Rep. of	LMC	ME&NA	15.24 (7)	15.47 (14)	18.03	ns	15.47* (0.0007)
El Salvador	LMC	LA&C	na	na	(18)	na	1.27
Eritrea	LIC	SSA	na	na	(16)	na	−33.70
Ethiopia	LIC	SSA	na	4.41 (14)	5.21 (13)	na	18.14* (0.008)
Ghana	LIC	SSA	10.97 (16)	8.49 (14)	8.83 (13)	−22.61* (0.005)	ns
Guatemala	LMC	LA&C	15.69 (16)	15.35 (14)	16.40 (13)	ns	ns
Guinea	LIC	SSA	na	4.52 (7)	3.90 (13)	na	−13.72* (0.0001)
Haiti	LIC	LA&C	na	na	(10)	na	−38.98
Honduras	LMC	LA&C	13.95 (21)	15.65 (14)	20.17 (13)	12.19* (0.0008)	28.88* (6.72E-08)
India	LMC	SA	15.08 (21)	16.42 (14)	15.97 (13)	8.89* (0.0001)	ns
Indonesia	LMC	EA&P	9.87 (21)	17.86 (14)	27.28 (13)	80.95* (2.70E-06)	52.74* (1.82E-07)

continued

A12.1 continued

	Status	Region	Income	1960–80	1918–14	1995–2007	% change
Iran, Islamic Rep.	LMC	ME&NA	8.43 (16)	9.46 (14)	12.15 (13)	ns	28.44 (0.0008)
Jordan	LMC	ME&NA	11.38 (16)	13.06 (14)	16.50 (130	14.76* (0.013)	26.34* (3.25E-05)
Kazakhstan	UMC	E&CA	na	na	(13)	na	-18.92
Kenya	LIC	SSA	11.31 (21)	11.58 (14)	11.54 (13)	ns	ns
Kyrgyz Republic	LIC	E&CA	na	27.67 (5)	14.22 (13)	na	-48.61 (0.0008)
Lao PDR	LIC	EA&P	na	11.85 (6)	18.16 (13)	na	34.75* (2.22E-05)
Madagascar	LIC	SSA	na	10.78 (11)	12.39 (13)	na	14.94* (0.026)
Malawi	LIC	SSA	12.98 (6)	16.26 (14)	13.47 (13)	25.27* (0.004)	-17.16* (0.0008)
Malaysia	UMC	EA&P	13.55 (21)	22.20 (14)	29.17 (13)	63.84* (1.08E-07)	31.40* (2.50E-07)
Mali	LIC	SSA	6.89 (14)	7.66 (14)	4.14 (13)	ns	-85.02* (3.19E06)
Mexico	LMC	LA&C	21.90 (16)	21.99 (14)	19.82 (130	ns	-9.87 (0.004)
Morocco	LMC	ME&NA	na	18.25 (14)	17.02 (13)	na	-6.74* (0.001)
Mozambique	LIC	SSA	na	na	(18)	na	33.22
Myanmar	LIC	EA&P	9.56 (21)	8.28 (14)	6.90 (6)	-13.40* (0.003)	16.67* (0.001)
Nepal	LIC	SA	3.95 (16)	6.30 (14)	8.90 (13)	59.50* (0.0002)	41.27* (5.90E-05)
Nicaragua	LMC	LA&C	na	na	(14)	na	0.11
Niger	LIC	SSA	4.70 (12)	6.17 (14)	6.54 (9)	31.28* (0.001)	-24.78
Nigeria	LIC	SSA	na	na	(5)	na	ns
Pakistan	LIC	SA	15.13 (21)	16.34 (14)	16.55 (13)	8.00* (0.0001)	-25.94* (1.89E-05)
Papua New Guinea	LIC	EA&P	7.90 (11)	10.37 (14)	7.68 (13)	31.27* (0.001)	ns
Paraguay	LMC	LA&C	16.25 (21)	15.19 (14)	15.01 (13)	-6.52* (0.005)	-21.91* (0.009)
Peru	LMC	LA&C	19.70 (20)	21.69 (9)	16.07 (13)	ns	-8.38* (4.64E-09)
Philippines	LMC	EA&P	24.99 (21)	24.70 (14)	22.63 (13)	ns	-22.07
Poland	UMC	E&CA	na	na	(14)	na	-35.08
Romania	UMC	E&CA	na	na	(16)	na	7.76
Russian Federation	UMC	E&CA	na	na	(6)	na	-40.49* (4,32E-06)
Rwanda	LIC	SSA	7.33 (16)	13.93 (14)	8.29 (13)	90.04* (0.0002)	8.95* (0.002)
Senegal	LIC	SSA	na	14.64 (14)	15.95 (13)	ns	ns
Sierra Leone	LIC	SSA	5.84 (16)	6.35 (12)	4.80 (9)	ns	na
Somalia	LIC	SSA	5.61 (21)	4.96 (10)	na	ns	na
South Africa	UMC	SSA	21.75 (21)	22.66 (14)	19.27 (13)	4.18* (0.009)	-14.96* (7.49E-09)
Sri Lanka	LMC	SA	17.33 (21)	15.12 (140	17.47 (13)	-12.75* (0.0002)	15.54* (3.34E-05)
Sudan	LMC	SSA	6.63 (21)	7.56 (14)	7.62 (13)	14.03** (0.037)	ns
Syrian Arab Republic	LMC	ME&NA	na	na	(15)	na	-45.34

Country							
Tajikistan	LIC	E&CA	na	28.19 (10)	25.66 (13)	na	ns
Tanzania	LIC	SSA	na	na	(17)	na	−25.46
Thailand	LMC	EA&P	16.80 (21)	25.82 (14)	32.92	71.55* (6.03E-09)	21.57* (4.23E-08)
Togo	LIC	SSA	8.28 (21)	8.38 (14)	8.74 (11)	ns	ns
Tunisia	LMC	ME&NA	9.48 (16)	15.56 (14)	18.06 (13)	64.14* (4.92E-09)	15.07* (0.0006)
Turkey	UMC	E&CA	na	na	(10)	na	−26.34
Turkmenistan	LMC	E&CA	na	na	(11)	na	−24.34
Uganda	LIC	SSA	7.37 (21)	5.79 (14)	8.01 (13)	−21.44* (0.002)	38.34* (6.83E-06)
Ukraine	LMC	E&CA	na	na	(16)	na	−46.35
Uzbekistan	LIC	E&CA	na	na	(17)	na	−56.33
Venezuela R. B. de	UMC	LA&C	16.00 (12)	16.61 (14)	18.18 (11)	ns	ns
Vietnam	LIC	EA&P	na	16.93 (10)	18.81 (13)	na	ns
Yemen, Rep. of	LIC	ME&NA	na	na	(14)	na	−49.46
Zambia	LIC	SSA	14.03 (16)	27.30 (14)	11.84 (13)	94.58* (1.18E-05)	−56.63* (3.38E-06)
Zimbabwe	LIC	SSA	18.79 (16)	22.99 (14)	15.39 (10)	22.35* (2.23E-05)	−33.06* (4.32E-08)

Source: World Development Indicators; Country classification based on World Bank (2009: 351).

Notes

Not all countries had data available for all years in the specified periods. Thus all relevant observations in a given period have been used. The numbers in parentheses represent the number of observations in the respective periods. Since data are missing from either the beginning or the end of the time series, it is possible to work out the beginning and the end of the series from the reported observations for each period. The percentage change reported in the last two columns is reported only when the t-test indicated a significant difference across means. For many transition economies, data are available only for the third period or so. In these cases, the last column reports the difference between the first and last year for which data were available and this at times exceeds 13 i.e. the years normally covered in the third period between 1995 and 2007.

LIC = Low income country ($935 or less).

LMC = Lower middle income country ($936–$3,705).

UMC = Upper middle income country ($3,706–11,455).

SOM = Manufacturing value added as a % of GDP.

na = Not available.

ns = Difference not significant.

* = Significant at least at the 1 percent level.

** = Significant at least at the 5 percent level.

EE&P = East Asia and the Pacific.

E&CA = Europe and Central Asia.

LA&C = Latin America and the Caribbean.

ME&NA = Middle East and North Africa.

SA = South Asia.

SSA = Sub-Saharan Africa.

Notes

1 Thanks are due to extensive, detailed, and very valuable comments by Ha-Joon Chang, Helen Shapiro, and Ilene Grabel. Thanks are also due to Eva Paus and Tariq Banuri for comments on an earlier version of this chapter. The usual caveats apply.
2 The alternative scholarship is this regard is extensive and referred to in the systematic challenge to neo-liberalism put forward by Chang and Grabel (2004).
3 Refer to Robert Wade's and Helen Shapiro's chapters in this volume for a fuller response to this question.
4 The reference is to Locke Anderson who taught macroeconomics at the University of Michigan until the early 1980s. The metaphor has the limitation of suggesting that the triumph of an alternative is inevitable; most heterodox economists may agree that changing the mainstream discourse is an uphill struggle. Refer to Cohen and Harcourt (2003) for a retrospective on the capital controversy.
5 As will be explained later, the goal is an indigenous and endogenous technological capacity and increasing returns activities normally associated with industrialization. The expectation is that this will create livelihoods but just as growth may not necessarily reduce poverty as presumed by neo-liberalism, industrialization may not lead to mass employment.
6 Refer to Hayek (1944) and Lange (1936).
7 Among the common dictionary definitions of ideology is that it represents a set of beliefs. The implication here is that the beliefs trump evidence, something that neo-liberal economists would undoubtedly dispute. Wade (2004: 344) refers to paradigms "(parrot-times) talking past each other." In the social sciences, entrenched beliefs challenge method, data, or interpretation rather than concede a point.
8 This section draws on Khan (2007). Refer to Toye (2003) for a fuller overview of this debate including the 1990s and Calclough (1991), and Shapiro and Taylor (1990) for earlier reviews.
9 The reference here is to Kuhn (1970), although the use of approaches rather than paradigms is probably more appropriate for the social sciences.
10 Also refer to eds. Meier and Seers (1984). Krugman (1998) provides an account of why the interest generated by the early developmentalists was not sustained in the mainstream research on development economics.
11 Frank (1966) was a pioneer of this "impossibility hypothesis." Refer to Kay (1989) for a review of this literature.
12 The tools, such as effective rates of protection, of this critique have been challenged by Fine (2005: Chapter 4).
13 This chapter perhaps overemphasizes the role of the World Bank and IMF in shaping and implementing a neo-liberal agenda. The agency of private capital and governments is an important part of the story. However, there are two reasons for the emphasis on these institutions. First, they have been central in building the intellectual case for neo-liberalism; directly via in-house research and indirectly via support for such research. Second, private capital has in general followed the lead of these institutions in judging whether or not the countries are capital friendly. Being subject to the discipline of a structural adjustment program has been perceived as a positive signal in this regard. While there has been greater acceptance and a voluntary turn to neo-liberal policies in several countries, Grabel's qualifications (Chapter 6 in this volume) in this regard are also an important part of the story.
14 For a friendly critique that documented some of the early evidence in this regard refer to eds. Cornia *et al.* (1987).
15 www.house.gov/jec/imf/meltzer.htm.
16 Neo-colonialism is understood to mean the continued transfer of surplus from LICs to HICs via the agency of foreign trade, investment, loans, and conditioned aid.

17 The path to middle- and then higher-income status is not a linear one as the East Asian Contagion and the experience of Argentina show, but nonetheless it is often a steady one when viewed over generations, and doubts about the robustness of the East Asian growth experience (Young 1994) have abated. Refer to comments on the latter issue in "The new titans: A survey of the world economy," *The Economist*, September 16th, 2006: 10. Robert Wade, in presenting evidence regarding the "middle-income trap" in Chapter 2 of this volume, is not optimistic about middle-income countries following the East Asian ones into high-income status.

18 The two Asian giants have large labor markets, but, based on press reports, the rise in wages for skilled labor in China is already evident as are salaries in the information technology sector in India.

19 While Rostow's (1960) framework has been criticized for lacking theoretical content, as a descriptive framework it still has resonance.

20 Industrial policy is defined in the next section. Success is defined broadly as "increasing the size of the pie." Distributional issues became prominent later in the economic development literature when trickle-down was widely critiqued for not delivering broad based development. East Asian states contained social inequality since it could trigger social unrest; Chang (2006: Chapter 2).

21 The World Bank position evolves, notwithstanding strong support for neo-liberalism among the core group of economists at the Bank. Some critics contend that it co-opts the heterodox approaches of its critics such as in the case of participatory development, gender and development, or the broader encompassing approach of sustainable development, and does not do them justice. In this particular case, the position evolved from a focus on markets, to accepting the importance of social sectors, to promoting governance and institutions, partly based on highly debated empirics [refer to Burnside and Dollar (2000), Easterly *et al.* (2004), and Burnside and Dollar (2004)].

22 Reinert (2007) points out that "getting institutions right" is the latest of a long list of "getting something right" adopted as a mantra by the World Bank. Perhaps it is in the nature of an organization that defines its role as one of giving advice that it must adopt and implement certainties. Under Paul Wolfenson's leadership, the World Bank defined itself as a knowledge bank.

23 Qian (2003) argues that the importance of FDI in accounting for Chinese economic growth since the 1980s has been exaggerated and puts it into perspective by proffering alternative explanations that include a prominent role for the state. Also refer to Nolan and Rui (2004), Rodrik (2006) Gallagher and Shafaeddin, this book regarding industrial policy in China.

24 Refer to pp. 4–5 of the introduction.

25 While many had been saying this for years, the pronouncements from a prominent economist, who was the Chief Economist at the World Bank, drew more attention.

26 While the focus of this chapter is on industry, Chambers (2006) makes a similar case for eclecticism for rural development, that is neither neo-liberal nor neo-Fabian, which he refers to as "eclectic pluralism."

27 New developmentalism is discussed thoughout this volume. Refer in particular to Wade's and Ha-Joon Chang's chapters in Part I and to Gallagher and Shafaeddin's section on the theory of capability building (TCB) in Chapter 9 of this volume.

28 Refer to Ffrench-Davis (1988) and other articles in the same volume. Refer to Santiso (2006) for a contribution to a pragmatic rather than an ideological, approach to development in Latin America and UNCTAD (2007: Chapter 3) is written in the same vein for economic development in Africa.

29 The work of Joe Stiglitz and his associates added to the range of market failures including missing markets and imperfect information. Drawing on these, the policy agenda that emerged during his tenure as Chief Economist of the World Bank included a mix of the human development, institutional, and "new-developmentalist" approaches referred to as the Post-Washington Consensus. However, while this is a

candidate for an alternative, it does not incorporate all of what is being proposed in this chapter and others in this volume. Refer to Fine and Jomo (2005) and Öniş and Şenses (2005) on the Post-Washington Consensus. Cimoli *et al.* (2004) question market failure as a point of departure for heterodox analysis and policy since the ideal cannot be realized due to missing information and markets, and an ever changing world in which the focus on efficient market led resource allocation as the norm makes limited sense.

30 For other definitions refer to UNCTAD (2006: 196, fn. 2). For supportive expositions, refer to Amsden (2001), Wade (2004), Rodrik (2004), and Chang (2006). For a critique of industrial policy refer to Pack and Saggi (2006) and to Chang (2009) for a commonality seeking rejoinder. The industrial policy debate between World Banks's Justin Lin and Ha-Joon Chang (2009) is also important in this context. Lin apparently supports industrial policy but by arguing that it should be tied to comparative advantage effectively rids it of new developmentalist prescriptive content. Baumol *et al.* (2007: Chapter 6) also assume a critical position but concede that state guided capitalism may be effective during the stage when low-income countries borrow, adapt, and absorb technology ("imitate") but that they need to move beyond this to innovate, the ultimate diver of economic growth. For an extensive survey of the theory and broad evidence refer to Harrison and Rodriguez-Clare (2009) who are skeptical that the available evidence or the tests conducted justify industrial policy on welfare grounds.

31 Structural adjustment encompasses all aspects and sectors of the economy. Industrial policy is equally broad since its success is dependent on supportive sector policies.

32 While the celebrated Lewis model (1954) was explicit on the need for balanced development, one in which an agricultural revolution would sustain industrial growth by keeping wage goods cheap, capital accumulation and industrial development was nonetheless central to the model. Refer to Khan *et al.* (1997) on testing for the dynamic efficiencies of industrialization.

33 Bauer (1976) and Lal (2000) are prominent in this critique of the developmentalists or of what is referred to as dirigisme.

34 Wade (2004) captures this well with his term "governing the market."

35 This is much the same as associating the Marxist vision of social justice with the centralized high-handedness of the Soviet state.

36 While new developmentalism could be viewed as having emerged from the inductive method, the key architects are methodologically eclectic and equally comfortable with deductive, inductive, and descriptive approaches. While the reductionist methodological individualism of neo-classical economics is not explicitly refuted, it is for the most part irrelevant to the essence of new developmentalism.

37 For example, while discussing industrial policy, the World Bank (2005) makes no reference to the relevant work of Alice Amsden, Ha-Joon Chang, or Robert Wade.

38 Chang (2009) views exports as easy to monitor and preferable to internal performance criteria like profits, which could be influenced by market power.

39 Khan (2009) distinguishes between "learning rents" and "redistributive rents" and success in industrial policy depends on the specific internal political economy that conditions the state's ability to manage rents to ensure learning and prevent mere acquisition.

40 In the foggy world of economic policy setting, no precision is implied in setting policy or in the ex ante knowledge of outcomes. Mistakes are expected and inevitable, but overall the states got it right.

41 For various reasons, including declining terms of trade, developmentalists like Nurkse (1953) and structuralists like Prebish (1962) were pessimistic about primary exports providing a path to development, although Prebish identified the importance of manufactured exports.

42 The introductory chapter addresses this broad debate and Robert Wade spells out the theory more prescriptively in Chapter 2 of this volume. Much more work however is needed on this issue.

43 Easterly purports to be anti-ideology and endorses instead the "freedom of individuals and societies to choose their destinies." He concludes that this should be shaped by comparative advantage, gains from trade, market clearing prices, and trade-offs. The latter appears to be the core agenda of structural adjustment, and so it is difficult to gauge if Easterly is being disingenuous.

44 Schumacher (1973) is notable for the challenge to industrialization in this context. Lyuba Zarsky has addressed the issue of sustainable industrial development in Chapter 11 of this volume.

45 Refer to Gallager and Zarsky (2007) for an exposition in the context of the debate between neo-liberal and new developmentalist policies.

46 The "love canal" (http://headlice.org/lindane/lindane/love_canal.htm) in the USA is among the more notorious examples. China and India are already confronting environmental nightmares.

47 The rest of industry is viewed as complementing manufacturing in this regard.

48 The review of industrial policy in this section is brief and other chapters in this volume address the subject in much more detail. Refer in particular to the chapters by Wade, Shapiro, and Gallagher and Shafaeddin.

49 It is not being suggested here, nor does Rodrik make such a claim, that all these ideas were originated by him. However, his "cross-paradigm" appeal gives more currency to these ideas. Other prominent contributors include Chang (2006, 2009), Shapiro (2007), and Cimoli *et al.* (2009).

50 Other market failures include imperfect credit markets, resource flow immobility due to adjustment costs, externalities, lumpy investments with high gestation periods resulting in excessive risk aversion, and imperfect market structures (too much or too little competition).

51 Implicit in this view is a competition policy that balances adequate rents with market discipline.

52 In our view an entrepreneurial inclination is normally distributed across the population, though sociologists have rightly argued that the incidence may be higher as a self-defense mechanism among some minority communities, like the parsis in the Indian sub-continent, refer to ed. Kilby (1971).

53 Most LICs are likely to focus initially on imported technologies, adaptation, and imitation.

54 This issue has been elaborated on in detail by Evans (1995) in terms of the concept of embedded autonomy and also by Johnson (1982: 267) in exploring various forms of "deliberation councils" used in Japanese industrial policy with the Industrial Structure Council of 1964, including the economic bureaucracy, business, and finance, coming closest to this concept of open channels of communication between stakeholders. Refer to reservations with this concept of "top down" policy expressed by Shapiro in Chapter 5 of this volume.

55 Evans (1995: 61) uses the term "pockets of efficiency." Also refer to Shapiro (1994).

56 This would include coordination for social and environmental investments and safeguards.

57 Refer to the concise summary by Chang and Grabel (2004: 77–80). Chang (2009: 26) points to the importance of retaining flexibility regarding targets to address contingencies while resisting undue lobbying for advantage, a universal trait of businesses.

58 Refer to Singh (2009) for a new agenda for the Indian Planning Commission.

59 Refer to Abugattas and Paus (2008), Gallagher (2005), Amsden (2005), Chang (2005), Kumar and Gallagher (2007), and the chapters in Part III of this volume on the issue of closing policy space. Policy space includes options and the range over which an option, such as tariff policy, is exercised.

60 Also refer to Gallagher (2007) and Kumar and Gallagher (2007).

61 Pakistan's request for an extension for compliance with TRIPS was turned down.

62 However, these dispensations, and also safeguards for infant industry protection, now only extend to eight years rather than for an unlimited period, which was allowed under GATT.
63 Of course, the ability to provide subsidies at a low resource base may be non-existent. Abugattas and Paus (2008) usefully employ the distinction between internal constraints on policy space (including funds) and external constraints. Rodrik (2007: 226) is not persuaded by Amsden's more sanguine view of policy space.
64 As earlier indicated, we view economic growth as a necessary but not sufficient condition for poverty alleviation.
65 Refer to Reinert (2007, 2009).
66 See Toye (1991: 332–5) on nationalism in this context.
67 Putin is a case in point as someone who restored Russian pride with political and economic management, and therefore his autocratic tendencies did not shake his popularity ratings.
68 Amsden (2008) suggests that historical manufacturing experience makes the difference and sets apart late industrializers. Johnson (1982: 307) refers to "situational nationalism" unique to the country in question, though it is not clear how and why it evolves. Evans (1995) and Kohli (2004) present useful theories of the state in the context of industrialization for low- and middle-income countries. However, these appear deterministic and do not explain dramatic transitions or discrete changes such as witnessed in China or India. This remains an important research issue for state theorists.
69 Ha-Joon Chang pointed out that this is reflected in recent US proposals to broaden the definition of subsidies in the WTO.
70 That most noted terrorists are educated professionals from prosperous families requires a separate explanation, but the rich are generally not the grist for the suicide bombing mill.
71 Hausmann and Rodrik (2003).
72 Olsen (1971).

References

Abugattas, L. and Paus, E. 2008. "Policy Space for a Capability-Centered Development Strategy for Latin America." In: D. Sanchez-Ancochea and K. Shadlen eds., Responding to Globalization in the Americas: The Political Economy of Hemispheric Integration. New York: Palgrave Macmillan.
Amsden, A. H. 2008. "The Wild Ones: Industrial Policies in the Developing World." In: J. A. Ocampo, Jumo K. S., and R. Vos eds., Growth Divergences: Explaining Differences in Economic Performance. London: Zed Books.
Amsden, A. H. 2005. "Promoting Industry under WTO Law." In: K. P. Gallagher, eds., Putting Development First: The Importance of Policy Space in the WTO and Financial Institutions. London: Zed Books.
Amsdem, A. H. 2001. The Rise of "The Rest": Challenges to the West from Late-Industrializing Economies. Oxford: Oxford University Press.
Amsdem, A. H. 1989. Asia's Next Giant. New York: Oxford University Press.
Baran, P. A. 1952. "On the Political Economy of Backwardness." The Manchester School, 20(1), 66–84.
Bauer, P. T. 1976. Dissent on Development. Cambridge Mass.: Harvard University Press.
Baumol, W. J., Litan, R. E., and Schramm, C. J. 2007. Good Capitalism, Bad Capitalism and the Economics of Growth and Prosperity. New Haven: Yale University Press.
Burnside, C. and Dollar, D. 2000. "Aid, Policies, and Growth." American Economic Review, 90(4), 874–68.

Burnside, C. and Dollar, D. 2004. "Aid, Policies, and Growth: Reply." American Economic Review, 94(3), 874–68.

Calclough. C. 1991. "Structuralism vs. Neo-Liberalism." In: C. Calclough and J. Manor, eds., States or Markets? Neo-Liberalism and the Development Policy Debates." Oxford: Clarendon Press.

Chambers, R. 2006. "The State and Rural Development: Ideologies and an Agenda for the 1990s." In: M. C. Behera, ed., Globalizing Rural Development: Competing Paradigms and Emerging Realities. New Delhi: Sage Publications.

Chang, H.-J. 2009. "Industrial Policy: Can We Go Beyond an Unproductive Confrontation?" Plenary Paper for Annual World Bank Conference on Development Economic, Seoul, South Korea.

Chang, H.-J. 2008. Bad Samaritans: The Myth of Free Trade and the Secret History of Capitalism. New York: Bloomsbury Press.

Chang, H.-J. 2006. The East Asian Development Experience: The Miracle, the Crisis and the Future. London/Penang: Zed Books/Third World Network.

Chang, H.-J. 2005. "Kicking Away the Ladder: Good Policies and Good Institutions in Historical Perspective." In: K. P. Gallagher, eds., Putting Development First: The Importance of Policy Space in the WTO and Financial Institutions. London: Zed Books.

Chang, H.-J. 2005a. "Kicking Away the Ladder: "Good Policies" and "Good Institutions" in Historical Perspective." In: Gallagher, K. P. eds., 2005. *Putting Development First: The Importance of Policy Space in the WTO and Financial Institutions*. London: Zed Book.

Chang, H.-J. 2002. Kicking Away the Ladder: Development Strategy in Historical Perspective. London: Anthem Press.

Chang, H.-J., 2002a, "Breaking the Mould: An Institutionalist Political Economy Alternative to the Neo-Liberal Theory of the Market and the State." Cambridge Journal of Economics, 26(5), 539–59.

Chang, H.-J. and Grabel, I. 2004. Reclaiming Development: An Alternative Economic Policy Manual. London: Zed Books.

Cimoli, M. *et al.* 2006. "Institutions and Policies Shaping Industrial Development: An Introductory Note," LEM (Laboratory of Economics and Management) working paper serious, 2006/02, Sant'Anna School of Advanced Studies, Pisa, Italy.

Cimoli, M., Dosi, G., and Stiglitz, J. E. 2009. "The Future of Industrial Policies." In: M. Cimoli, G. Dosi, and J. E. Stiglitz. eds., Industrial Policy and Development: The Political Economy of Capabilities Accumulation. Oxford: Oxford University Press.

Cimoli, M., Dosi, G., and Stiglitz. J. E. eds., 2009. Industrial Policy and Development: The Political Economy of Capabilities Accumulation. Oxford: Oxford University Press.

Cohen, A. J. and Harcourt, G. C. 2003. "Retrospectives: Whatever Happened to the Cambridge Capital Theory Controversy." The Journal of Economic Perspectives, 17(1), 199–214.

Cornia, G. A., Jolly, R., and Stewart, F. 1987. Adjustment with a Human Face. Oxford: Clarendon Press.

Easterly, W. 2007. "The Ideology of Development." Foreign Policy, 161(July/August), 31–5.

Easterly, W., Levine, R. and Roodman, D. 2004. "Aid, Policies, and Growth: Comment." American Economic Review, 94(3), 874–68.

Evans, P. 1995. Embedded Autonomy: States and Industrial Transformation. Princeton, New Jersey: Princeton University Press.

Fine, B. 2005. "The Development State and Political Economy of Development." In: B. Fine and K. S. Jomo, eds., The New Development Economics: Post Washington Consensus Neo-Liberal Thinking. London: Zed Books.

Frank, A. G. 1966. "The Development of Underdevelopment." Monthly Review, 18(4), 17–31.

Ffrench-Davis, R. 1988. "An Outline of the Neo-Structural Approach." CEPAL Review, 34 (April), 45–62.

Gallagher, K. P. ed. 2005. *Putting Development First: The Importance of Policy Space in the WTO and Financial Institutions*. London: Zed Book.

Gallagher, K. P. 2007. "Measuring the Cost of Lost Policy Space in the WTO," IRC Americas Program Policy Brief, Washington, D.C.

Gallagher, K. P. and Zarsky, L. 2007. The Enclave Economy: Foreign Investment and Sustainable Development in Mexico's Silicon Valley. Cambridge, Massachusetts: The MIT Press.

Hausmann, R. and Rodrik, D. 2003. "Economic Development as Self-Discovery." Journal of Development Economics, 72(2), 603–33.

Haq, M. 1976. The Poverty Curtain: Choices for the Third World. New York: Columbia University Press.

Harrison, A. and Rodriguez-Clare, A. 2009. "Trade, Foreign Investment, and Industrial Policy for Developing Countries." National Bureau of Economic Research Working Paper 15261, Cambridge, MA, www.nber.org/papers/w15261.

Hayek, F. A. 1944. The Road to Serfdom. Chicago: Chicago University Press.

Hirschman, A. O. 1959. The Strategy of Economic Development. New Haven: Yale University Press.

Johnson, C. 1982. MITI and the Japanese Miracle. Stanford: Stanford University Press.

Kay, C. 1989. Latin American Theories of Development and Underdevelopment. London: Routeledge.

Khan, M. 2009. "The Political Economy of Industrial Policy." In: M. Cimoli, G. Dosi, and J. E. Stiglitz., eds. Industrial Policy and Development: The Political Economy of Capabilities Accumulation. Oxford: Oxford University Press.

Khan, S. R. 2007. "WTO, IMF and the closing of development policy space for low-income countries: a case for neo-developmentalism." Third World Quarterly, 28(6), 1073–90.

Khan, S. R., Bilginsoy, C., and Alam, M. S. 1997. "Dynamic Efficiencies of Industrialization and Economic Growth." Economia Internationale, 50(1), 85–98.

Kilby, P., ed. 1971. Entrepreneurship and Economic Development. New York: Macmillan.

Kohli, A. 2004. State-Directed Development: Political Power and Industrialization in the Global Periphery. Cambridge: Cambridge University Press.

Kuhn, T. S. 1970. The Structure of Scientific Revolutions. Chicago: University of Chicago Press.

Kumar, N. and Gallagher, K. P. 2007. "Relevance of 'Policy Space' for Development: Implications for Multilateral Trade Negotiations." RIS (Research and Information System) Discussion Paper #120, New Delhi.

Krugman, P. 1998. "The Fall and Rise of Development Economics." Development Geography and Economic Theory. Cambridge, Mass: MIT Press.

Lal, D. 2000. The Poverty of "Development Economics" 2nd. ed. Cambridge University Press: MIT Press.

Lange, O. 1936. "On the Economic Theory of Socialism," The Review of Economic Studies, 4(1), 53–71.

Lewis, W. A. 1954, "Economic Development with Unlimited Supplies of Labor." The Manchester School, 22(2), 139–91.

Lin, J. and Chang, H.-J. 2009. "Should Industrial Policy in Developing Countries

Conform to Comparative Advantage or Defy it? A Debate Between Justin Lin and Ha-Joon Chang," Development Policy Review, 27(5), 483–502.

Little, I., Scitovsky, T., and Scott, M. 1970. Industry and trade in some developing countries (Oxford: Oxford University Press for the O.E.C.D. Development Center).

Meier, G. and Seers, D. eds. 1984. Pioneers in Development. New York: Oxford University Press.

Nolan, P. and Rui, H. 2004. "Industrial Policy and Global Big Business Revolution: The Case of the Chinese Coal Industry." Journal of Chinese Economic and Business Studies, 2(2), 97–113.

Nurkse, R. 1953. Problems of Capital Formation in Underdeveloped Countries. Oxford: Basil Blackwell.

Öniş, Z. and Şenses, F. 2005. "Re-thinking the Emerging Post-Washington Consensus." Development and Change, 36(2), 263–90.

Olson, M. 1971. The Logic of Collective Action: Public Goods and the Theory of Groups. Cambridge, Massachusetts: Harvard University Press.

Pack, H. and Saggi, K. 2006. "Is There a Case for Industrial Policy? A Critical Survey." The World Bank Research Observer, 21(2), 267–97.

Panagariya, A. 2004. "India in the 1980s and 1990s: A Triumph of Reforms." International Monetary Fund Working Paper series No. 04/43, Washington, D.C.

Prebish, R. 1962. "The Economic Development of Latin America and its Principal Problems." Economic Commission for Latin America, Santiago, Chile.

Qian, Y. 2003. "How Reform Worked in China." In: D. Rodrik, ed., In Search of Prosperity. Princeton: Princeton University Press.

Reinert, E. 2009. "Emulation versus Comparative Advantage: Competing and Complementary Principles in the History of Economic Policy." In: M. Cimoli, G. Dosi, and J. E. Stiglitz, eds., Industrial Policy and Development: The Political Economy of Capabilities Accumulation. Oxford: Oxford University Press.

Reinert, E. 2007. How the Rich Countries Got Rich and Why Poor Countries Stay Poor. New York: Carroll and Graf.

Reinert, E. 2007a. "Development and Social Goals: Balancing Aid and Development to Prevent "Welfare Colonialism." In: A. Ocampo, K. S., Jumo and S. Khan, eds., Policy Matters: Economic and Social Policies to Sustain Equitable Development. Himayatnagar, Hyderabad/London/Penang, Malaysia: Orient Longmans/Zed Books/Third World Networks.

Rodrik, D. 1994. "King Kong Meets Godzilla: The World Bank and the East Asian Miracle." In: A. Fishlow et al. eds., Miracle or Design: Lessons from the East Asian Experience. Washington D.C.: Overseas Development Council.

Rodrik, D. 2008. "Industrial Policy: Don't Ask Why, Ask How." Middle East Development Journal (Demo Issue), 1–29.

Rodrik, D. 2007. One Economics Many Recipes: Globalization, Institutions, and Economic Growth. Princeton: Princeton University Press.

Rodrik, D. 2006. "What is So Special About China's Exports?"

Rodrik, D. and Subramanian, A. 2004. "From 'Hindu Growth' to Productivity Surge: The Mystery of the Indian Growth Transition." National Bureau Working Paper series No. 10376, Cambridge, Massachusetts. http://ksghome.harvard.edu/~drodrik/Chinaexports.pdf.

Rosenstein-Rodan, P. N. 1943. "Problems of Industrialization of Eastern and South-Eastern Europe." Economic Journal, 53 (June–September), 202–11.

Rustow, W. 1960. The Stages of Economic Growth: A Non-Communist Manifesto. Cambridge: Cambridge University Press.

Santiso, J. 2006. Latin America's Political Economy of the Possible: Beyond Good Revolutionaries and Free-Marketeers. Cambridge, Massachusetts: The MIT Press.

Schumacher, E. F. 1973. Small is Beautiful: Economics as if People Mattered. London: Blond and Briggs Ltd.

Seers, D. 1969. "The Meaning of Development." paper presented at the Eleventh World Conference for the Society of Economic Development, New Delhi, India.

Sen, A. K. 2000, "What is Development About?" In: G. M. Meier and J. E. Stiglitz, eds., Frontiers of Development Economics: The Future in Perspective. New York: Oxford University Press.

Shapiro, H. 2007. "Industrial Policy and Growth." In: J. A. Ocampo, K. S. Jomo and R. Vos, eds., Growth Divergences: Explaining Differences in Economic Performance. London: Zed Books.

Shapiro, H. 1994. Engines of Growth: The State and Transnational Auto Companies in Brazil. Cambridge: Cambridge University Press.

Shapiro, H. and Taylor, L. 1990. "The State and Industrial Strategy." World Development, 18(6), 861–78.

Singh, A. 2009. "The Past, Present, and Future of Industrial Policy in India: Adapting to the Changing Domestic and International Environment." In: M. Cimoli, G. Dosi, and J. E. Stiglitz., eds., Industrial Policy and Development: The Political Economy of Capabilities Accumulation. Oxford: Oxford University Press.

Stiglitz, J. E. 2002, *Globalization and its Discontents* (New York: W. W. Norton & Company).

Toye, J. 2003. "Changing Perspectives in Development Economics." In: Ha-Joon Chang, ed., Rethinking Development Economics. London: Anthem Press.

Toye, J. 1991. "Is There a New Political Economy of Development?" In: C. Calclough and J. Manor, eds., States or Markets? Neo-Liberalism and the Development Policy Debates. Oxford: Clarendon Press.

UNDP (United Nation Development Program). 2005. International Cooperation at a Crossroads: Aid, Trade and Security in an Unequal World; Human Development Report 2005. New York: Oxford University Press.

UNCTAD. 2007. "Towards a Developmental State." In: Economic Development in Africa: Reclaiming Policy Space: Domestic Resource Mobilization and Developmental States. Geneva: United Nations.

UNCTAD (United Nations Conference on Trade and Development). 2006. Trade and Development Report. New York: United Nations.

Vos, eds., Growth Divergences: Explaining Differences in Economic Performance. London: Zed Books.

Wade, R. H. 2005. "What Strategies Are Viable for Developing Countries Today? The World Trade Organization and the Shrinking of "Development Space." In: K. P. Gallagher, ed. 2005. *Putting Development First: The Importance of Policy Space in the WTO and Financial Institutions*. London: Zed Book.

Wade, R. H. 2004. Governing the Market: Economic Theory and the Role of Government in *East Asian Industrialization.* Princeton University Press.

Warren, B. 1980. Imperialism: Pioneer of Capitalism. London: Verso.

World Bank. 2005. Economic Growth in the 1990s: Learning from a Decade of Reform. Washington, D.C.: World Bank.

World Bank. 1993. The East Asian Miracle. Oxford: Oxford University Press.

Young, A. 1994. "Lessons from the East Asian NICS: A Contrarian View," European Economic Review, 38(3–4), 964–73.

Index

developmentalism and 8; protection against imports in 38; state industrial policies in 90; success of 254

East Asian Tigers 254

Easterly, William 39–40, 203, 257, 272n43

ecological challenges 7; see also climate-resilient development

Economic Commission for Latin America 25

economic competition, political corruption and 93

economic crisis of 2007–9, 21; characteristics of 22; current status of 17n3; lower external debt exposure and 127; neo-liberalism and 11, 42; privatized gains, socialized losses and 22–3; as wake-up call 24

economic development, exploring and naming *an* alternative to 3–18

economic growth: governance and 32–3; property rights and 33, **33**; self-sustaining 9; virtuous circles of 61

economic laws, presumed universality of 23

Economic Partnership Agreement 84n8; limitations of 9; palliative nature of 71; redesign of 75

economic policy *see also* fiscal space dilemma; policy coherence; policy credibility: coherence of 11; effective 8; ideologically driven 11; institutional interdependence with 114n11; and insulation from politics 103; NAFTA's impact on 100; rule-based 115n15

economic reform: first and second waves of 89; institutional focus in 92–3; state's role in 90; technocratic fix in 91–2

economic retrogression: causes of 10–11; examples of 63, **63**

economic structure, relationship with political stability and peace 75

economic theory, new-classical 102

economics, palliative *see* palliative economics

Ecuador, investor–state disputes in 140–1

education: Latin American resource needs for 123; tertiary, in China 193–4

embedded autonomy 96, 273n54

employment creation 75, 214

employment policy, pro-active 15

Energiebeau, as example of climate-resilient development 244

energy access, in developing countries 229, 232

Energy Research Institute 239

energy sources: fossil fuels 233; non-carbon 233

environmental indicators, in assessment of productive agglomeration 72

environmental issues, industrial policy and 15

environmental sustainability *see also* climate-resilient development: early development economics and 56–7; in new developmentalism 257–8

EP *see* export promotion

ersatz development 9, 48, 53–5

Europe, post-war reindustrialization of 59–60

Everything But Arms: limitations of 9; palliative nature of 71; redesign of 75

exchange rate: currency boards and 111; policy credibility and 106–7

Export Processing Zones: in Mexico 181; tax incentives and 135; WTO policy and 264

export promotion 6

export subsidy programs, rent-seeking assumptions about 95

externalities: neo-liberal omission of 241–2; products generating 23; Washington Consensus and 73

extractive industries, Latin American re-nationalization of 141

feudalism, modern forms of 61

FFF states 59–86; benchmarking per capita GDP **79**, **80**; de-industrialization and 69–71; and divergence from industrialized countries 64–5, 66, 75; economic characteristics of 66; economic structure in 62; globalization and 70; governance characteristics of 67; and transition from divergence to convergence 71–4; UK Department of International Development classification of 84n13; urbanization and 84n4

financial sector, regulation of 23

Financial Stability Forum, African membership in 221

fiscal policy space: defined 131; determination of 131; framework for analyzing 132, *133*; and globalization constraints in Latin America 132–41; income tax base and 142–55; MDGs and 131–2; public expenditures and 131–2; tax stabilization agreements and 136

fiscal space dilemma 119–53; analytical considerations in 130–2; and constraints from globalization 132–41; and constraints from internal production structure 141–5; globalization and 12; and mobilization of public resources 125–30; and resource needs for development 120–5; suggestions for solving 145–7

Florentine state theory 68

foreign aid *see* development aid

foreign direct investment: to African and low-income countries **205**; BITs and 140; in China 195–6; climate-resilient development and 238; investment agreements and 137, 140–1; knowledge spillovers and 249n3; limitations of growth based on 242; in Mexican development 180–4; tax competition and 134–6; tax stabilization agreements and 136

foreign investment: competition for 134–6; definition of 162; favored status in dispute settlements 156–7; favored status in investment treaties 167–9; in investment treaty arbitration 156–8; legal advantages of 13; market constraints due to 133; NAFTA privileging of 111–12; new developmentalism and 245–6

foreign technologies, East Asia acquisition of 38–9

fossil fuels, global climate change and 228–9

Fourth World countries, average income in 27–9, *28*

Fraga, Arminio 96n9

fragility *see also* FFF states: benchmarking 73

free trade *see also* NAFTA: premature exposure to 63

Gallagher, Kevin 6, 14

General Agreement on Tariffs and Trade 104

German Bundesbank Law 108

Germany, deindustrialization of 75

Global Adaptation Fund 238

global climate change 7; anthropogenic contribution to 228; impact on humans 229, *230*, **231**, 232; industrial development paths and 227–51; socioeconomic impacts of 229

global economy, impact of new entries into 121

globalization: and challenges and opportunities for Africa 222–3; and constraints on Latin American fiscal space 132–41; engagement with 3, 6–7; FFF states and 70; fiscal space and 12; industrial policy and 263–5; legal issues and 13; policy sphere and 130; productive structures and 64–5; state role debate and 31; sustainable model of 16, 243–4

Goodhart, David 24–5, 31

governance *see also* growth-enhancing governance; state role: in FFF states 67; followership *versus* leadership of 35; market-enhancing 32–4; new developmental/growth-enhancing 34–7

governance reforms, World Bank and 32

government policy, in China *versus* Mexico 14

government reform: in China 177–80, 187–96; in Mexico 177–87

government role *see* state role

government spending, brainwashing about 23

Grabel, Ilene 11

Gross Domestic Product: growth rates in Latin America 120; with MVA per capita in Chad, Ivory Coast, Somalia, Sudan 77; per capita for selected world regions **78**; per capita in selected countries **81**; per capita in South Korea, China, and India **76**; productive agglomeration and 72–3

growth-enhancing governance: apex coordination point in 35; in China 39; control of beneficiaries in 36; corruption and income inequality and 36; divergence-convergence trends and 72–3; in East Asia 37–9; implementation of 37; incentive schemes in 35–6; *versus* policies 36

Hamilton, Alexander 36

Harberler, Gottfried 36

Havana Charter 61, 68

health care, Latin American resource needs for 123

high income countries, property rights and economic growth in *33*, 33–4

Hirschman, Albert 56

human development, economic growth and 253

human development index 47

human welfare, non-income criteria for 47–8

Hydén, Göran 61–2

Ibn-Khaldun, on pre-industrial rent-seeking 61, 64

ideology, definition of 270n7

import monitoring, in East Asia 37–8

import substitution industrialization 6, 253; as basis for export promotion 257; in China 187–8; impacts of 94–5; macro imbalances and 10–11; in Mexico 181; underlying vision of 256

impossibility hypothesis 270n11

incentive schemes, in growth-enhancing governance capacity 35–6

income, regional, as percentage of North 25–6, *26*, *27*

income distribution: civil war and 62; in early development economics 56; state mobility matrix for 27–9, *28*

income inequality: in African countries 215; determining trends in 25; Kuznets inverted-U and 23–4; Latin American tax system and 143–4; neo-liberalism and 24–5, 25–30, 41

income tax base, as constraint on Latin American fiscal space 142–4

increasing returns: absence of 62, 75; argument of 68; and "coo-petitive" diffusion of means 72;

knowledge-intensive services and 84n3; positive-sum-game and 68–9; rapid urbanization and 84n4

increasing returns industries, nation-state development and 64

India: climate-resilient development in 236–7; GDP per capita **76**; resistance to Washington Consensus in 70

industrial development: in China 14, 177–80, 187–96; in Mexico 177–87

industrial development paths, climate-resilient 227–51

industrial diversification, climate-resilient development and 237

industrial policy: climate and social justice sensitivity in 15; conceptualization and implementation of 262–3; defined 4, 255–6; economic globalization and 263–5; investment treaties and 166–9; in new developmentalism 256, 258; perspectives on 272n30; public sector and 262; rent-seeking paradigm and 93–6; Rodrik's approach to 262–3, 273n49

industrial tariffs 57n11; proposed abolishment of 52–3

industrial transformation, sustainable livelihoods and 233

industrialization: agricultural revolution and 272n32; in China under Mao 187–8; *versus* generation of sustainable livelihoods 227; market-led, in Mexico 182–3; in newly industrialized countries 254; palliative 69–71; role of learning in 178–80; state intervention for promoting 93–4

industrialized countries: benchmarking per capita GDP **79**; divergence between FFF states and 64–5, 66

industry policy: climate-resilient development and 234, 236–7; in new developmentalism models 245

industry promotion, tools of 53

infant industry argument 178

inflation, independent central banks and 107–8

informal economy, Latin American 142–3, *143*

infrastructure development: in Latin America *versus* East Asia 147n3; Latin American investment in 123, *124*

institutional constraints, on policy space 106–12

institutional development 3; in Latin America 125

institutional reform 92–3, 101

institutions: ideologically driven 11; interdependence with policy 114n11

Intergovernmental Panel on Climate Change, global warming imperative of 228–32

International Court for the Settlement of Investment Disputes 141

international financial institutions *see also* International Monetary Fund; World Bank: African voting rights in 222; conditional terms of 132–3; fiscal policy reevaluation by 133; relaxing conditionalities of 146

International Institute of Sustainable Development 239

International Monetary Fund: and constraints on Latin American fiscal space 132–3; and constraints on policy space 112–14; and cooperation with WTO 105–6; debt crisis of 1980s and 254; neo-liberal agenda and 11, 270n13; and opponents of neo-liberal conformance 113–14; policy coherence and 103–6

investment: alternate decision-making frameworks

For Product Safety Concerns and Information please contact our EU
representative GPSR@taylorandfrancis.com
Taylor & Francis Verlag GmbH, Kaufingerstraße 24, 80331 München, Germany

www.ingramcontent.com/pod-product-compliance
Ingram Content Group UK Ltd.
Pitfield, Milton Keynes, MK11 3LW, UK
UKHW021620240425
457818UK00018B/656